Fools
ON THE
HILL

Fools
ON THE
HILL

The Hooligans, Saboteurs,
Conspiracy Theorists, and Dunces
Who Burned Down the House

DANA MILBANK

Little, Brown and Company

New York   Boston   London

Little, Brown and Company
Hachette Book Group
1290 Avenue of the Americas, New York, NY 10104
littlebrown.com

First Edition: September 2024

Little, Brown and Company is a division of Hachette Book Group, Inc. The Little, Brown name and logo are trademarks of Hachette Book Group, Inc.

The publisher is not responsible for websites (or their content) that are not owned by the publisher.

The Hachette Speakers Bureau provides a wide range of authors for speaking events. To find out more, go to hachettespeakersbureau.com or email hachettespeakers@hbgusa.com.

Little, Brown and Company books may be purchased in bulk for business, educational, or promotional use. For information, please contact your local bookseller or the Hachette Book Group Special Markets Department at special.markets@hbgusa.com.

ISBN 9780316570923
Library of Congress Control Number: 2024941120

Printing 1, 2024

LSC-C

Printed in the United States of America

To Anna Greenberg

"I spend half my day as speaker of the House and the other half as a mental-health counselor."

—*House Speaker Mike Johnson,*
radio interview, May 28, 2024

CONTENTS

CONTENTS

Fools
ON THE
HILL

PROLOGUE

In November 2022, I assigned myself to the U.S. Capitol to cover the House of Representatives. For the previous 15 or so years, I had written a thrice-weekly syndicated column for the *Washington Post*, jumping from the White House to Congress to the Supreme Court to the campaign trail depending on the news of the day. But I had a feeling that what was about to happen in the People's House would be worthy of a singular focus. Republicans had just taken control of the House, but only barely, with a four-seat majority in the 435-member body. Because of that, combined with the large number of exotic characters and MAGA extremists in the House Republican conference and the weak slate of leaders, I suspected that this erratic crowd would provide some lively material.

They did not disappoint. What I could not have known then, however, was that I was about to witness the most ineffective session of Congress in a century, if not longer. The year began with chaos and incompetence. It ended in chaos and incompetence. In between were self-created crises and shocking moments of fratricide—interspersed with more chaos and incompetence.

House Republicans were immediately snarled in dysfunction with the 15-ballot marathon to elect Kevin McCarthy as speaker. This was followed by the first-in-history ouster of a speaker in midterm, then the 22-day attempt to elect a successor while the House was shuttered, followed by efforts to oust McCarthy's replacement, the hapless Mike Johnson. Along the way, the House majority came close to defaulting on the federal debt for the first time in American history and threatened, over and over again, to shut down the federal government.

They filled their committee hearings and their bills with white nationalist attacks on racial diversity and immigrants, attempts to ban abortion and to expand access to the sort of guns used in mass shootings, incessant harassment of LGBTQ Americans, and even routine potshots at the United States military. They tried to impeach President Biden without finding any evidence of wrongdoing, and they actually did impeach Homeland Security secretary Alejandro Mayorkas without identifying any high crimes or misdemeanors he had committed. They insulted each other's private parts, accused each other of sexual and financial crimes, and scuffled with each other in the Capitol basement. They screamed "Bullshit!" at Biden on the House floor during the State of the Union address. They used their official powers to spread conspiracy theories about the "Deep State" and for a year protected the serial fabulist in their caucus, the indicted George Santos. They stood up for the Confederacy, tried to ban abortion, and even claimed that the government was hiding space aliens.

After a year in power, they had almost nothing to show for it. A bipartisan debt deal (on which they promptly reneged) to avoid a default crisis that they themselves created. A pair of temporary spending bills (both passed with mostly Democratic votes) to avert a government shutdown crisis that they themselves created. They made hardly a dent in federal spending. Their attempts to stoke culture wars with poison-pill legislation went nowhere. Their monthslong failure to approve arms for Ukraine enabled Vladimir Putin to inflict punishing losses on Ukrainian forces. On the House floor, the Republican majority suffered one failure after another, even on routine procedural votes. By many measures—inexperience, incompetence, lack of productivity—this has been arguably the worst Congress ever, producing little other than mayhem and feuding. But don't take my word for it. Here's a sampling of some of the things House Republicans have said about themselves over the last year or so:

"Our Republican House majority has failed completely."
—Marjorie Taylor Greene, Georgia

"One thing. I want my Republican colleagues to give me one thing—one—that I can go campaign on and say we did."

—Chip Roy, Texas

"We're a party that can't govern." —Dave Joyce, Ohio

"The amount of damage they have done to this party and to this country is insurmountable." —Kevin McCarthy, California

"We're a ship that doesn't have a rudder."

—Mark Alford, Missouri

"We are a broken conference." —Troy Nehls, Texas

"You keep running lunatics, you're going to be in this position."
—Mike Lawler, New York

"We need to . . . get our heads out of our rear end."
—Mike Waltz, Florida

"This is embarrassing for the Republican Party. It's embarrassing for the nation." —McCarthy, again

"We put sharp knives in the hands of children, and they used them." —Tom Cole, Oklahoma

"Clearly, there's a lot of people that have serious issues."
—Tony Gonzales, Texas

"It makes us look like a bunch of idiots."

—Austin Scott, Georgia

"This is a continuation of a pretty dysfunctional disease."
—Dusty Johnson, South Dakota

"This is the worst team I've ever been on."

—Mike Kelly, Pennsylvania

And those were just a few of the examples of House Republicans' self-loathing you'll find in these pages.

For all of 2023 and into the early months of 2024 I hung out on Capitol Hill and produced weekly essays for the *Post* on this self-described "clown show." With the blessings of my editors, I built on those essays with additional reporting, analysis, and context to create this book. The events and scenes I recount are for the most part ones I witnessed in person or, when that was not possible, through the magic of C-SPAN. But I also relied on the work of a truly outstanding Capitol Hill press corps, which covers the place far more thoroughly and in much greater detail than it did when I was a young congressional reporter with the *Wall Street Journal* way back in the 1990s. I have credited my colleagues in the text and in the endnotes where I have relied on their reporting, and I apologize in advance for any I have overlooked.

I knew these House Republicans would furnish me with plenty of material. But there's another reason I focused on them and not, say, their GOP counterparts in the Senate minority. In the House, Republicans were in control, with a relatively free hand to set the agenda. This is what it looks like when MAGA Republicans try to govern. My last book, *The Destructionists: The Twenty-Five-Year Crack-Up of the Republican Party*, which came out in 2022, showed how trends within the GOP since the mid-1990s explained the emergence of Trump. If that book aimed to explain how we got here, the purpose of this one is to explain what "here" is.

This book comes out in the fall of 2024, with the general election in full swing and voters deciding whether to return Donald Trump to the White House and Republicans to control of Congress. In making that decision, voters ought to know that this is what they would get if they return MAGA Republicans to power: the chaos, the conspiracy theories, the lies, the constant cultural and political warfare. It has been plenty bad during divided government. It would be much worse if, for the first time, MAGA Republicans controlled both the White House and Congress. When Trump was last in the White House, Congress reined in some of his excesses; even when the House was under Republican rule, the relatively steady hand of Speaker Paul Ryan checked some of the far right's impulses. But MAGA Republicans now dominate the House GOP conference and are heading that way in the Senate.

As Nikki Haley liked to say during the Republican presidential prima-ries, "Chaos follows Trump." Chaos now also follows House Republicans, because they follow Trump. They won't temper his attacks on democracy, on the truth, on abortion and other freedoms, on migrants and minority groups, on basic decency. They will amplify those attacks. All the zany things House Republicans tried but failed to do in 2023 and 2024 could actually happen in 2025.

In the first section of this book, "Disinformation," I explain the broken politics that brought this bizarre assortment of misfits to power. In the second, "Dysfunction," I take you through the first year and more of comic incompetence and clownish missteps. In the third, "Disunion," I revisit key moments to show that while MAGA Republicans failed as legislators, they succeeded in injecting paranoia, white nationalism, and outrageous lies and conspiracy theories into the national bloodstream—most of it for the sole purpose of pleasing Donald Trump.

I have aimed to be as comprehensive as possible to give readers a sense of the sheer volume of crazy that has been produced by this House majority. Some incidents are well known, as when Greene displayed, at a televised committee hearing, photos of Hunter Biden engaging in sex acts. Others may be more obscure, such as Santos's visit to a karaoke bar, Colorado Re-publican Lauren Boebert's fascination with public urination, Greene telling Boebert she was a "little bitch" on the House floor, McCarthy delivering a "kidney punch" to the frame of Tennessee Republican Tim Burchett, and a fierce fight by Republicans to protect their right to carry loaded guns into committee hearings. But there is no way to capture all the nuttiness. As I write this, it is the spring of 2024, and in the last few weeks alone:

> The aforementioned Tony Gonzales, a Texas Republican, said of his right-wing colleagues: "I serve with some real scumbags." He told CNN's Dana Bash that "these people used to walk around with white hoods at night. Now they're walking around with white hoods in the daytime."
>
> Michigan Republican Tim Walberg had this to say about help for the people of Gaza: "We shouldn't be spending a dime on

humanitarian aid. It should be like Nagasaki and Hiroshima. Get it over quick." (He later said he meant the "exact opposite.")

Mike Johnson, the House speaker, described some of those who breached the Capitol on Jan. 6, 2021, as "people who were there and just happened to be walking through the building."

McCarthy, the former speaker, told an audience at Georgetown University "the truth why I'm not speaker: It's because one person, a member of Congress, wanted me to stop an ethics complaint because he slept with a 17-year-old." McCarthy was referring to Florida Republican Matt Gaetz.

Michael McCaul, chairman of the House Foreign Affairs Committee, could be heard at a committee meeting muttering "Go fuck yourself" to fellow Republican Darrell Issa of California, as the writer Ben Jacobs first reported.

Greene shared with her followers on social media that "God is sending America strong signs to tell us to repent. Earthquakes and eclipses and many more things to come." She seemed not to understand that the April 2024 solar eclipse was just the latest in a series of predictable astronomical phenomena that have been occurring for billions of years.

Greene, backed by two GOP colleagues, filed a motion to "vacate the chair" and oust Johnson from the speakership. The only reason Johnson is keeping his job (for now) is because Democrats, weary of all the chaos, voted to save him.

It's going to get even worse, because anybody with any sense in the House GOP is getting out. Five Republicans quit even before they could finish their current terms; the Republican majority at the moment is down to just one vote. Among the senior Republicans rushing to the exits are five committee chairs, eight subcommittee chairs, and former leaders such as Patrick McHenry of North Carolina, Cathy McMorris Rodgers of Washington, and McCarthy. I can't say I blame them.

It has long been the case that ideological extremists on the right do a bad job of governing. A January 2024 paper by Vanderbilt University and University of Virginia researchers for the Center for Effective Lawmaking found that over the last 50 years, conservative Republicans have been "notably less effective" than moderate Republicans, even when Republicans have been in the majority. That's in part because of their allergy to bipartisanship and compromise.

But now it's worse than just ideological intransigence. Now we must add in the woeful inexperience of this House majority (median tenure: just four years), the truly bizarre characters who have prevailed in Republican primaries in recent years, the disorienting disinformation churned out by Trump and the MAGA media echo chamber, and the House GOP leadership vacuum. It's no wonder that things are a mess and getting messier.

As you read on, keep in mind that this dysfunction is no accident. This is what MAGA Republican governance looks like.

Part I

DISINFORMATION

Chapter 1

"An Absolute Disaster for the Republican Party"

O N NOV. 8, 2022, HOUSE REPUBLICAN LEADERS ASSEMBLED THE PARTY faithful for an Election Night celebration that wasn't. The National Republican Congressional Committee had booked the capital's Westin City Center, the ballroom of which could hold 600 revelers. "I'm very optimistic," Ronna McDaniel, the Republican National Committee chairwoman, said in a Fox News live shot in front of the stage, decorated with "Take Back the House" signage, as polling places across the country began to close.

Republicans had been talking for months and months about a building "red wave" and even a "red tsunami" that would sweep President Joe Biden's party from control of the Senate and give Republicans a handsome majority in the House. The House Republican leader, Kevin McCarthy, who stood to rise from minority leader to speaker, had begun the midterm election cycle with an eye-popping prediction: Republicans might exceed the 63-seat pickup they had won in the Tea Party election of 2010 during the Obama presidency. Claiming that 70 Democratic-held seats were in play, McCarthy initially predicted "one of the biggest election losses for Democrats"—of all time!

Even later and more sober predictions had Republicans picking up 20 or 30 seats—far more than the five they needed to take control of the House. Almost everyone assumed a big night for Republicans, and with good reason: History was on their side. The incumbent president's party almost always loses seats in the midterms: Democrats lost 52 seats under

Bill Clinton in '94, Republicans lost 30 under George W. Bush in '06, and Republicans lost 40 under Donald Trump in '18. The political fundamentals also favored Republicans: Inflation was high, Biden's popularity was low, and Americans were worried about crime.

Before the results rolled in, the Election Night atmosphere had been festive at a private NRCC reception for party high rollers, with McCarthy and McDaniel in attendance, before the main event in the Westin ballroom. As the larger, would-be victory celebration for the masses kicked off at 8 p.m., Republican staffers and lobbyists fanned out to the several open bars in the ballroom in giddy anticipation of the first results. They tuned the TVs to Fox News—all TVs at such gatherings are always tuned to Fox—and prepared to celebrate.

But the early signs showed surprisingly tight contests. By 10 p.m., even the cheerleaders on Fox News could not mask their sense that something had gone badly wrong. Republicans had hoped to flip Democratic-held seats in Virginia, Rhode Island, and Connecticut, but Democrats were leading. "I'm not quite sure about this," host Bill Hemmer said. That vaunted red wave? "We have not seen that."

"Not a wave," agreed Mark Penn, a former Democratic pollster and now a Democratic detractor.

But host Bret Baier knew his audience and was not giving up hope. "It could be a pretty big swing in the House," he ventured.

As lackluster results continued to trickle in, the crowd at the Westin trickled out. Reflecting the party's initial confidence, McCarthy had planned to give a victory speech around 10 p.m. But the hour came and went in confused disappointment as McCarthy hid offstage. On Fox, the right-wing contributor Guy Benson was acknowledging that "if there's a national wave building for the Republicans, it hasn't quite materialized yet."

By 11 p.m., Republican losses were piling up, with Democrats holding on to seats in New Hampshire, Pennsylvania, Virginia, and even Ohio that Republicans had hoped to take. "I think Republicans will have some soul-searching to do here," proposed Fox's Dana Perino. The network's straight-shooting chief congressional correspondent, Chad Pergram, appeared on-screen to tell viewers it clearly would be a "smaller majority for Kevin McCarthy if he becomes speaker and Republicans win the

House. That means possibly more headaches for him." In remarks that would quickly prove prescient, Pergram said House GOP hardliners "could play Russian roulette with the debt ceiling." A small majority meant just a few dissidents could tank any item on the Republican leaders' agenda.

Baier grasped for hope. "You had the 30 seats [GOP gain forecast], now maybe we're down to 20 or even fewer, but it's still a majority," he said.

After midnight, it became clear that Democrats were having a good night in Arizona, and Democrat John Fetterman, despite having suffered a stroke during the campaign, had beaten the Republican TV personality Mehmet Oz in the Pennsylvania Senate race.

A *Politico* reporter who was at the Westin heard a woman cry, "Oh no!"

The ballroom was by then all but empty. Aides, desperate to keep some semblance of a crowd, negotiated to keep the bars open past the planned closing time of 1 a.m., *Politico*'s Olivia Beavers and Hailey Fuchs reported. Only two rank-and-file House Republican lawmakers—Tom Massie of Kentucky and Debbie Lesko of Arizona—were on hand for the "celebration," and Lesko skipped out early.

Now, late into the night, it had become clear that Democrats were going to maintain control of the Senate. It wasn't even a sure thing that Republicans would secure the net gain of just five seats they needed to take the House, as had been universally expected. Against the sky-high expectations for Republicans in the midterm elections, this was a debacle.

"That is a searing indictment of the Republican Party," conservative Fox contributor and *Washington Post* columnist Marc Thiessen said on the air at 1:25 a.m. "This is an absolute disaster for the Republican Party." Even Baier had thrown in the towel. "This night turned out a lot different than a lot of people thought," he acknowledged.

THE DISAPPOINTING REALITY WAS SETTING IN, BUT REPUBLICANS WERE refusing to accept it. Around the country, defeated Republican candidates were already howling, Trump style, about election fraud. In Arizona, the failed gubernatorial nominee, Kari Lake, took the stage at a Republican election-watch party in Scottsdale and spewed invective: "Corruption." "Cheaters and crooks." "BS and garbage." "Incompetent people running the show in Arizona." "Propagandists." "Fake media." "Incompetency."

Earlier in the night, before the results came in, Arizona Republicans, aligned with their D.C. counterparts, had been predicting a "red wave," a "red tide," and a "red tsunami." Now Lake refused to concede defeat. "We will take the victory when it comes," she said. As she departed the stage, Twisted Sister's "We're Not Gonna Take It" blasted from the loudspeakers.

Finally, around 2 a.m., staffers at the GOP party in Washington rounded up the remaining stragglers, now numbering in the double digits. To create the illusion of a packed room, aides gave the attendees signs to wave and moved them close to the stage. Fox alerted its dozing viewers: "I think we have Kevin McCarthy coming to the stage," Baier said at 1:57 a.m. "This will be interesting."

The aspiring speaker took the stage with McDaniel and Tom Emmer of Wisconsin, who as chairman of the NRCC had presided over the debacle. Emmer, a bear of a man, tried to pump up the applause. McCarthy forced a big grin. "It is clear that we are going to take back the House," he said. Reading closely from his text, in his trademark singsong delivery, he added: "You are out late, but when you wake up tomorrow, we will be in the majority and Nancy Pelosi will be in the minority."

The talking heads on Fox News were not buying it. "Not the night that he hoped for, certainly not," host Martha MacCallum said.

Baier agreed, noting that Republicans had thought it possible they would gain 35 or more seats. "It's probably going to be 10 or less," he deduced, correctly.

Republicans had not secured a majority by the next morning. Or the next morning. Or the morning after that. Eventually, more than a week after the election, enough votes had been counted for news outlets to project that the Republicans would control the House by a meager four seats. That was the same number the Democrats had had in their majority before the election. Technically, the GOP had gained control of the House (while the Senate remained under Democratic control). But nothing about it felt like a win.

The last time Republicans had seized control of the House, during Barack Obama's first term a dozen years earlier, Election Night had been a resounding triumph. John Boehner, the man who would become speaker, had broken into tears as he addressed the cheering throng on Election

Night in another D.C. hotel ballroom. "I've spent my whole life chasing the American dream," he told them. The crowd chanted "USA" to give him a chance to regain his composure. "I started out mopping floors, waiting tables, and tending bar at my dad's tavern."

McCarthy's win, if it could be called that, came with no joy. Twice before, when Boehner resigned in 2015 and when McCarthy led House Republicans into the 2020 election, he had grasped for the speakership and been denied. Now that he'd won, he heard only recriminations. "The RED WAVE did not happen," tweeted Mayra Flores, a Texas Republican, after being ousted by a Democrat. "Republicans and Independents stayed home. DO NOT COMPLAIN ABOUT THE RESULTS IF YOU DID NOT DO YOUR PART!"

How did this happen? Why had Republicans, despite the benefit of historic tailwinds, failed to rise to the moment? No doubt, the Supreme Court's overturning of *Roe v. Wade,* which unleashed fury and fear on the left, had hurt Republicans in the midterms. But at least as important was another factor, politely dubbed "candidate quality" by Republicans such as Mitch McConnell, the Senate GOP leader. Put another way, Republicans stumbled because they had nominated an extraordinary assortment of hooligans, conspiracy theorists, saboteurs, insurrectionists, white nationalists, eccentrics, extremists, ignoramuses, and oddballs—many of whom had received Donald Trump's endorsement. Not surprisingly, many of them lost.

They came from all walks of life, but for the most part they shared a common trait: They had lied about themselves and sold a bill of goods to the voters. They promulgated bogus conspiracy beliefs and conjured imaginary threats, policies, and programs. They lied about their opponents; they lied about the insurrection. Whether they believed such nonsense or whether they were cynically deceiving voters didn't matter. Either way, theirs was a campaign of deception. These charlatans had hoped to ride a "red wave," but the voters, thankfully, had no use for much of this flotsam.

Consider Ohio's J. R. Majewski, who lavishly promoted QAnon conspiracy themes, bypassed police barriers outside the Capitol on Jan. 6 (he was "pissed off at myself" that he didn't breach the Capitol building), and used 120 gallons of paint to turn his entire lawn into an enormous

Trump banner. He issued a call to "abolish all unconstitutional three-letter agencies," including the CIA. He said he was game to fight a civil war, and he made a campaign video in which he carried a rifle and said he would "bring this country back to its former glory" by doing "whatever it takes."

One of the things "it takes," apparently, is fabricating military and professional achievements. Majewski presented himself as an Air Force "combat veteran" whose "squadron was one of the first on the ground in Afghanistan after 9/11." But his military records showed that Majewski had never deployed to Afghanistan and never engaged in combat; he spent six months helping to load planes at an air base in Qatar. Majewski also called himself "an executive" at the company where he worked, but his employer did not list him among its executives.

During the campaign, Majewski had visited Washington, where he held forth at a nightclub from a table announcing him as "Congressman J. R. Majewski," the *Daily Beast* reported. The district in which he was running had been redrawn to favor Republicans, but "Congressman" Majewski still managed to lose to the incumbent Democrat, Marcy Kaptur.

Similarly, an ad for the Minnesota candidate Tyler Kistner by a super-PAC affiliated with House Republican leadership claimed he had "four combat deployments." In reality, he'd served four tours in noncombat regions (the ad was withdrawn). Kistner himself had previously claimed that he "put the enemy six feet under." The incumbent Democrat, Angie Craig, a top target for Republicans, prevailed.

In North Carolina, candidate Sandy Smith's ex-husband claimed she tried to run him over with a car and menaced him with a frying pan. Another ex-husband alleged that she had bashed his head with an alarm clock while he was sleeping. Court records showed her own daughter at one point said Smith "held me down by my hair and punched me in the face with a closed fist." In response to the allegations, Smith tweeted, "I never ran over anyone with a car and I never hit anyone in the head with a frying pan."

But her assaults on reality could not be denied. She proclaimed that after the so-called fraud in the 2020 election (she blamed Dominion voting machines), there should be "trails [sic] & executions of those found guilty of treason." She shared another social media post that invoked a conspiracy belief that alien lizards control the government. "Mike Pence is an extension of what the lizards want you to believe is 'failed Republican leadership,'" it said. "That's a psyOp. What's REAL is that Mike Pence acted as an integral player in a deep state operation to pull off a Marxist Coup, usher in full communism, steal an election, disenfranchise the American right to vote and force a Bioweapon on the American populace." Republicans had seen the open seat as a pickup opportunity, but that was before the alien lizards got involved, and Democrat Don Davis, a state senator, prevailed.

In Michigan, Trump-backed John Gibbs ousted an incumbent Republican in the primary (who had voted to impeach Trump)—only to lose the GOP-held seat to a Democrat, Hillary Scholten. Gibbs repeatedly offered bizarre claims on social media that Hillary Clinton's 2016 campaign chairman, John Podesta, participated in a satanic ritual involving the drinking of blood and other bodily fluids. In college, Gibbs had written that women don't "posess [sic] the characteristics necessary to govern" and that "the United States has suffered as a result of women's suffrage" (because they rely on "emotional reasoning" and are responsible for "increasing the size and scope of government"). Though a Black man, he invoked the white nationalist belief that Democrats are "eroding the white population."

North Carolina's Bo Hines lost a seat that had belonged to Republicans. The Trump-backed political neophyte had drawn national attention when he maintained during a radio interview that the term "banana republic" referred not to an underdeveloped nation but rather to a clothing retailer. "A lot of people . . . say we're in a banana republic," Hines said. "I think that's an insult to Banana Republics across the country. I mean, at least the manager of Banana Republic, unlike our president, knows where he is and why he's there and what he's doing." A Democratic state senator, Wiley Nickel, took that seat.

In Virginia, Republicans hoped Yesli Vega could oust the Democratic incumbent Abigail Spanberger in a competitive district. But then Vega responded favorably to a questioner's speculation that "it's harder for a woman to get pregnant if she's been raped." Vega commented that "it wouldn't surprise me, because it's not something that's happening organically. Right? You're forcing it."

Among the other failures:

Colorado's newly drawn Eighth Congressional District was expected to go to Republican Barbara Kirkmeyer, who once led an attempt by 11 counties to secede and become their own state. Democrat Yadira Caraveo prevailed instead. Meanwhile, Colorado's Seventh Congressional District was up for grabs because the Democratic incumbent had retired. Republican Erik Aadland, who followed the Proud Boys and other extremists on social media and who claimed the country was "on the brink of being taken over by a communist government," lost to Democrat Brittany Pettersen.

New Hampshire's First Congressional District, held by Democrat Chris Pappas, was one of Republicans' top pickup opportunities. But their candidate was a 25-year-old former Trump White House staffer who had spread lies about the 2020 election and claimed that climate change "is a manufactured crisis by the Democrat Party."

New Hampshire's Second Congressional District, held by Democrat Ann Kuster, was also potentially in play. Her pro-Trump Republican challenger, Robert Burns, claimed that before an abortion could be performed to save the life of a woman, "we would need a panel in this sort of situation" to decide whether she could get the lifesaving procedure.

Washington's Third Congressional District had been held by a Republican for 12 years. But the incumbent, Jaime Herrera Beutler, had voted to impeach Trump and was ousted in a primary. The Trump-backed nominee, Joe Kent, claimed that the Jan. 6 insurrection was an "intelligence operation," that those facing trial for attacking the Capitol were "political prisoners," and that the 2020 election was "rigged and stolen." He lost, and Democrat Marie Gluesenkamp Perez picked up the seat.

Republicans had redrawn Arizona's Fourth Congressional District in hopes of ousting the Democratic incumbent, Greg Stanton. But their candidate, Kelly Cooper, ran on a demand for the immediate release of those facing charges for their role in the insurrection. Cooper also likened IRS agents to the Gestapo. He lost.

Virginia's Tenth Congressional District, held by Democrat Jennifer Wexton, had been another Republican target. But the GOP candidate, Hung Cao, did himself no favors with his over-the-top championing of guns, including the preposterous claim that, among homicide victims, "most people get bludgeoned to death and stabbed to death," not shot. In truth, firearms cause nearly 75 percent of homicides, compared to 13 percent for blunt-object and stabbing homicides combined. Hung Cao became another Republican casualty.

Nevada's newly drawn Fourth Congressional District was within Republicans' grasp. But their nominee, Sam Peters, who used QAnon's "QArmy" hashtag and characterized those facing charges for the insurrection as "civically engaged American citizens exercising their constitutional freedoms," lost to Democratic congressman Steven Horsford.

New Jersey's competitive Fifth Congressional District offered a chance to oust Democratic incumbent Josh Gottheimer. But the Republican candidate, Frank Pallotta, failed in a rematch of the 2020 election. Pallotta had called the Oath Keepers "good people" before they stormed the Capitol in 2021, saying, "I stand by them."

And, of course, there was the at-large House seat in Republican-leaning Alaska. The cartoonish former Republican governor, Sarah Palin, tried to use the race for a political comeback—and that helped hand the seat to Mary Peltola, the first Democrat to win it in 50 years.

Had Republicans put up credible candidates in all these races and others, it's plausible that they could have picked up the dozens of seats they had been expected to win. Instead, they floated a bunch of frauds—and the red wave never came.

Chapter 2

"Voting for the Craziest Son of a Bitch in the Race"

U LTIMATELY THE BIGGER PROBLEM CAUSED BY THE 2022 MIDTERMS FOR House Republican leaders—and for Congress—wasn't the large number of GOP crazies who lost. It was the large number who won.

Without a doubt, the losses by so many exotic Republican nominees for seats that might have been competitive cost Republicans a working majority. Swing voters and independents ran from the madness.

But for core Republican voters, crazy was not disqualifying. In many congressional districts, most of them safely Republican, where the winner of the GOP primary invariably wins the general election, the zanier candidates prevailed.

Take the case of Andy Ogles, now representing Tennessee's Fifth Congressional District, which had been a Democratic seat but was redrawn after 2020 to make it safely Republican. Ogles had previously identified himself as an "economist, tax policy expert" and "Graduate—Vanderbilt Owen School [of Business]." He continued to claim "I'm an economist" after his election to the House. And he claimed to have a degree in "International Relations."

But soon after the election, it became clear that Ogles had sold the voters a series of lies. Exhaustive reporting by Nashville's NewsChannel 5 found that Ogles had merely participated in nondegree classes at Vanderbilt. His bachelor's degree was in "Liberal Studies," not international relations. And he had taken only one course in economics, at a community college, and received a C.

Ogles also claimed during the campaign to be "a former member of law enforcement" and a "trained police officer." But it turned out he was merely a volunteer reserve deputy with a county sheriff's office, and he lost that unpaid position because he didn't attend meetings and made no progress in field training.

The *Washington Post*'s Glenn Kessler subsequently found that Ogles had falsely claimed to have been on the board of directors of various organizations. He also found that several business roles Ogles claimed to have had were exaggerated or "could not be corroborated"—including a consulting firm he claimed to have run for seven years that did not appear in Tennessee corporate records.

NewsChannel 5 even found that Ogles took in $25,000 in a GoFundMe campaign for a children's burial garden (he promoted it with a photo of his own stillborn child), but the garden "never happened," the station reported.

Also in the House Republicans' Class of '22: Anna Paulina Luna of Florida's Thirteenth Congressional District, which had been redrawn from a Democratic seat to one that comfortably favored Republicans. Luna, a self-proclaimed "pro-life extremist" and election denier, had been propelled to stardom by the former Trump adviser Steve Bannon and Mike Lindell, the MyPillow CEO. The *Washington Post*'s Jacqueline Alemany and Alice Crites found Luna had embellished many aspects of her life story. She spoke of the threat to her life from a 4 a.m. "home invasion" she suffered, but her roommate at the time could recall no such thing, and police records instead referred to a daytime break-in when nobody was home. Her campaign biography said her father "spent time in and out of incarceration" during her childhood, but the *Post* found no records of prison sentences. Luna said she was "raised as a Messianic Jew" by her father, but immigration records and three family members said he was Catholic; Luna's paternal grandfather served in the armed forces of Nazi Germany.

Months after joining Congress, Luna, pregnant with her first child, published a children's book in which a Biden figure, drawn as a banana, cheats to win a footrace against a Trump figure, represented by an orange.

She also was part of a four-person team pushing for a select committee to investigate UFOs.

From Wisconsin came Derrick Van Orden, who won his election after the incumbent Democrat retired rather than face likely defeat in the rural, increasingly Republican Third Congressional District. Van Orden had joined the crowd at the Capitol on Jan. 6. He reportedly even paid for the trip with $4,000 of campaign cash left over from his previous (but unsuccessful) run for Congress. He claimed he never entered the Capitol grounds, but social media posts showed otherwise, placing him inside a restricted area closed off by barriers.

Van Orden doesn't require an insurrection to be disruptive. In 2021, a 17-year-old library worker in Wisconsin said he threatened her because a gay pride book was on display at the library, shouting and "aggressively shoving the books around" and demanding to know who arranged the display so he could "teach them a lesson."

Once in Congress, he made a name for himself by yelling and cursing at high school students serving as Senate pages because they were taking photos from the floor of the Rotunda (it was their last week on the job). The representative called them "lazy shits" and told them to "get the fuck up," reported *Punchbowl News*. Van Orden refused to apologize.

Also elected in 2022 was Ohio's Max Miller, who had been a midlevel aide in Trump's White House. His former girlfriend from the time, White House press secretary Stephanie Grisham, accused him of physical abuse and violence. Grisham reported the alleged abuse by Miller to the president and First Lady, who seemed "totally unfazed." Miller's defamation lawsuit against Grisham was dismissed.

The eccentricities of Class of '22 member Ryan Zinke of Montana were already well known in Washington. As Donald Trump's secretary of the interior, he rode a horse to work on his first day, and he ordered the department to fly a special "secretarial flag" from the building's roof whenever Zinke was in residence. He resigned under pressure in 2018 in the face of multiple probes into his real estate dealings, and the Interior Department's inspector general found that Zinke repeatedly violated federal ethics rules while in office.

Just days after being sworn in as a member of the new Congress, Zinke went to the House floor to announce that he had triumphed over the "Deep State," which, in Zinke's imagination, is a cabal that secretly runs the government. "Despite the Deep State's repeatedly [*sic*] attempts to stop me, I stand before you as a duly elected member of the United States Congress and tell you that a Deep State exists, and it is perhaps the strongest covert weapon the left has against the American people."

Zinke went on to say that "the Deep State runs secret messaging campaigns with one goal in mind: to increase its power to censor and persuade the American people." Claiming that "shell organizations" funded by foreign investors "repeatedly attempt to destroy the American West," the lawmaker said "they want to wipe out the American cowboy completely."

Yee-haw.

WITH SUCH AN EXTRAORDINARY LINEUP OF LUNACY, IT WAS GOING TO BE difficult for members of the freshman class to distinguish themselves as the nuttiest of the nutty. But there were many fine attempts.

Florida Republican Cory Mills celebrated his appointments to the House Armed Services and Foreign Affairs committees by handing out grenades to members of Congress. He wrote in a note accompanying the munitions that "it is my pleasure to give you a 40 mm grenade, made for an MK19 grenade launcher" (not included). Only at the bottom of the page would recipients find an asterisk labeling the weapon "inert." (This was not Mills's first stint as arms dealer: The co-founder of a security business, he previously claimed to have "sold tear gas used on Black Lives Matter protesters.")

Mike Collins of Georgia, who carried an assault rifle in a campaign video, falsely claimed during the campaign that Trump had won the Peach State in 2020, and Collins spoke in support of defendants charged in the Jan. 6 insurrection. Once elected, Collins promptly hired as his chief of staff one Brandon Phillips, who had been arrested the previous month on a charge of animal cruelty for allegedly kicking a dog and cutting its belly, *Politico*'s Daniel Lippman reported. (Collins's office didn't respond to my request for an update.) The staffer had resigned as Trump's Georgia director in 2016 after his *prior* criminal history came out: He had pleaded guilty to battery. Collins further distinguished himself by speculating on the House floor in 2023 that a spate of train derailments was caused by "Norfolk Southern's DEI"—diversity, equity, and inclusion—"policies directing resources away from the important things like greasing wheel bearings." Added Collins: "This insanity must stop."

Trump-backed Harriet Hageman of Wyoming, who had ousted Liz Cheney in a primary, claimed during the campaign that the 2020 "election was rigged" and echoed a QAnon allegation that "Joe Biden is the largest or the most destructive human trafficker in our history." Her conspiracy theorizing at one hearing was so bizarre that the (Trump-appointed) FBI director Christopher Wray called it "insane."

Eli Crane of Arizona, another star of the Class of '22, referred to Black Americans as "colored people" on the floor of the House. (He said he "misspoke.") Iowa's Zach Nunn described the bloody insurrection as "a bunch of middle-aged individuals . . . walking onto the floor." And in court in 2021, Texas's Monica De La Cruz had overcome accusations by her estranged husband of "cruel and aggressive conduct" toward his then 14-year-old daughter. (De La Cruz denied it.)

And from Long Island, New York, came a young gay Republican who, on the strength of his extraordinary résumé, won an open seat previously held by a Democrat. Before long, George Santos would become the most famous of all the members of the Class of '22.

THIS WAS, WITHOUT A DOUBT, THE ZANIEST BUNCH OF LAWMAKERS TO ENTER the House of Representatives since . . . well, since the Class of '20.

That batch included Georgia's Marjorie Taylor Greene, who was famous for, among other things, promoting such beliefs as: Jewish space lasers start forest fires; Democratic officials ought to be executed; pandemic public health restrictions were akin to actions of Nazi Germany; joining the U.S. military is "like throwing your life away"; the 9/11 attacks were an inside job; various school shootings were faked; members of Congress are being spied on by "Nancy Pelosi's Gazpacho Police"; Bill Clinton and Barack Obama are murderers; and "the Democrats are a party of pedophiles."

Shortly after the 2022 election, she went to a gala held by the New York Young Republicans and shared with the crowd the latest outrage she had discovered. "You can pick up a butt plug or a dildo at Target and CVS nowadays," she informed them. She also offered thoughts on how the Jan. 6 insurrection could have succeeded. "I want to tell you something," Greene said. "If [former Trump strategist] Steve Bannon and I had organized that, we would have won. Not to mention, it would have been armed."

Also arriving in the House after the 2020 election was Lauren Boebert of Colorado, who said she would carry her Glock in Washington, joked about a Muslim congressional colleague's being a suicide bomber, blamed Anthony Fauci for causing puppies to be "eaten alive," indignantly proclaimed that "we're not a democracy," and routinely accused trans people and those on the left of "grooming" children for pedophiles. Her Christmas card photo showed her children posing with AR-15–style weapons.

In a signature moment, Boebert and her boyfriend were escorted out of a Denver performance of the musical *Beetlejuice* in September 2023 after the venue accused her of vaping, singing, recording, and "causing a disturbance." During the show, a pregnant woman said Boebert refused her request to stop vaping. The U.S. representative, in turn, blew smoke at the woman. Boebert denied the claims. Then the venue released video surveillance footage showing Boebert vaping, singing, using flash photography, and behaving aggressively toward staff. It also showed her boyfriend groping her breasts and Boebert groping his crotch. Boebert, then a 36-year-old grandmother, attributed her behavior to a "difficult divorce" she was going through.

And the divorce, complete with restraining order and public accusations, wasn't her only difficulty. Facing potential defeat by a Democrat, she announced at the end of 2023 that she would instead run for a vacant seat in a more Republican district.

Boebert's 2020 classmate Matt Rosendale of Montana also saw the personal overtake his political ambitions. In rapid succession, he withdrew his bid for the Senate and then his reelection to the House in early 2024, saying he was the victim of "false and defamatory rumors against me and my family." Former Democratic senator Heidi Heitkamp of North

Dakota had publicly floated a "rumor" that he "impregnated a 20-year-old staff person," which Rosendale denied.

The GOP Class of '20 also included a gun dealer, Andrew Clyde of Georgia. Clyde handed out AR-15 lapel pins to colleagues (who happily wore them), and he opposed the awarding of the Congressional Gold Medal to police officers who had defended the Capitol on Jan. 6. Clyde had famously called the attack a "normal tourist visit."

Nancy Mace of South Carolina, duly elected in 2020, was known for her erratic voting, office management (her chief of staff left in a mass staff exodus and then ran in a primary campaign against her), and public pronouncements. Speaking at an annual prayer breakfast, she informed the crowd that her fiancé "tried to pull me by my waist over this morning in bed," but she turned him down. "He can wait. I'll see him later tonight," Mace told the worshippers. The couple later split.

And rounding out the roster for the Class of '20 was Ronny Jackson of Texas, who as White House physician under Donald Trump was known as "Candyman" for liberally dispensing pills without paperwork. His subsequent nomination by Trump to be secretary of veterans affairs fell through over allegations that he had been drunk on the job, had an explosive temper, and fostered a toxic work environment.

The toxicity continued after his election. On the same day as a mass shooting at an Indiana mall and two months after the Uvalde school massacre in his home state, Jackson tweeted a photo of himself holding two AR-15s (one aimed at his toes) with the words "I will NEVER surrender my AR-15. If Democrats want to push an insane gun-grab, they can COME AND TAKE IT!" At a rodeo outside Amarillo in the summer of 2023, Jackson got into an altercation with a state trooper—disobeying the officer, lunging and jabbing at him, and calling him "a fucking full-on dick" who had "better recalculate, motherfucker." Jackson referred to himself as "a retired U.S. Navy Rear Admiral," but in fact the Navy had demoted him in 2022 because of his antics as White House doctor.

This extraordinary influx of dubious characters added to an already broad base of oddballs that had arrived during the Trump years:

Matt Gaetz of Florida, elected in 2016, a hotheaded champion of Trump and insurrectionists, liked to brag to his House colleagues about his sexual conquests. The Justice Department investigated Gaetz as part of a sex-trafficking probe that led to a friend of his being sentenced to 11 years in prison for offenses including sex trafficking of a minor. The probe ended without charges for Gaetz, but the House Ethics Committee then resumed its investigation into whether Gaetz "engaged in sexual misconduct and/or illicit drug use, shared inappropriate images or videos on the House floor," and more.

In a typical Gaetz move, he hired as his legislative assistant for military policy a former Army National Guard sergeant who had spent eight years in prison as a war criminal for murdering an Afghan civilian.

Ralph Norman of South Carolina was elected the same year as Gaetz. Norman called for Trump to bring out the military to overturn the 2020 election by declaring martial law—but didn't know how to spell it. "Our LAST HOPE is invoking Marshall Law!!" he wrote in a text to Trump's chief of staff.

Clay Higgins of Louisiana came to Congress after a career as a police officer in which he resigned from two separate police departments under clouds, first for alleged misconduct (he was accused of assaulting a Black bystander) and later for a video talking about the "animals" of a mostly Black gang. In Congress, he posts violence-themed messages on social media using military and police codes. In a typical post on Facebook, he threatened that if Black Lives Matter protesters came armed to a Louisiana protest, "I'll drop any 10 of you where you stand." He added that "we don't want to see your worthless ass" and vowed that "your journey will end, fast. How fast? 1,450 FPS fast." He was referring to the speed of a rifle bullet.

Also serving in Congress since 2017 was Louisiana's Mike Johnson, a far-right advocate of biblical "covenant marriage." He blamed legal abortion for mass shootings and entered into an electronic monitoring system with his teenage son that would send each an alert if the other accessed pornography. Johnson would tell a group of Christian nationalists in 2023 that God had chosen him to be the new Moses of the Republicans.

The more seasoned oddballs included Arizona's Paul Gosar, a former dentist with extensive ties to white nationalist leaders and groups, and Maryland's Andy Harris, an anesthesiologist who said he prescribed the deworming drug ivermectin to treat covid. Andy Biggs (Arizona) and Scott

Perry (Pennsylvania), had, along with Gaetz, sought preemptive pardons from Trump for their efforts to overturn the 2020 election, according to the Jan. 6 committee. (They denied this.) Biggs, for his part, was a class act. At an Election Night party in Arizona for the 2022 midterms, he joked about the hammer attack on Nancy Pelosi's husband at their home that left him with a fractured skull. According to Biggs, Pelosi was "losing the gavel but finding the hammer."

And Perry, who headed the right-wing House Freedom Caucus throughout 2023, was a conspiracy-theory devotee who saw Islamic terrorists around every corner. Text messages revealed in court filings showed that he texted constantly with Trump lawyers, White House officials, and state government leaders about his various schemes to block the certification of the 2020 election results. According to the congressional panel investigating the Jan. 6 attack on the Capitol, Perry even tried to sell the Trump administration on the idea that an Italian defense contractor had conspired with the CIA to use military satellites to change Trump votes to Biden votes—an idea a Trump Justice Department official called "pure insanity."

But insanity is no vice in this GOP. Perry, as head of the Freedom Caucus, was one of the most powerful figures in the House.

REPUBLICANS WERE NOT TRADING UP WITH THESE CHARACTERS. WITH EACH election cycle, more of the sensible members of the House Republican caucus retired, fed up with the growing power of the crazies—and were replaced with yet more crazies. Among the more reasonable and reputable House lawmakers who had been forced into retirement in 2022 by MAGA Republicans or quit in disgust were Liz Cheney, Adam Kinzinger, and six other Republicans who had voted to impeach Donald Trump after the Jan. 6 insurrection. Only two of the 10 who voted their conscience that day, David Valdao and Dan Newhouse, won reelection—and Trump was still pushing to oust Newhouse in a 2024 primary. Fred Upton of Michigan, well liked on both sides of the aisle, retired after 36 years in the House, citing, in part, regular death threats he had received. Among his offenses: voting for a bipartisan infrastructure deal, which prompted Marjorie Taylor Greene to brand him a "traitor" and post his phone number on social media. "You're a fucking piece of shit traitor. I hope you die," went one of the resulting voicemails, which Upton played on CNN. The caller also wished death upon Upton's family and staff.

And the attempted purging of moderates continues in the 2024 election cycle. After antiabortion activist Mark Houck was arrested and charged with assault at an abortion clinic (he was later acquitted), several House Republicans turned him into a celebrity. Perry brought him as his guest to the 2023 State of the Union address, the House Judiciary Committee featured him as a witness at a hearing, and lawmakers accused a "tyrannical" FBI of "raiding" his house. (In fact, agents knocked at his door, and he surrendered without incident.)

Houck then used his newfound fame to launch an unsuccessful primary challenge against one of the few Republican moderates in the House, Pennsylvania's Brian Fitzpatrick. Houck's campaign to oust Fitzpatrick included a call for an abortion ban without exceptions for rape or incest and Houck's tale of overcoming a pornography addiction. He said that he "didn't want to run for Congress" but was encouraged to challenge Fitzpatrick by Perry and three other House Republicans.

Similarly, far-right House Republicans endorsed a primary challenger to moderate Texas Republican Tony Gonzales. Gaetz's communications director gave the challenger, Brandon Herrera (a "known neo-Nazi," Gonzales alleged on CNN), a tour of the Capitol, which Herrera celebrated on Instagram. Gaetz joined Illinois Republican Mary Miller in endorsing a primary challenge to a mainstream Illinois Republican, Mike Bost, CNN's Melanie Zanona reported. And on and on.

AFTER SEVERAL ELECTION CYCLES OF PURGES, THE HOUSE GOP NO LONGER has a critical mass of grown-ups to stop the madness. The Congressional Research Service found that the average length of service in the House for members of both parties was 8.5 years, down from 10.3 years in 2009. But the median tenure for a House Republican was just *four years*. Most didn't know a time before Trump took a wrecking ball to the American political system.

It's no mystery why this has happened. Thanks in part to excessive gerrymandering, all but a handful of House seats are from uncompetitive districts. One of the best recent examples is North Carolina, where voters are about evenly split between Republicans and Democrats and where the 14 congressional seats are evenly split between the parties, 7–7. But Republicans, who control the state legislature, redrew a map in late 2023 so that 10 of the 14 congressional districts are all but guaranteed to elect a Republican—no matter who is on the ballot.

In this environment, where maps have been engineered to make seats uncompetitive in general elections, the surest way for a Republican to get elected and reelected to Congress is to appeal to the tiny, fanatical sliver of the electorate that participates in Republican primaries—the ones whose views are most informed, or rather misinformed, by Fox News and the darkest corners of the web.

In the summer of 2023, a nonpartisan election reform group, Unite America, issued a report finding that just 8 percent of voters had effectively elected 83 percent of the members of Congress. This is because not even one in five eligible voters participates in primaries, which in most districts are the only competitive elections.

Unite America, as my *Washington Post* colleague Karen Tumulty noted, looked at the elections of eight of the House Republicans best known for blocking the House from conducting its business: Biggs, Crane, Boebert, Gaetz, Greene, Rosendale, Dan Bishop of North Carolina, and Bob Good of Virginia. These eight leading troublemakers were effectively elected by just 12 percent of the voters in their districts, or 543,998 people—and these eight districts contain just 2 percent of the overall U.S. electorate.

In effect, this means that, in a country of 330 million, just over half a million people can, through their votes in Republican primaries, essentially bring the government to a halt. This is no way to run a country and certainly no way for a democracy to function. But this is our current reality.

This is not to absolve Democrats, who commit their own redistricting shenanigans and elect their share of exotic candidates. But there is a fundamental difference. The Democratic primary electorate is more ideologically diverse, with a larger proportion of moderates participating. In 2023, Gallup found that 72 percent of Republicans identified as conservative, whereas 54 percent of Democrats called themselves liberals. This results in fewer extremist Democrats winning primaries in safe districts and therefore holding fewer seats in the House. And this, in turn, helps to explain why the Democratic House in 2021 and 2022 was able to function with a slim five-seat majority but the Republican House in 2023, with a similarly slim majority, struggled to get anything done.

Ideological "polarization" is a misnomer, for there is far more extremism in the GOP. The nonpartisan Pew Research Center found that, from 1971 to 2022, House Democrats became 23 percent more liberal, while Republicans became more than 100 percent more conservative. On a left-to-right scale of −1.0 to 1.0, House Democrats are at −0.38, while House Republicans are at 0.51. The political scientists call this "asymmetric polarization": One side is measurably nuttier than the other.

Measured by numbers of extremists, there's no comparison. There are more than four times as many extremists in the Republicans' far right House Freedom Caucus than there are in the Democrats' nearest equivalent, the far-left "Squad," an informal group of eight—several of whom face primary challenges in 2024 from more centrist candidates. There are five overlapping ideological caucuses in the House GOP, dubbed the "five families," in reference to the 1930s mafia crime families: the relatively moderate (and bipartisan) Problem Solvers, Republican Governance Group, and Main Street Caucus; the conservative Republican Study Group; and the far-right Freedom Caucus. But the Freedom Caucus routinely prevails over the others because of its constant threats to blow up the legislative process.

Republicans who stray too far from far-right orthodoxy in Congress are punished back home. In 2021, for example, county Republican parties censured 21 of their fellow Republicans, the website Five ThirtyEight found, compared to five Democrats censured by county Democratic parties. In North Carolina, the state GOP voted to censure Republican Senator Thom Tillis for an unforgivable sin: working with Democrats on immigration, LGBTQ rights, and gun-violence prevention. In 2024, the Oklahoma Republican Party censured conservative Republican senator James Lankford because he dared to negotiate a border security compromise with Democrats.

Tom Massie of Kentucky, one of the two rank-and-file lawmakers who bothered to attend McCarthy's Election Night fete, often tells the story of when he first won election to Congress, in 2012. He thought GOP primary voters favored libertarians. Eventually, it dawned on him that philosophy had little to do with it. "What I realized is they're not voting for the libertarian leaning, you know, Republican ideology," he said. "They're voting for the craziest son of a bitch in the race. And I happened to be that."

This cycle of extremism, repeated every two years, has left House Republicans without a grown-up in the room to stop the wildest impulses of the conspiracy crowd. And, as the 118th Congress began, the "craziest SOBs" held the balance of power in the U.S. House of Representatives.

Chapter 3

"Look, There's a Lot of Frauds in Congress. I Mean, George Santos Is the Least of This Country's Worries"

N EW YORK WAS ONE OF THE FEW BRIGHT SPOTS FOR REPUBLICANS ON Election Night 2022. They picked up three seats that Democrats had held. In the Third Congressional District, which extends from Queens into Long Island's wealthy North Shore, George Santos scored a mild upset, winning an open seat that had previously belonged to a Democrat.

The Trump-backing 34-year-old, who identified himself as a gay man and a "proud American Jew," the grandson of Holocaust survivors and son of a Latino-immigrant mother who was in the South Tower of the World Trade Center on 9/11, had a compelling life story.

He said that he had been a star volleyball player at Baruch College, then went on to get a business degree from New York University, score top jobs at Citigroup and Goldman Sachs, and amass a fortune in real estate. He had a successful acting career on the side and helped produce a Broadway hit. He knew tragedy—four employees at one of his companies were killed in the Orlando gay nightclub shooting—and was full of compassion, creating a charity that saved the lives of more than 2,500 dogs and cats.

As the world now knows, all of it was a lie. In real life, George Santos had been a drag queen in Brazil. And he would soon be indicted for fraudulently receiving unemployment insurance and for stealing donors' identities and using their credit cards to enrich himself. Republican leaders knew he was a fraud, yet they kept voters in the dark, and even helped Santos, with their endorsements and money, win a seat in Congress.

Worse, House Republican leaders stood by Santos even after he was exposed as a fraud. The reason was simple, if craven—and it said everything you need to know about their nihilistic pursuit of power. Kevin McCarthy needed Santos's vote, first to be elected speaker in a vote of the House and then, because Republicans had only a four-seat majority, to pass the Republican agenda on the House floor.

McCarthy could have refused to seat Santos, daring him to challenge the decision in court, or expelled him immediately after seating him—but he did neither. Instead, McCarthy—even as he removed Democrat Adam Schiff from the House Intelligence Committee because he allegedly "lied to the American people" during Trump's first impeachment—named Santos to the Small Business Committee and the Science, Space, and Technology Committee.

In fairness, Santos *did* have relevant small-business experience. He went from having only $55,000 in earned income in 2020 to claiming that he loaned his campaign $700,000 in the 2022 cycle, apparently earned from a "family firm" that had $80 million in assets but no listed clients. (Later, Santos voluntarily surrendered the assignments.)

"You know why I'm standing by him?" McCarthy said of Santos. "Because his constituents voted for him." Constituents whom Santos deceived—with McCarthy's complicity. McCarthy continued to stand by Santos even after federal prosecutors in May 2023 indicted him on 13 counts of wire fraud, money laundering, stealing public funds, and lying in his federal disclosures.

McCarthy stood by Santos even after a paid fundraiser for Santos was indicted on federal charges of wire fraud and identity theft for impersonating McCarthy's own chief of staff in a bid to coerce contributions to Santos's campaign.

This is why the Santos affair was a damning distillation of what House Republicans had allowed themselves to become. Santos was a charlatan, but charlatans have been elected to Congress since the Founding. What distinguished Santos was that party leaders helped him get elected even though they knew better, and then they kept him in office for nearly a year even though it was obvious he had no business being there. Only one thing mattered: They needed his vote.

Perhaps there was another reason why McCarthy and his House GOP leadership team stuck with Santos for nearly a year. Santos was, in a sense, showing the party what it had become, just as Trump had done eight years earlier. Trump recognized that the party faithful were awash in conspiracy theories and paranoia, fueled by Fox News and the rest of the right-wing echo chamber; they had been conditioned to embrace "alternative facts," in a Trump aide's immortal formulation, and Trump supplied them. Compared to Trump's insurrection-provoking lies, Santos's inventions were relatively easy to swallow. "Really, who lies about playing college volleyball?" Congresswoman Nancy Mace, the South Carolina Republican, joked onstage at a Washington gala. "If you're going to lie, at least make it about something big, like you actually won the 2020 presidential election."

Or, as Republican congressman Tony Gonzales of Texas put it on CBS's *Face the Nation:* "Look, there's a lot of frauds in Congress. I mean, George Santos is the least of this country's worries."

Another Trump innovation was the discovery that, because of intense tribal partisanship in the GOP, there was no longer such a thing as shame or disgrace. Trump, caught in wrongdoing or scandal, blamed the "Deep State" or the "globalists"—and the party rallied to his defense. This politics of victimhood was the essence of Trump (who could, and did, claim it was sunny when it was raining). Trump loved to complain about the "witch-hunts" and the "hoaxes" and how unfairly he was treated by the "fake news"—and many Republicans believed him. Naturally, the technique filtered down to the rank and file. Where once there was shame, there was now only grievance, directed at imagined conspiracies of dark forces. When Luna and Ogles were caught fabricating their past, they played the victim, claiming persecution by leftists. Santos, too, used this playbook. His lies are everybody else's fault—honest!

Like Trump, Santos claimed to be the victim of a "witch-hunt" by "desperate journalists" and "enemies" in the press who are "not interested in covering the facts." He complained that the "weaponized justice system is going after conservatives," adding, "If they can do it to Trump, imagine what they can do to us." He alleged victimization by "politicians" and "party leaders"—including Republican officials who he suggested doctored his résumé without his knowledge to include fake test scores and a fake MBA from New York University.

The Long Island liar blamed unnamed others for financial irregularities at his bogus pet-rescue charity. He blamed Portuguese translators for his wild claim that he survived an assassination attempt. He suggested that unknown others framed him 12 years ago by setting up a Wikipedia page attributing to him a successful drag and acting career. "I have to sit down and endure people say[ing] things about me that are absolutely not true," Santos protested.

People saying untrue things? The nerve!

He complained about his "uncomfortable" fame. "I can't stand it," said the guy who came early to snag a center-aisle seat at the State of the Union. Sad! Particularly because all Santos wanted was to be "a good servant to the American people . . . giving back what I've been able to reap." (From that Ponzi scheme where he worked, perchance?)

Yet one element of Santos's defense rang true to me. "If the media put the equal amount of effort and resources," he said, "on all 435 members of the House and 100 members of the Senate, I think the American people would have more clarity about who represents them in Congress."

I agree. The vast majority of House members, because they don't face competitive general elections, never get a proper vetting because the parties can't be bothered, and local media has been decimated. How many others have faked their way to high office with bogus claims, or have claimed backgrounds and associations that wouldn't hold up to scrutiny in the light of day? This shared vulnerability was likely one more reason so many of Santos's Republican colleagues refused to expel this fraud. That, and the utter absence of leadership.

THERE HAVE ALWAYS BEEN ODDBALLS, EXTREMISTS, AND CONSPIRACY THEORISTS on Capitol Hill. But now there's a crucial difference. Until recently, congressional leaders kept the fanatics in line. They criticized them publicly or denied them plum committee assignments.

John Boehner, the Republican speaker of the House from 2011 through 2015, did battle with what he called the "crazy caucus," a euphemism for the far-right Freedom Caucus. After attempts by the hardliners to force him out as speaker, he resigned in disgust. Similarly, Paul Ryan, the Republican speaker for three years starting in late 2015, struggled to keep the growing crazy caucus under control before he quit, also in failure. Though not as courageous as Boehner (Ryan joined Fox Corporation as a director), Ryan did, in 2021, condemn "yes-men and flatterers flocking to Mar-a-Lago."

Alas for Republicans, and for the country, Kevin McCarthy, elected in 2018 to succeed Ryan as the House GOP leader, was a thorough yes-man and flatterer who did flock to Mar-a-Lago for Trump's approval after fleetingly criticizing Trump for instigating the Jan. 6 attack.

In essence, McCarthy and his leadership team, after watching the failures of Boehner and Ryan, concluded that the only way to lead the extremists was to be led by them. To further their own ambition, the cowards would enable the crazies.

One member of McCarthy's leadership team didn't merely enable the crazies but became one herself after undergoing a thorough reinvention. Once upon a time, Elise Stefanik of New York, a Harvard graduate who co-chaired a small group of Republican moderates in the House, boasted about her bipartisan efforts, rejected the party's tax-cutting orthodoxy, and condemned Trump's "insulting" treatment of women, his "untruthful statements," and his proposed Muslim ban and border wall. But after Trump won in 2016, she reinvented herself as a MAGA Republican, and she ultimately succeeded in ousting, and replacing, Trump critic Liz Cheney as House Republican Conference chairwoman.

McCarthy, by contrast, had never shown any interest in ideology, nor in policy. He was perfectly malleable on matters of principle, adopting whatever sincerely held belief matched the moment. He was a savvy operator and a master at the backslapping aspect of politics, and he was by all accounts well liked among colleagues. But when it comes to substance, he was an amiable dunce, as he demonstrated memorably and repeatedly over the years.

Back in 2021, when McCarthy had made a typically mindless claim that mask-wearing during the pandemic wasn't supported by "science," NBC News' Frank Thorp asked then-speaker Nancy Pelosi for a response.

"He's such a moron," Pelosi replied.

That was a matter of opinion. But what McCarthy did next was, well, moronic. He launched a fundraising campaign in which, for a contribution of $25 or more, he would send the donor a T-shirt that said "MORON" in big letters. "You're a top patriot and HE NEEDS YOU to get this t-shirt to oppose HER & the Radical Socialist Left," the solicitation urged.

It was a remarkable self-own. McCarthy figured that his supporters would enjoy identifying themselves as morons as much as he enjoyed the label. The moron T-shirt offer fizzled.

Such moments had been something of a McCarthy signature.

After just one term in Congress, he had ascended to Republican chief deputy whip in 2009, and one of his first major projects was to build a new website for House Republicans, called americaspeakingout.com. The idea was for Republicans to crowd-source policy ideas and have people vote them up or down. McCarthy was *very* proud of the software. "I personally traveled to Washington state and discovered a Microsoft program that helped NASA map the moon," he boasted.

Using lunar software was appropriate, because the responses to the Republicans' request for policy ideas were far out:

"End Child Labor Laws," suggested one helpful participant. "We coddle children too much. They need to spend their youth in the factories."

"A 'teacher' told my child in class that dolphins were mammals and not fish!" another complained. "And the same thing about whales! We need TRADITIONAL VALUES in all areas of education. If it swims in the water, it is a FISH. Period! End of Story."

"I know this guy in Nigeria he says he's going to inherit a lot of money . . ."

The website was overrun by pranksters, and McCarthy's brainchild was shut down.

But McCarthy endured, rising to majority whip, then Republican leader. He famously lost a chance to be speaker in 2015 when he admitted to Fox's Sean Hannity that Republicans had created a select committee to probe the terrorist attack on U.S. diplomats in Benghazi, Libya, for the express purpose of hurting Hillary Clinton's presidential prospects. "Her numbers are dropping. Why? Because she's untrustable," McCarthy said in his inimitable way.

In 2016, McCarthy told fellow Republicans he believed Donald Trump was on Vladimir Putin's payroll—"swear to God." Aghast, then-speaker Paul Ryan silenced McCarthy.

In 2018, McCarthy tweeted, then deleted, a warning that three men of Jewish descent, George Soros, Tom Steyer, and Mike Bloomberg, wanted "to BUY this election!"

On *60 Minutes* in 2019, McCarthy was asked about then-president Donald Trump's infamous request of the Ukrainian president, "I'd like you to do us a favor, though." McCarthy, unaware this was a verbatim quote from the White House transcript, accused CBS of doctoring it.

Later, McCarthy trumpeted on Fox News an apocryphal report that Biden "is going to control how much meat you can eat." McCarthy also claimed not to know about QAnon (which he called "Q-on"): "I don't know if I say it right. I don't even know what it is." He had spoken several times previously about QAnon, by name.

All along, he waged a brave, lonely battle against the English language. He joined other GOP leaders at weekly news conferences, at which he would invariably step to the microphone, open his eyes wide, and say something baffling.

In 2014, I chronicled McCarthy's musings on blind justice ("You see the Supreme Court, you see the statue sitting there, blinded in the process with the weights in between"), on Obamacare enrollment ("He only totes the 8 million... How can we fall going forward?"), and on charter schools ("This is a great strength of a change making an equalizer inside for economy throughout"). In a 2015 foreign policy address, he announced that he had visited "Hungria" and lamented that Russia is "keeping the place of the band on America." He also scolded the Department of Veterans Affairs for failing to assist returning service members "who fought to the death in Ramadi."

He sounded like part Yoda, part Google Translate. I asked McCarthy's then-communications director, Matt Sparks, if the leader had a speech disability (in which case I obviously wouldn't ridicule him). But Sparks made no such claim, instead calling my interest in McCarthy's words "a bit sad and very odd."

The very day Pelosi called him a moron, McCarthy complained on the House floor that the latest mask guidance came from a study in India (not so) of an unapproved vaccine (also not so) that "didn't even pass purr review." Meow!

The day after Pelosi called him a moron, he offered more McCarthyisms:

On President Biden: "The president, we sat to met with, that we wanted to be—keep our path be energy independent."

On a retired colleague: "Former liberal senator Barbara Boxer is now has the effect of being robbed in Oakland."

On Pelosi: "She will go at no elms to break the rules."

Later that year, McCarthy delivered an $8\frac{1}{2}$-hour speech on the House floor as a symbolic protest against Biden's agenda. Among the crucial questions he raised: "Does McDonald's still have the dollar meal?"

In December 2022, as he tried to rally support to win the speakership, he gave a news conference, with predictable results.

"We're Christmas season," he began. We are? He continued: "A talk of the majority right now who wants to put a small continuing resolution to bump all the members up two days before Christmas, to try to vote on a package they cannot read, written by two individuals who will not be here, on spending for the entire government."

Do not even attempt to diagram that sentence.

McCarthy's allies in the House, facing the House Freedom Caucus members' increasingly noisy threats to deny McCarthy the speakership, searched for a way to right his listing bid for the speakership. In an attempted show of support, they passed out pro-McCarthy lapel buttons: stars on a field of blue with a red band in the middle that proclaimed, simply, "O.K."

It was meant to signify "Only Kevin," as CNN's Melanie Zanona reported, intended as a rejoinder to the "Never McCarthy" hardliners on the right. But the message had an unfortunate double meaning that highlighted the doubts about their always-a-bridesmaid-never-a-bride candidate for speaker. McCarthy is just that: okay. As in: Not great. Not even above average. Just okay. They might as well have made up pro-McCarthy buttons that said "Meh."

The "O.K." buttons fared no better than the "Moron" T-shirts. After the initial wave of ridicule, I went to the House floor and couldn't find a single member wearing one.

Bill Thomas, a retired Republican lawmaker and former House Ways and Means Committee chairman, knew McCarthy better than most. McCarthy had worked for Thomas for 15 years, and Thomas anointed McCarthy as his successor in his Bakersfield, California–area seat. But as McCarthy struggled to gain the speakership, Thomas told the *New Yorker*'s Jonathan Blitzer that he didn't recognize what McCarthy had become. "Kevin basically is whatever you want him to be. He lies. He'll change the lie if necessary. How can anyone trust his word?"

Thomas said that McCarthy would say whatever he needed to say to win the votes to be speaker. But then what? "What do you do after?" Thomas asked. "What have you got that keeps them tied to you?"

It was prescient. Nearly a year later, in September 2023, when McCarthy's nemesis Gaetz began his bid to oust McCarthy from the speakership, Gaetz said on the House floor that "we struggle with trust with Mr. McCarthy. Because, time and again, his viewpoints, his positions, they shift like sands underneath you."

But McCarthy, if lacking a discernible ideology and a firm grasp of policy, had a keen instinct for survival. He correctly assessed that this motley assortment of prevaricators and conspiracy theorists had come to hold the balance of power in his House Republican Caucus. And he would advance his own ambition by surrendering to them—the country be damned.

He began this capitulation by wooing Congresswoman Jewish Space Lasers herself. While still in the minority, he began inviting Greene to his Capitol office as often as once a week, and in between the meetings the pair exchanged a "constant stream of text messages," as Jonathan Swan and Catie Edmondson of the *New York Times* later recounted. He even had his general counsel intervene with Twitter executives to reactivate her account after she was banned because of her covid disinformation. He added her to House GOP leaders' strategy sessions on policy, and he gave priority to some of her pet projects: cutting off funds for Ukraine as it fights off the invasion by Vladimir Putin's Russia and hampering uptake of the lifesaving covid-19 vaccine.

She returned the favor, becoming a crucial figure in his struggle to secure the speakership. Once in power, McCarthy immediately reinstated her committee assignments (she and Gosar had been stripped of their committees in the last Congress because they had publicly fantasized about killing Democratic colleagues), placing her on the high-profile House Oversight Committee and the select committee probing covid-19's origins. "I will never leave that woman," McCarthy told a friend, in Swan and Edmondson's account. "I will always take care of her."

And she would take care of him. Before long, their tender friendship even had them sharing a personal toiletry item. At a caucus meeting, House GOP leaders, to raise money for the National Republican Congressional Committee auctioned off a lip balm that McCarthy had supposedly used. The winner: Greene, with a bid of $100,000.

AFTER EMPOWERING SUCH A DANGEROUS IDEOLOGUE AS GREENE, empowering a fraud such as Santos was relatively easy for McCarthy. And so, for the better part of a year, the fabulist lived a fabulous life in Congress.

He took a victory lap immediately after his election. "Meet the next Jewish Republican congressman from Long Island," announced a headline in the *Jewish Insider* on Nov. 10, in which Santos referred to "my mother's Jewish background beliefs, which are mine."

On Nov. 19, 2023, he took the stage at the Republican Jewish Coalition's convention in Las Vegas. "Good morning and shabbat shalom," he told the crowd, before boasting that he would increase the number of Republican "Jewish folks in Congress" to three and telling them of his "grandfather fleeing Ukraine in [the] 1920s to Belgium, then fleeing Belgium to Brazil in 1940."

He took his act to WNYC's *Brian Lehrer Show* on Nov. 21. Introduced as the "gay son of Latino and Jewish migrants" and a graduate of the City University of New York, he spoke in personal terms about the 2016 mass shooting at a gay nightclub in Orlando. "My company at the time, we lost four employees that were at Pulse nightclub," he said.

Everybody wanted a piece of Santos. He appeared on a Brazilian podcast on Dec. 7 and, in Portuguese, delivered the horrifying news that "we have already suffered an attempt on my life, an assassination attempt." The previous year, he added, he was mugged in broad daylight on Fifth Avenue and 55th Street in Manhattan, where two men took his briefcase, shoes, and watch. "They stole your shoes in the middle of Fifth Avenue?" asked the incredulous host.

"In the middle of Fifth Avenue," Santos affirmed.

On Dec. 9, he was a guest of honor at the New York Young Republican Club gala, where he rubbed elbows with a variety of white nationalists and conspiracy theorists.

Alas, Santos's excellent adventure took a dark turn on Dec. 19, when the *New York Times* published a bombshell report questioning "key parts of the résumé that he sold to voters." Citigroup and Goldman Sachs had no record of Santos working for them, as he claimed. Officials at CUNY's Baruch College, from which Santos said he graduated in 2010, had no record of him, either. And though he claimed his family fortune came from real estate, there was no evidence that he owned any properties.

Two days later, *The Forward*, a Jewish publication, reported that he apparently didn't have Jewish grandparents who fled Europe during World War II. They were in Brazil well before the Nazis came to power, and there was no sign that they were Jewish.

The floodgates opened, and over the next few weeks virtually every element of Santos's life story disintegrated. Eventually, his bio could be summarized as follows:

He didn't attend Horace Mann Prep high school, where he wasn't forced to leave because of financial difficulties. He didn't graduate from (nor attend) Baruch, where he did not get summa cum laude honors, did not earn a 3.89 GPA, and did not have a volleyball scholarship that led him to get two knee replacements. He didn't get an MBA from New York

University or get a 710 on the GMAT. He did not work for Citigroup, where the division he did not work for did not exist, nor for Goldman Sachs, where the project he didn't manage didn't double in revenues.

Four of the employees of a business he apparently did not start in Orlando did not die in the Pulse nightclub shooting. He did not have trouble evicting tenants from his 13 rental properties because he did not own such properties (but he claimed in his own 2016 eviction proceedings that a mugger had taken his rent money). His nonprofit, Friends of Pets United, did not save 2,500 dogs and cats (although Santos *was* accused of stealing $3,000 from a GoFundMe for a disabled veteran's dying service dog).

He was not a "proud American Jew," nor a Jew of any variety; his grandparents weren't Holocaust refugees and they fled neither Ukraine nor Belgium. His mother wasn't a finance executive, and she wasn't in her office in the South Tower of the World Trade Center, or even in the United States, during the 9/11 attacks, which hadn't "claimed my mother's life," as he put it. She also did not succumb a "few years later" but rather died in 2016.

He didn't help produce the Broadway show *Spider-Man: Turn Off the Dark*. He didn't help kids with a rare genetic disorder. He did not appear in Disney's *Hannah Montana* or in a movie with Uma Thurman. It wasn't even clear whether his real name was George Santos, or Anthony Zabrovsky or Anthony Devolder.

The fabulist explained his fabrications with new lies. "I never claimed to be Jewish," he lied to the *New York Post*. "I said I was 'Jew-ish.'"

A rather different life story emerged in place of the one Santos had conjured. A photo surfaced identifying him as a Brazilian drag queen by the name of Kitara Ravache. He was also alleged to have been a deadbeat tenant and to have written fraudulent checks in Brazil, and he was accused by former roommates of stealing a Burberry scarf and wearing it to a "Stop the Steal" rally.

Of more interest to the feds were his real-life financial irregularities: collecting unemployment benefits while he earned a salary of $120,000 and using political contributions to buy himself clothing and to pay off his debts. He had also worked at an investment company that the Securities and Exchange Commission said defrauded investors in a "classic Ponzi scheme."

How could such a charlatan have been elected in the first place? It's not as if there weren't warning signs. A local newspaper, the *North Shore Leader,* reported on the dubious loan he made to his campaign and the "inexplicable rise in his alleged net worth" from zero to $11 million over two years, even though he rented an apartment in an attached row house in Queens. One Republican referred to him in the article as "The Talented Mr. Santos," after the conman book and movie, *The Talented Mr. Ripley.* The Democratic Congressional Campaign Committee, though it missed most of his inventions, cast doubt on the existence of his animal-rescue nonprofit.

I had no idea about Santos's faked résumé, though his bizarre claim that he lost his previous bid for the seat in 2020 because of election fraud led me to include him in an October 2022 column titled "Think You Already Know Crazy? Meet the House GOP Class of '22."

The most damning fact, however, was that some people *did know* he was a fraud: House Republican leaders. And yet they continued to support him.

"Senior House Republicans were apparently aware of the inaccuracies and embellishments in the member-elect's resume, and the topic became a 'running joke,' multiple insiders close to House GOP leadership told The [New York] Post," the newspaper reported as Santos's stories unraveled. "'As far as questions about George in general, that was always something that was brought up whenever we talked about this race,' said one senior GOP leadership aide. 'It was a running joke at a certain point. This is the second time he's run and these issues we assumed would be worked out by the voters.'"

Worked out by the voters? The voters had no clue—and Republican leaders kept it that way.

The *Times* reported that a routine background check on Santos by his own campaign uncovered his elaborate deceptions, and members of his campaign team quit. Party leaders would almost certainly have been aware of all this. Yet McCarthy endorsed Santos in the Republican primary, and a political action committee aligned with him supported Santos financially. Santos raised money off the endorsement of House GOP

Conference chair Elise Stefanik. The National Republican Congressional Committee honored Santos as an "On the Radar" candidate in its "Young Guns" program.

McCarthy did a fundraiser for Santos. He later said, at a forum arranged by the *New York Times*, that at the time his "gut feeling" was that "something's going to come out on this guy." But he concluded that "you couldn't beat him," so he didn't try. Republicans kept their concerns quiet—lest word get out and help the Democrats win the seat.

In Washington, Santos lived his best life, clearly enjoying the notoriety. He brought Dunkin' donuts to the reporters staking out his office in the Longworth House Office Building. Those were well received, so he followed those with cupcakes and Chick-fil-A sandwiches. He wore an attention-grabbing lapel pin of an AR-15 assault rifle.

One evening, Santos, pursued by his round-the-clock media detail, went to Washington's Hill Country Barbecue for some karaoke. My source in the bar told me Santos chose to sing "I Will Survive"—but apparently lost his nerve when his turn came.

He routinely dodged reporters' questions about his lies and his legal problems. Other members of the public joined journalists in the fun of following Santos around. "Congressman Santos, who do you think is going to win *Drag Race* this season?" somebody asked Santos as he called for an elevator. The Instagram account DCHomos posted a video of his reaction: He froze, then turned around with his mouth open and gaped at the questioner.

On the House floor, he typically chose to sit with members of the far-right House Freedom Caucus, off the center aisle toward the back of the chamber. On State of the Union night, his center-aisle seat assured that he would be seen on TV greeting luminaries. There he got into a confrontation with Senator Mitt Romney of Utah. Santos recounted the inaudible exchange to *Semafor*'s Kadia Goba.

ROMNEY: "You don't belong here."
SANTOS: "Go tell that to the 142,000 that voted for me."
ROMNEY: "You're an ass."
SANTOS: "You're a much bigger asshole."

Romney later explained that Santos "should be sitting in the back row and staying quiet." The back-row comment inspired Santos to assume yet another fake persona for himself—that of a civil rights icon. "Mitt Romney... tells me, a Latino gay man, that I shouldn't sit in the front, that I should be in the back?" Santos said on a conservative podcast. "Well, guess what? Rosa Parks didn't sit in the back, and neither am I gonna sit in the back."

He shall overcome.

On Piers Morgan's show, he passed off his previous claims to be Jewish as a joke—a "party favorite." He claimed that at his speech to the Republican Jewish Coalition, "people were hysterically laughing" at his joke about being "Jew-ish." (The recording showed no such joke, and no such laughter.) Worse, Santos complained about Jews and others offended by his false story about his family fleeing the Holocaust. "Now that everybody's canceling me, everybody's pounding down for a pound of flesh," he protested.

Yes, "pound of flesh" comes from Shylock, the greedy Jew in Shakespeare's *Merchant of Venice.* Oy gevalt.

Santos spoke of how terribly sorry for himself he felt. "There's people who are granted that opportunity to apologize and redeem themselves, and there's people who are thrown into the fire pit and the media and everyone else around them are hell-bound on making sure that person's life is hell," he said. "I'm in the latter part." Still, the self-pitying prevaricator said, he would selflessly use his infamy "to the advantage of uplifting my legislative priorities for the American people."

About those legislative priorities: By the fall of 2023, the House had not acted on one of the 37 bills Santos introduced. As for constituent service, a report in July by the *Roll Call* newspaper found that the IRS and the Small Business Administration hadn't received a single bit of correspondence from Santos on behalf of the people back home.

With that record of achievement, Santos announced on Twitter on April 17, 2023, with a siren emoji: "I am proudly announcing my bid for re-election."

McCarthy, asked by CNN's Manu Raju if he would be supporting Santos for reelection, responded with a laugh, saying he would "wait and see" who else runs.

An Economist/YouGov poll in Santos's district in January 2023 found that 55 percent said he should resign, compared to 20 percent who thought he should stay (the rest were unsure). That included a plurality of Republicans who wanted him out. New York and local Republican officials demanded he resign. But McCarthy stood bravely with the young liar. "The voters elected him to serve," he maintained.

Implicit in McCarthy's claim that he's honoring the voters' wishes: that Long Islanders *knew* Santos was a phony—and they elected him anyway. Maybe Long Islanders simply love a scoundrel!

There is some evidence for this. Some of the greatest phonies of all time have made Long Island home: Bernie Madoff, Donald Trump Jr., Joey Buttafuoco, Sean Hannity, Bill O'Reilly. Santos now joined this august list.

In January 2023, an ad hoc group calling itself Concerned Citizens of NY-03 gathered in Great Neck, New York, to rebut McCarthy's "insulting" view that Long Islanders intended to elect a total fraud. "The people who voted for him didn't actually vote for him, they voted for an illusion he created," argued one of the organizers, Susan Rosenfeld Naftol. "This was not the will of the voters."

THE MORE IMMEDIATE THREAT TO SANTOS WASN'T THE WILL OF THE VOTERS but the votes of the jurors. Grand juries aren't generally known for their comic timing, but you've got to give credit to the one that indicted Santos in early May.

The jurors, sitting in Central Islip, New York, returned their indictment on May 9, 2023, charging Santos with, among other things, "fraudulent application for and receipt of unemployment benefits." The very next day, House Republicans began debate on the House floor of H.R. 1163, the "Protecting Taxpayers and Victims of Unemployment Fraud Act." One of the 35 cosponsors of the bill? George Santos.

"The Protecting Taxpayers and Victims of Unemployment Fraud Act takes much needed overdue action to recover fraudulently paid COVID benefits, prevent future fraud, and prosecute the criminals responsible," proclaimed the irony-challenged Jason Smith, a Missouri Republican and chairman of the Ways and Means Committee.

It got worse. Massachusetts Democrat Jim McGovern revealed during the floor debate that, according to the Labor Department, the GOP unemployment fraud bill actually "defunds the program that helps them catch fraud . . . Now maybe that's why George Santos cosponsored it." McGovern went on, "What's that old horror movie saying? The call is coming from inside the house? . . . The fraud is coming from inside the Republican conference."

Even as the House was debating the unemployment fraud bill, Santos was being arrested and arraigned for unemployment fraud. Outside the courthouse after the arraignment, he thanked House GOP leaders for their support. "I appreciate leadership for being patient," he said. "The way I look at it I'll be the chairman of a committee in a couple of years." But for the moment, he said, "I have to go back and vote tomorrow."

And he did. The House passed the unemployment fraud bill, 230–200. Among the ayes was Santos.

Post-indictment, Santos continued his unraveling. After another one of his campaign treasurers resigned, Santos appointed himself to the job before learning that this isn't allowed. He then named his fifth treasurer in as many months. And, though a couple of Santos's House Republican colleagues from New York demanded that he resign, GOP leaders continued to cover for him.

Democrats forced a vote on expelling Santos from Congress, but the 221 Republicans present, including Santos, unanimously blocked it, instead referring Santos's case to the House Ethics Committee, where it already was. The Ethics Committee is known for its glacial investigations in the best of times, and that was before House Republicans' rules package for the 118th Congress, adopted that January, gutted aspects of the ethics process.

Santos wrote thank-you notes to his GOP colleagues, and *Politico*'s congressional correspondent Olivia Beavers intercepted one. "I want to personally thank you," he wrote. Lamenting this "especially difficult time in my life," he went on: "Now more than ever, the Republican majority needs to stick together, and you demonstrated great dedication and courage by putting differences aside to allow the proper process to play out."

Dedication and courage? That's one way of looking at it. Another perspective came from Congressman Dan Goldman, a New York Democrat. "You are the party of George Santos!" he scolded on the House floor in June. "The guy is an alleged and acknowledged liar, and indicted, and you protect him every day . . . It's pathetic, and it's beneath you and it's beneath this body."

Goldman was right that House Republicans, by protecting the fabulist, had become the party of Santos. But he was wrong about one thing: In the post-factual, post-shame era, nothing was beneath this body.

IN LATE OCTOBER 2023, FEDERAL PROSECUTORS IN NEW YORK UNSEALED A superseding indictment against Santos, alleging, in addition to the original charges, that he stole the identities of his campaign donors and charged their credit cards for his personal purposes, while also faking his campaign finances to swindle Republican Party leaders into thinking he was a fundraising powerhouse.

In November, lawmakers tried again to expel Santos. Once again, Republicans rallied to protect him—and thereby preserve their four-seat majority.

Five endangered New York Republicans whose reelection prospects had been harmed by the Santos scandal wrote a "Dear Colleague" letter to fellow Republicans urging them to vote to expel Santos. "Some of our colleagues have said that removing Santos would further risk our already slim majority," they wrote. "To that, we say this issue is not a political one, but a moral one. Plain and simple—this is a question of right and wrong."

Their fellow Republicans took that into consideration—and decided to go with "wrong." This time, 24 Republicans voted to expel him. Fully 182 Republicans opposed the expulsion—and Santos won a reprieve.

During the debate, Santos couldn't find a single colleague to speak in his defense. So he awarded time to Democrat Goldman. "I rise today in support of this resolution to expel George Santos from Congress," Goldman began.

Santos, wearing his trademark sweater under his jacket, claimed he was a victim of the Deep State: "It is unconscionable to think that this body, who is at war with the D.O.J. over their politically motivated practices, would blindly accept their accusation against a member of another branch of government." The man who had fabricated every element of his life story and his campaign warned that "we risk losing the trust the American people place in us by passing judgment without due process." And Santos said he was "fighting, by God's grace," to clear his name.

Arguing for expulsion, New York Republican Nick LaLota told the House that Santos had "shown a consistent disregard for the principles of bipartisanship, servant leadership, good governance and civil discourse."

This was true—but if that were the standard for expulsion, House Republicans by that point would have been able to fit their entire caucus into an elevator car.

After the vote, Santos celebrated. He posted on social media (and later deleted) a doctored photo of himself wearing a crown with the caption: "If you come for me, you best not miss."

Arkansas Republican Steve Womack joked on social media after the vote: "Last night, the House saw its shadow. Unfortunately, this means there will be two more weeks of Santos."

Two weeks later, the Ethics Committee finally issued its findings—that it had uncovered "additional uncharged and unlawful conduct," and that Santos had "brought severe discredit upon the House." The report had outlandish new details: Santos had used campaign cash for Botox and spas, for visits to the Hamptons, for a $4,127.80 purchase at Hermès, for shopping at beauty-care retailer Sephora and shoe designer Ferragamo, and for Only Fans a live pornography site. It also found that the six-figure "loans" he made to his campaign were fictitious—but the "repayment" he took from his campaign for them was real. At the time when he was claiming in his financial disclosures to have more than $1 million in a savings account, the balance in the account was $3,068.63, and his checking account balance was $35.15.

"Representative Santos sought to fraudulently exploit every aspect of his House candidacy for his own personal financial profit," the panel concluded. "He blatantly stole from his campaign. He deceived donors into providing what they thought were contributions to his campaign but were in fact payments for his personal benefit."

By this time, Santos's former campaign treasurer and a campaign fundraiser had both pleaded guilty in related cases. And now the chairman of the House Ethics Committee himself was introducing a resolution to expel Santos—the third such attempt.

Santos announced that he would not seek reelection—but in a bizarre rant on social media he decried the Ethics Committee's "politicized smear" and demanded . . . a constitutional convention. "All this Congress wants to do is attack their political enemies with tit for tat unconstitutional censures, impeachments, expulsions and ethics investigations," he wrote. "THE TIME IS NOW FOR THE STATES TO RISE UP AND COMMENCE AN ARTICLE V CONSTITUTIONAL CONVENTION!"

IN THE PAST, WHEN CONFRONTED WITH A SCANDAL OF THIS MAGNITUDE, THE offender would typically resign. But Santos had no shame and wasn't about to start doing the right thing at this late stage in his congressional career. Because expulsion requires a two-thirds vote, Republicans were in control of Santos's fate. Some worried about setting a bad precedent—the only five members of the House expelled in U.S. history were either Confederates or convicts.

But really, the debate was about politics. Some Republicans didn't want to see their four-vote majority become a three-vote majority; others, particularly New York Republicans, worried that Santos would drag the party down in the next year's elections. Nobody actually cared about Santos, of course.

With an expulsion vote coming on Friday, Dec. 1, Santos went to the floor on Tuesday night, Nov. 28, to deliver a one-hour special-order speech in his own defense. It lasted six minutes. With a maroon double-breasted jacket stretching across his middle and a sweater in place underneath it as usual, he boasted about his achievements in office, which turned out to be routine constituent service: nominating kids to service academies, hosting a "congressional app challenge," and helping constituents with passports and immigration issues. "I will not be resigning," he concluded before the empty chamber.

The fabulist was about to be expelled from Congress, but not before he created a bit more mayhem. "Today at noon, I'm going to be introducing a privileged motion for expulsion of convicted and guilty-pleaded Congressman Jamaal Bowman," he announced, referring to a New York Democrat who pulled a fire alarm in a House building during a vote.

He alleged that "many members of Congress have rap sheets" (he didn't name them) and said "I will be filing a slew of complaints in the coming hours of today and tomorrow" with the Ethics Committee against his soon-to-be-former colleagues.

And he continued bashing the institution that was about to oust him. "It represents chaos—chaos—because we have a House that doesn't work for the people," he said, where "no real work is getting done." And he vowed to "take that story back to the American people."

But for himself, Santos saw boundless possibilities. Asked what he planned to do after his expected expulsion, the former Brazilian drag queen who faked his way to national fame proclaimed: "The future is endless . . . You can do whatever you want next. And I'm just going to do whatever I want." As long as he can do it from a prison cell.

Behind Santos, a Capitol garbage truck beeped. Off to the side, behind barricades, spectators taunted him when he finished: "Hey bitch, you ready to go back to jail? How much money did you spend on porn?"

Iowa Republican Zach Nunn walked by the Santos circus and, in remarks overheard by *Punchbowl News*' Mica Soellner, observed: "What a joke."

But the "joke" was on Santos's soon-to-be-former Republican colleagues, because Santos was loving every minute of the attention. "Today is my second-year wedding anniversary, and I'm going to enjoy it and try to forget the fact that it's been one year from hell," he said, promising to schedule yet more sessions with the press on his way out.

Santos pronounced himself "proud of the work I put forward" in Congress. "I wish I could do more," he said, but "if this is it, this is it."

In one sense, Santos was just the latest in a long line of congressional scoundrels. Still serving was the indicted senator Bob Menendez, a New Jersey Democrat found in possession of gold bars and cash stuffed into the pockets of a jacket with his name on it. In the House, Democrat Henry Cuellar of Texas was indicted in May 2024 for receiving bribes from an Azerbaijani oil company and a Mexican bank. Before that were Madison

Cawthorn, who faced various gun and driving charges and accused his colleagues of drug-fueled orgies; Duke Cunningham, who accepted a yacht, luxury cars, furniture, rugs, and other items listed on a bribe menu he provided to interested parties; William Jefferson, found with $90,000 in cash in his freezer wrapped in aluminum foil; and Jim Traficant, the last lawmaker to be expelled, convicted of bribery and other charges, who ended his speeches on the House floor with the phrase "Beam me up."

But in another sense, Santos was different from the others because he was a perfect distillation of the moment. At a time when Trump's Republican Party has been flooding the national debate with disinformation and conspiracy theories, Santos showed just how far one could go with a lie. And—also like Trump—he was endlessly entertaining in telling the lie.

During the expulsion debate on the floor, even those on Santos's side didn't really defend him. "I rise not to defend George Santos, whoever he is, but to defend the very precedent my colleagues are willing to shatter," argued Matt Gaetz. "Whatever Mr. Santos did with Botox or OnlyFans is far less concerning to me than the indictment against Senator Menendez who is holding gold bars inscribed with Arabic."

Santos winced and shook his head at the mention of his Botox and porn.

Troy Nehls of Texas rose to speak in defense of "George Soros," before catching himself.

And Louisiana's Clay Higgins called Santos's expulsion "the congressional equivalent of a public crucifixion."

Santos, in his defense, offered another denunciation of the Republican majority. "The most damning feature of this farce is the total perversion of the priorities of this body and this conference," he said on the floor, listing failed bills, votes, and policies.

The other side, mostly New York Republicans, denounced their colleague with contempt.

"George Santos is a liar," Anthony D'Esposito said, kicking off the debate.

LaLota declared that "there's no more provable case of election fraud before this Congress than George Santos's 2022 election fraud."

"Dear God," added Marc Molinaro, to laughter from the gallery. "My future former colleague is divorced from reality. He has manufactured his entire life to defraud the voters of his district."

And Max Miller, of Ohio, given just 15 seconds of floor time to close the debate, declared, "You, sir, are a crook!"—then hurried from the chamber.

Santos tried, unsuccessfully, to strike down Miller's words. He then reminded the House that Miller "is accused of being a woman beater."

Seconds later, he piously declared, "I'm not going to stand here and use the time I have to say ill things about my colleagues."

And with that final contradiction, the Great Prevaricator rested his case. "Take the vote," he told them. "I am at peace."

Republican leaders, more concerned about the loss of Santos's seat than the institution's loss of dignity, made a last-ditch attempt to save Santos. Speaker Johnson announced his opposition earlier in the week, and then, before the vote, majority leader Steve Scalise, whip Tom Emmer, and conference chairwoman Elise Stefanik all came out against expulsion.

For a moment, it appeared Santos might survive. But Republican members of the Ethics Committee threatened to resign from the panel in protest.

In the vote, Republicans overall narrowly opposed expulsion. But, in the end, 105 Republican votes for expulsion, combined with 206 Democratic votes, easily cleared the two-thirds threshold. "To hell with this place," Santos said as he left.

Santos departed in a flurry of recriminations against his colleagues, most of which were no more accurate than his previous utterances. But there was one thing that Santos said that struck me as unassailably true. Asked by one interviewer whether the current Congress is the most "ineffective" in modern history, as it is often described, Santos replied: "Yes, 100 percent. The worst. We have spent the bulk of our time figuring out who we are as a Republican conference while stalling progress... We have passed 21 pieces of legislation that the president has signed, none really consequential, most of them just giving money to other people and other places. And quite frankly, we have spent so much time censuring one another, expelling one another, going after one another, we're doing absolutely nothing."

I couldn't have said it better. At that point in the session, only 22 bills (Santos's count was slightly out of date) had become law, compared to 69 at the same point in the previous Congress and 77 at that point in the 2019–2020 Congress, which also operated under divided government.

"It's like a dog that's chasing its own tail. It's abysmal," Santos said.

Clearly, House Republicans had to expel this guy—and fast. The only thing worse for them than a lying Santos was one who told the truth.

Part II

DYSFUNCTION

Chapter 4

"A Speaker Has Not Been Elected"

E VER SINCE THE 20TH AMENDMENT TO THE CONSTITUTION IN 1933 SET the modern legislative calendar, each new Congress has met at noon on the third day of January and, as its first order of business, elected a speaker of the House. This had always been a formality in the modern era: The majority party nominated its candidate, and that person was elected speaker on the first ballot. You had to go back 100 years to find a speaker's race that went to a second ballot, and back to the eve of the Civil War to find one that required 10 or more ballots.

But Kevin McCarthy was about to make history.

The extent of the Republican leader's troubles had been evident since the disappointing showing in the midterms. Members of the far-right House Freedom Caucus made noises about opposing him, and, on Nov. 14, the night before House Republicans' secret ballot to elect its new leaders, Andy Biggs made it official: The Arizona Republican, a gadfly who was allegedly among those who had sought a pardon from Trump for his Jan. 6 activities, told the right-wing outlet *Newsmax* that he would run against McCarthy for speaker. "We need to change the trajectory of this place," he said.

Change it they did—by sending it into a doom spiral. "I'm not voting for Kevin McCarthy," Florida's Matt Gaetz said on MAGA provocateur Charlie Kirk's podcast the day before House Republicans assembled. "I'm not voting for him on the floor. And I am certain that there is a critical mass of people who hold my precise view. And so the sooner we can sort of dispense with the notion that Kevin is going to be speaker, then we can get to the important work."

There was a critical mass: In the secret ballot the next day, 31 House Republicans voted for Biggs. Sure, McCarthy won 188 votes, easily securing the nomination. But to win the speakership he needed a majority of the full House, which meant 218 of the 222 Republicans. He had six weeks to win over his opponents—and it didn't look promising.

McCarthy, in the closed-door meeting, said he deserved credit for delivering a Republican majority, no matter how tenuous. "They don't give out gavels in small, medium and large. We have the majority and we have the gavels," he told colleagues, in remarks leaked to CNN. Later, McCarthy told reporters his pitch to colleagues had been simple: "The No. 1 message was, 'We won.'"

It didn't feel that way—and now Republicans turned against each other. McCarthy's new ally Marjorie Taylor Greene delighted in the coming fratricide. "I'm not afraid of the civil war in the GOP—I lean into it," she said on former Trump adviser Steve Bannon's podcast.

Gaetz shot back with a reference to Greene's antisemitic lunacy: "Whatever Kevin has promised Marjorie Taylor Greene, I guarantee you this: At the first opportunity, he will zap her faster than you can say 'Jewish space laser.'"

McCarthy dangled goodies before the holdouts: multiple Hunter Biden investigations. A select committee to investigate the Afghanistan pullout. A select committee to investigate China. An investigation of the Jan. 6 investigation. Investigations of Anthony Fauci and the U.S. Chamber of Commerce. And a panoply of probes into the Justice Department and the FBI. Still, they resisted him.

Before the election, McCarthy said he didn't think anybody in the Biden administration deserved impeachment. But the Biggs challenge forced a U-turn. Two weeks after the election, McCarthy threatened Alejandro Mayorkas, Biden's Homeland Security secretary, with impeachment. Biggs boasted to me and other reporters that it happened only "after he knew that he was facing somebody who was gonna possibly deny him the speakership."

The hardliners demanded ever more groveling from McCarthy. They demanded cuts to food stamps. They insisted McCarthy include right-wing poison pills in future debt ceiling increases and must-pass bills—all prescriptions for defaults and shutdowns.

When Greene informed McCarthy that she would be launching an effort to cut off funds to help Ukraine repeal Russia's invasion (McCarthy adamantly supported aiding Ukraine), the discussion went like this: "I said, 'I'm having a press conference at four,'" Greene recounted. "And he said, 'Okay.'"

Of course he did. The crazies were all knocking at his door. And if he wanted to be speaker, there was only one answer to their demands: "Okay."

In the coming days and weeks, it became clear that McCarthy would say okay to whatever the hardliners asked, even if it made the speaker, and the speakership, powerless. A grim pattern had set in: McCarthy was willing to destroy the institution to save himself.

When Nancy Pelosi went to the House floor in November 2022 to announce that she was stepping down as the House Democratic leader, most Republicans couldn't be bothered to attend. A few lobbed taunts instead ("Good riddance!" declared Colorado's Lauren Boebert). Among the missing was McCarthy, who explained: "I had meetings." Classy.

It's too bad McCarthy missed Pelosi's speech, for he could have learned much from her about how an effective leader ran the House.

After two decades as party leader and two stints as House Speaker, Pelosi was departing on her own terms. Though her Democrats technically lost their majority, their better-than-expected showing in the 2022 midterms felt much like a victory. She blessed a new slate of leaders and, with high-fives and hugs, Democrats elected them by acclamation at their own caucus meeting two weeks after the Republicans' contentious affair.

As House Republicans bickered among themselves and McCarthy tried throughout the month of December to appease the extremists blocking his ascent to the speakership, Pelosi went out in a last burst of productivity, churning out legislation before the chamber became a lawmaking dead zone in 2023. Landmark gay rights legislation codified marriage equality. Congress approved a bill averting a ruinous rail strike, legislation to avoid a repeat of Trump's 2020 election abuses, the National Defense Authorization Act, and a massive 2023 spending package that provided arms to Ukraine, a boost in defense spending and veterans' healthcare, and disaster aid.

She was a master tactician, with a genius for keeping her ranks unified. This can be seen in the major achievements of her speakership: Obamacare, the economic rescue, Dodd-Frank, covid relief, infrastructure investment, and the climate bill, not to mention Trump's two impeachments. But it can also be seen in what she did as opposition leader: thwarting attempts to kill Obamacare and negotiating a Medicare overhaul.

I wrote after the 2016 elections that she and other septuagenarian leaders should step aside. But I'm glad she didn't, because she had precisely the vote-whipping skills needed to limit the damage of Trump's antidemocratic depredations. Pelosi stands all of 5 feet 4 inches tall, not counting the stiletto heels. But a more towering figure hadn't walked these halls in a generation.

Pelosi, on the eve of her departure from leadership, seemed at peace as she addressed reporters. Crossing her ankles behind the lectern, and battling a cold with sniffles and a tissue, she joked with a Fox News correspondent and referred to Trump as "you know who" and he "who shall remain nameless here." She volunteered a lesson on the 18th-century economist Adam Smith. She made a passionate plea for paid sick leave. And she offered this wish for her successors: "As one who has served so long, my dream is that they do better. And I think everybody who has a position of responsibility always wants their successors to do better."

But that was one dream certain not to come true.

It wasn't just that Pelosi made a devilishly difficult job look easy. It was also that her immediate successor as speaker was guaranteed instant chaos, dysfunction, and backstabbing from fellow Republicans.

The trials awaiting McCarthy could be previewed often during the lame-duck session of the 117th Congress, the two months between Election Day and the new Congress's debut in January.

In late November, for example, McCarthy received a devastating vote of no confidence from an unexpected source: Kevin McCarthy.

Right-wing senators such as Ted Cruz wrote a letter to Senate GOP leader Mitch McConnell insisting that Senate Republicans "must not accept anything other than a short-term continuing resolution" until Republicans took control of the House. That would have set up a show-down in January in which the government would shut down unless the new Republican House leadership and the Democratic Senate could strike a deal.

But McCarthy, evidently lacking faith in his own ability to get a deal through the House, was pushing for lawmakers to get it done before he was in charge. Continuing resolutions "are not where we want to be," he said in early December. As *Politico* artfully put it: "Nobody trusts McCarthy to pass anything (not even McCarthy)."

Because of their lack of confidence in McCarthy, Senate Republicans scrambled to negotiate a $1.7 trillion spending bill with the House's Democratic majority before McCarthy took over that would cover all of fiscal year 2023. As they successfully negotiated the spending bill with Democrats in December 2022, Republican senators openly doubted McCarthy's competence. Senator Roger Wicker of Mississippi told *Politico* that "it's too much to ask" of McCarthy. Senator Kevin Cramer of North Dakota told *Semafor* that "for Kevin's sake . . . some Republicans just feel like we should relieve him of that burden."

A band of Senate conservatives resisted fellow Republicans' rush to cut a deal before McCarthy took over. At a news conference in the Senate TV studio, Senator Mike Lee of Utah said he disagreed with several Re-publicans who told him "it'll be too hard for Kevin McCarthy."

Senator Rick Scott of Florida urged a postponement to give "House Republican leadership opportunity to . . . come up with a plan."

But the Senate band was small: only four lawmakers. Cruz, billed as a participant in the news conference, was a no-show. A reporter asked if the sparse attendance meant that Senate Republicans are "tacitly admitting that House Republicans just aren't ready."

"Umm," replied Lee, "those who are making that point are not doing so tacitly. They're doing so explicitly."

McCarthy, of course, shared Senate Republicans' distrust of his abili-ties, at least at first. But as Senate Republicans and Democrats negotiated the massive 2023 omnibus spending bill on a bipartisan basis, House hardliners stepped up their efforts to thwart the effort. Chip Roy of Texas, one of the House zealots, fired off a letter signed by more than 30 House Republicans to their Republican colleagues in the Senate, demanding that they block the spending bill. If not, they wrote, they would "do everything in our power to thwart even the smallest legislative and policy efforts of those senators" who support the omnibus.

Recurring theme alert: McCarthy caved to the hardliners' rebellion. He retweeted Roy's message with his endorsement. "Agreed," he wrote. "When I'm speaker their bills will be dead on arrival in the House if this nearly $2 T[rillion] monstrosity is allowed to move forward."

Just a few hours later, Senate Republicans showed how little they thought of McCarthy's threats. Twenty-one of them voted to proceed with the omnibus bill. McConnell, the main target of McCarthy's threat, reacted with pity. "I'm pulling for Kevin," he told reporters. "I hope he makes it."

Later, as the House speaker election turned into an epic humiliation for McCarthy on the House floor, these Senate Republicans claimed vindication. "I've been told you shouldn't vote for the $1.7 trillion spending bill because [when] the House is Republican, they'll make it better," Lindsey Graham told *Politico*. "I don't think that theory is holding up too well."

December's rail strike debate, likewise, gave an indication of the dysfunction to come. With a threatened Dec. 9 rail walkout that would have crippled travel and business in the holiday season, the White House worked with Democrats and Republicans in Congress to impose a settlement on the railroads and unions. It cleared the Senate by a lopsided 80–15. In the House, Representative Sam Graves, a Missouri Republican, warned colleagues that failure to pass the bill would lead to "obviously a catastrophic economic disaster." But when the roll call came, 129 Republicans voted no—including McCarthy. Sixty percent of the Republican caucus would rather cause an economic calamity than be caught cooperating with Democrats.

AN HOUR BEFORE THE NEW CONGRESS CONVENED TO ELECT A SPEAKER ON Tuesday, Jan. 3, an email went out from the Capitol Police: The Capitol's

"Duress Alarm System" had gone offline. Too bad, because McCarthy's duress was just beginning.

All indications were that McCarthy had not won over a sufficient number of Republicans to secure the speakership on the first ballot. In a final appeal to colleagues during a caucus meeting before the vote, McCarthy told Republicans that he had earned the job, "god dammit," then executed a literal mic drop. Replied Boebert: "This is bullshit!"

She walked out and told reporters: "Now here we are being sworn at instead of being sworn in."

Gaetz, at her side, said (no doubt disingenuously) that he would "take no joy in this discomfort" that the rebels were about to impose in voting down McCarthy. "But if you want to drain the swamp," he added, "you cannot put the biggest alligator in charge of the exercise."

McCarthy, in turn, vowed to bore the rebels into submission. "Look," he told reporters before heading to the floor, "I have the record for the longest speech ever on the floor. I don't have a problem getting a record for the most votes for speaker too."

But it quickly became clear that the anti-McCarthy Republicans were more numerous than expected. The first roll call produced 19 Republican votes against McCarthy. Each one set off a wave of murmurs in the chamber: Biggs. Bishop. Boebert. Brecheen. Cloud. Within the first few minutes of the alphabetical roll call, McCarthy's defeat was already assured—the first time in a century a speaker hadn't been chosen on the first ballot.

McCarthy greeted each defection with a wan smile. He jiggled his leg. He tapped his reading glasses. He scrolled on his phone. He whispered to an aide. And when the clerk's tally made his loss official, he acted as if he had won, shaking hands, smiling, waving.

It was much the same for subsequent votes, as he endured insult after insult:

"The last time an election for speaker went to a second ballot, Leader Jeffries's beloved New York Yankees had not yet won a World Series," Democratic whip Pete Aguilar, of California, pointed out.

Gaetz referred to McCarthy as "someone who has sold shares of themselves for more than a decade" to get the job.

On the third vote, Byron Donalds of Florida joined the rebels. "It's clear right now that Kevin doesn't have the votes," he told a group of us after his switch. "We do not reward not being able to close deals."

After three failed votes, the House adjourned for the night, with the clerk presiding over the chamber because there (still) was no speaker.

The next day brought more of the same. On the fourth vote, Victoria Spartz of Indiana switched her vote from McCarthy to "present."

McCarthy's supporters were flagging. Representative Ken Buck, a Colorado Republican who backed McCarthy for speaker, warned that McCarthy allies would waver: "We're with you for a few more rounds but the welcome mat's going to be taken away at some point," he told a group of us.

Congressman Mike Gallagher of Wisconsin, nominating McCarthy for the fourth ballot, complained that Democrats and the media were enjoying the House Republicans' meltdown too much.

"In some ways they're salivating," the Republican complained in his speech re-re-renominating McCarthy. "There's headlines about the chaos, this and that. Yesterday, our colleagues on the other side of the aisle were tweeting their bags of popcorn that they had out. They love it. The schadenfreude is palpable."

The earnest legislator, a 39-year-old Princeton graduate and former Marine captain with a PhD in international relations, then sought to explain that the mayhem in the People's House was in fact a good thing—a sign of robust political health.

"Sure, it looks messy," he went on. Democrats applauded to signify their agreement with this observation. "But democracy is messy, by design!" The Democrats laughed at this notion that the Founders, in their wisdom, created a system in which a small band of lunatics could hijack the House for days in vote after fruitless vote to choose a leader for the chamber. "That's a feature, not a bug, of our system," Gallagher continued. "We air it all out in the open for the American people to see."

No doubt some were taking pleasure in the Republicans' pain. But, watching this spectacle from the gallery, I didn't see anything enjoyable about it. I had been writing about politics in Washington for the better part of three decades, with a specialty for finding the absurdities in our political system. But nothing even close to this had happened before. This wasn't political theater. This was anarchy.

This was what happened when a political party, for years, systematically destroyed the norms and institutions of democracy. This was what happened when those expert at tearing things down were put in charge of governing. The dysfunction had been building over years of government shutdowns, debt default showdowns, and other fabricated crises, and now antigovernment Republicans had used their new majority to bring the House itself to a halt. The saboteurs were officially in command.

This was insurrection by other means: Two years to the day since the Jan. 6 invasion of the Capitol, Republicans were still attacking the functioning of government. McCarthy opened the door to the chaos by excusing Donald Trump's fomenting of the insurrection and welcoming a new class of election deniers to his caucus. Now, trying to save his own political ambitions, he had agreed to institutionalize the chaos—not just for the next two years but for future Congresses as well.

Nominating McCarthy for the fifth ballot, Warren Davidson of Ohio asked: "Does it really boil down to this, that 20 or more of my colleagues will never trust Kevin McCarthy as speaker?"

One of the rebels, Pennsylvania's Scott Perry, head of the right-wing House Freedom Caucus, claimed that his opposition to McCarthy "is not about personalities." This prompted laughter from the Democratic side.

As the fifth vote was being taken, a foreign journalist in the press gallery fell asleep, facedown on the table.

On the sixth ballot, Representative Kat Cammack of Florida began her McCarthy nomination speech by telling the House: "Well it's Groundhog Day, again."

And after each tally, the clerk repeated the same refrain: "A speaker has not been elected."

The Republican fratricide visible on the House floor spread far from the Capitol. Republican influencer (and failed candidate) Laura Loomer called Marjorie Taylor Greene "Benedict Arnold in drag" for backing McCarthy. Right-winger Ali Alexander, an organizer of the Jan. 6 protest, called Greene a "harlot" and a "whore." On Fox News, host Brian Kilmeade called the holdouts "insurrectionists" before softening that to "saboteurs."

McCarthy's supporters railed about the unfairness being perpetrated against their man by these "frauds." Dusty Johnson, of South Dakota, protested that "the 5 percent do not get to roll the 95 percent." Kelly Armstrong, of North Dakota, spoke of the "enviable political position" of the holdouts, who "win when they lose" and never have "the responsibility of having to govern."

Republicans referred to the holdouts in their ranks as the "Taliban 20" and "terrorists" and "hostage takers" and the "chaos caucus." Gaetz sent a letter to the Architect of the Capitol, the office in charge of Capitol grounds, challenging McCarthy for prematurely occupying the speaker's office: "How long will he remain there before he is considered a squatter?"

"This is a self-inflicted wound," complained Congressman Don Bacon of Nebraska, a rare Republican voice of moderation. "These guys should be embarrassed by the start they gave us."

But shame was in short supply on the House floor. Nancy Mace, a South Carolina Republican, conveyed her respect for the institution by voting with her dog in her arms. Two of the far-right holdouts torturing McCarthy gave floor speeches claiming to be acting in the tradition of Martin Luther King Jr. and Frederick Douglass. Dan Bishop, a white Republican from the South, accused Cori Bush, a Black Democrat, of "grotesquely racist rhetoric." Kat Cammack insinuated groundlessly in her speech re-re-re-renominating McCarthy that Democrats were drunk on the job—enjoying "popcorn and blankets and alcohol."

Democrats howled for her words to be struck from the record, but because there was no speaker, there was nothing to be done. "There are no rules," McCarthy said from his seat on the floor.

McCarthy's allies on and off the floor freely admitted that the leadership pratfall had been "messy." But this went well beyond messy and into the realm of stupidity.

One of the 21 anti-McCarthy holdouts, Representative Ralph Norman of South Carolina (the one who urged Trump to declare "Marshall [sic] Law" before the Jan. 6 insurrection), told me and others on the second day of fruitless balloting that he would support McCarthy only if he agreed to "shut the government down" rather than "raise the debt ceiling." In reality, one has nothing to do with the other.

But such people were now running the show. McCarthy clearly couldn't control them. Even Trump couldn't control them. Rebel Boebert, just a few seats away from McCarthy on the floor, told the House that Trump, rather than lobbying for McCarthy, "needs to tell Kevin McCarthy that, sir, you do not have the votes and it's time to withdraw."

McCarthy forced a grin.

No rules. No functioning. And, essentially, no House. The elected members of Congress could not be sworn in (although the office of George Santos, recently exposed as a serial liar, somehow issued a press release stating that he had been sworn in). Bills couldn't be introduced. Committee memberships and chairmanships couldn't be assigned, and staff couldn't be hired. Newly elected lawmakers couldn't access emails or office supplies. House Republican Conference chair Elise Stefanik even called off her colleagues' feeding. "Due to the House adjourning, there will not be pizza and salads tonight," announced an email from her office the first evening of the failed speaker votes.

Because there were no rules, the government no longer controlled the TV cameras in the House chamber, and C-SPAN was free to broadcast however it chose. Thus, Americans at home could watch leaders huddling with rebels, far-right Gaetz conferring with far-left Alexandria Ocasio-Cortez, and the serial fabricator Santos sitting alone, discreetly picking his nose.

But sabotaging government was no joke. The incoming Republican chairmen of the Armed Services, Foreign Affairs, and Intelligence committees warned that the standoff could "place the safety and security of the United States at risk." Even House chaplain Margaret Kibben sounded the alarm. "Protect us that in this imbroglio of indecision we do not expose ourselves to the incursion of our adversary," she prayed at the start of the Jan. 5 session. "Watch over the seeming discontinuity of our governance and perceived vulnerability of national security."

Outside the House chamber, corridors smelling of cigar smoke and body odor became scenes of mayhem: As I and other reporters chased McCarthy from the floor to his office, the unruly scrum knocked aside an unsuspecting Michael McCaul, incoming chairman of the Foreign Affairs Committee, as he gave a live interview on Fox News. Inside the chamber, lawmakers shouted at the House clerk—the only semblance of authority that existed in the leaderless House—as she struggled to maintain order.

The new majority couldn't even manage the most routine business without chaos. At the end of the second day of failed balloting, on Jan. 4, a GOP attempt to adjourn for the night nearly failed. Lawmakers, who hadn't been expecting the vote, sprinted into the chamber to register their votes before the clerk closed the vote. The next morning, Republicans celebrated their two-vote win on the adjournment. "Yesterday, we experienced very briefly our first win," new member-elect John James, a Michigan Republican, said in his speech re-re-re-re-re-renominating McCarthy. "It was a small victory, but didn't it feel good? We've been working hard for that victory."

Not many would call it a "win" to adjourn the House after failing to elect a speaker—but even that minor victory was short-lived. On Jan. 5, the third day of balloting, Republicans held vote after failed vote in their fruitless attempt to elect McCarthy. The reason they kept voting? This time it took them eight hours to corral enough votes to adjourn.

But on the floor, McCarthy kept smiling, back-patting, waving to his family in the gallery, pumping his fist as if in victory. During one roll call he was so distracted that he didn't respond at first when the clerk called his name—and he was distracted for good reason: He had already begun the process of surrendering.

The concessions began to flow after the second day of failed balloting, and they flooded out during talks on the third day. As the GOP rebels held the line on the floor that day, rejecting McCarthy five more times, McCarthy's representatives were one floor below, in the office of Republican whip Tom Emmer, giving away the store.

They had given the holdouts essentially everything they had asked for—and still the extremists demanded more. "A deal is NOT done," the Freedom Caucus's Perry tweeted that afternoon.

"Somebody should check and make sure Kevin McCarthy still has two kidneys," Adam Smith of Washington, the top Democrat on the Armed Services Committee, quipped on the fourth day of balloting.

Among McCarthy's giveaways: He agreed to allow any single member of the House to force a vote at will to "vacate" his speakership. In theory, lawmakers had almost always had the power, but nobody had been crazy enough to actually attempt it, and Pelosi in 2019 had formally removed the power. But far-right Republicans insisted on restoring the "motion to vacate"—and, unlike in the past, these guys might just be crazy enough to use it.

McCarthy's surrender to the rebels meant that he was in constant danger of a no-confidence vote—and all it would take to evict him from the speakership would be for five disaffected Republicans to join with Democrats.

McCarthy also agreed to put rebels on the Rules Committee, giving them sway over what gets a vote on the House floor. He let rebels cut in line ahead of more senior Republicans for key committee leadership posts, including the chairmanship of the Homeland Security Committee. He promised to have votes on cockamamie proposals, legislation abolishing all federal income taxes in favor of a new consumption tax. He promised to launch an investigation into the Jan. 6 committee—another Republican attempt to "investigate the investigators."

He promised to have the House vote individually on each of the 12 annual spending bills and to allow lawmakers to offer unlimited amendments—making it far more difficult to fund the government before hitting government-shutdown deadlines. He pledged that the House would not raise the government's borrowing limit unless coupled with spending cuts Republicans sought—putting the government on a path to default on the federal debt.

It all invited mayhem—and that's exactly what McCarthy got.

Perhaps worst of all, a McCarthy-aligned super-PAC, the Conservative Leadership Fund, agreed that it would no longer work against far-right extremists in the vast majority of Republican primaries. Essentially, McCarthy tried to placate the crazies in his caucus by surrendering every tool he had to maintain order in the House—and by guaranteeing that there will be even more extremists in Congress with each successive election.

Having surrendered so abjectly to the extremists, McCarthy had turned the speakership into a prize not worth having. Regardless of who held the title of speaker, the position would be powerless. The saboteurs had won.

His leadership had been characteristically erratic, and at times absent, throughout the crisis. At one point he infuriated his opponents by delaying a formal response to their demands. At another point he and his allies enraged them further by shaming them publicly and threatening to take away their committee assignments. When the voting started, he tried to beat them through attrition, forcing 11 votes in the first three days that he lost by nearly identical tallies. But throughout the ordeal, what worked best for McCarthy was capitulation. "Cavin' Kevin" is what Gaetz called him.

The one thing McCarthy didn't try? Negotiating with Democrats. They could easily have given him the votes he needed to become speaker, in exchange for concessions. But bipartisanship was a nonstarter in McCarthy's caucus—which left him perpetually at the mercy of a few hooligans, during the speaker election and on virtually every vote that followed.

It was a matter of basic arithmetic. In the 435-member House, you need 218 votes (assuming full attendance) to either elect a speaker or pass a bill. Because McCarthy had ruled out the possibility of bipartisanship, that meant that he could lose no more than 4 of the 222 Republicans on any vote. "All of us are powerful," observed Marjorie Taylor Greene. And dozens of them were willing to use that power to extort their leaders on a daily basis.

By Friday evening, Jan. 6, after the speakership saga had dragged on for four days on the House floor, the rebels could hardly believe the breadth of McCarthy's capitulation. "We're running out of things to ask for," Gaetz marveled.

Yet still they tortured McCarthy. One vote shy at the end of the 14th ballot that night, McCarthy publicly humiliated himself by walking over to Gaetz and pressuring him to switch his vote. In view of the whole House and the TV cameras, Gaetz rebuffed him.

Next, in a moment captured by the C-SPAN cameras that would come to symbolize the chaotic balloting, Mike Rogers of Alabama, the incoming chairman of the Armed Services Committee, lunged at holdout Gaetz and had to be pulled away.

McCarthy retreated. "We'll do it again," he said angrily.

Finally, on the 15th ballot early Saturday morning, Jan. 7, McCarthy's total surrender secured him the speakership, at least temporarily. But it was the most pyrrhic of victories. To save himself, he sacrificed the Congress itself.

At the core of McCarthy's appeasement was a fundamental fallacy. He believed that if he simply gave the 50 or so hardliners what they asked for, he would earn their loyalty. But, as McCarthy would discover, he was not dealing with rational actors. McCarthy was, rather, trying to negotiate with people who came from, and were chosen by, the fringiest elements of the right wing, who marinated in disinformation, who had distorted views of what was and wasn't possible in a democratic system, and who had little interest in the enterprise of governing. They were, as McCarthy would eventually discover, though too late, "individuals that just want to burn the whole place down."

Chapter 5

"What a Turd Sandwich This 'Deal' Is"

IT'S A SET PIECE OF MODERN POLITICAL THEATER: AFTER THEIR FIRST 100 days in office, presidents, or Speakers of the House, celebrate their promises kept and agenda items enacted. But what to do if you don't have any achievements to talk about?

This was the quandary facing Kevin McCarthy as he approached his 100th day as speaker, for his dysfunctional House Republicans had precious little to show for their time in power.

But if McCarthy hadn't accomplished much legislative change, he had achieved significant success with *venue* change. The new speaker, delighting in the ceremonial trappings of the job, had a new bidet installed in the speaker's office, having it rolled in on a Saturday night, March 11, to avoid attracting attention. He had also taken to sampling various backdrops in the Capitol for his public appearances. He did one in Statuary Hall. Another near the statue of Will Rogers. A few in the small rotunda outside his office. Several in the TV studio. Then, to celebrate his majority's first 100 days in mid-April, he led his Republican colleagues on a grand expedition, marching them out the west side of the Capitol, down the marble stairs, and onto the upper terrace.

"See, it's a new place!" he gushed to his leadership team. "You like it?"

Tom Emmer, the majority whip, hurried to indulge him: "I like it! Very nice!"

Republican caucus chair Elise Stefanik was not about to be outdone in the suck-up department. "I like it too," she chimed in.

But the venue, no matter how dazzling, could not disguise a couple of obvious problems. First, the 100-day mark had passed four days earlier, unobserved. For this, McCarthy had a nifty workaround: He would celebrate 100 days since lawmakers were sworn in—a helpful reminder that it had taken him 15 rounds of voting to get the job.

The larger problem remained, however, and it was the new majority's lack of legislative success in its first 100 days, or, for that matter, in its first 104 days. So McCarthy and his leadership team settled on an elegant solution: They would simply make stuff up.

"We defunded Biden's army of 87,000 IRS agents," Emmer boomed from the Capitol terrace. "We stopped the selling of strategic petroleum oil in our reserve to China. We tackled inflation with the Rein In Act. We defended parents' rights with the Parents Bill of Rights Act. And we lowered energy costs with our signature legislation, the Lower Energy Costs Act."

Um, no. They actually didn't do any of those things. The House did pass *bills* on those subjects, but not one of them had become law. That would require bipartisan negotiation and compromise—which this new majority was not willing to do. The only legislation that did become law in the new Congress's unproductive first 100 days was inconsequential: officially declaring the pandemic over, declassifying information about covid's origins, and rejecting the District of Columbia's criminal code.

The New Deal it wasn't.

"Today is a historical day," McCarthy began, aiming for "historic" but overshooting. He rattled off some statistics (182 roll call votes!) and, in his inimitable way with words, said this "shows a great contrast to the difference to the last Congress to this."

"It becomes a new, effective House," he elaborated. "An effective House looks very different than a Senate that Schumer has become unproductive."

This was as nonsensical factually as it was linguistically. By the 100-day mark in the last Congress, seven bills had already become law, including major legislation such as the American Rescue Plan and the Paycheck Protection Program extension.

By contrast, McCarthy's leadership team hadn't even kept the promises that were entirely within their control. Before Republicans took over the chamber, the incoming majority leader, Steve Scalise of Louisiana, sent Republican lawmakers a list of 11 bills that "we plan to bring to the House Floor in the first two weeks of 2023."

The first two weeks came and went. So did the next 10 weeks. As the 100th day approached, only five of the 11 had been passed by the chamber. Intraparty feuding had delayed the others, on abortion, the border, crime, and more.

And this wasn't even the hard stuff. Congress's main job is to fund the government, and House Republicans hadn't passed a budget, nor any of the 12 annual appropriations bills. "We haven't passed one of the must-pass bills this year," Representative Blake Moore of Utah, a vice chairman of the moderate Republican Governance Group, told the *Wall Street Journal* as Republicans convened in Florida in late March for a retreat.

The House's only major achievement, if it could be called that, was to put the government on a path to defaulting on the federal debt for the first time in U.S. history. The federal government would hit the debt ceiling in early June, about six weeks from when McCarthy and his colleagues stood on the Capitol terrace, and if Congress didn't raise the borrowing limit by then, the government would be unable to make its interest payments on the debt. This would risk a collapse in financial markets, potentially shocking the economy into recession, raising the cost of borrowing, and jeopardizing the dollar's status as the world's reserve currency. Yet McCarthy's House Republicans were playing chicken with the American economy.

For most of the 100 years since the debt ceiling was established in law, Congress had raised it as needed without fanfare. During the Trump administration, when the debt was soaring, Congress raised the debt cciling three times, with Democratic support.

But the modern Republican Party takes a different view, agreeing to raise the debt ceiling only when there is a Republican in the White House. The *Washington Post*'s Aaron Blake looked at all debt ceiling votes since 2000 and found that 65 percent of House Republicans voted for debt ceiling increases when Republicans were president, but only 24 percent of them approved increases when Democrats were president. (House Democrats approved the increases under both Republican and Democratic presidents.)

House Republicans had brought the nation to the cusp of default once before, in 2011, when Barack Obama was in the White House. That brinkmanship led Standard & Poor's to downgrade its rating of U.S. debt for the first time in history. Now, with a Democrat back in the White House, it was time for House Republicans to stage another showdown—and time for America's credit to take another hit.

A week after House Republicans celebrated their 100 days in power, the credit agency Fitch Ratings warned: "Repeated near-default episodes brought on by debt limit debates could erode confidence that the US government's repayment capacity is resilient to political dysfunction and may affect Fitch's view of the sovereign credit profile." (Three months later, Fitch did downgrade U.S. debt, citing "repeated debt-limit political standoffs.") JPMorgan in April proclaimed a "non-trivial risk" of a federal default, and trading in credit default swaps showed an even higher expectation of default than there had been during the 2011 standoff.

There was good reason for concern. McCarthy, pressured by the hardliners, was taking America's credit hostage and demanding that Biden pay him a ransom of $5 trillion. Even then, his plan called for having another debt limit showdown a year later to extort still more from Biden.

The hardliners wanted a showdown, and a showdown they would get. In March, members of the House Freedom Caucus joined a couple of like-minded Republican senators in the Senate television studio to list their demands. There, they proclaimed their determination not to increase the debt ceiling without large spending cuts—even if that meant default—and they provided a long list of other ransom demands that they would insist on for any debt ceiling increase: changes to student loans, covid policy, IRS funding, environmental programs, welfare, and immigration. In effect, they were saying that if Biden didn't accept their *entire* agenda, they would bring about economic collapse.

They floated the dangerous falsehood that failing to raise the debt ceiling wouldn't be so bad. "You can blow past the debt ceiling increase deadline," proposed Senator Mike Lee of Utah. "Yes, that causes problems... but that is not itself a default." Those "problems" it would cause? Stopping Social Security checks, paychecks for the troops, and the like.

Lauren Boebert, of Colorado, said the federal debt is causing "more suf-frage for the American people" (she presumably was going for "suffering") and said of Biden: "When the shutdown comes, it's on him!" Like other hostage takers, Boebert seemed unaware that failure to raise the debt ceiling causes default, which has nothing to do with a government shutdown.

Byron Donalds, of Florida, contributed this patriarchal take on Biden's budgeting: "Every wife in America would shudder if that was her husband."

The hardliners, confused though they were, made clear that they weren't wavering on the debt ceiling. "This is not the Republican Party of the past that will surrender," said Representative Bob Good of Virginia. "We made history in January," he said of their 15-ballot humiliation of McCarthy. "You're going to see us make history again."

And so they did. But not in a good way. Republicans were gambling with the full faith and credit of the United States. And it was abundantly clear that they had no idea what they were doing.

AT THE ROOT OF THE NEW MAJORITY'S DYSFUNCTION WAS SOME GOOD OLD-fashioned incompetence. Back at the end of 2022, as McCarthy tried to corral support on the right for his speakership bid, he offered a bold new proposal on Facebook: "Next year, Republicans will start every day of Congress with prayer and the Pledge of Allegiance. No exceptions." People quickly pointed out that Congress *already* started every day with a prayer and the pledge—and had been doing so for years, because it's enshrined in House rules. McCarthy later took down the post.

McCarthy then floated a new scheme: "On the very first day of the new Republican-led Congress, we will read every single word of the Constitution aloud from the floor of the House—something that hasn't been done in years." Alas, even this promise proved too difficult to keep. The reading of the Constitution came not on Day 1 but on Day 35. And, unlike for previous readings in 2011, 2015, and 2017, this time Republicans did it without Democrats.

As House Republicans began their term, they quickly found them-selves defeated even by basic things. They had planned in January to vote on a pair of symbolic resolutions expressing support for law enforcement. But they had to pull the bills from the floor; they didn't have the votes. Some Republicans worried that the benign language in the resolution—"expressing support for the nation's law enforcement agencies"—might signal support for the FBI, which in their fantasy was now a "weaponized" arm of the Deep State.

In another entry in their rapidly expanding annals of dysfunction, House leadership decided, as part of McCarthy's commitment to give the hardliners more say, to try an "open rule"—unlimited amendments to a bill—on the House floor for one of their first bills. Lawmakers introduced 143 amendments to the bill. It took two full days to get through all the speeches, points of order, and votes. At that rate of productivity, this two-year Congress would have to stay in session for about seven years to get its work done.

And all this time was wasted in service of a pointless gesture: The bill, restricting a president's ability to tap the Strategic Petroleum Reserve, was going nowhere in the Senate and, even if it did, faced a certain Biden veto.

Much of the dysfunction was rooted in the giveaways McCarthy had made to hardliners to get the job. The very first act of the new Congress—passing the rules that would govern proceedings for the next two years—became a brouhaha when *Punchbowl News* reported on Jan. 9 that McCarthy's team had inked a secret three-page "addendum" to the rules package outlining backroom giveaways he bartered with holdouts denying him the speakership.

It was all the more absurd because this secret addendum was part of what Stefanik called "the most transparent rules package in history." McCarthy, in a caucus meeting, denied that the secret addendum existed. Alas for McCarthy, other Republican lawmakers claimed to have read the very document whose existence McCarthy denied.

Representative Ken Calvert, a California Republican, told *Axios* he was personally reviewing the secret addendum. McCarthy ally Richard Hudson, of North Carolina, said he had seen it, too. Rules Committee Chairman Tom Cole of Oklahoma acknowledged that the addendum "has to be out there."

Nancy Mace of South Carolina, who had gone on CBS's *Face the Nation* to complain that "we don't have any idea what promises were made," told a group of us after hearing from Republican leaders that there remained "questions that I think many of us have about what side deals may or may not have been made."

On the floor, where Democrats were hollering about the "secret three-page addendum," Texas's Chip Roy, who negotiated much of the secret deal, countered that it was "classic swamp speak" to be "talking about secret deals." But negotiating such secret deals in the first place was, apparently, totally fine.

One change Republicans did make public was gutting the Office of Government Ethics. It was blocked from hiring new staff when current employees left. The shrunken ethics office made it more likely lawmakers could shield any wrongdoing from public scrutiny.

Another of McCarthy's concessions to the hard right that was made public: His promises to vote on a bill abolishing the IRS and another bill eliminating all income and corporate taxes.

To put numbers behind McCarthy's surrender to the right: His leadership team had given members of the right-wing House Freedom Caucus, who constituted about 20 percent of the GOP caucus, fully 38 percent of the seats on the high-profile Oversight and Accountability Committee, 44 percent of the seats on the equally visible Judiciary Committee and the select subcommittee probing the covid-19 response, and 50 percent of the "weaponization of the federal government" select committee, the *Washington Post*'s Blake calculated. Much of the speaker's power comes from his influence over who gets assigned to the standing (permanent) committees and his absolute control over who gets assigned to the select (temporary) committees.

With so many committees overloaded with loons, it was but a matter of time until things blew up. In an embrace of mayhem, the House Republicans' campaign arm, the National Republican Congressional Committee, adopted a new slogan, "Bring the Tiger," as *Politico*'s Olivia Beavers reported. This was a reference to a mock lip-reading video of McCarthy's viral standoff on the House floor with Gaetz, in which McCarthy was made to say: "I brought the tiger."

Yep. He brought the tiger, and now he had to ride it.

It didn't have to be this way. At every step, McCarthy had the option of working with the minority Democrats to reach consensus. This wasn't just theoretical. Mike Gallagher, the Marine captain and PhD from Wisconsin, had been put in charge of the new House Select Committee on the Chinese Communist Party—and, as the chairman, he turned his panel into everything the rest of the House wasn't: bipartisan, serious, and productive.

"This is an existential struggle over what life will look like in the 21st century, and the most fundamental freedoms are at stake," he said as he launched the panel with a prime-time hearing in late February. "Time is not on our side. Just because this Congress is divided, we cannot afford to waste the next two years lingering in legislative limbo or pandering to the press. We must act with a sense of urgency."

He took no partisan shots, and he screened "a joint video that the ranking member and I put together to help set the stage for the hearing." That ranking Democrat, Raja Krishnamoorthi of Illinois, reciprocated, acknowledging that "both Democrats and Republicans underestimated the CCP" and praising the bipartisanship and "our unity as Americans."

The witnesses, including two former Trump advisers, and other lawmakers maintained the feel-good sentiment—what Darin LaHood, an Illinois Republican, described as "Republicans and Democrats working together to expose the malign activities of the CCP."

The only dissent in the room came from a pair of hecklers from the far-left group Code Pink, waving signs that said "China Is Not Our Enemy" and "Stop Asian Hate."

Gallagher waited patiently for them to be removed. "Your sign is upside down," he told the person holding the "Stop Asian Hate" sign.

A couple of the Democrats obliquely referenced the racist remarks recently made by Congressman Lance Gooden, a Texas Republican, who (on Fox News, naturally) challenged the loyalty to the United States of California Democrat Judy Chu, who is Chinese American. But Gallagher had already called that "out of bounds" during a joint interview with Krishnamoorthi on *Face the Nation*—one of multiple joint appearances and statements by the pair.

Gallagher was exactly the sort of person you'd want in the role as China's growing aggression pushes us toward a new cold war. He noted with satisfaction that his panel had "no bomb throwers." Gallagher, by Krishnamoorthi's account, worked closely with Democrats to draft a rules package to guide the panel during this Congress's session—"a bipartisan agreement that has my full support." It passed without debate, amendment, or a single dissenting vote.

That's what happens when a public official puts country before party. But Republicans like Gallagher are on the outs in today's GOP. A year into the new Congress, Gallagher, after receiving a torrent of abuse from his fellow Republicans over one of his disagreements with them, announced that he wouldn't run for reelection. Soon after that, he announced that he would quit Congress before his term even expired.

THE DEBT CEILING CRISIS, LIKE MANY OF THE TROUBLES OF THE NEW CONGRESS, could be traced directly to the concessions McCarthy had made to the Freedom Caucus holdouts. McCarthy had promised them that he would deliver a 10-year balanced budget. But he also promised not to touch Social Security and Medicare—the largest sources of the budget imbalance. On top of all that, Republicans committed not to allow cuts to defense spending and veterans' pensions, nor to allow the Trump tax cuts to lapse.

This left them in an impossible situation. The nonpartisan Congressional Budget Office, at Democrats' request, ran the numbers on those promises and found that to keep all those pledges, Republicans would literally have to eliminate everything—*everything*—else the government does: No more Homeland Security, no more Border Patrol or FBI; no more Coast Guard, air traffic control, or federal funds for education or highways; no agricultural programs; no housing, food, or disaster assistance; no cancer research or veterans' healthcare; no diplomacy or space exploration; no courts—and no Congress.

Forget "defund the police." This was defund America. Even then, Republicans would still be slightly in the red after 10 years.

Not surprisingly, McCarthy and his lieutenants attempted some backtracking. House Budget Committee chairman Jodey Arrington, of Texas, revised the 10-year balanced budget promise to be merely "aspirational." Then Republicans quietly shelved plans to pass any budget at all.

Instead, Arrington touted a separate House GOP proposal to set 2024 spending at 2022 levels, which would require smaller (though still severe) cuts but wouldn't come close to balancing the budget. And they decided they would take the debt limit hostage to force Biden to negotiate federal spending at these lower levels: Meet our demands or the country will default.

Even before McCarthy started down this path, Senate Republican leader Mitch McConnell, a savvy veteran of many spending battles, made clear that he wanted no part in forcing a debt ceiling standoff. "I think it's entirely reasonable for the new speaker and his team to put spending reduction on the table. I wish him well in talking to the president. That's where a solution lies," he said in January. "I think the final solution to this particular episode lies between Speaker McCarthy and the president," he repeated. McCarthy was on his own.

The White House presented Biden's proposed fiscal year 2024 budget in early March 2023. By increasing taxes on the wealthy and closing tax loopholes, it proposed $2.9 trillion in deficit reduction over a decade while still expanding spending by $2.6 trillion. McCarthy immediately dismissed the White House budget as "completely unserious."

But Republicans, having abandoned their own attempt at a budget, had no alternative. Had they produced a budget, it would have to have been something as extreme as the budget outline produced by Senator Rick Scott, a Florida Republican, which called for terminating all federal programs, including Social Security and Medicare, after five years. (After an outcry, he quietly edited his plan to exempt Social Security and Medicare from the axe.)

Instead, McCarthy demanded a meeting with Biden, saying it was up to the president to suggest spending cuts. The White House, refusing to negotiate with itself, responded with a simple mantra: Show us your budget. And for weeks nothing happened.

The small band of moderate House Republicans, worried (with good reason) that McCarthy would again surrender to the hardliners' demands on the debt ceiling, tried to issue their own conditions. "Defund defense or allow anti-immigration legislation on the House floor and I am a NO on the debt ceiling," Tony Gonzales of Texas posted.

As the deadline approached, with no progress being made, Brian Fitzpatrick of Pennsylvania and other House Republican moderates indicated their lack of faith in McCarthy by beginning talks with Democrats about a "discharge petition." That rarely used maneuver would have circumvented GOP leaders and cleared the way for a bipartisan vote on the House floor to increase the debt limit, thus ending the crisis.

Adding to the sense of mayhem, Buddy Carter, a Georgia Republican, went to the House floor to make a pitch for his plan to abolish all income taxes in favor of a 23 percent national sales tax, on which McCarthy had allegedly promised a vote. "The pimps and the prostitutes—they're going to be paying taxes because they consume," Carter argued. "They go out and buy groceries."

In the end, McCarthy followed his go-to strategy: He embraced what the hardliners wanted and then tried to force the rest of his caucus to swallow it. In this case, it meant voting for unspecified cuts adding up to nearly $5 trillion over a decade, abolishing green-energy tax credits, cutting funds to the IRS, and imposing new work requirements to receive food stamps and Medicaid. Even then, the Republican plan called for scheduling another debt ceiling showdown in March 2024.

McCarthy then muscled the bill through the House by the thinnest of margins, 217–215 on April 26, with four Republicans joining all Democrats in opposition. Immediately after passage, he rushed into Statuary Hall to claim victory.

"We've done our job," he exulted. "You've underestimated us," he added.

His colleagues, likewise, were all backslaps and cheers on the House floor when the bill passed.

It was quite a bit of exuberance for a bill that, as many Republicans said aloud, was intended only to force Biden to the negotiating table. And even that came at an extraordinary cost.

Soon after Republicans assumed the House majority in January, McCarthy had said that "our very first responsibility" was "to pass a budget." But the majority hadn't passed a budget.

McCarthy promised, as part of his speakership bid, to come up with a plan to eliminate the federal deficit within 10 years. But the majority had come up with no such plan.

McCarthy vowed to restore "regular order" in the House, promising that legislation would work its way through committees. "You can't just throw something on the floor," he'd said in January. But only six of the first 30 bills followed "regular order," according to a tally by Democrats on the House Rules Committee that Republicans did not dispute. And on April 26, McCarthy had thrown on the floor, without a single committee hearing, "the largest spending cut in American history" (as Kevin Hern, head of the 173-member House Republican Study Committee, put it).

Members of McCarthy's leadership team had said they would not change the debt limit legislation to appease GOP holdouts, decreeing that "we're done negotiating" and vowing that they're "not opening this up" to changes. McCarthy then made a slew of last-minute changes to win over the holdouts.

House GOP leaders initially dismissed as unworkable a demand by Gaetz to impose, almost immediately, sweeping new work requirements on millions of food stamp and Medicaid recipients. They then amended the legislation to include the unworkable provision. (And Gaetz still voted against the bill.)

McCarthy had promised, as part of his speakership bid, an "open amendment process" on the House floor. Yet he'd allowed no amendments to the debt bill on the House floor.

Republicans had long howled about "giant bills negotiated in secret, then jammed through on a party-line vote in the middle of the night." They objected, in particular, to Democrats' use of a legislative trick called a "self-executing rule" that allowed them to "deem and pass" legislation (including part of Obamacare) without a straight up-or-down vote. But then they jammed their giant, secretly negotiated debt limit bill through the Rules Committee on a party-line vote—at 2:18 a.m. on April 26. And they did it with a "deem-and-pass" rule.

Even then, after all the reversals and surrenders, the bill came within one vote of failing. The lawmaker who cast the final, deciding vote? George Santos.

How apt that this legislation, built on one broken promise after another, would be carried over the finish line by the world's second most famous liar. This was why they didn't want to expel the man.

It's just as well that Santos, by dramatically delaying his vote until the end of the roll call, made himself the face of the debt bill. Those who ordinarily would have drafted such an important bill had no interest in claiming paternity.

At the Rules Committee hearing on the bill, the ranking Democrat, Jim McGovern of Massachusetts, asked Ways and Means Committee Chairman Jason Smith, a Missouri Republican, why Republicans circumvented the committee process.

"I'm not—I'm not in charge," protested Smith, looking around incredulously with wide eyes.

In a sense, nobody was in charge. The rookie Ways and Means chairman, just three months on the job, didn't know which end was up. Neither did the rookie Budget Committee chairman, Arrington, who was sidelined during the debt showdown by the rookie speaker, who presided over a caucus where the median congressional tenure was, as noted earlier, just four years.

At the start of this manufactured debt limit crisis, I had worried that ideological extremism might drive the nation to a first-ever default. But, in the end, an equal threat to America's credit rating was incompetence. Those in the House majority didn't know what they didn't know.

The Treasury was forecast to go into default in June. But Representative Tim Burchett of Tennessee, emerging from the GOP caucus meeting, told a group of us that "we're not going to default." Why? "I think September's the actual drop-dead date, so we're good." He *thinks*?

Coming out of the same meeting, Ralph Norman, of South Carolina, remained confused about what happens when the government defaults, mistaking it with a government shutdown. "Let the Senate shut the government down," he proclaimed. "Let them take the heat for shutting it down."

And House majority whip Emmer and others, trying to rebut criticism that they circumvented the committee process, erroneously claimed that they drafted the debt limit bill using a process known as the "committee of the whole" on the House floor. As the *Washington Post*'s Paul Kane noted, that is an actual procedure on the floor—but it had absolutely nothing to do with the backroom shenanigans Republicans used to write their bill.

The bill was going nowhere, of course; it was only intended to force Biden to the negotiating table. But to get it through the House, McCarthy had obliged about 30 Republicans from swing districts to cast potentially ruinous votes. It put 217 House Republicans on record in favor of demolishing popular government services enjoyed by their constituents.

One of the vulnerable Republicans, first-term representative Jen Kiggans of Virginia, had the haunted look of a woman about to walk the plank when she stood during the debate on the bill to justify her vote. She barely took her eyes off her text as she read it aloud, tripping over words and using her fingers to keep her place on the page.

"I do have serious concerns with the provision of this legislation that repeals clean-energy investment tax credits, particularly for wind energy," she read. "These credits have been very beneficial to my constituents, attracting significant investment and new manufacturing jobs for businesses in southeast Virginia."

Directing a question to the Republicans' chief deputy whip, Guy Reschenthaler of Pennsylvania, she asked for "the gentleman's assurance that I will be able to address these concerns as we move forward in negotiations and advocate for the interests of my district."

The gentleman offered no such assurance. "I support repealing these tax credits," he replied, offering only the noncommittal promise to "continue to work with the gentlewoman from Virginia, just like we will with all members." Kiggans then cast her vote to abolish the clean-energy credits her constituents find so "beneficial."

Many other Republicans also swallowed their misgivings. South Carolina's Mace complained to my *Washington Post* colleagues about the repeal of green-energy tax credits and said the bill "doesn't do anything to balance the budget." She voted yes anyway.

Indiana's Victoria Spartz, during the floor debate, protested the lack of action in reforming entitlement programs. "Ninety percent of spending is not even considered by this institution," she said. She voted yes anyway.

Spartz was absolutely right about the scope of the problem. Any serious effort to tackle the federal debt would need to deal with all parts of the problem: entitlement programs, taxes, defense, and domestic spending. Biden, in his budget, proposed a higher Medicare tax on the wealthy and closed tax loopholes that benefit the superrich.

FOOLS ON THE HILL

But by refusing to consider entitlement and revenues and by ruling out defense cuts, Republicans were wringing 100 percent of the cuts from just 15 to 20 percent of the budget. For all the trauma House Republicans were threatening to cause the country, their proposed solution was not going to do anything to resolve the federal government's finances.

On May 9, with three weeks to go until the United States defaulted on its debt, congressional leaders met with Biden in the White House, then stepped into the West Wing driveway to offer their thoughts.

"The solution lies with two people," McConnell said, washing his hands of the matter as he had been doing since January. "The president of the United States . . . and the speaker of the House."

Two minutes later, McCarthy stood in the same spot and passed the buck—to the Senate Democratic leader. The resolution of the standoff "would come down really to Chuck Schumer and the president," he said.

The next day, Trump weighed in. The Republican standard-bearer told CNN's Kaitlan Collins that the United States should default if Biden didn't accept everything Republicans demanded.

"Well, you might as well do it now," Trump said.

Collins, pointing out that Trump, as president, said the debt ceiling could not be used as a negotiating tool, asked him what had changed.

"Because now I'm not president," he said.

Confused? So was McCarthy.

After a subsequent debt limit negotiating session at the White House, he returned to the Capitol and offered reporters an update. "Let me be very clear," he said. "From the first day I sat with the president, there's two criterias I told him," McCarthy said, raising two fingers. "We're not going to raise taxes because we bring in more money than we ever have. And we're not going to pass a clean debt ceiling. And we've got to spend less than we spent this year."

Let me be very clear, Mr. Speaker. Those are three, er, "criterias."

This was one of the more worrying aspects of the default standoff: The full faith and credit of the United States was hanging in the balance, and the man sitting across the negotiating table from the president seemed

91

to be genuinely off-kilter. For House Republicans, that instability was the source of their power.

Whipsawed by public pressure from the Freedom Caucus and from Trump, McCarthy at one moment praised the "honesty" and "professionalism" of White House negotiators and the next moment attacked the other side as "socialist." He gave daily (sometimes hourly) updates packed with fake statistics, nonsense anecdotes, and malapropisms. His negotiators walked out of talks only to resume them hours later. It was at a GOP caucus meeting during the height of these negotiations that he auctioned off his lip balm to Marjorie Taylor Greene.

House Republicans issued Biden a long and growing list of demands, yet, with just days to go until a possible default, not a single concession—unless you count a possible willingness not to tank the American economy. Even that "concession" wasn't assured. Some sounded as if they were expecting a default and hoping that voters would blame the incumbent president for the resulting economic collapse. McCarthy said, "Don't blame me," and "Don't blame us Republicans," and "It is not my fault."

In foreign affairs, Richard Nixon pioneered the "madman theory": If you could make your foe think you were crazy and reckless enough to launch a nuclear attack, he would back down. House Republicans were doing much the same with a debt default—although the "madman" component seemed to be more genuine than theatrical.

Their nihilism definitely gave them leverage. "I think my conservative colleagues . . . don't feel like we should negotiate with our hostage," Gaetz told *Semafor*.

Willingness to shoot the hostage gave McCarthy an enviably strong hand. Biden, as talks unfolded, offered to freeze 2024 spending at the current levels, which would have saved $1 trillion over 10 years; that was enough to make liberals howl that he had given away the store. Yet House Republicans rejected it out of hand.

In past debt-limit showdowns, there was always a sense that grown-ups in the GOP would stop short of default. But there were no grown-ups this time: McCarthy, during his 15-round bid for the speakership, had surrendered to the far right the ability to toss him out of the job—"vacate the chair"—at will. And to McCarthy, nothing mattered more than keeping his job, even if it meant following the Freedom Caucus to default.

On the morning of May 18, an upbeat McCarthy told CNN's Manu Raju in Statuary Hall: "I see the path that we could come to an agreement," perhaps by the weekend.

But about four hours later, the Freedom Caucus put the kibosh on that, demanding that "there should be no further discussion" unless the Democratic Senate accepted all the House Republicans' demands. (Trump later echoed this: "REPUBLICANS SHOULD NOT MAKE A DEAL ON THE DEBT CEILING UNLESS THEY GET EVERYTHING THEY WANT [Including the 'kitchen sink'] . . . DO NOT FOLD!!!")

The next morning, McCarthy's negotiators called off talks, saying they'd "decided to press pause, because it's just not productive."

The wild swing between ebullience and despair recurred three days later. In the White House driveway after a negotiating session, McCarthy and one of his negotiators used the word "productive" at least 11 times, along with "professional," "intelligent," and "respectful." But the very next morning, McCarthy, facing his restive caucus in a closed-door meeting at Republican National Committee headquarters, told them they were "nowhere near a deal."

As the world waited to see whether McCarthy would shoot his hostage, the speaker provided regular glimpses into his erratic thought process. Democrats, he claimed, had "increased the amount of spending to the highest level we've ever had at any time in American history, especially to GDP." In reality, federal spending at the time as a percentage of GDP was barely more than half of the all-time high.

In the White House driveway, McCarthy asked: "Is it so arcane to say, should we look at where we're if we're spending higher than we average do in 50 years? Should it be arcane that we pull money back that we appropriated during COVID but wasn't spent?"

Is it so arcane to ask if the speaker knows what "arcane" means? No matter: We're spending higher than we average do!

Over and over again, McCarthy compared the federal government to a child.

May 16: "This is the equivalent of your child having a credit card."

Later on May 16: "This is giving your child a credit card."

May 21: "Think about what a debt ceiling is. It is your child having a credit card."

May 22: "If you were to give your child a credit card . . ."

Later on May 22: "To me a debt ceiling is providing your child a credit card."

Still later on May 22: "It's like having a child, giving them a credit card."

May 24: "A debt ceiling, so the American people understand, is having a credit card."

The mindless repetition didn't make the analogy any less bogus. The United States isn't a child. It's the world's largest economy and guarantor of the world's reserve currency, it has the unquestioned ability to raise whatever revenue it needs, and it has a solemn obligation to honor its sovereign debt as it has throughout history.

Those would be the relevant "criterias." Unless you were dealing with a madman.

SUNDAY, MAY 28, WAS BOTH THE HIGH-WATER MARK OF McCARTHY'S SPEAKERship and the beginning of his downfall. Defying the far right for once, he struck a perfectly reasonable compromise with Biden that raised the government's borrowing limit into 2025 and avoided a default.

The MAGA Republicans' opposition was categorical. It was also scatological.

Many of the same House GOP extremists who nearly denied McCarthy the speakership did their utmost to tank the bipartisan debt and budget agreement.

Chip Roy wanted colleagues to know "what a turd sandwich this 'deal' is."

Dan Bishop, of North Carolina, told me and other reporters that the hardliners needed "to fix this shit sandwich."

Florida's Byron Donalds, at a news conference, declared it "crap."

And Greene said she needed a sweetener if she was "to eat this shit sandwich." Proposed Greene: "Everyone loves dessert, and that's impeachment."

Members of the House Freedom Caucus gathered outside the Capitol to denounce the accord as an "insult," a "violation," and "un-American," in Norman's view.

"Trillions and trillions of dollars in debt for crumbs," protested Freedom Caucus chairman Perry.

Added Congressman Andrew Clyde of Georgia, wearing one of his AR-15 pins on his tie, the barrel pointed at his head: "It's a win for Washington."

The assembled murmured their agreement when Donalds complained that "this bill keeps all of Joe Biden's policy, all of Joe Biden's spending, intact."

The Freedom Caucus members began murmuring threats to punish McCarthy by hobbling, if not terminating, his speakership. "There's going to be a reckoning," Roy threatened, speculating (incorrectly, it turned out) that McCarthy didn't have "a majority of his own conference" supporting the deal.

Asked at the news conference whether they would consider a "motion to vacate" to depose the speaker Bishop's hand shot up. He accused McCarthy of "lying," of "total betrayal," and he said his confidence in the speaker is "none—zero."

Another dissident, Colorado's Ken Buck, told reporters to "stay tuned" for a "discussion on the motion to vacate."

But the renegades started in a weak position. Only 11 of the Freedom Caucus's 50-odd members joined the event at which they tried, in vain, to rally opposition to the deal. They looked like street protesters, not lawmakers. Immediately behind them, two ambulances and a paramedic van, lights on and beeping, attended to a stricken tourist. A pro-Trump demonstrator dressed as a Hassidic Jew and carrying a bullhorn wandered around in the background with a banner proclaiming "Traitor Kevin McCarthy/Shame on You!"

The House Freedom Caucus hardliners called for reinforcements, but the cavalry never came. Freedom Caucus founder Jim Jordan, co-opted by McCarthy with a pair of committee chairmanships, threw his support behind the "darn good deal." Provocateur Greene, now embraced by McCarthy as an ally, willingly devoured the feces sandwich under the rationale that Republicans could then move on to more important matters, such as impeaching Biden.

Self-proclaimed debt hawk Tom Massie of Kentucky—he carries a digital debt clock in his breast pocket instead of a handkerchief—could have used his seat on the Rules Committee (won as a concession during the speakership battle) to kill the bill before it got to the floor. Instead, Massie, perhaps to protect the subcommittee chairmanship he also secured during the speakership battle, cast the deciding vote for it—after some grandstanding. "I'm reluctant to disclose how I might vote on this rule at this moment, because then all the cameras leave," he said. "Dramatic pause," he narrated, before announcing his support.

The two other hardliners who had won seats on the Rules panel during the speakership fight flailed uselessly against the bill. Norman, revealing his true motive, suggested that deeper budget cuts were needed to "punish" the government—and those who rely on it. Likening government to a corporation, he asked: "Is that really a punishment if you tell the business we're going to really punish you, we're going to cut your business income 1 percent but we're going to leave 99 percent intact?"

Roy, the other dissident on the panel, denounced the deal as a "four-trillion-dollar increase" in the federal debt with "no teeth" to cut spending. "We all know who the big winner will be: government."

Republicans unsuccessfully came to the panel with more than 60 amendments to toughen the legislation. Colorado's Boebert, who attempted to insert 15 different poison pills, demanded that Congress "stop spending money we don't have." Added Boebert, who had just filed for divorce: "It has been an argument my husband and I often had."

The right-wingers expressed many irreconcilable differences with McCarthy's deal. The package rescinded only 2 percent of Biden's $80 billion expansion of the IRS. The work requirements for government programs had so many exemptions that the government would wind up spending more money on them, the Congressional Budget Office forecast. The package had no provision to enforce spending discipline after the first two years.

To answer his critics, McCarthy had a ready approach: He would make stuff up.

He gathered the rank and file for a closed-door caucus meeting, fed them cartloads of We, The Pizza pies, and told them: "I'm going to go on record and vote for the biggest spending cuts in history!"

This wasn't remotely true, but McCarthy repeated it endlessly over the following days.

"Tonight we are going to vote for the largest savings in American history," he said (wrong), "over $2.1 trillion" (also wrong). "We capped the ability of growth, of spending and government for the next six years," he said (wrong again). "History will write this is the largest cut in American history," he continued (still wrong).

But the facts didn't matter; McCarthy had the votes.

During the floor debate, the zealots used a parliamentary maneuver, attempting to derail the package by voting against the "rule" that allowed the debate to begin. Such rules routinely pass on strictly party-line votes, but this time 29 GOP holdouts cast no votes in protest—enough to kill the bill if Democrats hadn't intervened. House Democratic leader Hakeem Jeffries let McCarthy squirm for about 45 minutes (it was supposed to have been a 15-minute vote) before he raised a green card to allow Democrats to break ranks and vote for the GOP-written rule. Fifty-two of them did, bailing out McCarthy and the debt deal.

Later, during the debate, Jeffries gloated about saving McCarthy from his MAGA hardliners. "Earlier today 29 House Republicans voted to default on our nation's debt and against an agreement that you negotiated," he needled. "It's an extraordinary act that indicates just the nature of the extremism that is out of control on the other side of the aisle. Extreme MAGA Republicans attempted to take control of the House floor. Democrats took it back for the American people. And we will continue to do what is necessary."

McCarthy's allies didn't appreciate the taunt. The presiding officer, Brad Wenstrup of Ohio, took the extraordinary step of gaveling down the Democratic leader mid-speech, for the minor offense of referring to Republicans as "you" instead of "they."

(It was the second time Republicans had gaveled down the Democratic leader mid-speech. Steve Womack of Arkansas had done the same to Jeffries a month earlier. In a complaint to the House parliamentarian, McGovern, the top Democrat on the Rules Committee, noted that, under Democratic control of the chamber, McCarthy had committed the same "you" offense more than a dozen times—but was never gaveled down mid-speech.)

When the clerk called the roll for final passage of the debt bill, Jeffries's Democrats bailed out McCarthy again. In the final tally, most of the no votes came from Republicans; most of the yes votes came from Democrats.

IT WASN'T CLEAR WHETHER MCCARTHY MADE A CONSCIOUS DECISION TO PUT the country above his own job security, or whether, as Democrats and House Freedom Caucus members suspect, he simply got bested in the negotiations. As Brad Sherman, a California Democrat, told Bloomberg's Erik Wasson after the vote: "Now we are allowed to say it: We rolled them."

Whatever the motive, McCarthy did the right thing. For once, McCarthy didn't cower and cave. He told the right-wing hooligans to stuff it, and three days later he took his debt compromise to the House floor—where something remarkable happened.

More than two-thirds of Republicans stuck with McCarthy, leaving the 71 holdouts isolated.

At the same time, nearly 80 percent of Democrats voted for the package, putting more D's than R's in the yes column and lifting the bill to passage by a lopsided 314–117.

Watching from the gallery, I felt a rare (and, it turned out, fleeting) moment of hope for our politics. For a day, the madness had stopped.

McCarthy discovered that if he was willing to be reasonable, Democrats would lend him their support. He also proved that the Trumpian forces within his party could be sidelined—if sensible Republicans would only show some courage.

All the usual forces of destruction on the right were aligned against the debt-and-budget deal, and, by logical extension, in favor of default: Sean Hannity, Laura Ingraham, and the rest of the Fox Industrial Complex; Ron DeSantis, the House Freedom Caucus, Heritage Action, and the Club for Growth; former Trump aides Steve Bannon, Peter Navarro, and Russ Vought. Donald Trump himself, though he went quiet as the vote neared, told Republicans they should default rather than budge from their original, absurd demands for nearly $5 trillion in deficit reduction and the repeal of much of Biden's agenda.

Instead, McCarthy accepted a modest $1.5 trillion in projected savings over 10 years and left Biden's agenda intact, while agreeing that there would be no more debt limit hostage-taking before the election. Most Republicans tolerated the compromise, and Democrats leaped at it.

"This is fabulous," McCarthy replied at a post-vote news conference when the *Washington Post*'s Leigh Ann Caldwell asked him to square the overwhelming Democratic support with his claims that Democrats got "nothing" in the negotiations. "This is one of the best nights I've ever been here," he went on with exaggerated cheer. "I thought it would be almost impossible just to get to 218 [votes]."

There was nothing to celebrate in the *way* the debt agreement came about. Republicans manufactured a crisis and played a(nother) reckless game with the credit of the United States. They took tax revenues, entitlement programs, defense, and veterans' benefits off the table, requiring all cuts to come from a small sliver—about 11 percent—of the federal budget.

This made substantial debt reduction impossible, and the two sides struck a deal that was necessarily small-bore. Republicans won a modest slowdown in some categories of spending. Democrats protected their gains of the Biden years and removed Republican threats to tank the economy during Biden's reelection campaign.

Yet some real good could have come from the episode, if McCarthy had continued to work with Democrats and marginalize the extremists in his own caucus. During the speaker's 40-minute celebratory news conference in the Capitol's Rayburn Room after the vote, PBS's Lisa Desjardins asked if the bipartisan debt deal could be a "template for other issues."

Unfortunately, McCarthy sounded more interested in patching things up with the extremists. "I watched Congress divided today; I watched my own conference," he said. "I'll work to make sure everybody comes back."

But for one night, at least, McCarthy was king of the world. "Tonight we made history," he announced of the bipartisan success. "There's a whole new day here," he proclaimed.

He then proceeded to do the legislative equivalent of slipping on a banana peel, pulling down the drapes, knocking over a fully laden buffet, and face-planting into the wedding cake.

As the House's first order of business after the debt deal, McCarthy's leadership team decided to follow the classic culture-war script: Conjure up a crisis—in this case, the canard that the Biden administration was coming to take away your gas stove—and then force votes on legislation to counter the nonexistent threat.

"That's what we're seeing from the Biden administration, literally a plan to ban gas stoves," Scalise declared in a news conference about the upcoming votes on the Gas Stove Protection and Freedom Act and the Save Our Gas Stoves Act.

Biden "has a war against gas stoves!" added Debbie Lesko, an Arizona Republican.

Biden literally had no such plan, other than the usual rules requiring higher efficiency in future appliance models as technology improved. (One of the Consumer Products Safety Commission members had mused idly about a ban on future gas stoves, but the idea was immediately shut down by his superiors.) Regardless, the House GOP leaders' cooked-up stove crisis had the desired effect of causing everybody to retreat behind party lines.

At a House Rules Committee hearing on what Republicans called the Biden administration's "proposal to ban gas stoves," Democrat Mary Gay Scanlon of Pennsylvania tore into what she called "this whole insane, ridiculous gas-stove conspiracy theory. It is so absurd. It really is off the charts even for this House majority." She closed her remarks: "This is bullshit. Sorry."

On the Republican side of the panel, Massie tried to burn Representative Frank Pallone of New Jersey, the top Democrat on the Energy and

Commerce Committee. "Mr. Pallone, do you own a gas stove?" Massie demanded. "Does it meet the new standards or not?"

Pallone allowed that he hadn't "checked the stove before I came here."

Massie said that he was "trying to figure out, does my stove" meet the standard?

Pallone assured him that "it doesn't affect any stove that you have now. You don't have to change it. You don't have to throw it out."

Democrat Jared Moskowitz of Florida gave the half-baked bills the ridicule they deserved, offering the Rules Committee several amendments, because "I don't think the bills go far enough." He proposed renaming the bill "'The Appliance Bill of Rights,' to put it on par with some of our most important rights as Americans." He also proposed erecting "a stainless steel, six-burner double oven in Statuary Hall" to give gas stoves "the honor that they deserve." And he sought to appoint a "supreme allied gas commander" in the Energy Department to guard gas stoves.

"Just when Americans think Congress can't handle the big issues," Moskowitz told the panel, "we're here to show them we can do so by tackling the war on gas stoves."

The House had returned to pointless partisan sniping over a fake crisis addressed by legislation that stood no chance of becoming law. McCarthy's plan to appease the far right appeared to be working!

But then the rebels struck. Freedom Caucus members took their revenge on McCarthy—by making sure he couldn't pass the gas bill.

Just six days after McCarthy's debt ceiling triumph, a small band of right-wing zealots used parliamentary tactics to bring proceedings on the House floor to a halt, in the first protest of its kind in more than two decades.

Without warning, 11 of them voted with Democrats against the "rule" for the debate (the same tactic they attempted during the debt-ceiling fight) without which the debate could not proceed. The presiding officer had ordered a five-minute vote, but it lasted 53 minutes as GOP leaders, upon discovering the rebellion, tried to persuade the Freedom Caucus holdouts to relent. The vote failed—the first time a rule had failed under either party's leadership since 2002. The great stove debate could not begin.

The House went into recess. Journalists launched a thousand painful puns. "House Republicans couldn't pass gas," ventured *Politico*.

It wasn't that the right-wingers were opposed to McCarthy's gas stoves stunt—far from it—but they were determined to punish McCarthy by bringing the House to a standstill. And because he was trying to pass purely partisan legislation with only Republican votes, he had given them the power to do so.

The rebels shut down the House for a couple of hours, then for the entire day, then for the next day. Finally, on the third day of paralysis, House GOP leaders surrendered to the saboteurs with a whip notice: "Members are advised that votes are no longer expected in the House this week ... Thank you for your patience."

The mutineers were in command of the ship. They blamed McCarthy for betraying them. Negotiations went nowhere. And the People's House ceased to function.

For three days, the rebels went in and out of McCarthy's office. Scalise tried to placate them by promising to schedule a vote on a separate bill, offered by Georgia's Clyde, to roll back gun regulations despite a plague of mass shootings. (Clyde had claimed that GOP leaders threatened to kill his bill as punishment for opposing the debt deal.) But that didn't stem the rebellion.

McCarthy gallantly placed culpability for the debacle on Scalise ("the majority leader runs the floor"), specifically his "miscalculation, or misinterpretation," relating to Clyde.

Scalise returned the favor, telling *Punchbowl News* that there's "a lot of anger" at McCarthy, and the speaker has to "resolve those issues."

But trying to satisfy the extremists (who, as McCarthy accurately noted, hadn't articulated coherent demands) was a fool's errand. As long as McCarthy attempted to appease them, any hope of actual legislative achievement would be on the back burner. And any hope for a successful speakership would go up in smoke.

McCarthy tried to be upbeat. "In the end, when I look back, this may be a very big positive thing," he ventured, after the zealots shut down the House. Instead, it was the beginning of his end.

Chapter 6

"This Place Is Crazier Than Usual"

I T WAS PERFECTLY OBVIOUS THAT, AFTER THREE MONTHS ON THE JOB, THE House Republican majority of the 118th Congress had accomplished nothing of substance on the top issues facing the country. But nobody could accuse them of failing to address the "Number One" issue.

In late March, the House Committee Oversight and Accountability hauled District of Columbia government officials before Congress to grill them on what Republicans called the "crisis" of crime in the capital, one of dozens of "crises" the GOP majority had by that point proclaimed. And Representative Lauren Boebert was just bursting with a stream of invective.

"Did you or did you not decriminalize public urination in Washington, D.C.?" the Colorado Republican, fairly shouting, demanded of a witness, D.C. council member Charles Allen.

Allen looked puzzled. "I did not," he replied.

Boebert rephrased. "Did you lead the charge to decriminalize public urination in Washington, D.C.?"

"No, ma'am," Allen answered.

Boebert persisted. "Did you ever vote in favor of decriminalizing public urination?"

To the contrary, Allen said, he had voted to keep public urination as a criminal offense.

"We have records that show you were in favor of removing that criminal offense and allowing public urination!" Boebert charged.

The councilman explained that although the D.C. criminal-code reform commission had proposed making public urination a civil offense, the council voted to maintain it as a criminal offense.

Thus did the floodgates open on the Great Public Pee Pee Debate of 2023.

"I continue to be amazed by what the majority chooses to spend our limited time on," remarked Becca Balint of Vermont, a Democrat on the panel. Turning to the witnesses, she joked: "You have anything additional you want to say about public urination? Now's your time."

Boebert blurted out: "I do!"

There was laughter in the committee room. "No, not you," an exasperated Balint said.

Boebert just couldn't hold it. "I do have something else to say!"

Glenn Grothman, a Wisconsin Republican, volunteered his thoughts on the matter to the committee. "You've got to decide how many times a person's done something and how in-public it is, but I'm not sure public urination should be criminally charged," he opined, before adding that the D.C. officials "don't want me to tell you how to do your job."

Yet that's exactly what Republicans were doing. The voters had entrusted them with a House majority and the ability to set the agenda as they chose. And Republicans were devoting their time in power to micromanaging D.C. and its criminal code, including the precise penalties for public urination.

Two days earlier, on March 27, a killer had gunned down six people in a school shooting in Nashville. But when it came to ending the near-daily plague of mass shootings, Republicans had decided that "we're not gonna fix it," as Tim Burchett, a Tennessee Republican, drawled. "Criminals are gonna be criminals." But maybe they could hike the punishment for peeing in the nation's capital.

"Do you think parents," Florida Democrat Jared Moskowitz asked the witnesses, "are worried about public urination in Washington, D.C.? Or do you think they're worried about sending their kid to school and their kid not coming home?"

To be fair, urination wasn't the only priority in evidence among members of the House majority. Virginia Foxx of North Carolina declared, at the same hearing, her disapproval of bike lanes. Paul Gosar of Arizona, with his extensive white nationalist ties, complained about the D.C. mayor's naming of Black Lives Matter Plaza in June 2020. (Republicans demanded she revoke the name, calling BLM a "terrorist sympathizer group.")

In the same week as the pee hearing, House Republicans used no fewer than three other hearings to opine on Hunter Biden's laptop. They held an entire hearing on the "crisis" posed to our national security by a migrant invasion—from Canada. At another hearing, on the supposedly "woke" U.S. military, Gosar declared that "today's military leadership has become the world's laughingstock," that the "military is recruiting mentally troubled people," and that "military schools are focused on describing oral sex, masturbation and pornography."

IN ELECTION DAY EXIT POLLS IN 2022, VOTERS SAID THAT INFLATION WAS the issue that mattered most to them, followed by abortion (most favored the protection of abortion rights), then crime, gun control, and immigration. But House Republicans plunged into an agenda that bore almost no resemblance to the voters' priorities. They were attacking teachers' unions and trans kids. They were trying to expand access to the guns used in mass killings and decrease access to abortions. They were seeking to outlaw programs that promoted racial cohesion in the military and books that mentioned LGBTQ issues. They were trying to defund the FBI, dock the pay of the defense secretary, block the IRS from going after rich tax cheats, and impeach the Homeland Security secretary. Instead of dealing with the threats to national security posed by Russia, China, and climate change, they were seeking to ignite culture wars that nobody had asked them to fight.

Well, not nobody. They were answering to that small and unrepresentative sliver of the electorate that participates in Republican primaries and therefore controls the fate of the vast majority of House Republicans. This tiny sliver of America is the most susceptible to the Fox News disinformation machine, which had convinced them that terrorists were streaming across an "open border," that trans athletes dominated school sports, and that infants were being murdered by abortion doctors. It was a case of garbage in, garbage out.

In the first days of the 118th Congress, members of the new majority rushed to introduce legislation on the issues that mattered most to them:

H.R. 25: "Abolishing the Internal Revenue Service."

H.R. 29: "To authorize the Secretary of Homeland Security to suspend the entry of aliens."

H.R. 69: "To abolish the Occupational Safety and Health Administration."

H.R. 79: "To withdraw the United States from the . . . World Health Organization."

H.R. 81: "To prohibit funding to the Special Representative for Racial Equity and Justice of the Department of State."

H.R. 83: "To repeal the National Voter Registration Act of 1993."

H.R. 151: "To remove short-barreled shotguns from the definition of firearms."

H.R. 216: "To prohibit Federal education funds from being provided to elementary schools that do not require teachers to obtain written parental consent prior to teaching lessons specifically related to gender identity, sexual orientation, or transgender studies."

H.R. 112: "To repeal the Patient Protection and Affordable Care Act."

Thirteen years later, they were still trying to repeal Obamacare.

At best, the new majority was serving up an array of solutions in search of problems. But just as often, they were addressing actual problems, such as the scourge of gun violence, by making them worse.

First up for the new Congress was a bill to protect wealthy tax cheats. In August 2022, the prior Congress, during Pelosi's speakership, had enacted legislation to rebuild the IRS after decades of downsizing. The agency would get an additional $79 billion over 10 years, including $46 billion for enforcement. This would boost tax receipts by $180 billion, the Congressional Budget Office (CBO) projected.

The Biden administration said that increased audits under the legislation would target those among the wealthiest 1 percent of Americans who defraud the government, and fellow taxpayers, of more than $160 billion a year in tax revenue. Biden's Treasury Department issued a directive that the new funds could not be used to increase audits on households earning less than $400,000. The CBO calculated that only a "small fraction" of the increased tax receipts would come from those earning under $400,000, in part because "voluntary compliance will increase for all taxpayers."

But now the new GOP majority wanted to repeal the 2022 law, or most of it. And they would do it by making stuff up once again. Majority leader Steve Scalise, boasting about Republicans' "bill to repeal those 87,000 IRS agents," claimed that the CBO "confirmed" that those agents would "go after people making less than $200,000 a year," including "the single mom who's working two shifts at a restaurant."

In reality, the IRS was hiring only about 6,500 agents—over the course of a decade. In addition to its view that only a "small fraction" of increased revenue would come from taxpayers who aren't super wealthy, the CBO also projected that the Republicans' bill to cut funds to the IRS would add $114 billion to the deficit. So much for fiscal responsibility.

But Republicans spent the entire debate repeating the outright falsehood that 87,000 "agents" would "target American working-class families," as Ways and Means Committee chairman Jason Smith put it.

California Republican Michelle Steel alleged that the Biden administration "rammed through $80 billion to hire 87,000 new IRS agents to harass and spy on middle-class and low-income families."

Claudia Tenney of New York falsely said the CBO had projected "as many as 700,000 more audits, [of] Americans making less than $75,000 a year."

And Beth Van Duyne of Texas added the inventive claim that the fake agents would "make the IRS larger than the Pentagon, State Department, FBI, and Border Control together." The Pentagon alone employs about 3 million people.

Maryland Democrat Steny Hoyer, the former majority leader, told the House that the lies about the IRS were the "most dishonest, demagogic rhetoric that I have seen."

The dishonesty was just beginning.

THE NEW HOUSE MAJORITY PROMPTLY MOVED ON TO ITS NEXT PRIORITY: protecting babies from bloodthirsty abortionists who want to kill them even *after* they are born.

"If a baby is born alive, outside the womb, alive, how could you kill that baby and that be legal?" Scalise asked during debate on the Republicans' "born alive" abortion bill. "And yet in a number of states, it is legal and happening today."

No, it isn't. Infanticide is and always has been murder. In case anyone doubted this obvious truth, a 2002 "born alive" law affirmed that.

The real dispute was about whether a fetus born or aborted with a medical condition that isn't survivable should be treated with heroic measures to keep it alive briefly or whether it should be given compassionate care until nature takes its course. Infanticide wasn't on the table.

But for this up-is-down crowd, the false infanticide narrative was now on the table. The bill was one of three antiabortion measures House Republicans prioritized in their first week: new House rules promising a vote on permanently banning federal abortion funds, a denunciation of violence against antiabortion groups, and the "born alive" bill.

It was also a curious response to the 2022 elections, when voters angered by the Supreme Court's overturning of *Roe v. Wade* propelled Democrats to better-than-expected results and abortion rights supporters prevailed even in red states such as Kentucky and Kansas. "We learned nothing from the midterms if this is how we're going to operate in the first week," complained Nancy Mace, a South Carolina Republican. "What are we doing to protect victims of rape and victims of incest? Nothing." She said her GOP colleagues were only "muddying the waters and paying lip service."

Eventually, GOP leaders relented, dropping their plan to impose a permanent federal funding ban on abortion and going after insurance plans that cover abortion.

But the attempts to ban abortions wouldn't stop. How could they? This was, after all, a caucus led by the likes of Jim Jordan, the Judiciary Committee chairman and very nearly speaker of the House, who nine years before the *Dobbs* decision had sponsored legislation banning abortion nationwide from "the moment of fertilization." More than half of the House GOP caucus, 125 Republicans, signed on as cosponsors of the Life at Conception Act, which would ban all abortion nationwide and even shut down in vitro fertilization.

It was also the caucus of Marjorie Taylor Greene, who had called Mace "the trash in the GOP conference" and "pro-abort" because Mace, a rape survivor, wanted abortion bans to have exceptions for rape and incest.

And it was the caucus of Anna Paulina Luna, of Florida, who at the hearing on the D.C. criminal code displayed posters showing graphic images of fetuses. Given these "born alive" fetuses names such as "Phoenix, Holly and Angel," Luna said that they were "dismembered and mutilated to the point that they were in pieces." And because of these murders, she said, the District of Columbia's home rule, in place for half a century, should be repealed.

A witness calmly explained to Luna that there had been no change to D.C. law to allow infanticide.

Republicans used the dozen annual appropriations bills to attempt to block abortion access across the country. In the bill funding the Agriculture Department and the Food and Drug Administration, they added a provision blocking the commonly used abortion pill mifepristone from being dispensed by mail and at retail pharmacies. The bill eventually failed in September 2023 when 27 Republicans joined Democrats in opposition.

The bill funding the Commerce and Justice Departments similarly proposed to block the federal government from suing state or local governments over their abortion restrictions. It also limited abortions for those in federal prisons and blocked the Justice Department from covering the costs of abortions in most instances. The bill funding the Labor, Health and Human Services, and Education departments, in turn, blocked Medicaid from covering abortions, stripped funding for family planning, defunded an abortion counseling hotline, and curtailed research using fetal tissue. The bill funding the Pentagon blocked the military from covering the travel expenses for women service members who travel to get an abortion in states where it is legal.

The bill funding the Department of Veterans Affairs reimposed a gag rule blocking funds from going to nongovernmental organizations that provide abortions, and it curbed abortions at VA facilities except in cases of rape, incest, and endangerment of a mother's life. Even that wasn't good enough for Andy Ogles; the Tennessee Republican pushed for an amendment eliminating the exceptions.

California Republican John Duarte, one of a small group of Republicans who opposed the ubiquitous attempts to ban abortion, told *Axios*'s Andrew Solender: "We're just sick of every appropriations bill being a vehicle for some off-the-wall abortion policy."

Noting that voters in the November 2023 off-year elections again favored abortion rights, this time in Ohio and elsewhere, Duarte said, "The American people are about fed up with abortion regulations being stuffed into every aspect of their lives."

In a broader sense, the frenzy to inject antiabortion provisions was a pointless exercise. The Democratic Senate and the president would never swallow these poison pills on abortion or any of the other culture-war issues the far right inserted into the spending bills. And when the spending for the 2024 fiscal year finally cleared Congress—half a year late—virtually none of the poison pills remained. Yet House Republicans wasted more than a year fighting for these inane policies that they knew would never become law. It's as if they took pride in their ineffectiveness.

They reveled in do-nothingness once more after the Alabama Supreme Court ruled in February 2024 that embryos were children, effectively putting IVF treatments for fertility in jeopardy in that state. Republican lawmakers rushed to assure the public that they did not want to abolish fertility treatment. But this reassurance was at odds with the Life at Conception Act, backed by 125 House Republicans, which would have the effect of shutting down IVF treatment nationwide.

One swing district Republican, Michelle Steel of California, said she had withdrawn as a cosponsor of the Life at Conception Act—two days after she won a primary. Instead, she cosponsored a House resolution affirming that IVF "is necessary for women who cannot conceive naturally." This resolution was nonbinding, and it wasn't going anywhere: Only 10 Republicans, mostly from swing districts, signed up as sponsors or cosponsors. The House majority was well on its way to protecting IVF the way it has handled most of its agenda—by doing nothing. Then, in March, 2024, the House Republican Study Committee, which counts 80 percent of House Republicans as members, eliminated all doubt on where the caucus stood. It put out a budget proposal that embraced a nationwide ban on abortion from the moment of conception and the rescinding of approval of the abortion pill mifepristone.

IN ADDITION TO THE INCOHERENT BASKET OF GRIEVANCES AND CULTURAL skirmishes that passed for an "agenda," the new majority embraced the bizarre. On the very first day of the new Congress, even before they had elected a speaker, the new House GOP majority removed the metal detectors that had been put outside entrances to the House chamber after the Jan. 6 rioting.

The magnetometers annoyed them, and several Republicans refused to pass through them. Why? Well, perhaps because they set them off. Andy Harris, a Maryland Republican, set the detector off in 2021 near the House floor, because he was carrying a concealed gun. Congressional regulations, though allowing lawmakers to keep guns in their offices or transport them unloaded and securely wrapped, do not allow firearms on the House floor. Yet several Republicans, including Colorado's Boebert, said they had no intention of obeying this rule.

Three weeks into the new Congress, the House Natural Resources Committee proposed new rules for the panel that jettisoned restrictions on carrying firearms in the committee room. Jared Huffman, a California Democrat on the committee, proposed an amendment to reinstate the restrictions, noting that some of his colleagues "have vowed to take guns everywhere," which was in violation of the law and traditional House rules.

Boebert responded by displaying a poster portraying Huffman wearing a tinfoil hat. "With threats against members of Congress at an all-time high, I would like to remind the gentleman that now is not the time to be stripping members of our constitutional right to defend ourselves," she argued.

Huffman asked his colleagues how many of them "feel like they are so threatened . . . that they would need to bring weapons to our committee hearings."

"I need one everywhere here," Boebert replied.

"Would those be loaded weapons?"

"Not an unloaded weapon," Boebert affirmed.

Luna said she would "reserve the right to carry my firearm in whatever capacity I want to, without your permission." But she helpfully assured Democrats that "we would never hurt you" with their guns.

Tom McClintock, a California Republican, mockingly told the Democrats that if they "believe that there is a homicidal maniac amongst us . . . I would challenge them right now to name the names and present the evidence before such a catastrophe confronts us."

To which Democrat Alexandria Ocasio-Cortez of New York replied: "I believe that from what I've witnessed, the competence of some members may be something that I would be willing to question."

On a party-line vote of 25–14, Republicans got what they wanted: they could pack heat in the committee room.

As mass shootings have become a daily fixture in the United States, polls show that about three-fifths of Americans favor stricter gun laws, while less than a fifth want more lenient laws. But House Republicans had no more regard for public opinion on guns than they did on abortion. In the spring of 2023, the House majority decided to address the gun violence crisis. How? Republicans would pass, largely along party lines, a bill making it *easier* to obtain firearms. They voted, in effect, to protect a powerful and deadly type of handgun that had been used in several recent massacres, including in Nashville, Boulder, Colorado Springs, and Dayton. They did this by voting to strike down new rules by the Biden administration regulating "stabilizing braces" used on handguns.

The House Judiciary Committee had originally planned to take up the measure in March, but they delayed the bill's markup, or drafting session, because, the day before, the Nashville shooter had used one of these pistol braces in that massacre. "Democrats were going to turn this tragic event into a political thing," the committee's chairman, Jim

Jordan, told *The Hill* in explaining the three-week delay. He was clearly inconvenienced by the mass killing.

What's more, the primary sponsor of the legislation embracing pistol braces was Georgia Republican Andrew Clyde, a gun dealer by trade. If that conflict of interest weren't jarring enough, the Republican floor leader for part of the debate was Kentucky representative Tom Massie, known as one of several lawmakers to send out Christmas cards showing each member of the family around the Christmas tree holding an AR-style weapon.

As we know, the "posing-with-guns family photo" was a habit many members had adopted.

In the floor debate where they argued over their proposed pistol brace legislation, Massie, railing against gun-free zones, told the House about a former aide whose husband was shot in a bar. The lesson of this story? She couldn't fire back, as she had left her own gun in her car because "the sign said, 'No Guns Inside' because they served alcohol."

An incredulous Jim McGovern, the Massachusetts Democrat on the Rules Committee, took issue with Massie "suggesting that it's okay for people to carry guns into bars when they are drunk." He added: "This place is crazier than usual." And that was a high bar.

Texas Republican Wesley Hunt admitted on the House floor that "we do have a mass-shooting problem in this country, and my colleagues on the left would, of course, blame the AR-15. But I stand before you to blame the homicidal maniac!"

It was the same phrase McClintock had used to explain why lawmakers should be free to carry guns in the committee room. At its core was a fundamentally anti-American sentiment: that the high level of gun deaths in the United States isn't because of the hundreds of millions of guns on the street but because America must have a higher percentage of homicidal maniacs than other countries.

As with abortion, House Republicans also used spending bills to further their obsession about guns.

They attempted huge cuts to the Bureau of Alcohol, Tobacco, Firearms and Explosives, and they sought to cut the FBI's salaries and expenses by about 5 percent and federal prosecutors by 12 percent. They also proposed to block the government from regulating DIY "ghost guns," from getting reports when an individual buys multiple rifles or shotguns at once, from implementing "red flag" laws to keep guns away from those prone to violence, from offering gun buybacks, and from implementing several other initiatives to reduce gun violence. They tried to stop the Centers for Disease Control from even researching firearms injury and mortality prevention.

IN CONGRESS AND ACROSS THE COUNTRY, REPUBLICAN CULTURE WARRIORS were exceptionally busy in the early months of 2023 making sure that American schoolchildren are freed from the terrible burden of learning.

Among the treatises being removed from classrooms across the country, the *Washington Post*'s Hannah Natanson reported: Mary Wollstonecraft's 18th-century classic *A Vindication of the Rights of Woman;* Mark Twain's *Adventures of Huckleberry Finn;* John Steinbeck's *Of Mice and Men;* Anne Frank's *The Diary of a Young Girl;* and Christopher Columbus's journal. In one study, nearly a quarter of teachers said their classes had been affected by the new educational gag rules.

House Republicans didn't want to be left out of this exciting trend, and in March, the House Committee on Education and the Workforce took up the battle to dumb down America's youth. It marked up a national Parents Bill of Rights and a companion bill aimed at keeping trans girls from competing in youth sports.

Both were solutions to imaginary problems. Controversies involving trans kids in sports nationwide numbered only in the double digits—hardly enough to merit federal action that further stigmatizes children who are already vulnerable and have high suicide rates. And despite Republicans' "parents' rights" crusade, in reality parents report that they are largely satisfied with their children's education.

But the panel's Republicans were not to be persuaded. They claimed to be doing God's will. Chairwoman Virginia Foxx announced that parents' "God-given right to make decisions for their children has been ignored and at times attacked."

Virginia's Bob Good declared that "Democrats reject the God-created science of sex" and further informed the panel that "the fact is, God does not make mistakes. He creates us perfectly unique as individuals, and all of us are either immutably male or immutably female."

Utah's Burgess Owens affirmed that "parental-rights are non-negotiable. Parents have a God-given right to make decisions for their children."

Illinois Republican Mary Miller absurdly alleged, apropos of nothing, that Biden had acted to "force young girls to share locker rooms with 18-year-old men."

This paranoia over the supposed LGBTQ menace, though not on American voters' radar screen, was a recurring theme for congressional Republicans, who purported to speak exclusively for both God and America's parents.

At a Rules Committee hearing, Texas Republican Chip Roy repeatedly railed against a book called *Flamer*, which he called "a graphic book about young boys performing sexual acts at a summer camp." He seemed not to have read the book nor to have understood what it was, for it isn't "graphic" (meaning explicit) but rather a "graphic novel" (as in illustrated).

The Parents Bill of Rights passed the House along party lines, and—like so many of their efforts—had no chance of being taken up in the Democratic Senate. But House Republicans could tell their most ardent supporters that they had finally taken action to make sure that schools get parental consent before honoring a child's request to change pronouns.

The Education Committee didn't do much about education, however. At the same time that its Republican members were fanning trans hysteria, 161 House Republicans, or nearly three-quarters of the caucus, voted on March 24 for a provision that would eliminate the entire federal Department of Education. That included a supermajority of Republicans on the Education Committee. It was the equivalent of having a supermajority of Republicans on the Armed Services Committee support abolishing the military.

When that didn't work out, Republicans once again used the annual appropriations process to further their culture war, this time trying to defund the Education Department. They attempted a 28 percent cut to the department, including a $15 billion cut in aid to low-income Title I schools.

This might explain why the Education Committee was so conspicuously unproductive. In its first seven months, it focused almost entirely on the cultural rather than the educational: asserting "parents' rights," blocking transgender athletes and Biden's student debt relief, protecting sugar-added whole milk in schools—and drafting two bills opposing the use of school facilities to shelter "aliens."

That last one was yet another solution in search of a problem. But in July the House took up its second bill in as many months combating the supposed scourge of schools sheltering migrants.

"In May, New York City contemplated an unthinkable action: They planned on using public elementary and secondary schools to house migrants seeking asylum," Oklahoma Republican Tom Cole, chairman of the Rules Committee, said as the second bill went through his panel.

Had any school *actually* housed migrants? Education Committee chairwoman Foxx had apparently not bothered to find this out. She blithely claimed that it was happening "in blue-state strongholds across the nation" (where, she imagined, these "adult males" endanger schoolchildren).

Democrat Teresa Leger Fernandez of New Mexico told Foxx that there is only "one state that we do know of that has housed migrants" in schools. "Do you know what state that is, Madam Chairwoman?"

"No idea," replied Foxx.

"It was actually a red state," Leger Fernandez informed her. "Texas has housed migrants as shelter in schools."

"Had not heard that," the incurious Foxx replied.

Democrat Joe Neguse of Colorado pressed the chairwoman on the woeful record of her (anti-) Education Committee. He asked whether her panel had moved any bills related to teacher pay, gun violence in schools, pandemic learning loss, or school meals and hunger.

Foxx admitted she had not done anything on those important topics. But she had time to mark up two bills on a topic over which her committee has no jurisdiction: persecuting migrants, including those legally seeking asylum. She was also among those voting to abolish the Department of Education. As Foxx explained to Neguse: "If the Lord put me in charge, I would get the federal government out of education in a heartbeat."

THERE WAS NO LIMIT TO THE UGLINESS THAT THE CULTURAL WARRIORS displayed. Marjorie Taylor Greene, appearing in a *60 Minutes* segment in early April 2023, defended her claim that "Democrats are a party of pedophiles." She explained to Lesley Stahl: "Democrats support, even Joe Biden, the president himself, supports children being sexualized and having transgender surgeries. Sexualizing children is what pedophiles do to children."

Republicans loaded their 12 appropriations bills with riders targeting LGBTQ Americans: barring funds for gender-affirming care; blocking the federal government from suing states over anti-transgender laws; banning "drag queen workshops, performances or documentaries"; prohibiting the Pride flag from being flown at federal facilities; and protecting those who discriminate against same-sex couples.

In July, Republicans on the Appropriations Committee took the normally humdrum bill funding the Department of Transportation and the Department of Housing and Urban Development and turned it into a vehicle for overt bigotry against gay and lesbian Americans.

Republicans on the panel combed through all 2,680 earmarks that had been cleared for inclusion in the bill by Republicans and Democrats, then issued an amendment striking precisely three of them—all programs providing housing and related assistance for those in need within the LGBTQ community. To add insult to injury, the amendment also banned the display of "extraneous flags" (read: Pride flags) at funded facilities and forbade discrimination "against a person who speaks or acts in accordance with a sincerely held religious belief or moral conviction of what constitutes traditional marriage."

Republicans were so determined to enshrine the anti-gay sentiment into law that they violated longtime bipartisan procedures and nixed the grants even though they all qualified for inclusion on their merits.

Andy Harris of Maryland (the guy caught heading to the House floor with a gun), championing the anti-gay amendment at a hearing that July, didn't conceal his ugly intentions. He alleged without evidence that the programs "groom young children" and "groom seven-year-olds." He likened the programs to the "Ku Klux Klan" while also saying they support communists. His spokeswoman didn't respond to my request to substantiate his allegations. (Harris is a nasty piece of work. During an Appropriations Committee hearing earlier in the year, he informed the secretary of health and human services that gender-affirming surgeries for trans people were actually "gender-denying mutilation surgery.")

But no longer were Republicans content to harass the small number of transgender Americans by portraying them as predators in bathrooms. By July they had regressed to a frontal attack on tens of millions of gay Americans and their allies.

Democrats bitterly denounced the amendment. Debbie Wasserman Schultz of Florida called the proposal "a clear but ugly signal to the entire world that America's House is now governed by hatred and bigotry."

Mark Pocan of Wisconsin, who is gay, made a powerful, personal appeal. "If you were to take away earmarks because they went to the NAACP or the Urban League, you would, rightfully so, be called racist bigots!" he shouted. "But when you do it to the LGBT community, it's another frickin' day in Congress."

Pocan spoke of when he received a piece of mail with the words "Dead Faggot" over his photo, and when he was beaten bloody and unconscious with a baseball bat after leaving a gay bar. "This is what you guys do by introducing amendments like this," he said, adding that the action was "spitting on every single person who is LGBTQ plus."

Repeatedly, Harris rose to demand that Democrats' words be "taken down" for impugning his motives. His hysterics forced Appropriations Committee chairwoman Kay Granger to call a series of recesses, causing the July hearing to drag on for hours.

But Harris's own words impugned his character more than any Democrat's could. The 30 other Republicans on the committee, witnesses to this ugly spectacle, had not one but two chances to distance themselves from such flagrant discrimination. But in a pair of party-line votes on the amendment, they instead planted themselves firmly on the side of prejudice.

THE RAGING CULTURAL CLASHES OVER THE PANDEMIC HAD FADED BY THE time Republicans took control of the House in January 2023, and most Americans had moved on. But one of the least understood side effects of the virus continued to plague Congress: long covidiocy.

House Republicans presented with a textbook case of the ailment in late February. The newly formed House Select Subcommittee on the Coronavirus Pandemic met for the first time for what its chairman, Brad Wenstrup of Ohio, said would be some "Monday-morning quarterbacking." It instead became a Tuesday afternoon of false starts and illegal blocks as Republicans used their new panel to spread yet more covid disinformation.

Republicans on the panel offered their predictable assessments. Debbie Lesko of Arizona kicked off with the unsupported allegation that "covid was intentionally released" from a Chinese lab because "it would be impossible for the virus to be accidentally leaked."

Rich McCormick of Georgia advanced the ball by informing the panel that covid booster shots "do more harm than good." Ronny Jackson of Texas, of "Candyman" fame during his tenure in the Trump White House, ran out of bounds with claims about the "safety" of "potential therapeutics" (hydroxychloroquine and ivermectin, presumably).

And then Greene scored with this extraordinary medical discovery: "Researchers found that the vaccinated are at least twice as likely to be infected with covid as the unvaccinated, and those with natural immunity."

Dr. Jewish Space Lasers was an obvious choice for the committee. Back in 2021, when asked at a news conference about her anti-vax rhetoric and whether she felt "any responsibility for keeping people in Georgia safe," Greene laughed and said, "You crack me up."

But the new panel's greatest contribution to the science of misdirection was to feature as witnesses three scientists who arguably did more than all others to champion a herd-immunity approach to covid. Two of them were authors of the "Great Barrington Declaration," put out by a Koch-backed group, which argued in 2020 for letting the virus run wild through the population while somehow segregating the old and vulnerable.

Had they prevailed in making herd immunity the official policy, hundreds of thousands more Americans might have died. As it was, Trump and GOP governors used these scientists' claims to disparage face masks, isolation recommendations, and vaccines—all to whip up resistance to public health mandates issued to help slow the spread of the pandemic.

One of the witnesses, Marty Makary, a Johns Hopkins surgeon and Fox News regular, used the committee meeting to present a new variant of covidiocy. He declared with absolute certainty that the virus came from a Wuhan lab.

"It's a no-brainer that it came from a lab," he declared. What's more, "at this point it's impossible to acquire any more information, and if you did it would only be in the affirmative." He even suggested that two of the nation's top virologists knew this but "changed their tunes" because they were bribed with grant money by Anthony Fauci.

Some intelligence and medical experts (including those in the Energy Department) believed the virus came from the lab. Others thought it occurred naturally. Nobody knew for sure—except Makary. And he knew with equal certainty that whatever unknown evidence might emerge would back him up.

You didn't need a peer-reviewed study to conclude that these were trustworthy sources.

Makary was the guy who claimed in late February 2021 that "covid will be mostly gone by April." He was also the source of Florida governor Ron DeSantis's dubious claim that face masks cause unhealthy levels of carbon dioxide in children's blood.

Another witness, Jay Bhattacharya of Stanford University (also a Fox News regular), had called covid testing "actively harmful" and warned about "great harm" and "danger" from vaccination. He worked on a study that claimed the covid death rate was similar to the flu's, and he argued in March 2020 that "there's little evidence" that "the novel coronavirus would kill millions" if left unchecked.

As congressional witnesses, the trio did not exactly look the part. Bhattacharya, in chinos, had a parka slung over his chair. Makary was wearing Hurley athletic socks with his gray business suit, the logo visible while he sat. The third witness, Martin Kulldorff, a Swedish epidemiologist affiliated with Harvard, wore a sports coat that was torn and unraveling at the elbow, with the frayed white lining sticking through.

They sounded less like medical authorities than *Newsmax* personalities. Kulldorff called covid restrictions "the worst assault" on the poor and middle-class "since segregation." Makary, mocking "King Fauci," claimed that "the greatest perpetrator of misinformation during the pandemic has been the United States government." Bhattacharya repeatedly complained that he and his fellow witnesses had been "censored," "marginalized," and "slandered" by public health "dictators."

Far from being marginalized, these critics were embraced by the Trump administration and became right-wing celebrities. Their ideas helped power resistance to masks and vaccines—at the cost of untold numbers of lives.

There would have been much to gain from a serious debate about the effectiveness of school closures and vaccine mandates. Officials working with limited information did make a lot of mistakes. But those seeking honest answers would have to look somewhere other than the select covidiocy committee.

Republicans, as if unaware that the pandemic had expired, once again tried to advance cockamamie ideas by adding riders to appropriations bills. This time they tried blocking funds from going to covid-19 vaccine mandates or face mask requirements. Things deteriorated further when the covid subcommittee convened again in April for the purpose of bashing the president of the American Federation of Teachers, Randi Weingarten. Here, again, was a chance for the panel to have a serious discussion—this time about the effectiveness of school closures. Instead, they tried to smear the witness.

Greene, displaying a chart, alleged without evidence that diagnoses of gender dysphoria—she called them "diagnosises"—increased as a "direct result" of school closures during the pandemic. She asked the labor leader: "Ms. Weingarten, are you a medical doctor?"

"I am not," Weingarten responded.

"Are you a mother?"

"I am a mother by marriage," Weingarten replied, "and my wife is here with me."

Greene, in a broadside against all kinds of stepparents and adoptive parents, then charged that Weingarten was "not a biological mother."

"People like you need to admit that you're just a political activist," Greene concluded. "You're not a mother and not a medical doctor."

Raul Ruiz, the panel's ranking Democrat, asked for Greene's outrage to be struck from the record. Wenstrup declined, saying "it was not a violation of the House rules."

Only a violation of common decency. After the hearing, Greene told a group of supporters: "We had an important witness come to our committee. You may have heard of her—if I can call her 'her,' I don't want to misgender her."

REPUBLICANS' PASSION TO INFLAME THE CULTURE WARS WAS SO GREAT THAT they trampled traditional conservative principles, including even their longtime reverence for the free market. Of course, that had been slipping since long before the GOP takeover of the House. Donald Trump routinely attacked the "globalists" of Goldman Sachs and the leaders of large U.S. corporations. Ron DeSantis used tax policy to attack the Walt Disney Company because it dared to disagree with his "don't say gay" legislation. Republican governors enacted laws overriding private employers' covid-19 vaccination policies. GOP-led states moved to disrupt interstate commerce by blocking the shipment and distribution of morning-after pills.

Congressional Republicans joined the anticapitalist party, holding multiple hearings to harass social media companies over alleged "censorship" of their views and intimidating Delta Airlines, United Airlines, and Major League Baseball over those businesses' support for voting rights. They also threatened to use taxpayer resources to retaliate against the U.S. Chamber of Commerce for backing a few Democrats.

In May, the former party of laissez-faire capitalism took another step toward reimagining itself as a Soviet state planning committee. Republican lawmakers decided that it was their job to tell investors which businesses they could and couldn't invest in—and which criteria investors would be permitted to consider.

The House Committee on Oversight and Reform staged a hearing to denounce asset managers for using environmental, social, and governance (ESG) criteria for making investment decisions.

"An unelected cabal of global elites are using ESG, a woke economic strategy, to hijack our capitalist system," declared an overwrought Steve Marshall, Alabama attorney general and one of two expert witnesses at the anti-investor hearing. In case his point wasn't clear, Marshall used the word "elites" 13 times and "woke" 20 times in his opening testimony.

The other GOP witness, Utah attorney general Sean Reyes, declared that there exists a "conspiracy" of ESG-minded investors. He was particularly worried that "asset managers who collectively own significant percentages of utilities' stock are improperly influencing the operations of those utilities." Once upon a time, it wasn't controversial for shareholders, who own a company, to influence its operations.

But now, the House was trying to stop new Biden administration regulations allowing—not requiring but *allowing*—retirement plan investors to consider ESG standards. The Democrats' witness, Illinois treasurer Michael Frerichs, called the Republicans' schemes "anti–free market and anti-investor." The GOP officials would block asset managers from even considering whether a pharmaceutical company "has exposure to massive lawsuits because of its role in the opioid epidemic" or whether "healthcare companies understaff their operations and jeopardize the safety of patients," Frerichs told the culture warriors.

Apparently, a lot of investors agree with him, because the accountancy firm PwC predicted that the value of ESG-related assets under management would grow to $33.9 trillion by 2026, or about one-fifth of the worldwide asset management total. ESG, lamented Oversight Committee chairman James Comer, "is gaining ground on Wall Street." Republicans were determined to stop the free market, no matter the cost to businesses.

In reality, the anticapitalist binge was not about economics but, as with so much of the GOP agenda, culture. Wisconsin Republican Glenn Grothman expressed his concern that ESG considerations would work against "certain disfavored groups in our society. People don't like men. People don't like people of European background." Other Republicans on the panel used their time to denounce the perceived "woke" wrongs of JPMorgan Chase, Nike, Anheuser-Busch, and others.

Frerichs, a Democrat, pointed out the absurdity "of me defending the free market against a Republican legislature trying to have a planned economy mandating what businesses have to invest in."

But the irony was lost on Comer, who tried to draw a link, however awkwardly, between his anticapitalist crusade and his simultaneous attempt to prove wrongdoing by Biden and his family. "We just had a press conference and showed bank records that showed the Biden family getting millions of dollars from places like China," he said. "I wonder what types of ESG policies China" has.

China doesn't have ESG standards, of course. It's an authoritarian country with a state-run economy. Ours is a free-market economy in which investors can make their own choices. Republicans once championed the free market—until they let their culture wars conquer everything they do.

Gone, too, was the internationalist Republican Party, defender of freedom around the globe. In its place was a nativist, America First party that couldn't bring itself to support a free and democratic Ukraine as it fought off an invasion by Vladimir Putin's Russia.

After the GOP won control of the House in November 2022, Republicans opposed to helping Ukraine launched their push. In the House television studio in the underground Capitol Visitor Center, Marjorie Taylor Greene and other members took the stage to announce plans to force a vote on ending funds for Ukraine. "Is Ukraine now the 51st state?" asked Greene, alleging an elaborate cryptocurrency conspiracy in which a military aide for Ukraine actually funded Democrats' campaigns.

Matt Gaetz agreed: "I will not vote for one more dollar to Ukraine!"

"Don't send another penny to Ukraine," concurred Tom Massie.

In one of her last acts as speaker, Nancy Pelosi hosted Ukraine's Volodymyr Zelensky at a joint session of Congress in December 2022. The Ukrainian president, 10 months into Russia's invasion of his country, received a hero's welcome.

On the Democratic side of the House, women (including Wyoming Republican Liz Cheney) wore Ukraine's light blue and yellow. Reps. Madeleine Dean, Lisa Blunt Rochester, and others unfurled a large Ukrainian flag. In the gallery, Ukrainian and Ukrainian American leaders shouted "Slava Ukraini!" and "God bless America!" Democrats, and many of the Republicans in attendance, lavished wave after wave of standing ovations on the wartime leader.

But McCarthy was a study in discomfiture. He stood at the floor leader's desk, restlessly playing with the microphone. As Zelensky stood in the chamber door, McCarthy checked his phone. As the adulation began, McCarthy clapped absently while chatting with then-Republican whip Steve Scalise.

Zelensky told the rapt chamber that "your money is not charity" but "an investment in the global security and democracy that we handle in the most responsible way." Lawmakers rose to applaud. McCarthy, who vowed to probe Ukraine's use of U.S. funds, froze in his chair for a while before lumbering to his feet.

Zelensky called on the Americans to "help us bring to justice everyone who started this unprovoked and criminal war." McCarthy sat out the standing ovation, drumming his fingers.

"Let the world see that the United States are here," Zelensky urged. McCarthy yawned.

Most GOP lawmakers skipped the speech entirely, and a few in attendance—Lauren Boebert, Matt Gaetz, Tim Burchett—sat through it sulking. Other Republicans trashed Zelensky, calling him "the Ukrainian lobbyist" (Massie), "the shadow president" (Greene), and a "welfare queen" (Donald Trump Jr.).

When Biden flew to Ukraine in February in a show of support around the one-year anniversary of Putin's invasion, an unofficial Kremlin Caucus within the House GOP erupted. Scott Perry of Pennsylvania called it "breathtaking that President Biden can show up in Ukraine to ensure their border is secure, but can't do the same for America."

Greene called the trip "incredibly insulting," saying Biden "chose Ukraine over America, while forcing the American people to pay for Ukraine's government and war. I cannot express how much Americans hate Joe Biden."

Senate Republican leader Mitch McConnell, speaking for the fast-retreating internationalist wing of the GOP, pushed back. "Reports about the death of Republican support for strong American leadership in the world have been greatly exaggerated," he said, vowing that Republican leaders "are committed to helping Ukraine."

But, as had become obvious, the old guard didn't speak for this GOP. In July, Gaetz offered a one-sentence amendment to the National Defense Authorization Act, stating that "no federal funds may be made available to provide security assistance to Ukraine." Seventy House Republicans—nearly a third of the caucus—voted for it. Greene offered an amendment to cut the aid to Ukraine by $300 million; 89 Republicans voted yes.

In August, the right-wing Freedom Caucus, again trying to hijack spending bills for its policy aims, announced that it wouldn't support any spending bills that funded Ukraine's defense. In September, McCarthy held an "emergency" meeting of the Rules Committee to strip Ukraine spending from the Pentagon's spending bill. He also omitted Ukraine aid from the temporary spending patch to keep the government open through mid-November.

In October, the Pentagon warned Congress that it was almost out of funds with which to replenish Ukraine's weaponry. But House Republicans passed another temporary spending patch that also denied Ukraine additional funds. The Kremlin Caucus had prevailed.

Did House Republicans realize they were endangering national security and destroying American moral leadership? Possibly not. This group includes, after all, the same people who scolded the energy secretary for taking "international travel" to Puerto Rico (Cathy McMorris Rodgers, of Washington) and who said they couldn't support humanitarian aid for women and children in Afghanistan because they couldn't find the provision in "my pocket Constitution" (Anna Paulina Luna, of Florida).

"I have a real concern of the aggression of Russia. I have a more greater concern of this axis of power coming together of China, Russia, North Korea, and Iran," McCarthy explained in his inimitable way in early 2023. "I watched this happen in the world another time before I was ever born."

Without explaining how that was possible, he continued: "Um, I think it is utmost important that Russia lose . . . I think it's a very responsibility that yes Russia loses in this aggression."

To explain current world affairs, McCarthy reached, with great difficulty, for historical precedent. "What should they have done when they first saw Hitler, Mussolini, and Japan getting together?" he asked. "What dependencies did they become weak upon? What aggressions did they look the other way? On building up a military of Hitler even though it went against the Treaty of Versailles. Or the movement in of Czechoslovakia and Austria. Or the movement into Crimea. Or the desire to take Taiwan. So walking through the pandemic thinking about where was America waking up to medical supplies?"

No wonder he couldn't make the case for Ukraine.

MANY OF THE HOUSE REPUBLICANS' POISON PILLS IN THE DOZEN ANNUAL spending bills were meant to ignite fights about race, abortion, LGBTQ issues, and guns. But there was also a random assortment of the bizarre:

> Blocking funding for research on climate change and for Biden's attempts to address climate change as a matter of national security.

> Denying security clearances to anybody who signed on to a 2020 statement defending Hunter Biden.

> Forbidding the District of Columbia from making a law that denies motorists their God-given right to make right turns on red.

None of these had a chance in the Senate, but House Republicans went on having their fun.

The military came in for its share of abuse. And this was a shift for Republicans. They had for years gone after government institutions such as the IRS, the ATF, the Education and Justice and State departments, and the courts, helping to drive down public respect for all of them. But Republicans didn't mess with the military.

Until now. They would sacrifice even the military to their culture wars.

The Senate had been a relative bastion of stability for much of 2023, as a bipartisan Senate majority declined to join the Republican House in careening from default scare to shutdown crises. But not so on military matters, thanks to just one man: Senator Tommy Tuberville, Alabama Republican.

Starting in February 2023, he led a one-man blockade preventing senior military officers from getting confirmed by the Senate—all to protest the "woke" military's policy of paying for service members stationed in states where abortion was illegal to travel to get the procedure in states where it was legal. His fellow Republicans, who agreed with him on the abortion provision, did nothing to stop him.

This went on for the better part of a year, and before Tuberville relented he had suspended nominations of more than 450 military officers, throwing military leadership into chaos and doing "great damage to our military," as a fellow Republican senator, South Carolina's Lindsey Graham, put it. The military was thrown into crisis when the commandant of the Marine Corps was hospitalized with heart problems (he had been working two jobs because the Senate had not confirmed his deputy), and because he had no deputy there was nobody to step in when the commandant was incapacitated.

Naturally, the culture warriors in the House took aim at the military, too. In March 2023, House Republicans staged a hearing dedicated to demonstrating that "progressivism" in the military is what's jeopardizing "force readiness."

There had been recent shortfalls in military recruitment, and research showed that economic and quality-of-life issues were to blame, as well as a declining percentage of young people who met eligibility standards. But Republicans argued that the real culprit was "woke" policies, even though they had no evidence of this. "Just because you don't have the data or we don't have the data doesn't mean there's no correlation," argued Scott Perry.

And so they blamed a decision by the Pentagon to order discussions on extremism in the ranks. They blamed the military's diversity training. They blamed critical race theory and policies on abortion and trans recruits. They blamed the covid-19 vaccine mandate and the military's planning for climate change.

Gosar criticized the military for holding training sessions about "imagined" white supremacy, and accused the chairman of the Joint Chiefs of Staff, Mark Milley, of conspiring "to overthrow the sitting president of the United States," Donald Trump. Gosar would go on to call the nation's top soldier a "traitor," saying that in a "better society," the "sodomy-promoting General Milley would be hung."

Never mind that the military brass said their inclusive policies enhanced cohesion, recruitment, and war-fighting capability. Never mind that the commandant of the Marine Corps had just told the defense news website Defense One that there was "zero evidence" that the military's diversity efforts detract from their combat missions.

Just as Republicans intervened to stop private investors from considering ESG factors because businesses believe it's in the best interest of their shareholders, the GOP was now intervening to deter the U.S. military from doing what its leadership believed to be in the best interest of troop morale and strength.

Louisiana Republican Clay Higgins, lamenting an "emasculation of our country" and citing evidence from the far-right publication *Epoch Times*, argued that young people shouldn't enlist in the "woke" military. "We're southern families, we're conservative families, and we're not going to encourage our young men and women to join and endure that stuff," he said.

Similar efforts to undermine the military came when the National Defense Authorization Act came to the floor in July. The sprawling $886 billion piece of legislation, which sets priorities for the U.S. military, sailed through committee on a 58–1 vote and was on its way to overwhelming passage on the House floor. But then the far-right hooligans intervened, demanding that the House vote on amendments designed to address all manner of imaginary problems.

Greene, now styling herself the foreign policy brains of the GOP, authored an amendment calling on the United States to quit NATO, which she blasted as "not a reliable partner."

Gaetz offered amendments to combat the imagined threat of "radical gender ideology permeating the Department of Defense," suggesting to the Rules Committee that military recruitment has been hurt because "women are having to shower with biological men."

Warren Davidson, of Ohio, wrote an amendment banning the Pride flag from military installations because, he told the Rules Committee, "it co-opts, you know, God's symbol of the rainbow to promote an agenda hostile to that doctrine."

Lauren Boebert drafted an amendment to stop the military from being undone by "pornographic and radical gender ideology books" in schools on military bases.

"We have drag shows at Malmstrom Air Force Base," Montana Republican Matt Rosendale said during the debate. "There are 150 ICBM missiles that are being controlled by that air force base and by these individuals. I do not want someone who doesn't know if they are a man or a woman with their hand on a missile button."

A sensible leader would have rejected such nonsense and stopped his caucus from playing games with the American military. But McCarthy couldn't tell the conspiracy peddlers to take a hike. He needed their votes to keep his job. And so they got their amendments, several of which passed, turning the defense authorization bill from a bipartisan triumph into a partisan donnybrook. It cleared the House on a party-line vote of 219–210 and months later still hadn't become law because of disagreements with the Senate—which, by contrast, passed the same legislation without the partisan poison pills by a lopsided 86–11.

The military would have to wait for five more months before congressional negotiators could finally strip the poison pills from the legislation and send the National Defense Authorization Act to the president. Once again, the zealots had produced nothing but chaos and outrage.

Chapter 7

"The Dysfunction Caucus at Work"

T HE DEBT CEILING DEAL KEVIN McCARTHY NEGOTIATED WITH THE
White House sailed through the House on the night of May 31, 2023,
earning the votes of two in three Republicans and four in five Democrats.
It gave the speaker a model for future success: He could stiff-arm the House
Freedom Caucus and other extremists on the right and govern from the
center, with Democrats' support.

But McCarthy took another path. Instead, as noted earlier, McCarthy
tried to win back the affections of the far-right hooligans in his caucus.
It was a fateful error.

Biden's signature on the debt bill hadn't even dried before the hard-
liners began demanding that McCarthy renege on the bipartisan deal.
And, just two weeks after the House passed the debt and spending bill,
McCarthy obliged them. He reneged.

Kay Granger, chairwoman of the Appropriations Committee, issued
a statement on June 12 declaring that the spending levels agreed in the
just-passed compromise were "a ceiling, not a floor, for Fiscal Year 2024
bills." Instead of honoring the agreement, House Republicans would pass
spending bills at the lower levels the hardliners demanded.

It was a total surrender by GOP leadership, but the rebels wanted
more—about $115 billion more. They wanted spending to be cut about
$200 billion below the levels agreed in the debt deal. Twenty-one of the
zealots wrote to McCarthy in July saying they would oppose spending
bills that didn't meet their new demands. They also proposed forcing Biden

to accept their border and immigration bills, passed on partisan lines. And they said they would oppose a House vote on any of the 12 annual appropriations bills until all 12 had cleared committee. All of this made the likelihood of a shutdown on Oct. 1 much more likely.

"This just seems like another week in Congress," an exasperated McCarthy told reporters after receiving the latest threats from the right.

As if that weren't extreme enough, Victoria Spartz, of Indiana, sent her own letter to McCarthy expressing her "utmost dissatisfaction with the lack of leadership" on spending, and vowing that she would "oppose all Republican rules going forward." That effectively reduced McCarthy's House majority to three.

The far right's piety about the nation's finances was particularly suspect, because shortly after the debt deal, House Republicans took up new legislation, with support throughout the GOP caucus, that would significantly increase the debt. During the debt ceiling standoff, McCarthy said he was fighting to relieve the crushing burden of the federal debt on future generations, insisting "it's got to end now."

But just two weeks later, the House Ways and Means Committee passed a three-part bill that would, over the following three years, add $343 billion to the federal debt, according to calculations made by Congress's bipartisan Joint Committee on Taxation. That would more than wipe out the $186 billion saved over the same period by the debt deal—which Republicans had nearly tanked the American economy to achieve just two weeks earlier.

"Republicans, including those on this committee, held our entire U.S. economy hostage, purportedly because you're concerned about Washington spending and our national debt," Democrat Mike Thompson, of California, protested at the daylong markup of the bills. "But now less than two weeks later you brought before us a bill that would add over a trillion dollars to our national debt." The trillion-dollar figure came from the Committee for a Responsible Federal Budget, which calculated that if temporary tax cuts in the bill were made permanent (as often occurs), the bill would actually add $1.1 trillion to the debt.

How to explain this sudden change of heart about the federal debt? Representative Greg Murphy tried objectivism. "I'm slogging through right now . . . a 1957 book written by a lady named Ayn Rand, called *Atlas Shrugged*," said the North Carolina Republican, who apparently just discovered the 20th-century champion of self-interest. He cautioned that "it's very laborious" but "a wonderful lesson."

Perhaps he was taken by Rand's admonition to "never live for the sake of another man." That could explain the House GOP's nihilistic embrace of the looming government shutdown.

By late July, inflation had calmed, the stock market had reached its highest point since 2021, illegal border crossings were down, unemployment was at its lowest in decades, and GDP growth came in better than expected. It was time for the Freedom Caucus to create some chaos.

The group had already shown just how nutty it could be when, in early July, its members announced that they had voted to remove Marjorie Taylor Greene as a member. Apparently, Congresswoman Jewish Space Lasers wasn't crazy enough for the Freedom Caucus; her embrace of political violence was fine, but her alliance with McCarthy was totally unacceptable. Greene dismissed her fellow zealots as "the drama club" and complained that she had only heard about her ouster from the press. This was apparently because she refused to take a call from the Freedom Caucus's chairman, Scott Perry, informing her of her ouster.

Now, in late July, members of the far-right group had gathered outside the Capitol to outline their priorities for the House when it returned in September from its six-week recess. The first order of business was to shut down the federal government.

"We don't fear a government shutdown," proclaimed Bob Good, of Virginia, who convened the Freedom Caucus news conference. Why not? "Most of what we do up here is bad anyway," reasoned Good, and "most of the American people won't even miss [it] if the government is shut down temporarily." (Good, notably, wasn't in Congress for any of the previous shutdowns.)

The Freedom Caucus was perfectly happy to shut down the government on Sept. 30. "We're going to pass a good Republican bill out of the House and force the Senate and the White House to accept it or we're not going to move forward," Good argued. "We ought to use the leverage, if necessary, to force a government shutdown."

This would potentially mean national parks closed, airports snarled, food safety inspections suspended, Social Security applications on hold, hundreds of thousands of federal workers furloughed, calls to the IRS unanswered, and courts, medical research, passports, small business loans, farm assistance, and immigration proceedings all slowed.

Good and his colleagues had a high pain tolerance. Though the heat had been oppressive in the capital, the six of them chose to hold their news conference outdoors, under a broiling midday sun. "Anybody got a sweater I can borrow?" joked Ralph Norman, of South Carolina. But that was nothing compared with the hurt they were poised to inflict on the American public.

In addition to their demands that McCarthy renege on the debt deal, and their further demands that Republicans cut spending by an additional $200 billion, the hardliners were now insisting that an apothecary full of poison-pill amendments be added to the 2024 spending bills: blocking abortion access, LGBTQ rights, and efforts to promote racial diversity. As usual, McCarthy quickly complied.

House Republicans were now on a seemingly inevitable collision course not just with Biden, who had promised to veto the bills, but also with their fellow Republicans in the Senate, who wanted to set spending at a level above the debt ceiling deal so that the military would get more funds.

At the end of July, the Senate Appropriations Committee completed passage of all 12 annual spending bills in overwhelmingly bipartisan fashion. In the House, by contrast, McCarthy's attempts to placate the far right had turned the spending bills into partisan slugfests that even some Republicans couldn't stomach. The House quit town a day early for its August recess, after failing to drum up enough GOP votes to pass one of its spending bills. Republican moderates refused to support the agriculture appropriations bill because it "would ban abortion nationwide," as New York Republican Mike Lawler put it.

"Members are advised votes are no longer expected in the House tomorrow," majority leader Steve Scalise told the chamber. Some cheered. Some on the Democratic side booed.

"Now the Republican conference is saying they are sending us home for six weeks without funding the government?" Katherine Clark, the Democratic whip, responded. "We have one [spending] bill, one bill out of 12 completed because extremists are holding your conference hostage … This is a reckless march to a MAGA shutdown, and for what? In pursuit of a national abortion ban?"

The two went back and forth, ending with Scalise yelling about socialists.

The rebellion by moderate Republicans that forced Scalise to abandon the agriculture bill was a rarity. A similar backlash by moderates had killed another abortion provision offered by Good several weeks earlier. But these were exceptions.

Moderates frequently squawked about the far right's hostage taking. "If it continues, we're going to have to come up with a different role with Democrats," Don Bacon, of Nebraska, told the *Washington Post*. "We're going to have to work around these guys." But these were empty words. In theory, moderates affiliated with mainstream groups such as the Republican Governance Group, the Main Street Caucus, or the bipartisan Problem Solvers Caucus could have isolated the fanatics by striking legislative deals with Democrats. In practice, they never did.

THE AUGUST RECESS DID NOT GO WELL. THE HOSTAGE TAKERS KEPT ADDING to their demands.

On Aug. 10, Chip Roy and 14 other Texas Republican House members declared that they would block funding for the Department of Homeland Security unless the Biden administration overhauled its policies on immigration and the border to suit Roy and his colleagues. Otherwise, no money would go to Homeland Security secretary Alejandro Mayorkas—or, as Roy now called him on NewsNation, "that smirking son of a bitch."

On Aug. 21, the Freedom Caucus proclaimed that its members would "oppose any spending measure" that didn't put an end to the Biden administration's border policies, eliminate the "unprecedented weaponization" of the Justice Department and FBI and "the left's cancerous woke policies in the Pentagon," and curtail military aid to Ukraine. They also vowed to fight "short-term funding extensions," which were about the only option left to avoid a government shutdown.

The House Republicans' shutdown fever worsened strains not just with Democrats and the White House but even with hard-right Republicans in the Senate. "I'm opposed to a shutdown. Period," Senator Josh Hawley, of Missouri, told *Punchbowl News*. "This way of doing business where we're in constant brinkmanship and real people suffer is just bad news."

Senator Ron Johnson, of Wisconsin, called the House hardliners' position "unfortunate," and Senator Rick Scott, of Florida, said he'd "better not" see a shutdown because of the chaos in the House.

None of this really mattered to the Freedom Caucus crowd. In their safe districts, among their far-right constituents who vote in primaries, shutdown brinkmanship was good politics. And lucrative: The Club for Growth in late July announced it would spend $20 million to help reelect the 20 zealots who tried to block McCarthy from the speakership. Nor did McCarthy, a prolific fundraiser, offer much of a counterweight. Protect the House 2024, a political action committee he launched, gave money to rebels such as Lauren Boebert, of Colorado, and Anna Paulina Luna, of Florida. There was no downside for the shutdown crowd.

The very first day back from recess, Sept. 12, Florida's Matt Gaetz went to the House floor to deliver what was, in effect, an ultimatum to McCarthy: Shut down the government or kiss the speakership goodbye.

There were only three or four lawmakers on the floor to deliver the day's five-minute speeches on any topic of their choosing. One of the few in attendance was George Santos, sitting in the front row. One member spoke about farming, another about a local swimmer, a third about the anniversary of the 9/11 attacks. Then Gaetz raised an index finger to be recognized.

"I rise to serve notice: Mr. Speaker, you are out of compliance with the agreement that allowed you to assume this role," he said. "The path forward for the House of Representatives is to either bring you into immediate, total compliance or remove you pursuant to a motion to vacate the chair."

Gaetz, waving his hands theatrically, ticked off McCarthy's long list of offenses: no votes on constitutional amendments to impose term limits or to require balanced budgets, the public release of all security footage from Jan. 6, issuing subpoenas to Hunter Biden, impeaching Joe Biden, defunding special counsel Jack Smith's prosecution of Trump. But mostly Gaetz was demanding that McCarthy retreat from plans to keep the government open with a continuing resolution (CR).

"Our leadership right now is asking us to vote for a continuing resolution. A vote for a continuing resolution is a vote to continue the Green New Deal and inflationary spending," he argued, even while acknowledging that "there is no way to pass all the individual appropriations bills now," before the Sept. 30 deadline.

"No continuing resolutions. Individual spending bills or bust," Gaetz said. "Do these things or face a motion to vacate the chair."

An hour before Gaetz was scheduled to deliver his ultimatum, McCarthy tried to preempt him with a hastily arranged appearance outside the speaker's office. "Today, I am directing our House committees to open a formal impeachment inquiry into President Joe Biden," he announced.

Nothing much had changed since before the recess, when McCarthy told his caucus that there weren't grounds to justify an impeachment inquiry. But now McCarthy urgently needed to toss a bone to the far right. Even for McCarthy, it was extraordinarily craven: ordering up the impeachment of the president to preserve his own position. And it didn't even work. His surrender earned him no goodwill whatsoever with the far right.

The next day, House Republican leaders brought to the floor the annual defense appropriations bill, which routinely passes year after year because, without it, U.S. troops would not be funded. Yet five minutes before the House gaveled in for its legislative session on Sept. 13 to conduct its first substantive business since July, the Republican whip's office announced that the House would instead go back into recess. Right-wingers from the House Freedom Caucus, angry that McCarthy had not (yet) caved to their long and growing list of demands for government-wide spending cuts and policy changes, blocked the House from even debating the defense bill, much less passing it.

Throughout House offices, televisions cut from the floor to a blue screen (a familiar sight for much of this dysfunctional year) announcing: "The House is in recess subject to the call of the chair." More than four hours later, House GOP leaders still hadn't come up with the votes to begin debate. They called off the day's session and shelved the defense bill for the rest of the week.

By Sept. 14, with the House at a standstill and shutdown fast approaching, McCarthy was reduced to shouting obscenities at his Republican colleagues about a "fucking motion" to oust him as speaker ("vacate the chair," in legislative parlance). "You think I'm scared of a motion to vacate? Go fucking ahead and do it. I'm not scared," he said in a closed-door meeting.

Asked by reporters whether he had a plan for the next week, a defeated McCarthy replied: "I had a plan for this week. It didn't turn out exactly as I planned."

Across the rotunda, Republicans in the Senate looked with pity on the powerless speaker. (Though a couple of Senate Republicans were stalling floor action on spending bills, they all commanded broad support.) McCarthy is "under a lot of pressure over there," Senate Republican whip John Thune told reporters.

Ya think? With two weeks to go before the government funding deadline, the hard right in the House had bottled up 11 of the 12 appropriations bills, as well as all attempts at a short-term patch to keep the lights on.

Freedom Caucus hardliners scoffed at the notion that McCarthy's impeachment gambit would make them more flexible in their hostage taking. "Him starting an impeachment inquiry gives him no—zero—cushion, relief, brace, as it applies to spending," Bob Good told *Politico*.

It was foolish of McCarthy even to try, because these far-right saboteurs would never be appeased. Consider their escalating demands. First, they forced him to renege on the spending agreement he had reached with Biden in the spring. Then they sent him the pair of ransom letters over the summer with ever-zanier demands: Deeper cuts to spending! A radical crackdown on asylum seekers! Defund the FBI and the Justice

Department! Cut off military aid to Ukraine! Lard up the spending bills with poison-pill, culture-war provocations—and shut down the government if the Senate and the president don't swallow them.

Even after McCarthy's cave on impeachment, Gaetz had still gone to the House floor an hour later to deliver his previously scheduled jeremiad. The terms of this "agreement" McCarthy supposedly violated were shrouded in mystery, because the right-wingers wouldn't produce its text. Asked about this on his conference call following his floor speech, Gaetz claimed that "Chip Roy holds my copy."

Roy, asked about this later in the day, replied, "Yeah, I'm not going to get into that."

The terms didn't really matter, because Gaetz and his co-conspirators just kept adding more demands—and insults. "Much of the McCarthy regime has been a failure theater," Gaetz said on the conference call, vowing to demand a vote to oust McCarthy every day if the speaker didn't bend to the far right's various spending demands. "If we have to begin every single day in Congress with the prayer, the pledge, and the motion to vacate, then so be it," the Florida congressman said.

McCarthy responded with a low blow befitting his lowly stature, alluding to Gaetz's alleged sexual misconduct with a minor. "Matt is upset about an ethics complaint," he told CNN's Manu Raju.

It seemed clear that the far right wanted a shutdown—or, as Scott Perry put it, "a pause in government funding." Another of the firebrands, Andy Ogles, of Tennessee's Fifth Congressional District, told a group of reporters that the "fearmongering" about a shutdown from "woke folks" was misplaced: "A temporary shutdown isn't going to stop Social Security checks from being delivered. It's not going to stop veterans' benefits from being delivered. And quite frankly, if the government is not open, we're not wasting taxpayer dollars."

This would explain the vague and disorganized list of spending demands outlined at a Freedom Caucus news conference on Sept. 12, during the first week back from recess. Cheered on outside the Capitol by right-wing activists, including the mother of slain Jan. 6 rioter Ashli Babbitt, the lawmakers' grievances were all over the lot.

"A government that tells you you can't buy the stove you want or drive the car you want is a government of tyranny, and there is no freedom in America," Perry offered.

Senator Rick Scott, joining his House counterparts, howled about excessive spending yet also incongruously complained that the federal government won't "give money to my farmers and my ranchers for the hurricane."

Roy expressed outrage about, in no particular order, "covid tyranny," "the Wuhan lab leak," sex trafficking, and parents' rights.

Curiously, one of the Freedom Caucus lawmakers at the event, the usually outspoken Boebert, left early, without speaking. Shortly after the event, a possible explanation emerged: This was the afternoon the *Denver Post* broke the news that she had been escorted out of a performance of the musical *Beetlejuice*.

MARTIN LUTHER nailed his theses to a church door. MATT GAETZ displayed his in the men's room.

Specifically, the congressman (or somebody) left a draft of his "Motion to Vacate" on a baby changing table in a restroom downstairs from the House chamber in mid-September, where it was found by journalist Matt Laslo. "H. Res. __," it began. "Resolved, that the Office of Speaker of the House of Representatives is hereby declared to be vacant."

But while the resolution to vacate the chair hung over McCarthy, it had become clear that, for all practical purposes, the chair was already vacant.

Just two weeks before government funding expired, the leaderless Republican caucus stumbled toward a shutdown. The hardliners attempting to force the shutdown and other Republicans in the caucus were now hurling abuse at each other: "Clown show." "Clowns." "Foolishness." "Weak." "Terribly misguided." "Selective amnesia." "Stupidity." "Failure to lead." "Lunatics." "Disgraceful." "New low." "Enabling Chairman Xi." "People that have serious issues." "Pathetic."

Amid the epithets, Republicans brought the House to another standstill. For the second time in as many weeks, the zealots blocked the House from even considering a bill to fund the troops. Two days later, on Sept. 21, they blocked it for a third time. They also forced party leaders to pull from the floor their plan to avert a shutdown—a plan that in reality would do nothing to avert a shutdown even if it passed.

Walking into yet another grievance-airing session among House Republicans in the House basement, first-term Representative Rich McCormick of Georgia remarked to a colleague: "I think we should call this the Dance of the Dragons." That was a *Game of Thrones* reference to a civil war in which (spoiler alert) both of the aspirants to the Targaryen throne died, along with several of their children and most of the dragons. McCormick later developed the metaphor for me: "We have a lot of powerful people in one room who are ferocious," he explained, and "it's going to get even uglier."

McCarthy's allies put their best gloss on the chaos in their caucus. "It's a bottom-up approach," Patrick McHenry, of North Carolina, explained to a group of reporters. "It's messy from time to time, out in the public a lot. That's what this Congress has shown us."

The speaker tried to resolve the latest standoff with another of his trademark surrenders to the far right's demands—accepting spending levels that further reneged on the deal he had negotiated with Biden while also blocking disaster relief funds and military aid to Ukraine. Even if this somehow cleared the House, the Senate would, on a bipartisan basis, restore spending to the previously agreed levels while adding the disaster and Ukraine funds.

House Republicans would then again be deadlocked, just days before an Oct. 1 shutdown. At that point, McCarthy would face a choice: cut a deal with Democrats to keep the government running, and thereby risk a motion to vacate the chair, or give the far-right saboteurs the shutdown they desired, and thereby prove beyond a doubt that the speakership was already vacant.

Senate GOP leader Mitch McConnell spoke of McCarthy with pity: "We're pulling for the speaker and hoping we can move forward."

THE WEEK BEGAN WITH HOPES THAT A COMPROMISE BROKERED BY FAR-RIGHT and moderate Republicans (McCarthy, with his "bottom-up" leadership style, sat out the negotiations). But that deal, announced on a Sunday night, was dead by Tuesday morning, after several hardliners rejected it.

On September 18, Victoria Spartz took direct aim at the "weak speaker," posting on social media: "Unfortunately, real leadership takes courage and willingness to fight for the country, not for power and a picture on the wall."

McCarthy offered a petty response, criticizing Spartz for "quitting" and not seeking reelection.

"I don't think it's a good idea for him to go personal like that," Spartz told a few of us, joking that she might change her previously announced plan to retire just to spite McCarthy.

Gaetz condemned McCarthy's "disgraceful" remark about Spartz, saying, "Kevin would never understand subjugating ambition for anything, or anyone."

Asked by reporters about Gaetz's attacks, McCarthy responded with ridicule: "Oh my God, I'm going to lose the speakership because somebody tweeted about me."

Outside the Republican caucus meeting on Sept. 19, right-wingers were squabbling with one another. Gaetz said he was building "a large enough coalition to defeat the Donalds continuing resolution," referring to a bid by Byron Donalds of Florida to keep the government open at a reduced spending level—but not reduced enough for Gaetz.

Donalds, who like Gaetz was considering a 2026 run for Florida governor, responded, "I don't care about that foolishness."

Gaetz said his "friend" Donalds was "terribly misguided" and called the Donalds plan a "surrender" to Biden.

After one of Gaetz's (many) hallway news conferences, reporters asked Republican Mike Lawler, from a competitive New York district, to say a few words. "You want me to follow that clown show?" he said of Gaetz. "These folks don't have a plan," Lawler told us. "They don't know how to take 'yes' for an answer. They don't know what it is to work as a team. They don't know how to define a win."

In a separate interview with CNN's Manu Raju, Lawler said of his "clown show" colleagues: "This is stupidity ... You keep running lunatics, you're going to be in this position."

Louisiana Republican Garret Graves, for his part, accused the holdouts of "holding disaster victims hostage."

And McCarthy bumbled on. "We're going to try to put the CR on the floor," Bacon, the moderate McCarthy ally, told us. Within two hours, they had pulled the continuing resolution from the floor.

Asked about pulling the ballyhooed compromise bill, McCarthy replied, "No, no. I'm just re-circling it."

Re-circling?

Republican lawmakers crowded into the office of majority whip Tom Emmer to try to redraw the legislation. Holdouts enumerated their ransom demands. Greene showed up with a printout of six amendments she was insisting on.

"It feels like Festivus, the airing of the grievances, in there," Nick LaLota, of New York, told NBC News.

"There's yelling, there's screaming, there's crying, there's venting," Kelly Armstrong, of North Dakota, told the *Washington Post.*

On the House floor, meanwhile, yet another rebellion, this time by five far-right lawmakers, had once again blocked the House from taking up the defense appropriations bill. McCarthy's team seemed caught off guard by the revolt, even though a similar rebellion had blocked the same spending bill a week earlier. For 14 extra minutes, Republican leaders held open the vote on the rule that would allow the debate to begin as they tried to strong-arm the holdouts on the floor. Yet as soon as they got Spartz to switch her vote to an aye, Colorado's Ken Buck switched his vote to a no.

"The dysfunction caucus at work," Bacon said to reporters.

As though to illustrate that point, former GOP congressman Madison Cawthorn (the one who accused his then-colleagues of having cocaine-fueled orgies) returned to the House floor for a visit—where he was warmly received by serial liar Santos.

"They just handed a win to the Chinese Communist Party," California Republican Mike Garcia said of the rebels.

Armed Services Committee chairman Mike Rogers told *Politico* that "we've got five clowns that don't know what they want except attention."

To Raju of CNN, moderate Texas Republican Tony Gonzales said the failed vote "showed just how broken we are."

Besieged by reporters after the vote, McCarthy was asked by Fox News' Chad Pergram whether this was "another blow" to his leadership.

McCarthy snapped at the genial newsman. "I assume when something hard happens in your life, you quit?" he said. "I don't quit."

He wasn't quitting, but neither was he leading. On Sept. 20, with the legislative agenda snarled, the House took up minor matters such as increasing the number of judges on the Court of Appeals for Veterans' Claims. (It passed, 423–0.) During the vote, McCarthy, rather than button-holing lawmakers, sat for much of the time with Greene and Kentucky's Tom Massie, yukking it up.

Later, Republicans retired to the Capitol basement for another caucus meeting. This one stretched to $2\frac{1}{2}$ hours as they haggled. About 100 journalists crowded the hallway outside. "Holy crap!" Wisconsin Republican Derrick Van Orden said when he saw the throng. (The journalists had no interest in Van Orden, however, who described himself to a Capitol maintenance worker as "chairman of the not-important-enough-to-talk-to committee.")

Midway through the caucus meeting, Montana's Ryan Zinke emerged. How was it going? "Greeaaat!" he said with sarcasm. Then: "I'm going to the men's room. I'm going to do something productive."

Florida's Mario Díaz-Balart tried to be optimistic. "That's how the democratic process is supposed to work," he said. "It's not pretty."

Republican leaders thought McCarthy's latest capitulation to the far right had, at the very least, flipped the two votes he needed to end the blockade of the Pentagon spending bill.

On the floor on Sept. 21, two of the holdouts—Buck and Norman—did switch their votes to yes. But two other hardliners, Greene and Eli Crane of Arizona, switched their votes to no, and the vote failed again. Defeating "the rule," as this is called, had been unheard of for years; in McCarthy's House, it had become routine. "Obviously, they can't count," Tim Burchett, of Tennessee, said of GOP leadership as he acknowledged the obvious: "We are very dysfunctional right now."

McCarthy, defeated again, said as he left the chamber: "This is a whole new concept of individuals that just want to burn the whole place down."

Now that he had had this belated realization, maybe the speaker would finally stop appeasing them?

He would not.

From Mar-a-Lago came orders for House Republicans to shut down the federal government in order "to defund these political prosecutions against me." Trump further ordered them: "UNLESS YOU GET EVERY-THING, SHUT IT DOWN!"

This explains why, as the last days slipped away before the federal government's funding expired, House Republicans weren't even trying to avert the shutdown. Instead, on the House floor, they wasted days debating spending bills that would, even if passed, do nothing to avoid the looming disaster. And then, just two days before the shutdown dead-line, they staged the first hearing of their "impeachment inquiry" into Biden—an embarrassing session in which even their own witnesses said they didn't have the goods on Biden.

In the Senate, by contrast, Republicans and Democrats negotiated a short-term deal to avoid the shutdown. As it advanced through the Senate by overwhelming votes of 77–19 and 76–22, Senate Republican leader McConnell pleaded with colleagues to avoid the "actively harmful proposition" of a shutdown that would cost taxpayers billions of dollars and "take the important progress being made on a number of key issues and drag it backward."

But McCarthy said he wouldn't even allow the House to consider the bipartisan Senate compromise.

And so, barring some deus ex machina, millions of U.S. troops and other government employees were about to be forced to work without pay. Other federal workers were about to be furloughed, and millions of women, infants, and children would be denied food assistance. But House Republicans did take action to protect and insulate one crucial government function from the ravages of a shutdown. They designated their impeachment inquiry into Biden an "essential" operation, CNN's Annie Grayer and Melanie Zanona reported, so vital to the national interest that it must continue undisturbed during a shutdown.

How was that for a set of priorities? The troops wouldn't be paid and infants wouldn't be fed—but the pursuit of Biden must go on.

BY NOW, IT WAS BECOMING HARD TO KEEP TRACK OF MCCARTHY'S SURRENDERS. When right-wingers howled about the bipartisan debt ceiling deal that

McCarthy had struck with Biden in the spring, McCarthy promptly reneged on the deal—setting the country on its current course toward a shutdown. When some of the same right-wingers threatened to oust McCarthy if he didn't launch impeachment proceedings against Biden, McCarthy launched the impeachment inquiry. And when the right-wingers threatened to cause more havoc unless he cut off military aid to Ukraine, McCarthy ordered up an "emergency" meeting of the Rules Committee to zero out funds for Ukraine from the Pentagon spending bill.

"It's like every room the speaker goes into is an escape room," observed Massachusetts's James McGovern, ranking Democrat on the Rules Committee, when the emergency defunding of Ukraine came before the panel. "He just does whatever he needs to do to get out, even if it means caving to MAGA Republicans every single time."

But this time there was no plausible escape. That's because the MAGA Republicans actually wanted a shutdown. As House GOP leaders ignored the looming deadline, Democrats used a procedural tactic, a "point of order," to force a brief floor debate on the government shutdown.

This infuriated Roy, who shouted that Democrats were only forcing a discussion about the government shutdown because "they don't want to talk about Hunter Biden."

Louisiana Republican Mike Johnson, a McCarthy ally, quarreled with the notion "that somehow Republicans are in favor of a government shutdown. No one desires a government shutdown."

No?

Brendan Boyle, of Pennsylvania, ranking Democrat on the Budget Committee, replied, "I have the quotes right here."

Among those on Boyle's list:

"We shouldn't fear a government shutdown . . . Most Americans won't even miss it." (Bob Good)

"It's time to call a halt to spending, and if the government shuts down, let's shut it down." (Ralph Norman)

"I'm not afraid of shutdowns." (Byron Donalds)

"Swamp dwellers hand-wringing over a possible shutdown."
(Chip Roy himself)

"Kevin McCarthy's fault that the government is going to shut
down." (Gaetz)

Boyle missed a few. Greg Steube, of Florida, told Fox News that "people
in my district are willing to shut the government down for more conservative fiscal policy." And Andy Ogles thought a shutdown would be "fine."

McCarthy, trapped in a no-escape escape room, attempted to create
a diversion. He issued a last-minute ransom note to Biden: Republicans
would let the government remain open if the president closed the southern border. Never mind that McCarthy probably couldn't deliver on his
end of the deal. Had the speaker forgotten that Trump shut down the
government in 2018 for the same reason? It didn't end well.

"Look, this isn't that difficult to happen," McCarthy told reporters.
"All the president has to do: Call us up. Let's go sit down and get this done
before the end of the week. He's changed this by a simple stroke of his
own words of how this border is happening."

Stroke of his own words?

A shutdown was imminent—and the only man who could stop it
was talking gibberish.

Even McCarthy's Republican colleagues were baffled. "Mr. Speaker,
leaders lead from the FRONT," Perry, head of the House Freedom Caucus,
posted on social media. "We need your plan."

By now, McCarthy's team had had to pull the Republican-drafted
Pentagon spending bill from the floor three times because of Republican
holdouts. On Thursday, Sept. 28—two days before the government's
funding lapsed—Republican dissidents defeated the Republican-drafted
agriculture appropriations bill on the House floor.

On Sept. 29, a day before the deadline, McCarthy finally made his
first attempt at keeping the government open. It was a sop to the right
wing and had no chance of clearing the Senate: slashing much of domestic spending by nearly 30 percent while requiring a return to the
construction of a border wall, in exchange for keeping the government

funded for just 30 days. Twenty-one Republican holdouts joined with Democrats to defeat it.

In private, Republicans shouted and cursed at each other in caucus meetings in the Capitol basement. In public, they called each other some new names, adding "charlatan" and "joke" to an epithet repository that already included "lunatics," "pathetic," "weak," and "clowns."

Outside the Sept. 29 evening caucus meeting, Steve Womack, of Arkansas, a seven-term Republican on the Appropriations Committee, swung between metaphors for the Republican caucus. One moment, he told a group of us, House Republicans were a football team using "the wrong snap count"—and the next they were a spaceship disintegrating on reentry into Earth's atmosphere. "You make a lot of mistakes when you are tired and mad, and we are both right now," he said, predicting with confidence that at midnight Oct. 1 "the lights are going to go out."

Republicans were hopelessly divided. A seven-day continuing resolution? Fourteen days? Thirty days? A spending level of $1.47 trillion or $1.56 trillion? What about the border? They couldn't reach consensus on any of it. Gaetz and another holdout, North Carolina's Dan Bishop, walked out of the meeting. Another dissident, Bob Good, left shouting, claiming McCarthy had "surrendered to the Senate," where a bipartisan stopgap spending bill was moving.

Marjorie Taylor Greene was actively cheering for a shutdown, as some sort of punishment for Washington, D.C., because of covid restrictions. "People here in Washington need to understand how it feels to be shut down," she told reporters.

Even George Santos was honest about the chaos in the room: "We're just screaming at each other at this point," he told *Axios*'s Andrew Solender.

THINGS HADN'T IMPROVED BY THE MORNING OF SEPT. 30, WHEN REPUBLICANS met again—this time to hear their majority whip, Tom Emmer, tell them that they didn't have enough votes to pass any continuing resolution of any duration—14 days, 30 days, or 45 days. Instead, they would let the government shut down, while taking up a few bills (paying the troops, extending flood insurance) to mitigate the pain.

And then, just like that, McCarthy became an adult. In a sudden epiphany, he saw the truth that had eluded him for months: There was no way to placate the extremists in his caucus.

"We're going to be adults in the room and we're going to keep government open while we solve this problem," McCarthy told reporters just 12 hours before a shutdown as he rushed to the floor a last-ditch attempt to fund the government at current levels for another 45 days.

And if Gaetz and other juvenile delinquents tried to evict him from the speakership with their threatened motion to vacate the chair?

"You know what? If somebody wants to remove [me] because I want to be the adult in the room, go ahead and try," McCarthy dared them. "But I think this country's too important."

Who was this man and what had he done with Kevin McCarthy?

For eight months, there had been no adults working in the House Republican daycare center. Day after day, the toddlers of the far right threw tantrum after tantrum. But instead of putting the juvenile delinquents in his caucus into a time-out, their caregiver, McCarthy, routinely had tried to quiet them with all the lollipops, ice cream, and sugary drinks they could consume.

Finally, McCarthy declared himself a grown-up. He did the right thing—after he had exhausted all other options.

Democrats initially suspected a trick when McCarthy announced the "clean" continuing resolution, with no changes to spending levels or policies. He hadn't consulted them at all and wouldn't even grant their request to have 90 minutes to study it. But after they stalled for time to read the 71-page bill, they wholeheartedly embraced it: While House Republicans were split on the bill, voting 126–90 for it, Democrats approved it by a near-unanimous 209–1.

It wasn't an ideal fix. It merely delayed the shutdown threat until just before Thanksgiving, and it didn't provide urgently needed funds for Ukraine to hold off Russia's invasion. But it was, at long last, a nod to sanity—especially considering that a day earlier House Republicans had tried to slash government spending by some 30 percent, and just a few hours earlier Republicans had been willing to let the government shut down without any attempt to avoid it.

"MAGA Republicans have surrendered," Hakeem Jeffries, the House Democratic leader, exulted after the vote.

Actually, they hadn't surrendered; they had been sidelined. Asked before the vote whether he had any support from the wingnuts in his caucus, McCarthy laughed. "No," he said. "Look, I had tried that for eight months."

The crisis had been postponed, but it could hardly have been handled any worse. With much fanfare, House Republicans had adopted a rule at the beginning of the year requiring the text of bills to be distributed 72 hours before a floor vote. This time, they released the text a few minutes before bringing the bill to the floor. Democrats delayed—a vote to adjourn, and a mini-filibuster by Jeffries—while staff combed the bill.

Adding to the chaos of the moment, hotheaded Jamaal Bowman, a New York Democrat, pulled a fire alarm in the Cannon House Office Building, requiring an evacuation; he was caught on tape. Bowman claimed it was an accident, but Republicans sought punishment. "Jamaal knew what he was doing and I have put the timeline together to prove it," Santos declared. Honest!

Immediately after the vote, it was time for some of the 90 Republicans who opposed McCarthy's clean CR to set off alarms. Andy Biggs of Arizona complained that "McCarthy sided with 209 Democrats" on "Biden-Pelosi-Schumer spending," then asked on social media: "Should he remain speaker of the House?"

Gaetz already had an answer to that question. Immediately after the vote, he stood at a microphone on the House floor, gesturing to be recognized. But the presiding officer, Womack, quickly slammed the gavel and adjourned the House until the next week—postponing McCarthy's reckoning for at least 48 hours. McCarthy's speakership, Gaetz promised, "is on tenuous ground."

Jeffries, asked whether Democrats would help the speaker keep his job, only said, "We'll cross that bridge when we get to it."

But Democrats had good reason not to trust McCarthy; he was, after all, the man who weeks earlier had tried to placate the far right by beginning impeachment proceedings against Biden without an iota of evidence of wrongdoing. And even if McCarthy could be trusted, how much more of his incompetence could a poor nation stand?

On Oct. 2, two days after McCarthy defied the terrorists in his caucus for a second time, they struck back. Gaetz went to the floor to allege—almost certainly falsely—that McCarthy had made a "secret side deal on Ukraine" with the White House. "It is going to be difficult for my Republican friends to keep calling President Biden feeble while he continues to take Speaker McCarthy's lunch money in every negotiation," Gaetz taunted.

Referring to his planned motion to vacate McCarthy's speakership, Gaetz teased that "there may be other votes coming today or later this week."

On social media, McCarthy played the tough guy. "Bring it on," he wrote.

And Gaetz did. That evening, after a series of post office namings and just before Pennsylvania Republican Glenn Thompson gave a speech congratulating Mifflinburg Hose Company No. 1 on 125 years of service, Gaetz introduced his resolution "declaring the Office of the Speaker of the House of Representatives to be vacant."

The next day, which would turn out to be McCarthy's last one as speaker, proceeded like the others before it—in chaos.

It was clear that there were more than enough hardliners supporting Gaetz's motion to vacate that McCarthy would need some Democratic votes to keep the speakership. But he offered Democrats nothing for those votes except platitudes. McCarthy decided to go out the same way he had operated his speakership—by acting with Republican votes alone. "If five Republicans go with Democrats, then I'm out," he said after the Republican caucus meeting on the morning of Oct. 3.

"It sounds likely," ABC's Rachel Scott pointed out.

"Probably so," McCarthy admitted.

By stiffing Democrats once again, McCarthy sealed his fate. Offered nothing for bailing him out, they unified against him at their own caucus meeting. "Absent any significantly meaningful benefit for Maine's Second

District, I see no reason to vote for him," said Maine Democrat Jared Golden, co-chair of the centrist Blue Dogs and one of the most frequent crossover votes for McCarthy.

Jeffries made it official: "We are ready to find bipartisan common ground," he announced. "Our extreme colleagues have shown no willingness to do the same. They must find a way to end the House Republican Civil War."

On the House floor, the Republican combatants seemed ill-equipped to defuse the latest crisis they had created. Santos lifted up his sweater to reveal to Greene his SpongeBob SquarePants tie. Boebert played with her infant grandson.

"We need a speaker who will fight for something—anything—besides just staying or becoming speaker," said Good, one of the rebels.

McCarthy snickered and whispered with the member seated to his right, Juan Ciscomani of Arizona.

Tom Cole, the genial chairman of the Rules Committee, pleaded with those who "are willing to plunge this body into chaos and this country into uncertainty."

Retorted Gaetz: "Chaos is Speaker McCarthy! Chaos is somebody who we cannot trust with their word."

McCarthy drummed the armrest, put on reading glasses and perused his phone, then resumed whispering and chuckling with Ciscomani.

Republicans laughed, booed, and heckled Gaetz as he spoke. California's Mike Garcia called the rebels "Republicans running with scissors supported by Democrats."

Republican Tom McClintock, of California, appealing for "sobriety, wisdom and caution," warned of a "paralyzed" House. "The Democrats will revel in Republican dysfunction and the public will rightly be repulsed," he said. "There are only minutes left to come to our senses and realize the grave danger our country is in at this moment. Dear God, grant us the wisdom to see it."

Gaetz (only Good and Andy Biggs joined his side in the debate) parried his GOP colleagues with one-liners. When Republican conference chair Elise Stefanik improbably claimed that "this Republican majority has exceeded all expectations," Gaetz quipped: "If this House of

Representatives has exceeded all expectations, then we definitely need higher expectations."

Graves, of Louisiana, spoke bitterly of Gaetz using his motion to vacate to raise campaign cash. "It's disgusting," he said, and cries of "Shame!" came from the Republican side. "We need to stand behind the greatest speaker in modern history!" Graves proposed, producing guffaws from the Democrats.

Replied Gaetz: "I take no lecture on asking patriotic Americans to weigh in and contribute to this fight [against] those who would grovel and bend knee for the lobbyists and special interests who own our leadership." As his fellow Republicans jeered, he added: "Boo all you want!"

"You're no martyr!" a Republican heckled.

No, he wasn't. Gaetz, with his arched eyebrows and slicked-back hair, looked the part of a cartoon villain. More of a street thug than a legislator, he had done nothing in his seven years in Congress but tear things down. But this street thug made quick work of McCarthy. As the clerk called the roll, the doomed speaker, in the same seat he had occupied during January's 15 ballots, could be seen sitting silently, staring straight ahead.

At 4:45 p.m., the gavel fell on McCarthy's speakership.

"The Office of Speaker of the House of the United States House of Representatives is hereby declared vacant," the presiding officer, Arizona's Womack, announced after the 216–210 vote to oust McCarthy.

From the front row of the gallery, I heard gasps from the floor. And then, from the Republican side of the chamber, a lone woman's voice: "Now what?"

That was the operative question.

Chapter 8

"Let's Get Our Poop in a Group, People. We've Got to Figure This Out"

K EVIN MCCARTHY, WHOSE ONLY EVIDENT IDEOLOGY AS SPEAKER HAD been personal ambition, had obtained his place in history: the only speaker in U.S. history to be voted out by his peers. His chaotic nine months in the job was the shortest tenure since that of Michael C. Kerr in 1876, as *The Bulwark*'s Tim Miller pointed out. But Kerr's speakership ended because he died from tuberculosis. McCarthy, by contrast, was knifed by his fellow Republicans.

This is why McCarthy's ouster was much larger than McCarthy, for it made it clear, if there had been any doubt, that the Republican Party had ceased to function as a governing entity.

McCarthy's term began in chaos, with his 15 rounds of balloting. It lurched from crisis to manufactured crisis, with the needless debt ceiling showdown, failed votes and pulled bills on the floor, recriminations and name-calling in Republican caucus meetings, the launch of impeachment proceedings on fabricated charges, and finally the near shutdown of the government. Then it ended in chaos, with Republicans openly savaging each other on the House floor and all legislative functions ceasing while the majority party tried to pick its next leader.

Under "continuity of government" procedures—designed for terrorist decapitation of the government rather than partisan zealots offing their own speaker—a predesignated speaker pro tempore took temporary control of the house. That man, revealed to be Patrick McHenry of North Carolina, did the only thing he could. "It would be prudent to recess," he told the body, so that leaderless lawmakers could "meet and discuss the path forward."

The path forward, however, would prove elusive. In a sense, it didn't really matter whom Republicans chose to replace McCarthy, who announced shortly after his ouster that he wouldn't run again. Nobody could succeed in that role because the party itself had become ungovernable—and incapable of governing. No longer content merely to attack Democrats, government workers, and democratic institutions, this "chaos caucus" was now eating its own.

McHenry, when he declared the recess, slammed the gavel so hard it looked as though he were trying to ring the bell in a carnival strongman game. Perhaps McHenry hoped to hammer some sense into his feuding Republican colleagues? If so, he did not win the prize.

The same lethal combination of vindictiveness, name-calling, vulgarity, sabotage, and paralysis that had caused the meltdown on the House floor continued to consume the party off the floor:

> Republican lawmakers, on the verge of fisticuffs in their caucus meeting in the Capitol basement, burst out of the room complaining to reporters about the "bullshit" and "horseshit" decision by McHenry to have a weeklong adjournment to cool down.

> Mike Lawler of New York said he would lead an effort to expel Florida representative Matt Gaetz from the Republican caucus—part of the payback for the "eight selfish assholes" (as Lawler put it to *Axios*'s Andrew Solender) who ousted McCarthy.

> Though House rules gave McHenry the temporary speakership "for the sole purpose of electing a new speaker," McHenry promptly abused his power by evicting former House speaker Nancy Pelosi and former majority leader Steny Hoyer from their Capitol offices; Pelosi, in California for the funeral of Senator Dianne Feinstein, was told she must vacate immediately and the office would be "re-keyed."

FOOLS ON THE HILL

Republican lawmakers threatened to quit the bipartisan Problem Solvers Caucus. The moderate Republican Governance Group threatened to expel Nancy Mace, of South Carolina, because she had voted to oust McCarthy.

Former House Republican Markwayne Mullin, now in the Senate, went on CNN to describe how Gaetz used to "brag about how he would crush ED [erectile dysfunction] medicine and chase it with an energy drink so he could go all night." Another Senate Republican, John Cornyn, told *HuffPost*'s Igor Bobic that "the next speaker is going to be subjected to the same terrorist attacks" that bedeviled McCarthy.

Three members of the House GOP leadership team that failed so spectacularly over the previous nine months—Steve Scalise, Tom Emmer, and Elise Stefanik—all seemed to think they deserved a promotion. They signaled plans to move up the leadership ladder.

The election of a new speaker, which McHenry scheduled for the next Wednesday, Oct. 11, 2023, was in serious doubt. Neither of the announced candidates, Scalise and Ohio's Jim Jordan, had a clear path. Others threatened not to elect any speaker without rules changes to prevent a repeat of what happened to McCarthy. And Texas Republican Troy Nehls helpfully announced that he would "nominate Donald J. Trump for speaker of the House."

A casually dressed Garret Graves, of Louisiana, worked his way through the Capitol, warning journalists to settle in for a long slog. "This is potentially a setback of weeks and, I hate to say this, but potentially even longer," he told CBS's Nikole Killion.

Perfect. Just six weeks from the next government shutdown deadline, and with the United States unable to send weapons to Ukraine to hold off Russia's invasion, the House majority had ceased to function at all.

"My fear is the institution fell today," McCarthy said in his farewell-to-the-speakership news conference the night of his ouster. Going down to defeat, he kept claiming that his ouster wasn't "good for the institution" because "I believe in the institution" and "the institution was too important" to be so assaulted by Gaetz (and Democrats) who weren't "looking out for the country or the institution."

This was rich coming from a man who voted to overturn the 2020 election results, bowed and scraped at Mar-a-Lago after Jan. 6, destroyed a bipartisan Jan. 6 commission his own designee negotiated, sabotaged the Jan. 6 committee, released Jan. 6 security footage to Tucker Carlson, undermined the rule of law by attacking the prosecutions of Donald Trump, and launched the impeachment of Joe Biden without a shred of evidence of wrongdoing. Anybody who considered McCarthy a defender of "the institution" ought to be institutionalized.

The former speaker was correct, of course, that the House had failed. But he had the causation backward. It didn't fail because he was ousted; he was ousted because the House had already failed. And the ones who caused it to fail were McCarthy and his colleagues.

For years, they had taken every opportunity to trash the institutions of government—the FBI, the Justice Department, the IRS, the "woke" military, the Centers for Disease Control, the National Institutes of Health, the courts, the election system, the presidency. After laying waste to all other institutions, it was inevitable that House Republicans would also trash the one institution they controlled.

McCarthy's allies cast Gaetz as aberrant. But the same demagogic techniques that Gaetz used against McCarthy—dishonesty, conspiracy, vengeance—had been deployed routinely by House Republicans in recent years, and particularly for the previous nine months, against the Biden administration and congressional Democrats. Gaetz was merely doing as his Republican colleagues had taught him.

Moments before he called up the resolution that would topple McCarthy, Gaetz, carrying a folder with his speech notes, walked up to use one of the tables designated for Republican speakers during debates.

But Guy Reschenthaler, of Pennsylvania, the Republican chief deputy whip, turned him back. John Leganski, McCarthy's floor leader, added a contemptuous flourish, shooing Gaetz away with the back of his hand. Ultimately, Gaetz wandered across the aisle and parked himself at an empty lectern typically used by Democrats.

Then, in their closing argument in the debate that followed, McCarthy's allies had the chutzpah to attack Gaetz—for speaking from the Democratic side. "You need to look no further than where the opponents are sitting today in this chamber!" proclaimed Kelly Armstrong, of North Dakota, making the false insinuation that Gaetz was a Democratic tool. "They're not over here—they're over there!"

Republicans applauded Armstrong. "Yeah!" cheered a Republican lawmaker.

Gaetz, speaking truthfully for once, protested that "you sent me over here."

It was fitting that the McCarthy forces' closing argument against Gaetz—a man who in McCarthy's telling had never uttered "one true thing"—would itself be grounded in deceit.

In perhaps the most revealing moment of the debate, Tom Massie, of Kentucky, rose to plead for McCarthy. "This motion to vacate is a terrible idea," he said. He warned that "if you vote to vacate the speaker . . . [t]his institution will fail. Please do not vacate the speaker."

But Massie himself had begun the ruinous cycle of right-wingers purging speakers for being impure. As he acknowledged, he had been a cosponsor of the motion to vacate Speaker Boehner in 2015, and he was one of the prime antagonists who hounded both Boehner and, later, speaker Paul Ryan into retirement. Those ousting McCarthy were using the very technique Massie had pioneered—and now, too late, he wanted to recork that bottle. The poison had already escaped.

McCarthy and his defenders claimed Gaetz was acting out of personal retribution toward the speaker. "You know it was personal," McCarthy said, insinuating that Gaetz's real motive was pique over McCarthy's refusal to quash an ethics probe into sexual and other misconduct by Gaetz. ("I've seen the texts," McCarthy teased.)

Right, and McCarthy knew something about retribution, having led several efforts to censure Democrats and strip them of committee assignments in what Republicans explicitly acknowledged was revenge for things Democratic leaders had done.

McCarthy ally Graves piously denounced Gaetz during the debate for sending out fundraising solicitations that cited his motion to vacate—Gaetz's "disgusting" use of "official actions to raise money." Yet Gaetz was only doing precisely what two top lieutenants of McCarthy had done in the previous couple of weeks, as both Oversight Committee chairman James Comer and Ways and Means chairman Jason Smith had sent out fundraising appeals that cited their work on Biden's impeachment.

Armstrong, another McCarthy ally, was entirely correct when he said during the debate that instead of valuing loyalty, integrity, and competence, "we have descended to a place where clicks, TV hits, and the never-ending quest for . . . celebrity drives decisions and encourages juvenile behavior that is so far beneath this esteemed body." Yet then he claimed McCarthy "has done more in nine months to restore the People's House than any Speaker in decades." Er, by elevating Marjorie Taylor "Jewish Space Lasers" Greene to power and influence in the Republican caucus? Or by restoring the stature of Arizona Republican Paul Gosar, a white nationalist icon? Or by blocking attempts to expel the discredited George Santos?

McCarthy's defenders were furious about Gaetz's allegation that McCarthy had struck a "secret side deal" with Biden to send billions to Ukraine. But they were perfectly content to place Gaetz in a conspiracy theory of their own. "Is Gaetz secretly an agent for the Democratic Party?" former speaker Newt Gingrich, a McCarthy ally and longtime conspiracy theorist, posted on social media. McCarthy repeatedly alleged that Gaetz was working with Democrats to oust him.

In reality, plenty of Democrats would have voted to save McCarthy—but his own toxic partisanship prevented him from offering even small concessions in exchange for their support. Instead, he went on CBS's *Face the Nation* and claimed that the Democrats "tried to do everything" to stop a short-term spending bill from passing the House on Sept. 30 and "were willing to let government shut down." (Fully 209 of 210 Democrats voted for the bill.) Hours before the vote, McCarthy explained why he wouldn't offer Democrats even a crumb for their votes to save his speakership: "I win by Republicans and I lose by Republicans." And so he did.

A new speaker could easily pull back from this destructive madness by abandoning McCarthy's insistence on drafting and passing legislation with Republicans only. "The only way to defeat this," Nebraska's Don

Bacon, a moderate, said of the extremists in his caucus, "is to have more bipartisan spirit." Otherwise, no matter who succeeded McCarthy, "within a month they'll be having the speakership held over their head and the vacate-the-chair threats."

That would have been the one course that could have salvaged the House as an "institution." It was also the one course Bacon's fellow Republicans absolutely refused to take. "That doesn't work," McCarthy had said when asked about the possibility of governing with Democrats. "Our government's designed to have compromise, but look, we're in the majority. You—you don't surrender."

AFTER THE WEEKLONG RECESS MCHENRY DECLARED, REPUBLICANS RETURNED to Washington no closer to electing a speaker than they had been when they left. Over the weekend, on Oct. 7, Hamas had launched a devastating terrorist attack on Israel from Gaza. The Ukraine war effort, denied funding in the stopgap spending bill that the House finally passed, needed replenishment. And the government faced a new shutdown deadline of Nov. 17.

And House Republicans, as usual, were putting on some sort of goat rodeo.

As the conference gathered to hear from speaker candidates Scalise and Jordan, Representative Harriet Hageman, of Wyoming, the Trump-backed slayer of Liz Cheney, walked into the caucus meeting wearing a big smile and carrying a lasso. Was she planning to rope some goats? She didn't say.

A moment later, Nancy Mace, one of the eight Republicans who had voted out McCarthy, strolled into the caucus meeting with a big red *A* decal on her T-shirt. "I'm wearing the scarlet letter," she later explained to a group of us, "after the week that I just had last week, being a woman up here and being demonized for my vote." In her telling, wearing the 17th-century mark of an adulteress showed that "I'm going to do the right thing every single time."

There was little time to dwell on Mace's bold reinterpretation of Nathaniel Hawthorne, however, because the defrocked McCarthy himself soon emerged from the caucus meeting, which he left after leading the opening prayer. Recognizing that he had a captive audience in the 140 journalists crowding the hallway, he gave a 13-minute news conference repeating the same thoughts about Israel he had offered in a news conference the day before.

Sadly, the former speaker's oration was interrupted by the arrival of McHenry, the interim speaker. "Mr. Speaker!" some journalists shouted, trying to ask McCarthy questions. "Mr. Speaker!" other journalists shouted a moment later, trying to ask McHenry questions. The confusion was all the greater because neither man was, actually, the speaker. Republicans didn't have one of those.

No sooner had that commotion quieted than a new one erupted while the Republican members were meeting: Authorities had just unsealed additional charges against Santos, alleging that he had stolen the identities of his campaign donors, used their credit cards, and swindled the Republican Party. The famous fabricator was besieged by shouting reporters when he exited the caucus meeting: "Did you steal people's identities? Will you resign?"

"I did not have access to my phone," Santos pleaded. "I have no clue of what you are talking about." (This was plausible, for intraparty distrust had grown so intense that members had to check their phones at the door.) Reporters and TV crews chased Santos back to his office, crashing into furniture in the hallway. "How can you vote in the speaker election," asked CNN's Manu Raju, "when you've been charged with all these crimes?"

Santos slammed his office door in Raju's face.

This was going well.

Scalise, the House majority leader, emerged from the caucus meeting full of confidence that he would win the speakership the next day. "We need a Congress that's working tomorrow," he said.

His colleagues were not so sure. "What are the chances we have a speaker tomorrow?" a reporter asked Massie. Massie, in his 11th year in Congress, responded with a long pause, as if calculating the odds in his head.

"Two percent," he answered.

"Why two percent?"

Another long pause. "Uh, you know, it's just the way things are going for us," Massie replied.

Massie's handicapping was spot on. Republicans narrowly tapped Scalise to be speaker at another meeting the next day; he got 113 votes on a secret ballot, while Jordan and other candidates got 107. Applause sounded in the conference room at 1:03 p.m. when the tally was announced, and Scalise, rushing to build momentum, called for a speaker vote on the House floor at 3 p.m.

"We're going to have to go upstairs on the House floor and resolve this and then get the House open again," said the ebullient majority leader, referring to himself in the third person as "Speaker Scalise."

"Is it true you don't have the votes?" a reporter asked. Scalise walked away without answering.

Then, in rapid succession, a dozen House Republicans announced that they would oppose Scalise on the floor—and a dozen more threatened to do the same. Some were the same zealots who had stymied McCarthy back in January, when holdouts forced 15 rounds of balloting on the House floor. Others were first-time participants in the GOP dysfunction game. But there were well more than the five needed to deny Scalise the speakership.

Texas Republicans Chip Roy and Michael Cloud said they would oppose Scalise because of the "unacceptable" and "underhanded" rush to vote on the floor. Greene said she would oppose him because he was battling blood cancer—a cruel argument Trump also made. Massie announced his opposition because Scalise had not "articulated a viable plan" on government spending.

Mace, no longer wearing her scarlet *A*, tried to plant a KKK label on Scalise. "I personally cannot, in good conscience, vote for someone who attended a white supremacist conference and compared himself to David Duke," she said on CNN of Scalise's past comment that he was "David Duke without the baggage." (This apparently hadn't bothered Mace when she accepted Scalise's campaign help in 2020.)

Greg Murphy, of North Carolina, responded to Mace on social media: "#GetADamnLife."

"The House GOP conference is broken," Pennsylvania Republican Lloyd Smucker accurately observed, announcing his opposition to Scalise. Michael McCaul, chairman of the House Foreign Affairs Committee, pleaded with his colleagues for sanity, saying the speakership is "going to have to be worked out in the next several hours. We can't afford this dysfunction."

But when it came time for the 3 p.m. vote, McHenry instead sent the chamber into an indefinite recess. A few hours later, House GOP leaders called off all votes for the night.

Finally, the day of disarray ended in farce: Santos, facing renewed calls for his expulsion from the House, delivered one more blow to Scalise. Because Scalise hadn't reached out to the indicted liar, "I'm now declaring I'm an ANYONE but Scalise and come hell or high water I won't change my mind," Santos tweeted. "We need a speaker that leads by including every single member of the team."

Scalise, seeing his speakership slip away before it even began, set about doing what McCarthy had done in January: placating the hard-liners. Florida's Anna Paulina Luna, a holdout, stated her conditions for supporting Scalise: defunding the prosecution of Donald Trump by special counsel Jack Smith, issuing a subpoena to Hunter Biden, and having the House vote on impeaching President Biden. After meeting with Scalise, Luna pronounced herself "confident" he would meet her requirements.

Even then, she changed her mind within 24 hours, saying, "I will no longer be voting for Scalise."

By late in the day on Oct. 12, after the umpteenth Republican caucus meeting of the week dissolved in recriminations and paralysis, it was looking doubtful that Scalise could get enough GOP votes to be elected speaker. Around 8 p.m., he told colleagues he was withdrawing.

"I just shared with my colleagues that I was withdrawing my name as a candidate for speaker-designee," he then told reporters. "There's some folks that really need to look in the mirror over the next couple of days and decide: Are we going to get back on track, or are they going to try to pursue their own agenda? You can't do both."

Ten days after they voted out McCarthy and started this crisis, it still wasn't obvious that this fractured and feuding majority could coalesce around anyone. Only one thing was perfectly clear: Whoever Republicans chose to be speaker would be a leader in name only. This House GOP majority, ungovernable at best, had collapsed into anarchy.

A group of us were talking the night of Oct. 10 with Arizona's Juan Ciscomani, a McCarthy ally, about the chances that, of the 221 current House Republicans, the necessary 217 could agree on a candidate for speaker. "Do you think 217 of them can get behind anything at the moment, even if it's mom and apple pie?" asked the writer Ben Jacobs.

Replied Ciscomani: "That's to be seen tomorrow."

The next day, we got the answer: Baa! Baa!

As you can see from the highlights above, it had been a week of pure mayhem, and it had begun with former Speaker McCarthy offering himself as the future Speaker McCarthy.

Over the previous weekend, Republican National Committee chair Ronna McDaniel had said on Fox News that Hamas's attack on Israel was a "great opportunity" for Republicans. On Monday, Oct. 9, McCarthy had attempted to seize that supposed opportunity, accusing Biden of "appeasement" and left-wing Democrats of antisemitism. "Have we not understand the moment in life we are living?" McCarthy asked.

But the real purpose of this moment in life had been to dangle the possibility that he would return as speaker. Though he had previously said he wasn't running, he now said, "I'm going to allow the conference to do their work" and "the conference decides that."

This threw the speaker race into more confusion. In a caucus meeting in the Capitol basement, Carlos Giménez, of Florida, and a couple of others said the only candidate they would support for speaker was McCarthy.

Others used the gathering, the first since the day Republicans ousted McCarthy, to direct their fury at those who led the coup. "Matt Gaetz is, frankly, a vile person," Lawler told reporters outside the room. Inside, over a barbecue dinner, one lawmaker reportedly called the anti-McCarthy eight "chickenshit."

"They're just venting," said Tim Burchett, one of the eight. (Burchett, who had supported McCarthy in January's voting, turned against him when the best argument McCarthy could give Burchett for keeping the job was "I really want to be speaker.") The Tennessean said he wouldn't budge on McCarthy and called the process to find a new speaker "like junior high school."

Republican staffers confiscated lawmakers' phones at the door, in an attempt to prevent the likes of *Punchbowl News*' Jake Sherman and *Politico*'s Olivia Beavers from live-tweeting every utterance in the room as it leaked to them. But so deep was Gaetz's distrust of his colleagues that rather than check his phone at the door, he walked it all the way back to his office.

McCaul, after the meeting, made one of his appeals to "wake up the members of my conference" to rise above the brawling. "The world is watching. They are seeing a dysfunctional democracy," the Foreign Affairs chairman said. "This is what the ayatollah wants" and "Chairman Xi, when he talks about democracy does not work. We have to prove him wrong."

Other sensible lawmakers urged colleagues to revise the rule regarding the motion to vacate so that a single lawmaker could no longer call a vote to topple the speaker. It "gives power to the most loony parts," Bacon told several of us, "the most disaffected, the most fringe people in our conference." Rules Committee chairman Tom Cole offered a related metaphor to *Axios*'s Solender: "It's time to take the sharp knives away from the children."

For the candidates forum on Oct. 10, where those running to be speaker made their pitches, Republicans moved their meeting to the Ways and Means Committee room in the Longworth building. One hundred forty journalists crowded into "Gucci Gulch"—as the lobbyist-filled hallways outside the committee room are known—and, because the building is open to the public, so did some right-wing activists. One of them, Ivan Raiklin, informed me that "38,000 were murdered" by the coronavirus vaccine and explained how Trump could be installed as House speaker.

Another activist interrupted McCarthy's impromptu news conference in the hallway to inform him that it was the birthday of Ashli Babbitt, the woman fatally shot inside the Capitol as she tried to breach the House chamber on Jan. 6, and to demand the release of more security footage from the insurrection. "That's another day, another question," McCarthy said, asking reporters for a different question.

For the moment, there was really only one relevant question: "How do we get to 217 and how do we bring this party back to a functioning majority?" as California's Mike Garcia put it. And the answer to that was ... well, nobody knew.

Inside the forum, both Scalise and Jordan said the House would need to pass a continuing resolution to keep the government open after Nov. 17—even though it was McCarthy's passage of just such a CR that caused him to be booted from the speakership in the first place. The coup had achieved nothing.

Outside the forum, Marc Molinaro, of New York, went up to the microphones, shouting, for no particular reason: "George Santos should resign!"

But Santos, despite the latest indictment, still couldn't be forced out, because Republicans couldn't afford to see their four-vote majority become a three-vote majority as they struggled to elect a speaker. So what if the congressman was charged with identity theft and credit card fraud in addition to unemployment fraud and all the rest? Let he who is without a superseding indictment cast the first stone!

The next day opened with cursing and shouting even before the Republicans returned to the Longworth building to choose a speaker candidate. At a briefing for lawmakers on the war in Israel, Derrick Van Orden, the Wisconsin Republican who had made news for his obscene tirade at teenagers serving as Senate pages, launched an obscene tirade at the Biden administration officials giving the briefing.

The shouting was only beginning. Santos called a few reporters into his office (inexplicably, I was not one of them) to deliver a Mr. T–style rejoinder to colleagues threatening to oust him: "They can try to expel me, but I pity the fools that go ahead and do that."

Entering the caucus meeting for the day's voting on speaker candidates, increasingly cranky lawmakers again had their phones confiscated, then put in manila envelopes piled haphazardly into yellow plastic boxes. Texas's Roy offered a proposal designed to avoid a repeat of Republicans' January debacle by requiring them to have 217 votes for their speaker nominee before they went to the floor.

Scalise's allies roundly defeated that proposal. An hour later, Scalise had won the nomination with his slender majority, and his team, trying to railroad Jordan's supporters, made plans to go straight to the floor. The leader of the coup against McCarthy, Gaetz, pronounced himself thrilled. "Long live Speaker Scalise!" he cried.

But "Speaker Scalise" didn't make it to the floor that day. Trump, who had endorsed Jordan, did nothing to help Scalise. And, by various accounts, McCarthy was privately undermining his old rival by encouraging support for Jordan. The House Freedom Caucus met to discuss the matter—and more members announced opposition to Scalise.

The following day, McHenry opened the session and immediately declared another recess. Back in the House basement that afternoon, Republicans entered yet another caucus meeting while rumors swirled. Florida's Greg Steube told reporters that he had heard (incorrectly) from the MAGA outlet One America News Network that Scalise had dropped out of the running. Nehls said if Republicans hadn't elected a speaker by Oct. 15 they should "bring in the closer"—Trump—to serve as speaker.

An exasperated Dusty Johnson, chairman of the moderate Main Street Caucus, complained to us about colleagues "refusing to do your damn job." Rogers, chairman of the Armed Services committee, called his colleagues who ousted McCarthy "traitors."

Inside the room, Republicans resumed their venting. Missouri's Mark Alford told reporters it was "marriage therapy."

"We're celebrating our diversity," joked Brad Wenstrup, of Ohio, as he stepped into the hallway.

"Everything's at gridlock," Greene said, leaving the meeting. "It's not a good look for the Republican conference."

Santos delivered the plain truth about the grim state of affairs for the GOP. "It was a waste of time," he complained, "like every single meeting we've had."

As the meeting broke, lawmakers raged against their own incompetence. "If you see smoke, it's not a speaker—someone just set the place on fire," Ronny Jackson, of Texas, told NBC's Ali Vitali.

"This is the worst team I've ever been on," Mike Kelly, of Pennsylvania, told the *Huffington Post*'s Arthur Delaney.

"We are a broken conference," said Nehls.

"We're a ship that doesn't have a rudder," offered Alford.

"All thrust and no vector," added Garcia.

"Makes us look like a bunch of idiots," observed Austin Scott, of Georgia.

"We need to . . . get our heads out of our rear end," suggested Florida's Mike Waltz.

"This is a continuation of a pretty dysfunctional disease," is how Dusty Johnson phrased it. "That is not how any functional government or any functional marriage or any functional business works."

THE NEXT WEEK, AFTER 14 SPEAKERLESS DAYS, THE FRATRICIDAL REPUBLICANS would try again. And if they rejected Jordan, too? Georgia Republican Mike Collins had a proposal. "We should just have a lottery," he posted. "If you lose, you have to be speaker."

Scalise's allies were bitter that their man had been "kneecapped" by Jordan's forces, as Arizona's Steve Womack put it. "It was the most egregious act against a sitting member of our conference I have witnessed in my thirteen years of service."

Things were so desperate that Austin Scott nearly got elected speaker—by accident.

"When I woke up this morning, I had no intention of doing this," the little-known backbencher told reporters on the morning after Scalise was ousted. "Actually, I don't necessarily want to be speaker of the House."

But he tossed his hat into the ring anyway, to give his Republican colleagues at least some alternative to Jordan. And so great was the animosity toward Jordan that 81 Republicans threw their support behind Scott, whom even some Capitol Hill veterans couldn't have picked out of a lineup.

In a second vote, fully 55 House Republicans indicated that they would oppose Jordan on the House floor. Jordan postponed a floor vote until Oct. 16, and eventually until Oct. 17, to give him more time to twist arms.

In the hallways of the Longworth House Office Building, where Republicans were meeting in the Ways and Means Committee room, order was unraveling. Santos emerged from the office of Burchett carrying an infant. Was it his baby?

"Not yet," the famous prevaricator answered. (The child apparently belonged to a staffer.)

An anti-Israel activist took this moment to harass Santos over "genocide of the Palestinians." And the attention-loving Santos, after handing off the baby, returned to confront the activist in front of a mob of reporters. "He is a fucking terrorist sympathizer!" Santos screamed to the journalists, also calling the activist "human scum."

After the caucus meeting nominating Jordan, his allies fanned out to begin their intimidation campaign. Ralph Norman told us that Jordan's opponents' "phones are going to be lit up."

And so they were. Over the weekend, Jordan's allies mounted their campaign of terror. On Sunday, a Fox News producer for Sean Hannity sent an intimidating email to the holdouts—or "snowflakes," as Hannity called them on air—that was intercepted by *Axios*'s Juliegrace Brufke. Hannity also provided phone numbers so his audience could harass Jordan's foes.

On Oct. 16, many of Jordan's opponents, an assortment of institutionalists and moderates, did what they had done all year when confronted with the far right's threats: They wilted. For example, Missouri's Ann Wagner had called herself a "hell no" on Jordan, saying she would "absolutely not" back the firebrand. But after Jordan and his thugs gave her the treatment, Wagner said Jordan "has allayed my concerns."

Whip Tom Emmer, a notoriously inept vote counter during McCarthy's speakership, predicted victory for Jordan: "We're going to have a speaker tomorrow."

They didn't have a speaker the next day. Jordan had bullied most of his opponents into submission, but a brave band still opposed him: a combination of lawmakers on the Appropriations Committee (Jordan routinely votes against their appropriations bills), swing-district moderates (who feared the extremist label Jordan would give them), and a few old-bull institutionalists (who actually care about things such as honoring election results).

Bacon, a leader of the never-Jordan resistance, was looking appropriately battered the night of Oct. 16, with a scabbed-over wound on his right cheek. "I just can't abide by the fact that a small group violated the rules to get what they wanted," he told a group of us. "So I think we've got to have consequences and you've got to stand up for that . . . You just can't cave in."

Still, he was dreading the abuse he would receive from the Jordan forces during the alphabetical roll call on the floor. "Maybe I could change my name to Zacon," he mused aloud.

Drew Ferguson, of Georgia, reported that he and his family received death threats because of his opposition to Jordan. Ferguson had switched his vote away from Jordan in the first place because of the "threatening tactics and pressure campaigns Jordan and his allies were using." Mari-annette Miller-Meeks, of Iowa's First Congressional District, after turning against Jordan, said she, too, had received "credible death threats" and a barrage of abusive calls. "One thing I cannot stomach, or support, is a bully," she said in a statement.

New York's Nick LaLota, a Jordan foe, posted one of the obscene death threats he had received. Bacon reported that even his wife had received threatening emails and texts and vulgar voice messages, some of which he shared with *Politico*'s Beavers. "I hope your kids fucking burn alive," one caller told Bacon in another message, shared with *National Review*. Ken Buck reported that he was being evicted from his office in Windsor, Colorado, because the landlord was mad at his vote against Jordan.

Officially, Jordan condemned the threats, yet, curiously, they kept coming. Also curious: These were the same sorts of threats that have been visited on Jordan's usual opponents—Democratic lawmakers and targets of his committee probes—for years.

As his allies continued threatening holdouts, Jordan posted an appeal for unity: "We must stop attacking each other and come together." For him.

Inconveniently, Matt Gaetz shattered this phony call for harmony with a fundraising email: "RINO's are working RADICAL DEMOCRATS like AOC, ILHAN OMAR and RASHIDA TLAIB to BLOCK JIM JORDAN from becoming SPEAKER!!"

After an angry retort from Jordan opponent Lawler, Gaetz, hawker of hatred, blamed "a vendor."

Incredibly, Scott Perry, a Jordan ally, belittled the death threats. "All of us in Congress receive death threats," he told reporters. "That's nothing new. That is another red herring."

Perry, when he wasn't excusing death threats against colleagues, was also preparing a resolution "removing the Honorable Patrick McHenry ... from the position of elected speaker pro tempore." Florida's Greg Steube held a copy of the resolution on the House floor, and AP photographer Alex Brandon snapped a shot of it.

Winning over the remaining holdouts required serious persuasion, but Jordan only knew how to bully. His tool was the hammer, and his colleagues were all nails. "You can't have the same style with everybody," Jordan ally Byron Donalds admitted to a group of us. "I think that some of it did backfire."

Fortunately, 20 courageous Republicans blocked Jordan's terrorist takeover of the speaker's gavel. But this also meant that 200 House Republicans—including all House leaders and several self-styled moderates—voted for an extremist takeover of their majority. This was no aberration: The next day, 199 of them did it again in a second vote. Two days later, 194 of them did it a third time.

It's no longer a matter of the Republican establishment being disrupted by fanatics. As the Jordan votes show, the fanatics had become the establishment. It was the equivalent of 90 percent of House Democrats nominating Ilhan Omar or Rashida Tlaib to be speaker—except no member of "the Squad" ever fomented an attack on the Capitol.

Debbie Lesko, an Arizona Republican, issued a statement on the evening of Oct. 17, after Jordan's first failed vote on the House floor. She announced that she would not run for reelection. "Right now," she wrote, "Washington, D.C. is broken."

But Washington wasn't broken. The House of Representatives was broken—because she and her Republican colleagues broke it.

If there were any remaining doubt about this, one need only look at what Lesko and 199 of her Republican colleagues did on the House floor just four hours before she sent out her Washington-is-broken retirement missive. They voted to elect as speaker of the House:

An instigator of the Jan. 6 insurrection and facilitator of Trump's attempted coup who defied a duly issued subpoena from the congressional committee investigating the insurrection.

A legislator who hasn't enacted a single piece of legislation in his 16 years in Congress—but who issued 45 subpoenas this year alone.

A thuggish bully described as a "legislative terrorist" by Republican former speaker Boehner.

After Jordan's second failed vote on Oct. 18, Garcia, a swing-district Republican, stepped off the House floor and into the nineteenth century. "Clearly what we're doing right now is not working," he told a few of us reporters as he exited the Speaker's Lobby. "So we've got to get a different approach here."

Such as?

"It sounds silly, but let's go to Gettysburg or something," Garcia proposed, "so that the Republican Party can once again remember why we do what we do."

Perfect. What better way for feuding Republicans to hone tactics for their party's civil war than to go to the site of the bloodiest battle of the real Civil War? They could spend a pleasant day celebrating their ineffectiveness by reenacting Pickett's Charge.

Alas, getting to Pennsylvania posed a daunting logistical challenge for a group that couldn't even organize lunch. Republicans scheduled a caucus meeting for 1:30 that day in the Capitol basement after the failed vote, and I watched staffers wheel in a cart piled high with pizza boxes. But the meeting never happened, and the pies were scavenged by staffers, police, and reporters.

Garcia proposed that his colleagues could instead "do an off-site" nearby, either at Manassas or "somewhere else." The best option was just a short drive south on I-95, a Civil War site whose name perfectly matched the Republicans' situation: the Battle of the Wilderness.

Almost a year earlier, voters had entrusted Republicans with control of the House. And this is what they had done with it:

Fifteen rounds of voting to choose a speaker in January.

Nine months of lurching between crises and failed votes on the House floor.

A march to impeach Biden on fabricated charges.

The ouster of the speaker.

A successful coup to topple the man Republicans nominated to replace the ousted speaker.

Two failed speaker votes (and counting) on the House floor for the man who led the coup.

Seventeen days (and counting) without a functioning House of Representatives at a time of two wars and a looming government shutdown.

And no solution in sight.

Things were so topsy-turvy that Marjorie Taylor Greene started to sound like one of the sensible ones. Congresswoman Jewish Space Lasers left a GOP caucus meeting telling a group of us that it was "a venting session" with "mostly a lot of arguing" and "just airing grievances"—much like "every single meeting" lately.

"I've never wasted so much time," said Greene. "Even on vacation I'm busier."

On social media, Mike Collins of Georgia mocked his Republican colleagues' glacial pace: "Looking forward to clocking in around lunchtime today. No need to rush getting a speaker!" Then "I miss the good ole days when we used to do 2–3 votes a day for speaker. Gets it done faster." And "If we all get a chance to be voted on as speaker, are we going alphabetically or by class? Trying to plan Thanksgiving travel."

"My new favorite member of Congress," somebody replied.

"Low bar!" observed Collins.

Perhaps nobody embodied the Republican incoherence quite as well as Victoria Spartz. The Indiana representative was one of the holdouts who had blocked McCarthy from assuming the speakership in January. During the summer, she announced that she would vote to block all Republican bills from coming to the floor. She announced that she would retire from Congress—then teased that she would run again, then did run again. In the fall, she issued a statement threatening to resign immediately if the House didn't approve—of all things—a debt commission, pleading, "I cannot save this Republic alone."

In the speaker's race, she voted for Jordan in the Republican caucus meeting, then issued a statement the same day saying, "I rescind my support for Jordan for now," citing "backstabbing." Three days later, she reportedly broke into tears as she delivered an incomprehensible speech to her colleagues in another caucus meeting. The same day, pronouncing herself undecided in the speaker's race, she issued yet another baffling statement: "We fought a war not to have kings," and "Republicans are not sheep and will refuse to support [Jordan] if he will try to use the same McCarthy intimidation techniques on members on the floor." Two days later, she voted for Jordan.

Why? An impulsive decision, she explained, because she liked the nominating speech given moments before by Tom Cole. In between, she cast a ballot for Kentucky's Tom Massie (who wasn't running for speaker), explaining that it was another impulsive choice; she had planned to vote "present" but had a last-minute worry that such a vote could help elect a Democratic speaker.

Gettysburg was sounding better and better.

THE SCENE ON THE HOUSE FLOOR WAS A POORLY PRODUCED SEQUEL TO McCarthy's January vote-a-rama.

"Jim is the voice of the American people who have felt voiceless," Republican conference chairwoman Stefanik told the House in her speech nominating Jordan for the first ballot, "whether on the wrestling mat or in the committee room."

The Democrats erupted in hoots. Was Stefanik trying to remind everybody of the many allegations that Jordan, as a college wrestling coach, had turned a blind eye to sexual assaults on athletes?

Pete Aguilar, the Democratic conference chairman, countered that Jordan was "the architect of a nationwide abortion ban, a vocal election denier, and an insurrectionist."

Jordan laughed.

Aguilar pointed out that Jordan "has not passed a single bill" in Congress.

Gaetz applauded.

As in January, each no vote against the Republican nominee sent a murmur rippling through the chamber. As in January, the vote ended with the now common refrain: "A speaker has not been elected."

Cole told reporters it was time to convene "the Bourbon and Cigar Caucus."

Jordan made only a perfunctory attempt at buttonholing a few of his opponents on the floor. He and his staff spent the afternoon trying to blame Scalise for his failure.

Leaving an unproductive session with holdouts, Jordan held a hand-written note with a question he had apparently asked his detractors. Captured by Reuters photographer Leah Millis, it said: "What is the real reason?" (Answer: You're a legislative terrorist.)

"The question now occurs—" McHenry began on the afternoon of Oct. 18, before catching himself. "The question now *recurs*, on the election of a speaker." This time, there were 55 empty seats on the Republican side as McHenry called for nominations; GOP lawmakers apparently preferred to sit in the cloakroom rather than sit through the whole thing again.

Once again, Jordan lost the vote before the alphabetical roll call made it out of the D's. He swung the votes of two holdouts but gained four new opponents. One Jordan opponent voted for Boehner—to cheers from the Democrats. Another voted for Candice Miller, the public works commissioner of Macomb County, Michigan—momentarily baffling the clerk.

Nobody said they had to be rational. After voting for GOP whip Emmer for speaker in the first ballot, Ken Buck went on CNN.

"Do you really want Tom Emmer to be speaker?" host Dana Bash asked him.

"No, I don't," Buck replied. "I don't like Tom Emmer. I figured this would be the worst job in America."

Friends don't let friends become speaker of the House.

The next day, Oct. 19, Jordan called off what would have been a third failed vote on the House floor. Instead, he backed a plan to expand the powers of the temporary speaker, McHenry, to allow the House to function for the next three months—while Jordan spent that time putting thumbscrews to the holdouts.

But this caused the Republican caucus, meeting once more in the Capitol basement, to erupt in furor. Jordan's foes didn't want him to remain as the speaker nominee. And Jordan's hardline supporters didn't want to reopen the House.

Jim Banks, of Indiana, burst out of the meeting calling the idea "the biggest F.U. to Republican voters I've ever seen."

Virginia's Bob Good decried an "unconstitutional" and "highly dangerous coalition government arrangement with Democrats."

Nehls renewed his call to make Trump the speaker.

Inside the closed-door meeting, Gaetz and Mike Bost of Illinois came close to blows, *Politico*'s Beavers reported. McHenry reportedly threatened to resign, NBC's Scott Wong and Rebecca Kaplan reported.

That night, Greg Murphy, of North Carolina, got into a social media spat with South Carolina's Mace over her vote for McCarthy's ouster. Then he blocked her. Responded the congresswoman: "This is exactly what's wrong with this place—too many men here with no balls."

By Friday, Oct. 20, which would turn out to be his last day as House Republicans' speaker nominee, Jordan was clearly losing altitude. What to do about it? Why, call in the Wright Brothers, of course.

Jordan opened his 8 a.m. news conference in the Capitol with a long story about touring the Ohio home of Orville and Wilbur, seeing their bicycle shop and their "gadgets and gizmos." He marveled at their first flight, in Kitty Hawk, North Carolina, noting that it "barely" got off the ground. Then he reminded reporters that over the next 66 years, "we went from two guys flying 100 feet to putting a man on the moon."

Where was Jordan trying to go with this anecdote? That his campaign wasn't getting off the ground? That it would take him 66 years to win the speakership? He didn't really have a point, other than to conclude that "this is a great country . . . made up of great people."

Great! If there was any aviation metaphor to be drawn from the news conference, it was that his bombing run would continue—he said he saw nothing wrong with "multiple rounds of votes"—until he had blown up whatever vestiges of functionality were left in the House Republican caucus. Mercifully, his fellow Republicans shot Jordan down six hours later.

McCarthy gave the third nominating speech for Jordan on Oct. 20, announcing that the always intransigent Jordan (with no bills enacted in Congress) "is an effective legislator" and good at "reaching compromise."

Democrats guffawed. Republicans called for order.

After another failed speaker vote on the floor that morning—this time Jordan lost 25 Republicans, three more than in the last vote—the "crazy eight" (as McCarthy dubbed the Republicans who had ousted him) released a letter in which they said to their colleagues that if they elected Jordan as speaker, "we are prepared to accept censure, suspension, or removal from the conference" for leading the coup against McCarthy. (One of the signatories, Buck, promptly disavowed the letter bearing his name, reducing the band to the less-assonant "crazy seven.")

"If what these holdouts need is a pound of flesh, we're willing to give it to them," Gaetz said.

But nobody wanted his flesh.

"I will not vote for Jim Jordan," Florida's Carlos Giménez told reporters on the House steps. "It used to be that I was voting for McCarthy. Now I'm not voting for Jim Jordan."

And Jordan supporters were throwing in the towel. "There's no more runway," said Pat Fallon, of Texas. Nehls, a one-trick pony, said he would vote for Donald Trump on the next speaker ballot.

Republicans went to the Capitol basement for another gripe session. Once again, cartloads of pizza went in. An hour later, Jordan had been dethroned. In a secret ballot, only 86 Republicans said he should stay in the speaker race, while 112 wanted him out. Nineteen didn't even bother to attend; some had flown home for the weekend rather than participate in more pointless speaker votes on the floor.

Now the leaderless and rudderless Republicans had to start all over again. The earliest they could vote on the next nominee, their third, would be the next Tuesday, a full three weeks after they ousted McCarthy and shut down the House. And the next race would be a free-for-all, with nine candidates in the running.

"Back to the drawing board," a grim McCarthy said after Jordan dropped out. McCarthy blamed the seemingly endless chaos on the Republicans who ousted him, saying, "The amount of damage they have done to this party and to this country is insurmountable." Added the former speaker: "We are in a very bad position as a party."

They wouldn't even hold the next candidates forum for three days—what's the rush?—because "I think we need to give people a little bit of time to mourn," Dusty Johnson told us in the hallway.

Gaetz left the meeting in a rage. "The most popular Republican in the United States Congress was just knifed by a secret ballot, in a private meeting, in the basement of the Capitol," he fumed. "It is as swampy as swamp gets, and I am disgusted."

For the third time in as many weeks, a Republican leader had gone down in flames.

THE FOLLOWING WEEK, ON DAY 22 OF HOUSE REPUBLICANS' SLAPSTICK QUEST to find a new speaker, they were back once again in the Ways and Means Committee room, and once again bickering. This time, they were about to nominate whip Tom Emmer, their fourth-string choice for the speakership—and he would be shot down just a few hours after he was chosen.

"Let's get our poop in a group, people. We've got to figure this out," Bill Huizenga of Michigan admonished his GOP colleagues in a closed-door caucus meeting on Oct. 24. (The remarks, naturally, were immediately leaked to reporters.) "I don't want us to go out there and, in front of the entire world, puke on our shoes again. That's what we've been doing."

Grouping poop? Puking on shoes? The "chaos caucus" had finally found its new digs: in the sewer. Huizenga's was an unpleasant (if reasonably accurate) gastrointestinal diagnosis for what ailed House Republicans. But it was arguably preferable to the urological diagnosis being offered by some of his colleagues.

The evening before, Greene asked the panel of nine men then running for speaker whether they would impeach or otherwise harass various Biden administration officials. "I want to know which one of you have the balls to hold them accountable," she said, as relayed to Olivia Beavers of *Politico*.

This was the second time in a week that a woman in the GOP caucus had raised doubts about her colleagues' testicles.

Actually, the problem was almost certainly the opposite: a toxic overdose of testosterone, resulting in aggressive and risk-taking behavior.

Among the nine men who had entered the speakership race after Jordan's bid collapsed were some unknown backbenchers enjoying their 15 minutes of fame. "Mr. Scott! Mr. Scott!" reporters called after the previously invisible Austin Scott as he entered the candidates forum in the Longworth building on the night of Oct. 23. Flashes went off and reporters gave chase when Michigan Republican Jack Bergman walked down the hallway during his (brief) candidacy. Bergman, asked after the forum whether he had a "path forward" in the next day's voting, told reporters: "Well, I have a path at least to get up in the morning and get here."

Pennsylvania's Dan Meuser didn't even get that far. He made his pitch to lawmakers on the night of the 20th—and then immediately dropped out. Alabama's Gary Palmer gave out printed campaign cards detailing the "Palmer Principles." Kevin Hern, of Oklahoma, a former McDonald's franchisee, topped all contenders by delivering two cheeseburgers to each of his Republican colleagues.

Still, as voting on Oct. 24 would make clear, House Republicans were still a couple of fries short of a Happy Meal.

Emmer was the front-runner for the speakership on the morning of the caucus vote, and his supporters predicted a quick victory. But he had two big problems: Trump didn't like him, and Democrats did. Democrat Dean Phillips, of Minnesota, posted that he would "sit-out the speaker vote" to help Emmer win—if Emmer agreed to his conditions. But Trump shared on Truth Social a post by right-wing provocateur Laura Loomer calling Emmer a "NEVER TRUMPER and COMMUNIST ENABLER."

Emmer had 78 supporters on the first ballot to Mike Johnson's 34. But it took him four more ballots, with candidates eliminated in each, to get a narrow majority: 117 to Johnson's 97.

A roll-call vote showed that about two dozen wouldn't vote for Emmer on the floor. The usual suspects on the far right—Greene, Roy, Bob Good, Scott Perry, Arizona's Andy Biggs—were ready to tank his candidacy, and they had more than enough votes to do so. The legislative terrorists had taken another hostage.

Republicans recessed the caucus meeting for a couple of hours to give Emmer time to win converts. They also canceled nine committee hearings that had been scheduled for the day. Emmer kept the holdouts in the room, to see whether he could change their minds. But it was no use. Georgia's Rick Allen told Emmer that he needed to "get right with Jesus" because of Emmer's support for gay marriage, *Punchbowl News* reported.

Outside the room, Republicans went through another wave of despair.

"We've been three weeks without a speaker," McCarthy complained. "Every member is tired of this."

"It's disheartening," offered Brandon Williams, of New York.

"Distressing," said Marc Molinaro, another New Yorker.

"A disservice to the country," lamented Pennsylvania's Mike Kelly.

"We've got to figure out how to function," Dusty Johnson told us. "This is a mess."

Punchbowl's Max Cohen asked him about Mike Johnson as a backup option for Emmer. "You mean the backup to the backup to the backup to the backup?" the South Dakotan replied.

In what had become a familiar pattern, GOP lawmakers and others began to announce their formal opposition to the nominee. Jim Banks, of Indiana, called Emmer a "liberal" whose ascension would "betray our voters." Trump, who could see Emmer was going down, finished him off with a post calling him a "Globalist RINO."

Emmer, nominated by his colleagues at noon, surrendered by teatime.

181

By my watch, he had been the speaker-designate for four hours and seven minutes.

Emmer stormed out of the GOP conference meeting after withdrawing his doomed candidacy. Emerging through a wooden door marked Private, he rushed out of the building, leading dozens of journalists on a high-speed chase. In the stampede, journalists knocked into equipment and stanchions as they followed Emmer east on Independence Avenue, then south on New Jersey Avenue, where he frantically searched for the black SUV that would whisk him away.

Greene celebrated. "This is good," she told reporters. "The GOP conference has changed and it's changing to reflect America First."

Greene was right. The legislative terrorists had won yet again. They ousted McCarthy, blocked Scalise, nearly succeeded at installing Jordan, and blocked Emmer. And now, as Republicans prepared for another round of voting on the night of Oct. 24, the only candidates left standing were MAGA faithful. All five of them had voted to overturn the 2020 election. "Voting now. All candidates now 100 percent Trump," one of the candidates, Chuck Fleischmann of Tennessee, texted to a Trump aide. "All 5. I preached Trump in my speech." The sycophancy was too much even for Trump, who mockingly posted the message on social media.

"What's up, friends? Nothing? Or nothing?" Mike Gallagher asked reporters. We once again had been waiting for hours in the hallways of the Longworth House Office Building, this time as the Emmer candidacy came and went.

Scalise, recovering from his own failed speaker bid, followed behind him. "What Gallagher said!" Scalise seconded.

Dan Crenshaw, from the Houston area, blamed the Republicans' latest disarray on the outcome of the American League Championship Series. "I told people there would be problems if the Rangers won, and that's exactly what's happened," he said.

Gallagher, by contrast, saw an NFL analogy for his party's dysfunction. "As the Republican representative from Green Bay, it pains me to ask this question," he told a group of us, "but I'm not sure who sucks at team sports more right now—the Packers or the House Republican caucus."

That's easy: The Packers had only lost three in a row.

Republican dysfunction had gone from amusing to embarrassing to absurd to . . . well, no one had words anymore. In a huge scrum of reporters after Emmer quit, journalist Ben Jacobs asked Steve Womack whether the speakership chaos had become absurd. Replied Womack: "It was absurd last week."

The updates from Elise Stefanik, the GOP conference chair, had become a running joke.

"Congratulations Speaker-designate @SteveScalise!" she posted on Oct. 11.

"Congratulations Speaker-designate @Jim_Jordan!" she posted on Oct. 13.

"Congratulations Speaker-designate @GOPMajorityWhip [Emmer]!" she posted at 12:15 p.m. on Tuesday.

And finally: "Congratulations Speaker-designate @RepMikeJohnson!" she posted at 9:54 p.m. on Tuesday.

Over their three speakerless weeks, House Republicans heard from 12 candidates, including four who ran more than once. They held five votes on the House floor and about 15 behind closed doors. "I mean, what are we going to do, go down and just put everybody's name in a damn hat?" asked Troy Nehls.

Finally, at night on the 22nd speakerless day, House Republicans picked the name "Mike Johnson" out of the phone book. Though he held a junior leadership post, he was acceptable because he was relatively unknown on Capitol Hill, even to many Republicans. During the roll-call vote on the House floor on Oct. 25, Kay Granger, chair of the Appropriations Committee, rose and mistakenly voted for Mike Rogers—the chairman of the Armed Services Committee—before correcting herself to Mike Johnson. Paul Gosar, in a statement congratulating the new speaker, called him "Jim" Johnson Susan Collins of Maine, the top Republican on the Senate Appropriations Committee, told CNN's Lauren Fox that she'd have to Google the new speaker.

Johnson's anonymity was his greatest asset. In just his seventh year in Congress, he hadn't been around long enough, or had enough power, to make enemies. He was the least experienced speaker in a century and a half. But he was also an avid election denier, Trump defender, and promoter of the Deep State conspiracy theory, which appealed to the MAGA hardliners who had defeated McCarthy, Scalise, and Emmer.

Johnson had two other things going for him, too: exhaustion (about 25 Republicans skipped the final vote in the GOP caucus meeting that nominated him on the night of Oct. 24) and a fear that if yet another nominee failed, a small band of Republican institutionalists might actually make good on their threat to work with Democrats to return the chamber to functioning.

"If you do that, you're done," Texas Republican Wesley Hunt told us. "That's not even an option."

Heaven forbid.

Now, three weeks before the next deadline to avoid a government shutdown, Republicans had elected a no-name speaker with no experience and no agreement on a way forward. And the hardliners immediately started threatening him. Just minutes after Johnson won the speakership, Chip Roy, a Freedom Caucus ringleader, told Bloomberg News' Erik Wasson that any bill avoiding a shutdown on Nov. 17 would need to impose something like the 30 percent slashing of government spending that House Republicans had attempted previously.

New speaker. Same dysfunction.

"Because of the absolute nonsense of the last four weeks, I think the chance of a shutdown went from 10 percent four or five weeks ago to probably something more like a coin flip," Dusty Johnson told us, in between Emmer's four-hour reign and Mike Johnson's nomination. He allowed that "the last four weeks have not provided me with a lot of reason to be optimistic that Republicans are going to have our act together . . . We need to be aware that, any given day, eight or 10 people can decide they want to blow the whole thing up."

That was Johnson's problem now. On the third ballot, just before 10 p.m., Johnson claimed a majority. The hardliners had gotten their guy—and everybody else was too exhausted to object.

"This group here is ready to govern," Johnson declared, standing with a throng of his colleagues. "You're going to see this group looking, working like a well-oiled machine."

Not quite.

ABC News' Rachel Scott asked Johnson about his role in attempting to overturn the 2020 election. "Shut up! Shut up!" Virginia Foxx, of North Carolina, standing to Johnson's side, bellowed at the journalist.

Johnson smiled and shook his head. "Next question," he said.

Another reporter asked about Israel.

"Go away! Go away!" cried Foxx.

"We're not doing policy tonight," Johnson said.

Nor the next day. After Johnson's election on the House floor, GOP leadership called a "press conference" with the new speaker on the Capitol steps—but then he refused to take questions. The *Washington Post*'s Jacqueline Alemany buttonholed Johnson and asked about whether the 2020 election was stolen. "We're not talking about any issues today," he said.

On the House floor for the speakership vote to elect Johnson, Republicans quelled their anger at each other for the moment, leaving them free to vent it once more at Democrats.

"The federal government has been illegally weaponized against we the people," Stefanik said during her speech nominating Johnson.

Democrats groaned at the Deep State nonsense; Johnson applauded the line.

"I'll say it again: The federal government has been illegally weaponized," Stefanik repeated.

Speaking for the Democrats, caucus chairman Pete Aguilar, of California, told the House that the speaker squabble was "about who can appease Donald Trump."

On the Republican side, Nehls and others stood to applaud this sentiment.

Aguilar spoke of Johnson's role in discrediting the 2020 election.

"Damn right!" shouted Anna Paulina Luna.

Aguilar said that "if House Republicans choose, they can still join us on a bipartisan path forward."

Several Republicans shouted, "No!"

During the voting, Republicans unanimously rose to support the man Iowa's Zachary Nunn called "Miracle Mike."

When New Jersey Democrat Bonnie Watson Coleman voted for Democratic leader Hakeem Jeffries as "the only candidate that protects the integrity of this House," the Republican side erupted in boos and a shout of "Bullshit!"

And when Jeffries, who had the task of handing the gavel to Johnson, preceded it with a speech, he was treated to heckling from Greene, jeering and booing when he mentioned the Jan. 6 insurrection, shouts of "regular order" to cut him off, and finally a chant of "We want Mike!"

After shutting the House down for three weeks, they couldn't give the Democratic leader three minutes.

Johnson, accepting the gavel, alluded to the unexpected—and unlikely—nature of his ascent. It happened so "suddenly," he said, that his wife "couldn't get a flight in time." It was a gracious speech, and he won bipartisan applause when he announced: "The people's House is back in business."

Back in business—but, as the heckling of the hooligans on the House floor made clear, as dysfunctional as before.

Chapter 9

"It's the Same Clown Car with a Different Driver"

B EFORE MIKE JOHNSON'S SUDDEN RISE TO SPEAKER, AS THE *WASHINGTON Post* discovered, somebody Googling his name would have turned up "hits for a 'Bachelorette' contestant, the NHL's retired star of that name, a Mike Johnson in the tech start-up world, as well as one who runs a Toyota dealership in North Carolina and another who's famous for his steel guitar riffs in country music."

But the real Mike Johnson quickly became apparent. CNN and others dug up past writings in which he called homosexuality "inherently unnatural," a "bizarre choice," and a "dangerous lifestyle" that would lead to legalized pedophilia and bestiality. He argued for the criminalization of sodomy, calling it "same-sex deviate sexual intercourse."

Johnson, in his first TV interview as speaker, told Fox News' Sean Hannity: "People are curious: What does Mike Johnson think about any issue under the sun? Well, go pick up a Bible off your shelf and read it. That's my worldview."

In other writings, he blamed mass shootings on legal abortion, evolution, and no-fault divorce laws, and he blamed post–Hurricane Katrina looting in Louisiana on atheists and legalized gambling. He championed "covenant marriage," which imposes added barriers to divorce. He disparaged the "so-called separation of church and state." He has pushed to ban abortion nationwide, and he has acknowledged that he uses an "accountability software" program called Covenant Eyes in which his son will receive an alert if the elder Johnson ever accesses pornography.

Most famously, he led a legal challenge to the 2020 election and urged colleagues to reject the Electoral College count.

He didn't change a bit after becoming speaker. New on the job, he decided to break bread with a group of Christian nationalists. At the Museum of the Bible in Washington, D.C., in early December 2023, he gave the keynote address to the National Association of Christian Lawmakers, a group whose founder and leader, "proud" Christian nationalist Jason Rapert, has said: "I reject that being a Christian Nationalist is somehow unseemly or wrong."

Rapert's organization promoted the pine-tree "Appeal to Heaven" flag, which had been embraced by Christian nationalists and which was among the banners flown at the "Stop the Steal" rally on Jan. 6—and which, by total and remarkable coincidence, was proudly displayed outside Johnson's congressional office.

At the group's meeting in June, one of the speakers noted with approval that "the American colonies imposed the death penalty for sodomy." Confirmed speakers and award recipients for the gathering Johnson addressed included a man who proposed that gay people should be forced to wear "a label across their forehead, 'This can be hazardous to your health'"; a woman who blamed gay people for Noah's flood and more recent natural disasters; and various adherents of "dominionist" theology, which holds that the United States should be governed under biblical law by Christians.

Reporters were kicked out of the event before Johnson spoke, but the organizers later posted a video on Facebook, and a *Rolling Stone* writer spotted it before it was taken down. In it, Johnson thanked his hosts for banishing the journalists. "I'll tell you a secret since the media's not here," he said, informing them that God "had been speaking to me" about becoming speaker.

God told him, specifically, that "we're coming to a Red Sea moment" and he needed to be prepared—to be Moses! Throughout the speakership battle, "the Lord kept telling me to wait," Johnson recounted. "And it came to the end, and the Lord said, 'Now, step forward.'" Johnson told them that "only God saw the path through the roiling sea"—and that was by anointing him as the Republicans' Moses.

But the Lord also must have decided to keep the sea roiling, for the House spiraled into more chaos as soon as Johnson took over.

IN JOHNSON'S FIRST WEEK AS SPEAKER, GREENE FORCED A VOTE IN THE HOUSE on censuring Michigan Democrat Rashida Tlaib for being antisemitic. It was funny enough that Congresswoman Jewish Space Lasers herself was accusing somebody else of being antisemitic. But her censure resolution was so over the top—it accused Tlaib of "leading an insurrection"—that 23 Republicans joined all Democrats in tabling it.

After the vote, Chip Roy said the censure resolution "was deeply flawed and made legally and factually unverified claims, including the claim of leading an 'insurrection.'"

Greene shot back on social media: "You voted to kick me out of the Freedom Caucus, but keep CNN wannabe Ken Buck and vaping groping Lauren Boebert and you voted with the Democrats to protect Terrorist Tlaib."

(To unpack this Greene crazy: Buck had criticized fellow Republicans' plan to impeach Biden without any evidence, and Boebert had been kicked out of a *Beetlejuice* performance with her date after causing a disturbance that, it was later revealed, involved both vaping and groping.)

Asked about this accusation from Greene, Roy told *The Hill*'s Mychael Schnell: "Tell her to go chase so-called Jewish space lasers if she wants to spend time on that sort of thing." To this, Greene replied with a new post: "Oh shut up Colonel Sanders, you're not even from Texas, more like the DMV." Roy, who grew up in northern Virginia, has a white goatee not unlike the whiskers on the chin of the late founder of Kentucky Fried Chicken.

Greene had also been referring to Boebert as a "whore" in conversations with Trump and others, the *Daily Beast*'s Zachary Petrizzo reported.

The People's House was back in business!

In the 10 days since Johnson rose from the back benches on Oct. 25, the new speaker presided over a second failed attempt to expel the indicted George Santos, the introduction of not one but two resolutions to censure Tlaib, and a resolution to censure New York Democrat Jamaal Bowman for having pulled a fire alarm during a vote in September. Johnson managed to turn an area of near-unanimous support into a partisan brouhaha by making funds to help Israel defend itself against Hamas contingent on a provision making it easier for the wealthy to cheat on their taxes. With just two weeks to go until the federal government would run out of funding, Johnson was floating a cockamamie "laddered" approach that would replace the looming shutdown threat with multiple shutdown threats.

And the internecine feuding in the GOP had resumed immediately after Johnson's elevation. Ways and Means Committee chairman Jason Smith publicly blasted Gaetz for causing the crisis by ousting Kevin McCarthy as speaker. Gaetz responded by insinuating on social media that Smith is gay. Smith "called me a liar," Gaetz wrote. "It's a somewhat predictable projection. Because he lives a lie every day."

On Nov. 1, Johnson was caught telling a whopper by the nonpartisan Congressional Budget Office. Republicans claimed that their bill offering $14.5 billion in aid to Israel was "offset" by cutting the same amount from the IRS. But the Congressional Budget Office forecast that the cuts to the IRS would actually *cost* the federal government an additional $12.5 billion—as reduced enforcement makes it easier for people to cheat on their taxes.

"Only in Washington when you cut spending do they call it an increase in the deficit," Johnson responded to the Congressional Budget Office.

Only in Louisiana, apparently, do they think that if you stop collecting taxes your tax receipts will increase.

Johnson continued moving spending bills through the House along party lines, at levels that violated the bipartisan budget deal. In the Senate, by contrast, a package of spending bills passed that same week on a broadly bipartisan vote of 82–15. Patty Murray, chairwoman of the Senate Appropriations Committee, admonished her House counterparts "to get serious about governing, stick to the spending agreement they themselves negotiated, and work with us to finalize bipartisan bills."

But that wasn't about to happen. The House "chaos caucus," which ousted McCarthy and turned the lights out in the chamber for 22 days, had found its man. Johnson was well on his way to being a chaos speaker.

Before Mike Johnson became speaker, the House of Representatives had voted to censure one of its own members only seven times in 100 years. In the two weeks after Johnson became speaker, members of the House tried to censure each other eight times.

The House most definitely was not in order.

It wasn't just his inability to curb the tit-for-tat censure resolutions that turned the chamber into a seething den of recriminations. Just seven days before the federal government was to shut down, as the temporary extension in funding (which cost Kevin McCarthy the speakership) expired, Johnson was fumbling in the dark.

He squandered the week without passing, or even floating, a plan to avoid a shutdown. "I'm not going to tell you when we'll bring it to the floor, but it will be in time," Johnson declared in a news conference. "How about that? Trust us. We're working through the process in a way that I think the people will be proud of."

"Trust us" would not seem to be a compelling argument, given the early record of the Johnson speakership.

On Nov. 7, the House wasted hours debating and voting on amendments to the appropriations bill that would fund the Department of Transportation and the Department of Housing and Urban Development, only to pull it from the floor before the final vote because of a revolt by Republicans from the Northeast over cuts to Amtrak of more than $1 billion.

The House then wasted hours on Nov. 8 debating and voting on amendments to the Financial Services and General Government appropriations bill, only to pull it from the floor moments before the scheduled vote the next morning. This time, moderate Republicans rebelled over a provision in the bill that would allow employers in Washington, D.C., to discriminate against women who have an abortion or use contraception.

"I don't think the Lord Jesus himself could manage this group," Troy Nehls told NBC. Another Republican pronounced the GOP caucus "ungovernable."

Military aid to Israel was on ice because Johnson had attached it to a partisan attack on the IRS. Aid to Ukraine, which also commanded broad support, was similarly bottled up. Ohio Republican Max Miller, a strong supporter of Israel, voted for Johnson's bill tying Israel aid to IRS cuts, but he told *Jewish Insider* that pairing the two was "disgusting" and a "gimmick."

"I refuse to put people over politics," the new speaker wrote in a fund-raising email to supporters. Was this a typo? Or a statement of policy?

Nothing was clear. As Republicans held a closed-door caucus meeting in the House basement to discuss their plans for avoiding a shutdown, an aide to Georgia Republican Mike Collins held a poster featuring three images of Gru from *Despicable Me* and the message "Collins for Conference Vice Chair."

It was as good a plan as any: Republicans would avoid a shutdown by stealing the moon with a shrink ray. As part of his campaign for the junior leadership post (the position Johnson had held before his elevation), Collins also released a video that seemed to troll his fellow Republicans. It showed, among other things, Greg Steube showing off his military-grade pistols and high-capacity magazines during a House Judiciary Committee hearing, Nancy Mace inquiring about "non-human spacecraft" at another hearing, Anna Paulina Luna at a hearing asking a witness, "Do you believe that we should place a ban on spoons?," and Pat Fallon at still another hearing saying, "I'm going to get out my unicorn and ride it to a pool to visit my mermaid that was financed by a leprechaun."

"This is my team," Collins wrote in an accompanying message promising "to amplify our message." Inexplicably, he lost.

Outside the caucus meeting where House Republicans were debating their various options for avoiding a shutdown, lawmakers coming and going had no idea what plan their leaders would settle upon. They offered endless variations of evasions to reporters in the hallway: "Uh, we'll find out . . . Working on it . . . We're looking at all the options . . . What the what?"

Johnson, for his part, called the aimless session "a refreshing, constructive family conversation."

Drew Ferguson, of Georgia, told *Politico* that the plan was as "clear as mud." Others used the phrases "train wreck," "all over the place, like usual," and "I don't have an opinion on it because I don't understand it." House Appropriations Committee chairwoman Kay Granger assured the outlet that "we've got a plan" to avert a shutdown—"but I can't tell you until it's a real plan."

Still in the dark was Susan Collins, the top Republican on the Senate Appropriations Committee. She told NBC's Frank Thorp on Nov. 8 that "I'm getting anxious." Why? "Because we don't have a plan."

The absence of a plan was the one common thread connecting House Republicans' activities. The week's two major pieces of legislation, the Transportation–Housing and Urban Development and Financial Services spending bills, went down in flames. Similarly, the annual Agriculture, Rural Development, and Food and Drug Administration appropriations bill failed in the House in September over restrictions it would have imposed on the abortion drug mifepristone.

House Republicans couldn't even get two other spending bills out of committee because of partisan provisions and poison pills. Among the various riders: provisions dropping the pay of Defense secretary Lloyd Austin, Homeland Security secretary Alejandro Mayorkas, and Transportation secretary Pete Buttigieg to $1 apiece. They also attempted to cut the salary of the White House press secretary and the Securities and Exchange Commission chairman to $1, and to defund the office of Vice President Kamala Harris.

The serial failures on the House floor were the direct result of the GOP leadership's stubborn insistence on passing spending bills with Republican votes alone—in contrast to the Senate, where all 12 appropriations bills commanded bipartisan support.

Still, it would be unfair to dismiss the Johnson speakership as entirely unsuccessful so far. After all, he presided over a golden age of censure:

Jack Bergman filed a resolution to censure Tlaib.

Marjorie Taylor Greene filed a resolution to censure Tlaib.

Michigan Republican Lisa McClain filed a resolution to censure Bowman.

Greene filed another resolution to censure Tlaib.

Ohio Republican Max Miller filed a resolution to censure Tlaib.

Georgia's Rich McCormick filed a resolution to censure Tlaib.

In retaliation, Vermont Democrat Becca Balint filed a resolution to censure Greene, and California Democrat Sara Jacobs filed a resolution to censure Florida Republican Brian Mast.

The only one to pass was McCormick's censure of Tlaib—which was a source of intense jealousy to Greene. She produced a 13-minute video rant excoriating Republican leaders for favoring McCormick's censure over her "very harsh" alternative.

This had spun out of control. "If we are going to start censuring anybody who says something we don't like, all we will do from now on is censure each other all day," James McGovern, ranking Democrat on the Rules Committee, pointed out during the debate. "My Republican colleagues go on and on about cancel culture and here they are today trying to cancel someone."

BY MID-NOVEMBER, NEARLY 30 HOUSE LAWMAKERS HAD ANNOUNCED RE-tirement plans. Yet even the retirements couldn't be orderly. On Nov. 13, Texas's Fallon announced that he wouldn't run for reelection and would instead run for his old seat in the state senate. On Nov. 14, Fallon rescinded his retirement and announced that he would run for reelection to Congress after all. Mark Green likewise announced his retirement, then rescinded it.

The cause for the rush to the exits was obvious. "Impeach that person, censure that person. It's all political," Ken Buck, one of the retirees, complained to *Punchbowl*, calling the environment "stupid."

How stupid? Well, in mid-November, reasonable people could disagree about who was the most unreasonable member of Congress. At the time, there were many serious contenders:

James Comer, the Oversight Committee chairman, had just blown up at a hearing and called one of the Democrats a "Smurf."

Marjorie Taylor Greene, responding to a colleague who said she "lacks maturity," informed her 2.8 million followers on X that the man who called her immature was a "pussy" and that he did not have testicles.

And George Santos had just been found by the House Ethics Committee to have engaged in "additional uncharged and unlawful conduct" beyond his 23-count indictment.

But there was one thing about which there could be no debate: This was what Republican governance looked like in the year 2023. It had been one kidney punch after another to competent leadership.

And now the punches were real.

As the caucus meeting broke up, Tennessee Republican Tim Burchett was talking with NPR's Claudia Grisales in the hallway when "McCarthy shoved Burchett," Grisales recounted, and Burchett "lunged towards me."

Burchett chased after McCarthy, yelling, "You got no guts" and "You're pathetic, man." He then gave a series of interviews on the Capitol steps, telling CNN's Manu Raju that it was "a clean shot to the kidneys." The punch caused "a lot of pain," Burchett said.

As Burchett finished the interview, Florida Democrat Jared Moskowitz walked over and pretended to shove the startled Burchett. Later, on the House floor, Burchett received a hero's welcome. Buck gave Burchett a fist bump. Another colleague gave him a high five. Boebert, who had come to the floor carrying her grandchild, passed the infant to Burchett to hold. McCarthy sat in the back row, pretending to read an amendment sheet with great interest.

McCarthy denied he intentionally hit Burchett, saying that "if I kidney punched someone, they would be on the ground."

But McCarthy antagonist Gaetz immediately filed a complaint with the House Ethics Committee saying McCarthy "assaulted Representative Tim Burchett." Gaetz, the target of an Ethics Committee probe into alleged sexual misconduct, said the panel should be "interviewing, under oath, the alleged assailant."

Informed by reporters that Gaetz had filed the complaint, McCarthy responded with a smile: "I think Ethics is a good place for Gaetz to be."

In fairness, maybe Tim Burchett had it coming. Speaking with a few of us outside the GOP caucus meeting on the morning of Nov. 15 in the Capitol basement, the Tennessean, one of the eight Republicans who had ousted McCarthy, renewed his accusation that McCarthy "lied to me."

As if the fisticuffs in the basement weren't enough of a sign that things in the Capitol were out of control, it happened at about the same time that Senator Markwayne Mullin, an Oklahoma Republican, used a hearing of the Senate Health, Education, Labor and Pensions committee to challenge one of the witnesses to "stand your butt up" and fight him right there in the committee room.

Mullin, upset about Teamsters president Sean O'Brien's trash talk about Mullin on social media, told the witness: "If you want to run your mouth, we can be two consenting adults. We can finish it here."

"Okay, that's fine. Perfect," O'Brien answered.

"You want to do it right now?" asked Mullin, a McCarthy friend who had graduated from the House to the Senate in January 2023.

"I'd love to do it right now."

"Well, stand your butt up right now then."

"You stand your butt up, big guy."

Chairman Bernie Sanders intervened. "Sit down!" he admonished Mullin. "You're a United States senator."

Mullin, a former wrestler and mixed martial arts fighter, told reporters he had no regrets about his behavior. "How do you not handle it that way?" he asked. In a podcast after the incident, the senator elaborated on his strategy: "In a fight, I'm gonna bite," he said. "And I don't care where I bite, by the way."

The week, the last in session before Thanksgiving, had begun with a failed attempt on the House floor by Greene to force a snap impeachment of Homeland Security secretary Alejandro Mayorkas. It continued with a failed initial attempt to bring a temporary spending patch to the floor to keep the federal government open for another 60 days. And it ended in yet another failed vote on the floor, in which 19 Republicans blocked GOP leaders from beginning debate on the annual Commerce, Justice, and Science appropriations bill. In the past, it was unheard of for lawmakers to defy their own party leaders on such routine procedural votes; in 2023, it was commonplace.

After this last failure, which followed similar recent failures on the floor to pass four other appropriations bills because of intra-GOP squabbles, House leaders called off further votes for the week and sent lawmakers home early for Thanksgiving to "cool off," as Speaker Johnson put it.

Six weeks earlier, House Republicans had ousted McCarthy because he relied on Democratic votes to pass a "clean" temporary spending bill to keep the government open without demanding spending cuts. They shut the House down for 22 days while they found a new speaker.

Now Johnson had passed exactly the same sort of "clean" temporary bill that had cost McCarthy his job. And once again, GOP leadership had to come crawling to the Democrats to supply most of the votes. After all the trauma, House Republicans were right back where they started.

As Kelly Armstrong put it to *Politico*: "It's the same clown car with a different driver."

"We've had enough!" Freedom Caucus chief Scott Perry told reporters after he and his colleagues shut the House down yet again by blocking debate on the latest spending bill. "We're not going to be part of the failure theater anymore."

After the House called off votes for the rest of the week, Chip Roy held the floor for 55 minutes, railing against his own newly elected leadership. "What in the hell are we doing in this chamber?" he demanded. "I want my Republican colleagues to give me one thing—one—that I can go campaign on and say we did. One!" he shouted.

No takers.

Roy later tried to raise campaign cash from his bashing of Republican leaders. "I want Republicans in Congress to name one thing that we have done collectively to make your life better since we took back the House in January," he said in the appeal. "I need you to help me apply pressure and make them actually get off their butts and do something meaningful for the country."

When Moody's Investors Service lowered its outlook in November on the U.S. government's creditworthiness, it specifically cited Washington dysfunction: "renewed debt limit brinkmanship, the first ouster of a House Speaker in U.S. history, prolonged inability of Congress to select a new House Speaker, and increased threats of another partial government shutdown due to Congress' inability to agree on budgetary appropriations."

Johnson ignored all that, instead putting out a statement blaming Moody's action on "President Biden and Democrats." He then led the House through another week of dysfunction.

Johnson introduced a temporary extension of government funding, adopting a tiered approach with multiple expiration dates that had been proposed by the House Freedom Caucus. Members of the Freedom Caucus immediately trashed the very plan they had devised. Johnson met with the caucus on the night of Nov. 13 to try to sway them. But the next morning, the group issued a statement saying Johnson's plan "contains . . . not a single meaningful win for the American people."

"Not much of a honeymoon in this job," Johnson said on CNBC.

The House Rules Committee had met to take up the proposal. But five hours later, it adjourned without voting on it. It turned out Republicans didn't even have the votes to start debating the proposal on the House floor.

At their weekly caucus meeting, Republicans found themselves in a familiar state of paralysis. "The Republican conference is a colorful group," Dusty Johnson told us, "and we've got between 20 and 40 who find it almost impossible to get to yes."

Van Orden blamed the trouble on the "immature man child," Gaetz, for ousting McCarthy. Van Orden, by now well known for his outbursts directed at teenagers, complained that his colleagues "act out of emotion rather than logic."

At a GOP leadership news conference, Fox News' Chad Pergram pointed out that Johnson hadn't satisfied the "arch conservatives" in his party who were accusing him of surrendering to Democrats.

"I'm one of the arch conservatives," Johnson pleaded. But he argued that "you've got to fight fights that you can win."

At the same news conference, Emmer, the majority whip, urged: "Now is the time for House Republicans to stay united as a team."

Thereupon the team immediately divided. Members of the Freedom Caucus went to the floor and threatened to block GOP leaders from taking up that day's spending bill for the Departments of Labor and Health and Human Services. A group of 10 hardliners withheld their votes, forcing

Johnson to hold the vote open while he cajoled them in the center aisle; eventually they relented.

Because Johnson couldn't get Republican votes to take up the government funding resolution under normal procedures, he instead had to "suspend the rules" and pass it with a two-thirds majority. This meant Democrats would have to bail him out—just as they had McCarthy.

"Let us be very clear," Texas Democrat Sheila Jackson Lee taunted during the floor debate. "It is the Democrats who have come to save America and to stop this dastardly shutdown."

Even the few Republicans arguing for Johnson's plan in the debate went out of their way to say it was "not ideal" and "not my preferred method."

In the final tally on Nov. 14, 209 of 211 Democrats voted for Johnson's 60-day stopgap. But 93 Republicans voted against it—three more than the number had who opposed McCarthy's 45-day stopgap in September before they booted him from the speakership.

Still, Johnson, after three weeks on the job, had one thing in his favor that protected him from the same fate as McCarthy: House Republicans had proven beyond all doubt that absolutely nobody could govern them.

THE HOUSE RETURNED TO WORK AFTER NEARLY TWO WEEKS OFF FOR Thanksgiving—and immediately got down to its usual business of doing nothing. Internal disagreements within the GOP prevented them from taking up spending bills. Extraneous demands made by House Republicans kept Congress from acting on emergency aid to Israel and to Ukraine. Instead, the House took up a pair of symbolic resolutions on its first evening back, calling for Hamas to release hostages (this passed, 414–0) and reaffirming Israel's right to exist (only one Republican, Kentucky's Tom Massie, and one Democrat, Michigan's Rashida Tlaib, could not bring themselves to support this benign proposition).

With so little to show for themselves, Republicans began taking credit for pieces of legislation that they had voted against when they were passed by the previous, Democratic-controlled Congress. Speaker Johnson and Florida Republican Vern Buchanan held an event to celebrate a $100 million expansion of Sarasota Bradenton International Airport in

Florida. As *Punchbowl News* pointed out, some of the funds came from the infrastructure bill, which both men had opposed.

Similarly, the trade publication *E&E News*, which covers energy issues, reported that several Republicans hailed investments in their home states by the CHIPS Act of 2022, which they had opposed, including Jeff Duncan, William Timmons, and Joe Wilson in South Carolina; Maria Elvira Salazar and Carlos Giménez in Florida; Jason Smith in Missouri; and Claudia Tenney in New York. New York's Brandon Williams, who as a candidate opposed the CHIPS Act as "corporate welfare," was now boasting about New York becoming a "magnet of innovation and technological advancement"—thanks in part to funds from the bill he had opposed.

Right-wingers, angered that Johnson had kept the government open with a short-term continuing resolution and frustrated that he had bottled up military aid to Israel, were becoming increasingly harsh in their assessment of the new speaker. Max Miller called him a "joke," telling *Politico*'s Olivia Beavers that Johnson "did a 180 on everything he believed in" and made a "fucking dumb" decision to tie Israel's funds to cutting the IRS, which was "a slap in the face to every Jew."

Andy Biggs called Johnson's performance "unsatisfactory," and Chip Roy called it "plummeting."

Freedom Caucus chief Scott Perry did give Johnson one assist, by saying his group could accept a level of spending for 2024 that was $120 billion higher than what it had insisted on when McCarthy was speaker.

This was just one more thing that must have infuriated McCarthy. Speaking at a conference organized by the *New York Times*, the ousted speaker said there were some people in his caucus "I need to get medication for." The uninhibited McCarthy also suggested to *Politico* that his chief tormenter, Gaetz, "belongs in jail." And the *Washington Post*'s Jackie Alemany and Leigh Ann Caldwell reported on a phone call in which Trump, listing his grievances against the former speaker, told McCarthy why he didn't rescue his speakership. "Fuck you," McCarthy reportedly told Trump.

On Dec. 6, to the surprise of nobody, McCarthy announced his resignation, becoming the 31st lawmaker in the House not to seek reelection, as members of both parties stampeded to exit the dysfunctional chamber.

McCarthy, who had spent the first 10 months of the year saying "I do not quit," said he would quit at month's end, with a year left in his term.

Freshman Rich McCormick decried the "brain drain" in his party (veteran Republicans Patrick McHenry, Michael Burgess, and Brad Wenstrup also had called it quits), although, in fairness, there wasn't a whole lot of brain in the first place. Of more immediate concern to Republicans was a vote drain: After the Dec. 1 expulsion of George Santos and McCarthy's resignation, the GOP, paralyzed with a four-vote majority throughout 2023, would have just a two-vote majority to start 2024.

McCarthy, announcing his departure in a *Wall Street Journal* op-ed, reflected: "It often seems that the more Washington does, the worse America gets." By this standard, he should have been delighted with Congress. Famously unproductive during his tenure, it was now doing almost nothing.

Johnson said he wouldn't take up Ukraine support in the House unless Democrats swallowed House Republicans' entire wish list of border policies. That obstinance blew up negotiations in the Senate, where Oklahoma Republican James Lankford called Johnson's position "not rational," *Punchbowl News'* Andrew Desiderio reported.

After Johnson told Senate Republicans this demand was non-negotiable, Senator John Cornyn, a Texas Republican, explained to NBC's Sahil Kapur that "this is not a traditional negotiation, where we expect to come up with a bipartisan compromise on the border. This is a price that has to be paid." Johnson was, in effect, demanding a ransom to release the Ukraine funds he was holding hostage.

Johnson had already stalled military aid to Israel, and he had likewise bottled up spending talks for the rest of the fiscal year by failing to agree to the overall spending number that Senate Republicans and House and Senate Democrats all accepted.

In rare cases when Johnson did try to do something productive, his fellow Republicans denounced him. After a double flip-flop, the speaker finally blessed a compromise with Senate Democrats on the annual National Defense Authorization Act, including a temporary extension of the surveillance authority known as Section 702 of the Foreign Intelligence Surveillance Act. "Outrageous . . . a total sell-out," protested Marjorie

Taylor Greene. Chip Roy told *The Messenger*'s Lindsey McPherson this was "strike two and a half—if not more" against Johnson.

The new speaker even managed to divide the chamber on a matter where there had been virtually no disagreement: the need to denounce the recent rise in antisemitism. The House Education Committee held one of the best hearings of the year in December, in which the presidents of Harvard, the University of Pennsylvania, and MIT disgraced themselves by suggesting, in response to questions by Stefanik and others, that their students should feel free to run around calling for the genocide of Jews.

It was an entirely different picture on the House floor, where Republicans brought up their latest of several resolutions condemning antisemitism. This resolution, however, declared that "anti-Zionism is antisemitism," a dubious proposition equating criticism of Israel with hatred of Jews. A group of Jewish Democrats, arguing that "the safety of Jewish lives is not a game," urged colleagues to vote "present" in protest—and 92 did. But for Republicans, it *was* a game: After the vote, the National Republican Congressional Committee, the House GOP's political arm, put out a statement saying, "Extreme House Democrats just refused to denounce the . . . drastic rise of antisemitism."

Alas for the NRCC, the one genuinely antisemitic act from the episode came from Republican Tom Massie, who suggested in a post on X that "Zionism" was at odds with "American patriotism."

In lieu of doing anything productive, House Republicans continued their record-setting pace of censures. On Dec. 7, they made New York's Bowman their third victim of the year, for his fire-alarm-pulling episode more than two months earlier. "If extreme MAGA Republicans are going to continue to try to weaponize the censure," Democratic leader Hakeem Jeffries said on the House floor, "going after Democrats repeatedly, week after week after week because you have nothing better to do, then I volunteer: Censure me next! . . . That's how worthless your censure effort is."

The race to censure had become a competitive sport among Republicans. Beavers reported that after McCormick recently got a vote on *his* motion to censure Rashida Tlaib before Greene got a vote on *her* motion to censure Tlaib, Greene accused her fellow Georgian of "assault." McCormick said he merely shook Greene by the shoulders in a "friendly" gesture.

"THIS WILL GO DOWN AS . . . THE LEAST PRODUCTIVE CONGRESS SINCE THE Great Depression," Colorado Democrat Joe Neguse observed on Dec. 12 as the Rules Committee marked up House Republicans' year-end finale, a vote to formalize their impeachment inquiry into President Biden for imaginary crimes.

Bet Neguse almost certainly understates the case. While it's true, as the *Huffington Post*'s Jonathan Nicholson pointed out, that Congress got even less done in 1931, this was only because it didn't start its session that year until December. It seems probable that no Congress in American history spent so much time accomplishing so little as this one.

Among the 22 bills in 2023 that had become law by the time the House recessed for the year were landmark pieces of legislation such as H.R. 3672, "To Designate the Clinic of the Department of Veterans Affairs in Indian River, Michigan, as the 'Pfc. Justin T. Paton Department of Veterans Affairs Clinic.'" Also H.R. 5110, the "Protecting Hunting Heritage and Education Act," which authorized federal education funds "to purchase or use dangerous weapons" for instruction.

On Dec. 14, the House, exhausted from its labors, recessed for a three-week vacation, leaving behind a pile of urgent, unfinished business, including funds for Ukraine and to fortify the southern border. They would return with just eight legislative days to avoid the latest government shutdown—on which they had made no progress.

"It's been an up-and-down year," majority leader Steve Scalise said in a year-end news conference. (He was half right.) "I know for those of you in the press, there's never been a week where it was boring for you." (This was true.) "Next year is going to be just as busy," he went on. (That shouldn't be hard.) He acknowledged that "there's talk about how hard it's been," but he blamed the Democratic Senate for the inaction.

Nice try. This Senate, with a similar majority, had been highly productive in the last Congress. And Congress, even under divided government, had routinely found ways to function—until this gang took over the House.

The final week was typical. In the Senate, Democrats and Republicans feverishly tried to negotiate a deal on Ukraine and the border. Senate majority leader Chuck Schumer pleaded with Johnson to keep his chamber in session so that the emergency spending package could be passed before year-end. Johnson refused—prompting Senate Republican leader Mitch McConnell to say it would be "impossible" to pass the desperately needed bill.

Likewise, the House scheduled votes in its final week on two competing bills that would have reauthorized the FISA national security surveillance program. Johnson, who, as *Punchbowl News* noted, had "proven to be unwilling or unable to make tough decisions," declined to pick one bill over the other. So the House Republican Caucus devolved on the eve of the vote into yet another round of bickering, with Ohio's Warren Davidson accusing Intelligence Committee chairman Mike Turner of "fucking lying."

Once again paralyzed, House GOP leaders yanked both bills from consideration on the floor. Instead, they moved on to the Duck Stamp Modernization Act of 2023—no doubt a matter of great importance to waterfowl hunters.

The dysfunction showed every sign that it would continue in the new year. The House Freedom Caucus, whose members routinely derailed proceedings in the House in 2023, elected as their new leader Virginia's Bob Good, one of the most doctrinaire members of the caucus and one of the eight Republicans who had ousted McCarthy. Davidson, in a letter to colleagues obtained by *Axios*'s Juliegrace Brufke, alluded to Good's bomb-throwing tendencies and asked that the group "prayerfully consider electing someone else." They went with the legislative terrorist anyway.

As a holiday gift, Freedom Caucus members tried to lob one more bomb on the final day of the session. They were furious that their various attempts to ignite culture wars over abortion policy and LGBTQ rights had been stripped from the annual National Defense Authorization Act. So Freedom Caucus member Chip Roy and 22 other Republicans delayed its passage by forcing a vote on a motion to adjourn. The bill passed anyway—as usual, with mostly Democratic votes.

AFTER A YEAR OF FRATRICIDE AND FAILURE, THE HOUSE REPUBLICAN MAJORITY took four weeks off for the holidays to cool their tempers, gather their wits, regroup, and come up with a better plan for the second session of the 118th Congress.

Yet within 24 hours of their return to Washington in January 2024, they had already collapsed into their all-too-familiar dysfunction.

Right-wingers in the House, furious that during the break Mike Johnson had struck a spending deal with Democrats that was almost identical to the one their former speaker, Kevin McCarthy, had struck, made noises about ousting the new speaker, too. In the very first vote of the year (not counting a sparsely attended quorum call the night before), these far-right zealots protested by blocking the House from starting debate on three bills GOP leaders had brought to the floor. Thirteen of them joined Democrats to defeat the rule for debating a trio of Republican bills on labor standards, electric vehicles, and legal settlements. After this day 1 pratfall, Republican leaders called off the rest of the day's votes.

The People's House was back in session, and still thoroughly out of order.

Recall that in the 20 years before this crop of Republicans took control of Congress in 2023, the House hadn't experienced this particular type of parliamentary paralysis—defeating the rule that allows floor debate to begin—a single time. This was now the fifth time it had happened under the current GOP majority, in addition to the several other times GOP leaders pulled legislation from the floor in the face of certain defeat.

After Johnson reached his spending deal with Senate majority leader Chuck Schumer, the Freedom Caucus called it a "total failure." The group's new chairman, Bob Good, called it "another loss for America," adding, "At some point, having the House majority has to matter." Chip Roy, one of the group's more voluble members, threatened a "motion to vacate" Johnson's speakership. "I'm leaving it on the table," he said on a podcast.

Just a couple of months after Johnson was unanimously elected speaker by the caucus, one "well-plugged-in House Republican" who is not a Freedom Caucus loon gave this murderous blind quote to *Punchbowl*

News: "Significant concerns growing about Mike's ability to jump to this level and deliver conservative wins. Growing feeling that he's in way, way over his head . . . Mike is struggling to grow into the job and is just getting rolled even more than McCarthy did."

Hardliners blasted Johnson at the welcome-back meeting of the House Republican Caucus. Warren Davidson of Ohio, leaving the session, accused Johnson of "surrender" and spouting "drivel." Asked whether Johnson should be fired as speaker, Davidson replied: "He should never have been hired." He later called his vote for Johnson "one of the worst votes I've cast."

The first-day-back debacle set a new record for legislative incompetence. "No words," Arkansas Republican Steve Womack, leaving the chamber after the latest failed vote, told *Axios*'s Andrew Solender.

House Republicans immediately resumed their now-familiar infighting. "If you are a Republican member who constantly votes against the rule, who says Republicans haven't done anything this Congress, then perhaps you ought to look in a mirror and you will see the answer," Greg Murphy, of North Carolina, posted on X.

Senate Republicans watched their House brethren with pity and dismay. "They are going to have to figure out how to get their work done over there," John Thune, the number-two Senate GOP leader, told CNN's Lauren Fox, "because at some point, we're going to have to fund the government."

By early February 2024, Johnson had been speaker barely more than 100 days, but he had already accomplished the impossible: He made McCarthy look like a legislative genius. In just three months Johnson amassed a record of failure and dysfunction that his predecessor had labored for nine months to achieve. And, arguably, McCarthy never managed to match the level of combined incompetence and destructiveness that Johnson attained.

In the space of just three days in February, Johnson:

Killed a bipartisan border security bill, the toughest in decades, that he himself had demanded and senators had painstakingly negotiated.

Killed off funds to help Ukraine defend itself against Vladimir Putin's invasion.

Tried to pass military aid to Israel but watched it go down to defeat on the House floor.

Put the impeachment of Mayorkas on the House floor for a vote, and failed.

The House, which had begun its workweek on a Monday evening and ended it on Wednesday morning, left town with just four working days before the next deadline to keep the government from shutting down on March 1. Deadlines to reauthorize the Federal Aviation Administration and the Foreign International Surveillance Act came shortly thereafter. And lawmakers had made no discernible progress on any of this.

"It's hard to sit there and see it," Womack told CNN's Melanie Zanona. "It's tough. We're in a difficult spot right now."

Johnson tried to be philosophical after the twin failures of Israel aid and the Mayorkas impeachment on the House floor. "Democracy is messy," he told reporters, and "we're governing here—sometimes it's messy," and "you're seeing the messy sausage making," and "the process is messy sometimes."

The rookie speaker blamed Biden. He blamed Chuck Schumer. He blamed House Democrats. He blamed it on "the body itself and the place where we've come in this country." He blamed everybody and everything, in short, but himself. "I don't think that this is a reflection on the leader," Johnson said.

As if things weren't "messy" enough, Ohio Republican Mike Turner, chairman of the House Intelligence Committee, decided this would be a good time to spark a panic about a Russian nuclear attack. He issued an alarming public warning about a "serious national security threat" that turned out to be about a Russian nuclear weapon in space. In the frenzy that followed, the White House and leaders of the Senate Intelligence committee reassured the public that there was no threat to Earth and no cause for panic.

Meanwhile, Senate Republican leader McConnell, who had supported the border security legislation, formally attributed its failure to Johnson. "It's been made pretty clear to us by the speaker that it will not become law," he said.

And Johnson had no backup plan after killing the border security deal. Leaving a GOP caucus meeting, Dan Crenshaw, of Texas, told a group of us that it's "unacceptable" to do nothing about the border. Of GOP leadership, he said: "I just wish they . . . had a plan."

Johnson was barely coherent in explaining why he had just killed the border security bill he had been demanding. For years, he had been urging precisely such action. In February 2023, Johnson shared his view that "our immigration system is broken. Reforming that system is a job for Congress." He used exactly those same words in February 2021, and words very much like them at various points going back to 2018. He urged Biden to work with Republicans on "substantive legislation" on the border, and he said it was imperative that Congress "correct the longstanding loopholes that have encouraged illegal immigration and led to the crisis we face today."

"We have a catastrophe at our border," he said after winning the speakership in October. "Inaction is unacceptable, and we must come together and address the broken border." He felt so strongly about this that he insisted in October that border legislation must be enacted before he would allow emergency military aid to Ukraine to go through the House. "I explained that supplemental Ukraine funding is dependent upon enactment of transformative change to our nation's border security laws," he wrote after a White House meeting. He told House Republicans in a private meeting that the demand for border legislation would be their "hill to die on."

Other House Republicans had said much the same. Majority Leader Scalise argued: "This is a broken system that needs to be fixed. It takes congressional action. You need to change the law."

Some Senate Republicans, led by James Lankford, of Oklahoma, did exactly that, negotiating a border security compromise with Democrats and the White House. But then Donald Trump panned the very idea of legislation, saying "a border deal now would be another gift to the radical left Democrats."

Suddenly Johnson forgot everything he had previously said about border legislation. In an about-face, he decided Biden had "ample authority" without congressional action. But he didn't stop there. He went to the House floor and, in his first speech since accepting the gavel in October, he ridiculed the "so-called deal" sight unseen ("I'm working off of reports. I haven't seen the text") as "madness" and a "surrender."

The speech was a splendid heap of contradiction. On the one hand, he sounded alarms about an "open border" and a "soft invasion" by "military-age single men" from "terrorist regimes," "coming into our country to do only God knows what." On the other, he proposed to do absolutely nothing about it, saying Biden has "all the tools and the executive authority necessary."

Johnson had been right the first time. As the *Washington Post*'s Catherine Rampell described, Biden had taken more executive actions than Trump did on immigration; many of Trump's border actions were struck down in court, including by Trump-appointed judges; and other policies— such as to end catch-and-release—couldn't be implemented because Congress hadn't provided the funds.

Confusingly, Johnson still asserted, in his Jan. 31 speech on the floor, that legislation with "transformational policy changes" was still needed. But he was certain that the bipartisan Senate deal, which he hadn't seen, wasn't it. Yet even as he said that no immigration legislation was needed unless it was "transformational," Johnson brought four decidedly non-transformational immigration bills to the floor that week that mostly rehashed existing law.

"I think I need to go to the Capitol Physician and see if I can get a neck brace, because I have whiplash following the logic of some of my Republican friends," Democrat McGovern said during the floor debate. "We heard all year that we need to pass a bill in order to fix the immigration crisis at the border, and then . . . we're told we don't need a bill, we don't need a law. And then here we are today dealing with four more bills."

But this was the new standard. The hysteria about a crisis on the border is matched only by a determination to do nothing about it. Better to have an issue for the 2024 campaign than to solve the problem. It turned out House Republicans weren't actually looking for a solution to the fentanyl epidemic, MS-13 gangs, human trafficking, and illegal border crossings. They were looking for a campaign issue.

AT A JAN. 29 NEWS CONFERENCE, HOUSE REPUBLICANS INVOKED THE "CRISIS" on the border no fewer than 21 times and the "invasion" at least eight times. A separate news conference by Republican leaders brought a dozen more mentions of a crisis—an "unmitigated" and "historic" crisis, the "most pressing" in history. A Jan. 30 House Judiciary subcommittee hearing on the "southern border crisis" produced 19 more mentions of a crisis, and a whopping 113 mentions of an invasion.

"We are here to address an ongoing crisis," said Michael Burgess, of Texas, on the floor. "The word crisis has been a hard one for my friends on the other side to absorb . . . If this doesn't sound like a crisis to you, I don't know what would."

Responded McGovern: "He thinks this is Beetlejuice: If they say 'crisis' three times, the crisis goes away." To Republicans, he added: "Shame on you for ginning up all this hate and all this vitriol and not wanting to be part of the solution."

IN LATE FEBRUARY, HOUSE REPUBLICANS LOST THE CLOSELY WATCHED SPECIAL congressional election in New York to replace Santos. As the results came in, longtime Republican pollster Frank Luntz warned them that the result was "a rejection of House Republican chaos" and of a House majority that "gave voters nothing to vote for."

"Tonight is the final wakeup call for the @HouseGOP," he posted on X. "If they ignore or attempt to explain away why they lost, they will lose in November as well."

The next morning, House Republicans attempted to explain away the loss.

Walking out of a House Republican caucus meeting in the Capitol basement, Max Miller, of Ohio, explained to us that New York City, a sliver of which is in the district, is "a liberal cesspool"—and at the same time argued that the vanquished Republican "should have embraced Trump."

Marjorie Taylor Greene attributed it to "a bunch of stupid decisions" by a "bad campaign."

"Snow played a factor," offered Byron Donalds.

New York's Marc Molinaro, wearing a cheerful tie with an ice-cream-cone pattern, rationalized it by saying "special elections suck."

Surely it had absolutely nothing to do with the fact that House Republicans, after 14 months in the majority, had produced nothing but mayhem. To judge from House GOP leaders' message at their post-election press conference, the only thing they had to do differently was to call Joe Biden senile more often.

Caucus chairwoman Stefanik led off with her view that the president's "deteriorating mental state" left him "mentally unfit" to serve.

Majority whip Emmer concurred that Biden was "unfit" and had "zero business occupying the Oval Office."

To emphasize the point, they invited to the microphone the "candy-man," Ronny Jackson. "We need a cognitive test," the doctor ordered.

They certainly did.

And Speaker Mike Johnson, leaning as the others did on the medical expertise of special counsel Robert Hur, a Republican lawyer, opined: "A man too incapable of being held accountable for mishandling classified information is certainly unfit for the Oval Office."

But if there was anybody in public life whose actions scream out for the Montreal Cognitive Assessment, it was Johnson. A couple of weeks earlier, the Louisiana Republican got Israel and Iran mixed up in a *Meet the Press* appearance. Now he seemed to be forgetting what he had done just the previous week.

On Feb. 12, he issued a statement rejecting out of hand an emergency foreign aid package that was sailing through the Senate en route to passage by an overwhelming bipartisan vote of 70–29. "House Republicans were crystal clear from the very beginning of discussions that any so-called national security supplemental legislation must recognize that national security begins at our own border," he wrote.

Apparently, he just plum forgot that he was the one who, a week earlier, had killed a bipartisan border security bill—the toughest in a generation—that he had originally demanded but which he now called "dead on arrival."

If Johnson had not taken leave of his mental faculties, the alternative was worse: He was deliberately and knowingly sabotaging the functioning of the U.S. government.

He told Republicans on Feb. 14 that there was "no rush" to get military aid to Ukraine as it struggled to hold off Russian invaders and proposed discussing the legislation at the House GOP retreat—a month in the future.

It wasn't as though he had anything better to do. GOP leaders scheduled a vote on a bill, desired by New York Republicans, to expand deductions for state and local taxes. But 18 Republicans blocked it from being taken up for debate. For those who lost count, it was the sixth time during this Congress that a "rule" for debate had failed.

The majority also punted on plans to renew FISA, because of more GOP infighting; with hardliners howling about the Deep State spying on ordinary Americans, Republican leaders pulled the bill from the floor, canceled votes, and left for recess a day early.

At a news conference, PBS's Lisa Desjardins asked Johnson pointedly about his plans for border security and Ukraine: "Are you actually going to do nothing?"

Replied the speaker: "We are not going to be forced into action by the Senate." Nor, apparently, by anything else.

Johnson's growing trail of legislative destruction had already led to some dire consequences in the real world. As the *Washington Post*'s Nick Miroff first reported, the killing of the border security bill, which would have sent $6 billion in emergency funding for Immigration and Customs Enforcement (ICE), had forced ICE to prepare plans to release thousands of migrants from detention in order to cover a budget shortfall.

The consequences of the collapse of Ukraine aid were potentially worse. Writing in *The Hill*, British foreign secretary and former prime minister David Cameron thanked the Senate for acting and pleaded with House Republicans blocking the aid. "I believe our joint history shows the folly of giving in to tyrants in Europe who believe in redrawing boundaries by force," he wrote. "I do not want us to show the weakness displayed against Hitler in the 1930s. He came back for more, costing us far more lives to stop his aggression."

Asked about Cameron's words by Britain's Sky News, Marjorie Taylor Greene replied: "David Cameron needs to worry about his own country, and frankly he can kiss my ass."

In that, Congresswoman Jewish Space Lasers had an ally in Donald Trump, who had just threatened anew to blow up NATO if he was elected president in 2024 and said that he would not protect allies attacked by Russia if they hadn't spent more for their own defense. Instead, he would "encourage [Russia] to do whatever the hell they want."

Twenty-two Senate Republicans, including McConnell, defied Trump and stood by Ukraine. "Why am I so focused on this vote?" Thom Tillis, a North Carolina Republican and one of the honorable 22, asked on the Senate floor. "Because I don't want to be on the pages of history that we will regret if we walk away. You will see the alliance that is supporting Ukraine crumble. You will ultimately see China become emboldened, and I am not going to be on that page of history."

Another of the brave 22, Jerry Moran, of Kansas, urged his colleagues not to undo in a moment all that had been built, at a great cost in blood and treasure, in the years after World War II. "We owe something to those who served," he said. "We owe them to live up to our responsibility to preserve what they have defended and protected and made available to me, to Americans today."

Invoking Trump's nativist phrase, Moran went on: "I believe in America First. But, unfortunately, America First means we have to engage in the world. Taking a sober view of history, there should be no doubt of the importance of the outcome in Ukraine, the Middle East, in China, in the South Pacific, and what it means to the United States."

Cutting and running in Ukraine, abandoning an ally to Vladimir Putin's depredations, would, as Senator Angus King, a Maine independent, memorably put it, "echo throughout the history of this country and the history of the world for generations" as surely as the appeasement of Hitler had in 1938.

Opponents answered with more Russian propaganda. Alabama senator Tommy Tuberville, echoing Putin, claimed that "Russia is open to a peace agreement, while it is the DC warmongers who want to prolong this war." He also claimed that Ukraine "can't win" against Russia.

On the Senate floor, Ohio's J. D. Vance mixed his isolationism with a vulgar appeal to ethnonationalism. "Not a single country—not even the U.S.—within the NATO alliance has birthrates at replacement levels. We don't have enough families and children to continue as a nation and yet we're talking about problems 6,000 miles away."

In late February, Johnson could stall no longer. The federal government had been running on autopilot since Oct. 1 because of Congress's failure to pass spending bills. The latest of three short-term funding patches to keep the government running would expire at the start of March, and the government would shut down.

The House Freedom Caucus, as usual, was spoiling for a shutdown, demanding that Johnson fight for all the poison pills on abortion, race, and LGBTQ issues they had injected into the appropriations bills.

Chip Roy blasted Johnson's leadership on social media. "NO PLAN TO FIGHT," he protested, complaining that "GOP leaders are poised to ... INCREASE spending" with no "policy wins." He accused Republican leaders of squandering "a year of hard-fought negotiating" on spending. "We are told 'we can't risk shutdown,' but must eat HIGHER spending than Pelosi & temper expectations on so-called policy riders." Condemning the "capitulation," Roy charged: "Republicans are putting out the same tired excuses that we've been telling our voters for decades ... If we want to achieve something different, we have to do something different. Pick a fight and win it."

Roy was right about Johnson's intentions. House GOP leadership, surrendering to the inevitable, agreed to a massive, $460 billion spending package that averted a partial government shutdown. It rolled six of the 12 annual spending bills into one legislative package with more than 600 pages of earmarks; the other six would follow in a second tranche two weeks later.

It was precisely what House Republicans had spent the last year swearing they would not pass. The bill spent more money than Republicans had said they would spend, and they were stripped of virtually all the poison pills on culture-war issues that Republicans had fought for a year to include.

The hardliners, 83 of whom opposed the bill, were infuriated. "The fact of the matter is all of this is a shell game," Roy hollered on the House floor. "Republicans will go around and talk about how they scored major wins, how they somehow delivered for the American people. The fact of the matter is we did no such thing . . . The truth of the matter is, we didn't get any of the major wins that we worked all last year to get."

This was true enough. House Republicans had spent 15 months on threats, showdowns, drama, infighting, and a coup—and yet they had managed to achieve precisely nothing.

The right-wingers' anger boiled over two weeks later, when Johnson brought the second spending bill to the floor. On March 22, the House passed it, avoiding a partial government shutdown that would have occurred the next day and finally approving spending for fiscal year 2024, which was already half over. But this time, a majority of Republicans, 112–101, voted against the bill, which passed only because Democrats overwhelmingly approved it, 185–22.

In protest, Marjorie Taylor Greene filed a motion to vacate the chair. "This is a betrayal of the American people," Greene, mobbed by reporters on the Capitol steps, said of the latest spending bill. "This is a betrayal of Republican voters." She said the House needed a "new speaker of the House that will stand with Republicans and our Republican majority instead of standing with the Democrats."

It wasn't an immediate crisis. Greene hadn't filed the motion as a "privileged" resolution, so there was no deadline to hold a vote. And most Republicans, disinclined to humiliate themselves with another weeks-long search for a leader, tended to agree with New York Republican Mike Lawler's assessment of Greene's gambit: "Idiotic."

Lawmakers went home for a two-week recess, but Greene returned without any diminution of her belligerence. When the House came back into session, Republicans were greeted by a five-page "Dear Colleague" letter from Greene on April 9, explaining why they had no choice but to oust Johnson. "I will not tolerate our elected Republican Speaker Mike Johnson serving the Democrats and the Biden administration and helping them achieve their policies that are destroying our country."

And Johnson had a new problem. He had stalled for months on a foreign aid package for Ukraine and Israel (Biden had asked for the emergency funds way back on Oct. 20, and a demoralized Ukraine was short on ammunition), and now some Republicans were preparing to sign a "discharge petition" to force a vote. That would be a major rebuke to Johnson and further weaken his leadership. But if he called a vote, it would increase calls to vacate the chair.

Still, Johnson stalled. The announcement from the Rules Committee about what legislation would be taken up the week of April 15 showed how frivolous the House had become. As Ukraine ran out of bullets, the House would take up six bills, all of them about home appliances, with names such as the "Liberty in Laundry Act" and the "Refrigerator Freedom Act."

Finally, having exhausted all other possibilities, Johnson did the right thing. He called for a vote (actually, a series of votes) on foreign aid. "We have terrorists and tyrants and terrible leaders around the world like Putin and Xi and in Iran, and they're watching to see if America will stand up for its allies and our interests around the globe—and we will," he said. Later, he added: "To put it bluntly, I would rather send bullets to Ukraine than American boys. My son is going to begin in the Naval Academy this fall. This is a live-fire exercise for me as it is so many American families. This is not a game, this is not a joke."

It had taken him five months, but finally Johnson showed some leadership. Once Johnson allowed the House to work its will, aid to Ukraine sailed to passage, 311–112, on April 20.

Predictably, the far-right saboteurs reacted badly. One hundred twelve Republicans, again a majority of the caucus, voted against the Ukraine funds. The day after Johnson's announcement that he would let the House vote on Ukraine aid, Kentucky's Tom Massie told a gathering of the House Republican caucus that he would join Greene's motion to vacate. His colleagues booed. "It's a clusterfuck," one Republican told *Axios*'s Juliegrace Brufke. "We are screwed," said another.

Ukraine was saved, for the moment, but House Republicans were back in their familiar place of recriminations, sniping, and paralysis. Over in the Senate, North Carolina Republican Thom Tillis told CNN's Manu Raju and others: "I think these people need to grow up."

Massie and Greene alone had the ability to oust Johnson if Democrats didn't bail him out, because Republicans were down to just a one-seat majority. By now, Santos had been expelled, the disaffected McCarthy and Buck had resigned before their terms ended, and Gallagher, also abused by his extremist colleagues, was about to do the same.

The best thing Johnson had going for him? A near certainty that nobody else could do the job either. "You have to have a solution," Troy Nehls of Texas told reporters. "So who? Who we gonna put in there now? If it's not him, then who? Who can manage this conference? There isn't anybody in that room I just walked out of that can manage this conference."

He was right, of course. It didn't matter who held the title of "speaker." These guys were utterly ungovernable.

Democratic leaders, rather than watch Republicans shut the House down for another 22 days while they searched for yet another speaker, decided to save Republicans from themselves. Minority leader Hakeem Jeffries and his lieutenants announced on April 30 that they would block Greene's motion to vacate—a reward for Johnson's help passing Ukraine funds and a rebuke of the "pro-Putin Republican obstruction" of Greene and her comrades.

On May 8, Greene forced a vote on evicting Johnson, and 11 of the usual Republican suspects—including Biggs, Gosar, Roy, Spartz, and Crane—supported the move. That would have been more than enough to oust Johnson, but 163 Democrats voted to table Greene's attempt, keeping Johnson in the speakership. The House would remain in business—despite the best efforts of its ungovernable majority.

Part III

DISUNION

Chapter 10

"My Opinion of a White Nationalist, If Someone Wants to Call Them White Nationalist, to Me, Is an American"

THE CONSTANT FAILURES OF THE HOUSE REPUBLICANS TO GOVERN WERE, in one sense, comical. They were, truly, the gang that couldn't shoot straight. As a legislative body, they failed to enact any meaningful legislation, their zany policy riders never made their way into law, and they managed to do the most basic task of keeping the government funded only after months of squabbling and screaming.

But that is only part of the story. For while they failed to legislate, they used their majority powers quite effectively to sow division. They used those powers—control of the House floor, control of committees, the subpoena power—to legitimize white nationalism and to demonize migrants. They abused the most solemn power of the legislative branch by devoting 15 months to an ill-fated attempt to find something—anything— they could use to impeach Joe Biden. They used the House floor as a vehicle to settle scores, setting off an extraordinary cycle of censure and recriminations. They used their majority powers to give voice to Russian propaganda and to legitimize ludicrous conspiracy theories about an imagined Deep State operating within the federal government. And they used those same powers to assault the rule of law, attacking the FBI and the courts and sabotaging federal and local prosecutors while glorifying those who attacked the Capitol on Jan. 6, 2021—all in the cause of aiding the presidential prospects of Donald Trump.

They may have failed to pass laws, but they did an impressive job of spreading enmity and distrust. Let's start with the triumph of white nationalism under the House GOP majority.

IN THE EARLY 20TH CENTURY, DURING THE JIM CROW ERA, WHITE SUPREM-acists succeeded in naming several military bases across the South in honor of Confederate generals who had taken up arms against the United States.

A century later, a federal base-renaming commission proposed new names for the bases, which had been named for slavery's defenders as an overt reassertion of white power after the failure of Reconstruction.

But House Republicans stood with the Confederates.

Bob Good, a Virginia Republican who had been on the staff of the Jerry Falwell–founded Liberty University before coming to Congress, introduced an amendment to the National Defense Authorization Act (NDAA) to defund the base-renaming commission so that there could be no change to "the naming of items of the Department of Defense that commemorate the Confederate States of America."

"The intent of that commission was to try to rewrite our nation's history," Good said on the floor. He called for Congress to "fight these reckless efforts to destroy our country" and to "preserve our history and our Founders and our principles of our nation." Stripping the traitors' names from military bases would be a "tragedy," Good judged.

Adam Smith, the top Democrat on the Armed Services Committee, pointed out that "all of these bases that are named for our 'history,' as you describe it, are monuments to white supremacy." Forcing Black troops, and anyone who doesn't support white supremacy, to serve on Confederate-named bases "is the kind of thing that undermines good order and discipline in the military."

But in the vote on the amendment, 177 Republicans—80 percent of the caucus—stood with the Confederates. Good had so much fun with that vote that he and Georgia Republican Andrew Clyde made similar stands for Confederates in the energy and military construction spending bills.

If there were some doubt as to their motives, Arizona Republican Eli Crane had helped to spell them out earlier in the NDAA debate, in what may have been a Freudian slip on the House floor. Crane proposed an amendment that sought to limit the consideration of race in military training, education, and the like. "The military was never intended to be inclusive," he argued.

Ohio Democrat Joyce Beatty, who is Black, responded that "we take this very seriously and we take it very personally," recalling the time when "Black officers . . . were not allowed to serve."

Crane responded: "My amendment has nothing to do with whether or not colored people or Black people or anybody can serve."

Colored people? Beatty, outraged, called for "unanimous consent to take down the words . . . referring to me or any of my colleagues as 'colored people.'" Crane, after offering to amend his statement to "people of color," consented to the rebuke. He later issued a statement saying he had misspoken.

Yet it was hard not to see racial animus in the sheer number of poison pills Republicans added, or tried to add, to the NDAA—amendment after amendment eliminating any offices and positions that promote "diversity, equity and inclusion" (DEI), blocking the military from requiring any training on "race-based concepts," prohibiting anything that could even loosely qualify as "critical race theory." During the debate, Gaetz spoke up to attack the military for talking to the troops about the dangers of ideological extremism. He called it a "white supremacy snipe hunt"—as if no such thing as a white supremacist thought existed.

Nor was the NDAA an outlier. Republicans added provisions to various appropriations bills blocking funds from going to anything that might qualify as promoting "racial equity," critical race theory, DEI, or affirmative action. They added a provision excluding undocumented immigrants from census counts. Another one blocked funds for the Smithsonian Institution's National Museum of the American Latino.

Texas Republican Lance Gooden caused a furor with his allegation on Fox News in February that California Democrat Judy Chu should not have a security clearance because of her Chinese ancestry. "I question either her loyalty or her competence," he said of the American-born congresswoman, hinting that she was compromised because of alleged ties to Chinese communists. After a bipartisan outcry, Gooden repeated the slander, tweeting: "It's not 'xenophobic' to question where her loyalty lies."

California Republican Young Kim, who is Korean American, tried to intervene, holding a private meeting with Gooden. But when word of the meeting got out, Gooden alleged that Kim "has betrayed the trust of our visit."

During a hearing of the Armed Services Committee, chairman Mike Rogers of Alabama (who had joined Good on the House floor in arguing to protect Confederate base names) brought up an amendment by Democrat Ruben Gallego of Arizona, the son of Latino immigrants. Rogers called him "Rep. uh, Galeyo," then "Rep. Galaguh—Galeyo." Looking down the dais at Gallego, Rogers laughed. "Hey. He's definitely not from Alabama," the chairman said.

The Republican Conference chairwoman, Elise Stefanik, thought it advisable to hold a $150,000 fundraiser for the party in Buffalo, New York, with Carl Paladino. Paladino, a former candidate for Congress, was known for his sentiment, expressed in 2016, that Michelle Obama should be "let loose in the outback of Zimbabwe where she lives comfortably in a cave with Maxie, the gorilla." Among many such remarks, Paladino also suggested that Attorney General Merrick Garland "probably should be executed" and said that Hitler was "the kind of leader we need today."

Marjorie Taylor Greene is never one to be outdone in the provocation department. In 2022, she spoke at the white nationalist America First Political Action Conference, run by the white supremacist Nick Fuentes. Arizona's Paul Gosar addressed the same event the year before. McConnell condemned both of them, saying, "There's no place in the Republican Party for white supremacists or antisemitism."

Yet Greene took umbrage when, she said, outspoken New York Democrat Jamaal Bowman, who is Black, called her a white supremacist. She said it was the same as "calling a person of color the n-word."

She further said, at a news conference, that Bowman's "physical mannerisms are aggressive" and "I feel threatened by him." Explaining her angry-Black-man accusation, she said Bowman "has a history of aggression, not just toward others but toward me in particular and I'm very concerned about it."

Somebody call the gazpacho police!

Yet that was mild compared to the treatment given to Minnesota Democrat Ilhan Omar, who is both Black and a Muslim.

Just a few weeks after taking control of the House, GOP leaders declared an emergency.

Russia's invasion of Ukraine?

Inflation?

Violent crime?

Well, no. Their emergency was the need to kick Omar off the House Foreign Affairs Committee, lickety-split.

So House Republicans overrode the rule they had voted in just a couple of weeks earlier with great fanfare—that bills must be introduced 72 hours before receiving a vote. Apparently, having the Minnesota Democrat continue to serve on the panel for even one more day would be ruinous.

Steve Scalise, the majority leader, cited "concerns to national security" in claiming it "would create major problems if she were on the Foreign Affairs Committee" with "access to classified, sensitive information."

Omar had been hearing the same for years. In 2021, Lauren Boebert delighted MAGA crowds with jokes about Capitol police fearing Omar would blow up an elevator in the Capitol ("And I said, well, she doesn't have a backpack, we should be fine").

In a refreshing moment of candor, Republicans on the House Rules Committee admitted that there was no legitimate justification for their Omar undertaking. "This is raw politics. That's what this is," acknowledged Chip Roy of Texas.

Tom Massie, of Kentucky, concurred: "It's a partisan exercise."

Added Ralph Norman, of South Carolina: "The partisanship is real and I'm glad."

This was revenge, pure and simple. Two years before, Democrats had votes to remove Greene and Gosar from committees after both shared social media fantasies about killing Democratic colleagues; Greene had, among other things, "liked" a comment recommending a bullet to the head of then-speaker Pelosi, and Gosar had made a cartoon video in which he killed Alexandria Ocasio-Cortez. Republicans had already reinstated both to committees upon taking over.

Omar hadn't threatened violence against anyone. She had made anti-semitic remarks a few years earlier and, after an outcry from Democrats and Republicans alike, she apologized unequivocally—a detail omitted from the resolution denouncing her. Votes to remove Greene and Gosar were bipartisan; the vote to oust Omar was strictly partisan.

A few Republicans had qualms about what they were doing. "This is not my resolution; I didn't draft it," said Michael Guest of Mississippi, who, as chairman of the Ethics Committee, had the task of leading the debate on the House floor.

The naked vengeance inspired a rare moment of conscience for one House Republican. "We cannot have these kangaroo courts—it's unacceptable," said Victoria Spartz of Indiana.

"Speaker McCarthy needs to stop 'bread and circuses' in Congress and start governing for a change," Spartz said in a statement objecting to the "charade" of kicking members off their committees.

Emperor McCarthy grinned when Spartz's words were read to him. Asked how he would respond, he replied, "Not at all."

A week later, Spartz's conscientious objection was over. She announced that she would vote to remove Ilhan Omar from the Foreign Affairs Committee after all.

Maybe they should have heeded their consciences, for the debate was ugly. After Guest quickly ran out of speakers (only six enlisted), he spent much of the debate reserving his time and leaving the Democrats' allegations unrebutted. And they were lacerating:

"This is the very weaponization of antisemitism that I as a Jewish person find repulsive, dangerous and shameful," said Minnesota Democrat Dean Phillips.

New York's Alexandria Ocasio-Cortez, bouncing up and down with fury, accused Republicans of "racism and incitement of violence against women of color in this body."

Missouri Democrat Cori Bush saw a "blatantly Islamophobic and racist attack on Congresswoman Omar."

California Democrat Eric Swalwell shouted for Republicans to "look in your own damn mirror" for antisemitism.

"Unbelievable bigotry. Shame on you!" scolded Wisconsin Democrat Mark Pocan.

Michigan Democrat Rashida Tlaib, breaking into tears, said Republicans had turned "Congress into a place of fearmongering hate."

And Guest kept saying, "I reserve."

Omar stood with a poster showing her as a nine-year-old Somali refugee who fled civil war. "There is this idea that you are suspect if you are an immigrant, or if you are from certain parts of the world, or a certain skin tone, or a Muslim," she said, angrily reminding her Republican assailants: "I am an American—an American who was sent here by her constituents to represent them in Congress."

She closed with defiance. "My leadership and voice will not be diminished if I am not on this committee for one term," she said. "So take your votes or not. I am here to stay."

The hugs and tears she shared on the floor with her colleagues—Black and white, Jewish, Christian, and Muslim—were a powerful rejoinder to the Republicans' reign of fear and loathing.

But that reign continued all the same. Not content with kicking Omar off her committee, Republicans later attempted to censure her over remarks that she didn't actually utter. Greene said her remarks were "treasonous." House majority whip Tom Emmer accused Omar of "a direct violation of her oath of office," saying "she should resign in disgrace."

Republicans were basing their case on a translation they found somewhere online of remarks Omar made in Somali, in which she purportedly said she and other Somali Americans are "Somalians first, Muslims second," and that the U.S. government "must follow our orders." But actual translations showed that Omar had said nothing like this—and Republicans quietly dropped the effort.

In July, the GOP majority went after another woman of color. This time, the task was to humiliate Washington Democrat Pramila Jayapal, who is Asian American, for calling Israel a "racist state." After dozens of her Democratic colleagues and House Democratic leaders denounced her statement, she issued an apology and clarified that "I do not believe the idea of Israel as a nation is racist."

Still, House Republicans, sensing a political opportunity, rushed to the floor with a resolution affirming that "the State of Israel is not a racist or apartheid state" and that "Congress rejects all forms of antisemitism and xenophobia." Both were noble sentiments (it's one thing to call the Netanyahu regime racist but entirely different to so brand the entire Jewish state), and the resolution passed by an overwhelming 412–9. Jayapal herself was among the ayes.

Only one lawmaker spoke on the floor against the resolution: the Palestinian American Tlaib. Unlike Jayapal and Omar, who showed contrition and sought conciliation after causing offense, Tlaib was an unrepentant antisemite, spreading dark conspiracy theories about global Jewish domination and other absurd falsehoods (she claimed on the House floor that Israel's president "has long advocated against interracial marriage," when in fact he had said nothing about race).

In November 2023, it was Tlaib's turn. Republicans led a successful effort to censure her for antisemitic statements. Unlike in the Omar and Jayapal cases, Tlaib deserved reproach. She had outrageously accused Biden of supporting the "genocide" of Palestinians, and she promoted the chant "From the river to the sea, Palestine will be free." The "river to the sea" proposition leaves only two possibilities for millions of Jews in Israel: exile or death—though Tlaib implausibly denied that she meant it as it is widely understood, as a call for the destruction of the Jewish state. Maryland Democrat Jamie Raskin, though leading the debate against censuring Tlaib, told the House, "The phrase 'from the river to the sea' is abhorrent to me, even with her published explanation of what she means by it."

Yet the Tlaib episode took a racist turn. Montana Republican Ryan Zinke, echoing Trump's threatened "Muslim ban," introduced legislation barring Palestinians from entering the United States and revoking visas issued to Palestinians since the week before the fighting in Gaza began.

Ohio Republican Max Miller, on Fox News, declared: "I don't even want to call it the Palestinian flag because they're not a state, they're a territory, that's about to probably get eviscerated and go away here shortly, as we're going to turn that into a parking lot."

Greene, who absurdly accused Tlaib of inciting an "insurrection," produced a 13-minute video rant in which she repeatedly referred to "Terrorist Tlaib," saying: "We have a terrorist, Rashida Tlaib, serving as a member of Congress."

And Florida Republican Brian Mast, speaking on the House floor, said he objected to "the idea of innocent Palestinian civilians," calling it equivalent to "the term 'innocent Nazi civilians' during World War II." Mast then doubled down, telling a group of us that "Nazi is a pretty damn good comparison."

Predictably, the debate over censuring Tlaib degenerated into sobs, heckling, fist shaking, and screaming.

Miller, who is Jewish, violently pounded the lectern: "Never again, dammit, means never again!"

New York Republican Mike Lawler alleged that Tlaib "believes Israel should be eradicated."

"It is a lie!" Bush called out, and she and Ohio Democrat Summer Lee continued heckling.

Bush, in her own remarks, ignored the speaker's gavel and, yelling between gasps for breath, said the censure is "not surprising because this place is where 1,700 members of Congress, this elected body, enslaved Black people!"

From the back of the chamber, Ohio Republican Warren Davidson shouted: "Show some respect for this place!"

Bowman bellowed at the Republicans that "maybe because of your lack of diversity you lack the cognitive and emotional ability to recognize diverse opinions when they speak truth to power!"

"Pull a fire alarm!" taunted Texas Republican Pat Fallon, referring to Bowman's misdemeanor guilty plea for triggering an alarm during a key vote in September.

Georgia Republican Rich McCormick, who introduced the censure resolution, acknowledged that there had been "a lot of screaming, a lot of accusations, you could say, on both sides." He assured the chamber that "I don't really care what race, religion, gender or orientation you are."

"Yes you do!" Bush heckled.

MANY REPUBLICANS BRISTLED AT BEING LABELED "WHITE NATIONALISTS." But then there were Republicans such as Tommy Tuberville in the Senate. "Do you believe they should allow white nationalists in the military?" a radio interviewer asked him in May.

"Well, they call them that," the senator replied. "I call them Americans."

Tuberville elaborated to reporters on Capitol Hill. "I look at a white nationalist as a Trump Republican," he explained.

In July, he told CNN's Kaitlan Collins that while he opposed racism, "my opinion of a white nationalist, if someone wants to call them white nationalist, to me, is an American."

Told that white nationalists are racists, Tuberville replied: "Well, that's your opinion."

The next day Tuberville continued saying that it was a matter of "opinion" whether white nationalists are racists, before finally conceding the point.

But he never changed his white nationalist stripes. When Donald Trump said that immigrants were "poisoning the blood of our country"— words taken from *Mein Kampf*—Tuberville told reporters that he was "mad." Why? Because Trump "wasn't tougher than that."

In the House, Arizona's Gosar regularly took a similar line. He dined with white nationalists, traveled with them, spoke at their conferences, defended them on social media, and promoted their racist themes. He promoted fringe websites that called the Holocaust a hoax, praised Hitler, and condemned "Jewish warmongers" in the U.S. government. He repeatedly promoted the work of the white supremacist Fuentes. Members of his staff also had ties to Fuentes.

But House Republican leaders, in their wisdom, gave Gosar a seat on the House Oversight Committee. And Gosar repaid their confidence in him—by using one of the very first hearings of the committee to promote white nationalism. At a hearing on border security, Gosar read aloud headlines suggesting that the U.S. government has surrendered the border to drug cartels. "What is the answer to this mess for Biden and the Democrats?" he asked. "More big brother? More control? Even changing our culture?"

"Changing our culture." That is the essence of the racist "Great Replacement" conspiracy theory: that the left is deliberately importing immigrants to replace white people and white culture.

Democrats on the committee had anticipated a blue streak of white nationalism at the hearing. At its start, they tweeted a message of good luck to all except Republican lawmakers "who are using today's hearing to amplify white nationalist conspiracy theories." The tweet linked to a list of previous expressions of "Great Replacement" sentiments by panel Republicans, including chairman James Comer of Kentucky (who said Democrats are encouraging illegal immigration as "part of their social equality campaign to fundamentally change America") and Pennsylvania's Scott Perry (who claimed that "we're replacing national-born Americans, native-born Americans to permanently transform the landscape of this very nation").

Republicans saw red after the Democrats' mention of white nationalism—"offensive" and "inflammatory" was the view of Wisconsin's Glenn Grothman—but then proceeded to validate the accusation.

Greene decried "the illegal invasion into our country," and Boebert agreed that "there's an invasion at our southern border."

Louisiana's Clay Higgins informed the committee who the "million gotaways"—migrants who avoided capture over the preceding two years—are: "stout young men . . . wearing camouflage, they're rolling hard, they've got mil spec radios, they're carrying backpacks, they work for the drug cartels."

Arizona's Andy Biggs determined that border patrol "stopped 216,000" more—all "young, single adult males in camo carrying backpacks."

The Customs and Border Protection officials testifying at the hearing played it straight. Yes, they were overwhelmed by the number of migrants. But the agency's John Modlin testified that the real cause was disinformation. Apprehended migrants, he said, primarily tell border agents that they heard the border "was open." Said Modlin: "All it takes is a few people to say a few words and it travels."

Now, where would migrants get the impression that the U.S. border is open? Hmm.

"My constituents are hit hard by the Biden open-border crisis," Gosar told the committee.

Alabama's Gary Palmer declared that Democrats "are sold out completely for an open border."

Michigan's Lisa McClain recited problems that have "arisen because of the open-border crisis."

And Comer himself purported to analyze Democrats' "defense of an open border."

If Republicans were really worried that there's a conspiracy afoot to replace white people, they might pause for a moment to consider what's causing the supposed "invasion" of the border: their own malicious falsehoods.

But House Republicans just couldn't quit these white nationalists.

A week after the House Oversight Committee hearing, on Feb. 15, 2023, the gunman who killed 10 Black people in a racist massacre at a Buffalo, New York, supermarket in May 2022 was sentenced to life in prison. The killer had subscribed to the racist "Great Replacement" conspiracy theory.

On the same day the killer was sentenced, the House Committee on Energy and Commerce marked the solemn occasion by holding a field hearing in Texas, where it hosted as one of its witnesses a proponent of the very same "Great Replacement" conspiracy theory.

The witness, National Border Patrol Council president Brandon Judd, had alleged on Fox News in 2022 that the Biden administration had opened the southern border (itself a falsehood) because "they're trying to change the demographics of the electorate" in order to "stay in power." That's "replacement" theory in a nutshell. Judd has a history with far-right anti-immigration groups, and he argued that governors should be "declaring an invasion" at the border. On Newsmax, Judd falsely said that Biden wanted "amnesty for all the adults who knowingly violated our laws." Judd also participated in the filming of a Western-themed ad in 2022 in which a Republican Senate candidate fired a gun at actors portraying Biden, Nancy Pelosi, and Democratic senator Mark Kelly of Arizona.

Republicans on the Commerce Committee chimed in with inflammatory language of their own. Georgia's Rick Allen announced that "our nation is being invaded" and "we are at war."

Judd did not disappoint, alleging that "Biden's open-border policies" have "made the securing of our border impossible." And he testified that "we are constantly seizing backpacks filled with fentanyl" from migrants illegally crossing the border.

In reality, the vast majority of fentanyl comes into the United States through legal border crossings, often brought by U.S. citizens. But it's so much scarier to conjure images of brown people smuggling opioid-laden backpacks.

"You look at 1.2 million gotaways," Judd said. "If every single one of them was carrying a backpack of 90 pounds of drugs, that's an awful lot of drugs." (He acknowledged that not all migrants carry 90 pounds of fentanyl, implying that most do.)

That wasn't remotely what was happening at the border. Yet Republicans continued to smuggle such white nationalist propaganda into their hearings.

At another hearing, of the Judiciary Committee, committee chairman Jim Jordan fanned hysteria about "Mexican smuggling cartels exploiting the open border to terrorize U.S. communities." Darrell Issa of California pronounced the "borders wide open," while Mike Johnson of Louisiana, at that point not yet speaker, warned: "If we do not have a border we do not have a nation." The Louisianan had earlier invoked the "Great Replacement" theory, suggesting in 2022 that Democrats were trying "to turn all the illegals into voters ... That's why the border's open."

Never mind that U.S. authorities apprehended 2.2 million migrants that year at the supposedly "open border."

The Judiciary Committee hearing featured as a witness a man who is part of the far-right "constitutional sheriff" movement. Constitutional sheriffs—an outgrowth of the white nationalist posse comitatus movement—claim they are above federal and state government and are the ultimate arbiters of the law. The nonprofit Arizona Center for Investigative Reporting found that the witness, Cochise County sheriff

Mark Dannels, spoke at a "constitutional sheriff" event and supports nullifying laws.

Next, it was the House Homeland Security Committee's turn for some extremism. Its chairman, Mark Green, a Tennessee Republican, had invoked the "Great Replacement" conspiracy theory, saying Homeland Security secretary Alejandro Mayorkas's "intent" was to "fundamentally change the population of the United States, and I believe to empower the Democrat [*sic*] Party in perpetuity."

Green's panel hosted as a witness Pinal County (Arizona) sheriff Mark Lamb—another "constitutional sheriff." Though eschewing the term, Lamb is the front man for one "constitutional sheriff" group, has spoken to a second, and also supports the bogus right of sheriffs to "nullify" federal law, the Arizona Center for Investigative Reporting noted. A booster of the "Stop the Steal" (he called the Jan. 6 rioters "very loving, Christian people") and anti-vax movements (he refused to enforce the stay-at-home orders of Arizona's Republican governor), he responded to the Black Lives Matter movement by creating a "Citizens Posse" of residents to be deputized at his pleasure.

A week before he came to Washington, Lamb spoke at a Second Amendment rally attended by Oath Keepers, Proud Boys, and other extremists. He teased a Senate run and took photos with a few Proud Boys. And there he was, just nine days later, at the witness table in the Homeland Security Committee's hearing room. Green hailed Lamb's "essential role in defending our nation's homeland."

This was one of the ways in which Republican lawmakers brought dangerous extremists into the mainstream. And in case all of this was too subtle, seven congressional immigration hardliners assembled in the House TV studio and alleged that Biden was running "narco-slavery support programs."

But the new majority wasn't actually doing anything about the border. The GOP border bill, which GOP leaders had promised to bring to the floor in their first two weeks, instead got bogged down in intraparty disagreements over attempts to block legal immigration, including from those seeking asylum. When the seven hardliners were asked about the endangered legislation, Iowa's Ashley Hinson acknowledged: "I'm not sure where negotiations stand."

Where they stood was this: Tony Gonzales of Texas, co-chair of the Republicans' Congressional Hispanic Conference, had complained that the GOP bill was ungodly. "We can't allow the Republican Party to be hijacked," Gonzales said in late January 2023. "Trying to ban legitimate asylum claims—one, it's not Christian, and two, to me, it's very anti-American. So a lot is at stake."

The bill's author, Chip Roy, retorted that the current system was what's "un-Christian-like" and that "I'm tired of Republicans using rhetoric that is actually not addressing the problem." Eventually, the bill cleared the chamber after a compromise—but it was still so extreme that it had no chance of becoming law.

In their "invasion" hysteria, Republicans even saw a threat posed by the rogue state to our north. The House Homeland Security Committee assembled a panel to probe "Biden's Growing Border Crisis: Death, Drugs and Destruction on the Northern Border."

"It's really a crisis," New York Republican Claudia Tenney informed the subcommittee holding the hearing.

Pennsylvania Republican Mike Kelly said that as a result of this "crisis at the northern border," we're "totally unprotected." Concerned that an "infestation" of immigrants (more white nationalist language) was "corrupting us," Kelly claimed: "If they were wearing the uniform of a foreign country we'd think we were being invaded."

O Canada! Who knew you were so menacing?

In truth, illegal immigration from Canada (typically by Mexican nationals who fly to Canada and then cross into the United States) had risen—but from the double digits to the triple digits. A much bigger problem was going the other way: people crossing illegally from the United States into Canada. (Biden and Prime Minister Justin Trudeau struck an agreement to address the matter.)

Republicans had a choice. They could build a 5,525-mile-long wall along the Canadian border. Or they could heed the suggestion New York Democrat Brian Higgins gave the panel. "We cannot characterize our northern border and our northern neighbor as hostile," he said. "We in North America are surrounded by fish and friends."

THE HOUSE COMMITTEE ON HOMELAND SECURITY, CREATED IN THE AFTER-math of the 9/11 attacks, had for two decades been a place where lawmakers often took pride in overcoming partisanship for the sake of national security. Then came the GOP takeover of the House. In his wisdom, McCarthy named his friend Marjorie Taylor Greene to the Homeland Security Committee—and, in doing so, ended any possibility that the committee could still perform its vital work of protecting the American people.

Thanks to McCarthy's surrender to the crazies in his ranks, extrem-ists with white nationalist ties such as Greene had gone from gadflies to positions of prominence. Greene raised prodigious funds, which her GOP colleagues gladly accepted, and to avoid being canceled by her on social media, they defended her indefensible behavior.

The Georgia Republican got right to work on the committee, using her elevated status to praise Jack Teixeira, the National Guardsman arrested as the suspected leaker of highly classified U.S. intelligence about Ukraine, China, and more. "Jake [*sic*] Teixeira is white, male, christian, and antiwar. That makes him an enemy to the Biden regime," Greene tweeted. "Ask yourself who is the real enemy? A young low level national guardsmen? Or the administration that is waging war in Ukraine, a non-NATO nation, against nuclear Russia without war powers?"

But McCarthy's pick for the Homeland Security Committee wasn't con-tent merely to label the American president "the real enemy." Greene used her new perch to push for the impeachment of Mayorkas, a Cuban-born Jew serving as Biden's Homeland Security secretary. A cabinet officer had not been impeached since 1876, but Greene wanted to change that.

In a typical broadside in April, Greene used an appearance by Mayor-kas before the Homeland Security Committee to blame him for "killing people" with fentanyl. When he tried to defend himself, Greene cut him off, shouting: "You're a liar!"

Democrats objected. Chairman Mark Green concurred, silencing her for the rest of the hearing.

But it was the chairman himself who set the ugly tone. According to an audio recording obtained by the *New York Times,* the Tennessee Republican had told donors the week before: "Next week, get the popcorn—Alejandro Mayorkas comes before our committee, and it's going to be fun." (He later claimed he was somehow misquoted.)

Popcorn? Fun? He was playing with the nation's security.

I asked Mayorkas, who arrived 20 minutes early for the hearing, why he hadn't heeded the chairman's instructions to bring popcorn.

"Wrong movie," he replied. He was determined not to give his tormentors the satisfaction of getting under his skin—and he mostly succeeded.

Green opened with a bit of "Great Replacement" theory. "You have not secured our borders, Mr. Secretary, and I believe you've done so intentionally," he alleged, saying that administration policy was all about "moving people into the country," welcoming "illegal aliens," and "settl[ing] them into the interior of our country."

Epithets flew: "Reckless." "Insult." "Insane." In the hearing room, the decibel app on my iPhone at one point found Green's volume to be equivalent to that of a food processor. "Not only have you lied under oath, you just admitted your own incompetence!" (At least he didn't call Mayorkas a "liar.")

Mayorkas endured the shouting, finger-pointing, table-pounding, and impeachment talk with eyes straight ahead. Invited by Texas Democrat Sheila Jackson Lee to respond to one Republican's insults, he replied: "I've chosen not to, thank you."

It brought to mind the old admonition not to wrestle with a pig: You'll both get muddy, and the pig enjoys it.

For all the rhetoric, House Republicans passed a bill during the debt limit standoff that would have led to cuts of as many as 2,400 Customs and Border Protection agents, the Department of Homeland Security said. Instead of negotiating with Democrats and the White House on a comprehensive plan to beef up security while also protecting legal immigration, they jammed through a bill that dramatically cracks down on legal immigration and puts huge new burdens on employers to "e-verify" workers' immigration status.

Gonzales correctly pointed out that the House bill was going nowhere. "This crisis ends when President Biden signs a bill into law that strengthens border security and protects legal immigration," he said at a news conference with other Hispanic Republican lawmakers also insisting on protecting legal immigration. "Until the president signs that into law, it's just speaking into the wind."

For that and other truth-telling (he also supports gun-safety laws and gay marriage) Gonzales earned a primary challenge and the censure of the state GOP for "violations of Republican Party of Texas principles."

How inadvertently truthful! There was a time when Gonzales's principles—tough border security but a humane approach to immigration—were Republican principles. But where once there was civility and common sense, there was now slur and slander. Get the popcorn!

THE MAYORKAS IMPEACHMENT HAD BEEN IN THE WORKS SINCE BEFORE Republicans took over the House. In December 2022, Arizona Republican Andy Biggs, who was then mounting his stalking-horse challenge to McCarthy for the speakership, demanded the immediate impeachment of the secretary.

At a news conference, I listened for more than 40 minutes as Biggs and his colleagues (16 white men and two white women, by my count) took turns denouncing Mayorkas. Standing behind a campaign-style "Impeach Mayorkas" yard sign, they were strikingly personal in their attacks: "Regularly lies." "Malice against the people of the United States." "Intentional and knowing disregard for human life." "Disgusting." "Despicable." "Purposefully endangering the American people … for crass political purposes."

But they didn't have much in the way of high crimes and misdemeanors. Mostly, they objected to Biden's border policies. For example, Norman (of "Marshall Law" fame) claimed that Biden had said the border "is not a problem." (Biden said no such thing.)

Texas Republican Brian Babin complained that "sixteen thousand illegal aliens were apprehended crossing the southern border in the last 48 hours. Also in the last 48 hours, $97 million worth of narcotics were seized." Umm, so didn't that mean that the border laws were being enforced?

But the Biggs band had already forced McCarthy to support their cock-amamie impeachment scheme. Before the election, McCarthy had said he didn't think anybody in the Biden administration deserved impeachment. But two weeks after the election, McCarthy threatened Mayorkas with impeachment—a reversal that, Biggs boasted, happened only "after he knew that he was facing somebody who was gonna possibly deny him the speakership." McCarthy was in no hurry to take such an extreme step, particularly because the only offense Mayorkas had committed was implementing Biden's policies, which they did not like. But the right-wingers' impeachment clamor grew louder in the spring after Trump-imposed pandemic border restrictions expired. Never mind that the expiration didn't produce the expected surge in border crossings. Minnesota's Tom Emmer, the Republican whip, joined the call for impeachment.

In June, McCarthy gave in to the pressure and gave his blessing to formal impeachment proceedings against Mayorkas—they just weren't supposed to use the *i*-word. "We haven't even gotten to that word," Chairman Mark Green said at a news conference unveiling the GOP's don't-call-it-impeachment inquiry. This "five-phase deep dive" authorized by McCarthy would prove that Mayorkas "has been willfully derelict" and "disregarded his oath." Explained Green: "We're going to get more information about the failures of this secretary, and when we're done we'll make a recommendation to the Judiciary Committee."

By this time, Pat Fallon, Clay Higgins, Biggs, and Greene had all introduced articles of impeachment against Mayorkas with a combined 84 cosponsors. But Republicans didn't have the votes to impeach—in part because they didn't have the goods on Mayorkas.

Illegal crossings of the southern border had at that point dropped 70 percent from their record highs. That was due in part to toughened Biden administration policies, including restrictions on asylum. Heightened enforcement has also led to the seizure of record amounts of fentanyl.

Still, Green kicked off his news conference with a Trumpian flourish. "Murderers released into the United States! Rapists released into the United States!" he shouted in the House television studio. "One hundred seven thousand dead Americans . . . Alejandro Mayorkas's policies are the cause of all of this!"

The Mayorkas impeachment was hobbled by its competition with the simultaneous movement to impeach Biden (and various and sundry other moves to impeach other Biden administration officials). There was also the distraction of the dizzying array of crises proclaimed by the new majority.

By the end of March 2023, Republicans had identified not just a border crisis but an energy crisis, a debt crisis, a fentanyl crisis, an opioid crisis, a crime crisis, an inflation crisis, an economic crisis, a banking crisis, a crisis in East Palestine, Ohio, a crisis abroad, a crisis in the nation's capital, and a productivity crisis. Emmer declared "a host of crises." Many more matters qualified as "alarming," "startling," and "scary."

"We have reached an existential crisis in this country," submitted Biggs.

"This time, we really are in a crisis," asserted Grothman. "A complete crisis."

The Mayorkas impeachment proceedings, such as they were, dragged on, and on. Most House Republicans wanted to impeach Mayorkas, but in the fall of 2023, they still didn't have the votes—or the evidence. That may have been because they hadn't produced evidence of high crimes or misdemeanors.

So, as noted earlier, an impatient Greene in November used a "privileged resolution" to force a snap vote on impeaching the secretary without completing an impeachment inquiry. It was a parliamentary maneuver seldom used in the past, and then usually by party leaders, but one frequently abused in this Congress by Greene and others. As lawmakers carried on conversations, the House clerk read Greene's venomous resolution about "willful admittance of . . . terrorists," "the invasion of approximately 10 million," "border crossers who have invaded," "gotaways," "illegals," and even "illegal people."

Despite such white nationalist bromides, 201 Republicans sided with Greene. Among them was Gonzales, the one who had earlier called his fellow Republicans' border policies anti-American. But now Gonzales was facing primary challengers backed by members of the House Freedom Caucus, and he held a press conference at which he was "honored" to stand with his "good friend" Greene and thank her "for her leadership."

I asked Gonzales about all of Greene's "invasion" talk, which she repeated at the news conference. "I, I, uh—435 members, we all have different styles," he replied.

After her impeachment resolution went down, Greene railed, in a video posted on social media, against Republicans on the Judiciary Committee who thwarted her. "If we have people serving on Judiciary Committee that don't believe in impeachment, then why are they on this committee?" she demanded.

One of those lawmakers, California's Issa, told a few of us that Greene "lacks the maturity and the experience to understand what she was asking." This prompted Greene to allege that Issa "lacks" part of the male anatomy.

An undeterred Greene vowed to force another impeachment vote. A couple of days after her first attempt failed, she confronted Mayorkas as he testified before the House Homeland Security Committee and told him: "You can honorably resign, or we are going to impeach you—and it's happening very, very soon."

Greene introduced another privileged resolution to impeach Mayorkas three weeks later. This time House leaders got her to back down—by promising her that they would handle the impeachment themselves.

Greene reported that Republican leadership had assured her that the House "very soon" would usher her articles of impeachment through the Homeland Security Committee and to the floor for a vote. As usual, Greene was firmly in command of the House Republican caucus.

House Republicans' usual legal allies turned against them in their capricious attempt to impeach a cabinet secretary for the first time in 148 years. Alan Dershowitz, Michael Chertoff, and the *Wall Street Journal* editorial page criticized the Mayorkas impeachment, and law professor Jonathan Turley, an all-purpose Republican witness who reliably validates their claims, said there is no "cognizable basis here for impeachment."

In fact, there was only one, noncognizable basis for impeachment, and that was Greene.

The Homeland Security Committee staged a clownish pair of hearings to concoct a rationale for impeachment. At the first, Morgan Luttrell, Republican of Texas, asked law professor Frank Bowman whether selling deadly fentanyl could be "considered a high crime."

"I'm unaware that the secretary has sold any fentanyl," the professor replied.

The congressman then asked if Bowman would "consider slavery a high crime."

"Is there any evidence that Mr. Mayorkas has enslaved anyone?" the professor answered.

Thwarted, Luttrell abandoned his line of questioning. "This is getting a little bit more complicated than I thought it was going to be," he said.

"We take the use of impeachment extremely seriously," said chairman Mark Green—the same Green who had told donors to "get the popcorn."

Impeachment ringleader Greene offered the panel a lesson on the Constitutional Convention. "Historical evidence is overwhelming that the Founding Fathers intended impeachment to be used to deal with the commission of indicktable [*sic*] crimes and the abuse of power," she read.

Indicktable!

One measure of the quality of debate: New York Republican Nick LaLota denounced Mayorkas for failing to provide testimony ("the committee has yet to receive a response"), apparently unaware that, as the chairman had already noted, Mayorkas did provide testimony.

Democrats tried to amend the impeachment articles to note that much of the supporting material had been provided by anti-immigrant organizations termed hate groups by the Southern Poverty Law Center. Republicans responded by shutting down the hearing and approving the error-plagued articles without further debate.

"Yeah, we're not debating it," Green said after cutting off amendments.

In lieu of allegations of high crimes or misdemeanors, the impeachment articles charged that Mayorkas "terminated Asylum Cooperative Agreements" with Central American countries. There was just one problem with this: Secretary of State Antony Blinken was the one who terminated those.

The articles further charged that Mayorkas "willfully refused to comply with the detention mandate" in the Immigration and Nationality Act of 1952. In fact, that standard has *never* been met in the decades it has existed—because Congress has never provided the funds to enforce it.

And the articles proposed impeachment because Mayorkas "terminated contracts" for Trump's border wall. Congress's own investigative arm blessed the legality of the border wall "pause," which, in any event, was Biden's policy, not Mayorkas's.

GOP leaders had showed how seriously they took impeachment by naming Greene herself as one of the impeachment managers who would argue the case in the Senate. In another display of their sobriety, the official impeachment report accompanying the articles of impeachment said impeachment was "the process of deporting Secretary Mayorkas." So now they wanted to send the naturalized Mayorkas back to Cuba?

After the committee approved the articles of impeachment, Green presented the case at a closed-door meeting of the Republican caucus. Mayorkas had to be impeached, he argued, because "this reptile has no balls to resign."

The reptilian reference, first reported by *Politico*'s Olivia Beavers, evoked an age-old antisemitic trope. Biden White House official Ian Sams protested the "vile" remark about the Jewish Mayorkas, citing a line about "reptilian men" from the American Jewish Committee's glossary of antisemitic terms.

But it was looking like a close vote on the House floor. Tom McClintock of California, opposed to the impeachment "stunt," as he called it, warned his colleagues in a memo and in speeches in the caucus meeting and on the floor that they had failed "to identify an impeachable crime that Mayorkas has committed" and that their actions would "distort the Constitution" and "shatter the separation of powers."

"I think that it lowers the grounds of impeachment to a point where we can expect it to be leveled against every conservative Supreme Court justice, every future Republican president and cabinet member," he told a group of us.

Greene responded with the usual threats. Her colleagues "better pay attention to what the American people will think of them if they don't vote to impeach," she warned.

The floor debate was predictably lowbrow.

Greene alleged that Mayorkas facilitated "the complete invasion of our country by criminals, gang members, terrorists, murderers, rapists."

Bennie Thompson, a Mississippi Democrat, replied: "She also thinks Jewish space lasers cause wildfires."

Pat Fallon called Mayorkas "a sheep in sheep's clothing" and said, "We must fire this bum, this second coming of Benedict Arnold."

Clay Higgins, with Old Testament fire, foretold: "On this day, it shall be written in the historical record of the people's House that ... Mayorkas has been impeached. So shall it be written. So shall it be done."

The prophecy didn't age well.

For the vote, 86-year-old Republican Hal Rogers of Kentucky, recovering from a car accident, came in a massive neck brace. Seventy-six-year-old Democrat Al Green of Texas, who had just undergone surgery, was wheeled in wearing hospital clothes and no shoes. But the worst casualty was the Republican whip operation, which miscounted. Some Republicans had begun referring to the hapless majority whip, Tom Emmer, as "Emmer Fudd," the *New Republic*'s Pablo Manriquez reported.

Wisconsin's Mike Gallagher, who had warned his GOP colleagues not to "pry open the Pandora's box of perpetual impeachment," became the decisive third Republican vote against impeachment, dooming the effort. As Republican leaders held the vote open and Democrats howled for the vote to be closed with cries of "regular order," colleagues encircled Gallagher along the back aisle.

Georgia's Greene got in his face, clearly threatening him. Tennessee's Green screamed at him, wagging his index finger. Virginia Foxx, Jodey Arrington, and Guy Reschenthaler joined in the berating. From the first row of the gallery, I could see Gallagher, mouth agape, sometimes swallowing hard, as he took in the abuse. But he took it. Greene made a slashing gesture, indicating it was all over.

Watching the one-vote defeat from afar, the expelled Santos asked his former Republican colleagues in a post on X: "Miss me yet?"

Responded Matt Gaetz: "I've never missed Santos more. Whoever he is."

The following week, with more Republicans in attendance, the House held a re-vote and narrowly impeached Mayorkas. Even that dubious achievement, passed by a single vote, required a legislative sleight-of-hand: scheduling the vote right after Steve Scalise returned from weeks of cancer treatment and 90 minutes before the polls closed in a special election that gave Democrats an additional seat in the House.

But then GOP leaders decided to sit on the articles rather than send them over to the Senate, because they feared their articles would be dismissed without a trial. They had justified the impeachment in the first place by saying it was of the utmost urgency. "We cannot allow this man to remain in office any longer. The time for accountability is now," Green argued.

Louisiana's Mike Johnson argued that "it's an extreme measure" to impeach Mayorkas, "but extreme times call for extreme measures."

When then-speaker Pelosi, in late 2019, held on to Donald Trump's articles of impeachment for 28 days before sending them to the Senate, Johnson called the delay a "charade" that left Democrats with "no credibility." And Green said that "Democrats sat on the articles for four weeks because they knew they did such a terrible job establishing any evidence of an impeachable offense."

But House Republicans sat on the Mayorkas impeachment articles even longer—an acknowledgment, by their own standard, that their effort had been a "charade" and a "terrible job."

After 63 days, Green, Greene, Higgins, and the other designated impeachment managers walked their articles over to the Senate on May 16. The next day, the Senate Democratic majority ruled the two articles to be unconstitutional and dismissed them without a trial. Even with Senate Republicans' objections and motions to adjourn, the whole thing took only about three hours—exactly the quick and unceremonious end the frivolous case deserved after House Republicans' 15 months of fabrication.

Chapter 11

"Well, Unfortunately, We Can't Track Down the Informant"

P RESIDENT BIDEN TOOK THE OATH OF OFFICE ON JAN. 20, 2021. THE NEXT
day, Marjorie Taylor Greene filed articles of impeachment against him.

What had Biden done, in just one afternoon on the job, to trigger the grave constitutional "high crimes and misdemeanors" standard for his removal? Well, it turned out he had committed a most egregious offense: He fathered a son. In 1970.

The newly minted congresswoman, a self-professed adherent of the QAnon conspiracy belief that the U.S. government was secretly run by Satan-worshipping pedophiles, had decided that the son's misbehavior automatically accrued to the father. "Hunter Biden paid nonresident women who were nationals of Russia or other Eastern European countries and who appear to be linked to an 'Eastern European prostitution or human trafficking ring,'" Greene wrote, and "Hunter Biden received millions of dollars from foreign sources as a result of business relationships that he built during the period when his father was vice president."

Casting aside standards of evidence, logic, and common English usage, she concluded from this: "In so doing, Joseph R. Biden threatened the integrity of the democratic system, interfered with the peaceful transition of power, and imperiled a coordinate branch of government." A coordinate branch of government? And how did the younger Biden's alleged hiring of prostitutes interfere with the "peaceful transition of power"? Never mind—Greene was on a roll: "Wherefore President Biden, by such conduct, has demonstrated that he will remain a threat to national security, democracy, and the Constitution if allowed to remain in office …"

Wherefore? Clearly, Greene didn't know her whereas from her elbow, and in any event her impeachment articles were going nowhere in the Democratic House. Nor should they have. But two years later, House Republicans would attempt to impeach Biden on grounds nearly identical to the preposterous case that Congresswoman Jewish Space Lasers had made on day one.

Republicans, once they were in charge of the House, devoted three committees to the cause of impeachment, issuing subpoenas by the dozen and holding an endless stream of depositions and hearings. They would come up with not a shred of evidence of wrongdoing by Biden—only a profusion of zany accusations that never panned out.

This was a naked abuse of power, using the most powerful punishment provided to the legislative branch under the Constitution for the sole purpose of revenge—because Trump wanted revenge. He wanted revenge for his first impeachment, supported by Republican senator Mitt Romney of Utah, who said Trump was "guilty of an appalling abuse of public trust" and a "flagrant assault on our electoral rights, our national security and our fundamental values." He wanted revenge for his second impeachment, supported by 10 House Republicans, for fomenting the attack on the Capitol. Trump "summoned the mob, assembled the mob and lit the flame of this attack," as Wyoming Republican Liz Cheney put it.

To House Republicans in 2023, the facts didn't really matter. They were merely acting on orders from the 45th president. As Trump directed them on Truth Social: "Either IMPEACH the BUM or fade into OBLIVION. THEY DID IT TO US!" This was about nothing more than tribal revenge for the twice-impeached Trump. He spelled it out even more explicitly in a September 2023 radio interview with Megyn Kelly. "Had they not done it to me," he said, then "perhaps you wouldn't have it being done to them."

As they obeyed Trump's orders, the only thing House Republicans "discovered" in their year of probing to find any hint of corruption around President Biden was what had already been known: That Hunter Biden, in the throes of drug addiction, had engaged in the sleazy business of trading on his father's name to enrich himself and his partners. And that the younger Biden, during a decades-long addiction to alcohol and crack cocaine, went through failed rehabs, acknowledged "rampages" with women, an ugly divorce, a fling with his deceased brother's widow, a paternity fight over an unacknowledged child, and the apparent abandonment of his laptop at a repair shop that made its salacious contents public. After a yearslong federal probe and a botched plea deal, prosecutors charged Hunter Biden in September 2023 with tax crimes and lying about his drug use when buying a gun, then in December with more tax crimes.

But the younger Biden, who made millions by trading on his famous name, was a bit player in the influence-peddling racket compared to Donald Trump's family, which brought in billions this way. Trump's son-in-law, Jared Kushner, received a $2 billion investment for his private equity firm from a fund connected to the Saudi government, and hundreds of millions of dollars from United Arab Emirates and Qatar. A firm tied to the Qatari government bailed out a Kushner-family-owned office tower in New York to the tune of $1.2 billion while Kushner was working in the White House on Mideast diplomacy. Ivanka Trump received valuable trademarks from the Chinese government during her father's presidency—a time when Trump properties, which remained under the president's control, received millions from foreign governments.

More to the point, nothing Hunter did implicated the president. Still, House Republicans decided that, in the absence of anything better, they would visit the sins of the child on the father. It was a guilt-by-association smear of the most sordid kind. But in their zeal to bring down Biden, a smear would suffice. They would try to impeach the president over "bribery" for which they produced no evidence—because it never occurred.

A MONTH BEFORE THE 2022 MIDTERM ELECTIONS, CONGRESSMAN JAMES Comer of Kentucky, having served only four years, was already in line, if Republicans won control of the House, to become the chairman of the House Oversight Committee. It was the committee responsible for investigating the president.

He promised in an interview with *Time* magazine that he would use the gavel with the utmost gravity and discretion. As *Time* recounted: "He spoke of his frustration with some of his fellow Republicans and conservative media figures who have focused obsessively on sordid details from the younger Biden's personal life, such as a leaked video of him appearing to smoke crack with a prostitute. 'I think that's very counter to a credible investigation,' Comer says. 'I don't care anything about that.' Instead, he vowed to conduct a sober investigation if he assumes the committee's gavel, leaving aside the more salacious aspects of Biden's history that dominate right-wing talk shows."

But Comer quickly reneged on his promise to use the gavel with gravity and discretion, and by July 2023, he was hawking the same sordid details he had piously dismissed as irrelevant.

"I would like to let the committee and everyone watching at home know that parental discretion is advised," Greene, placed on Comer's Oversight Committee by Kevin McCarthy, said cheerily at a panel hearing. She then displayed, for a live television audience, three lightly redacted posters displaying blown-up images, apparently taken from Hunter Biden's laptop, of a nude woman Greene called a prostitute servicing the president's son's genitals manually, orally, and in other ways.

One of the posters had the text: "Hunter recorded multiple sex tapes with a prostitute he had paid for out of his law firm's bank account."

The panel's ranking Democrat, Jamie Raskin of Maryland, protested. "Should we be displaying this, Mr. Chairman?"

Evidently Comer thought they should, for he let Greene have extra time for her show, with no reprimand.

After the hearing, Comer fired off a letter to the Justice Department, with Greene as his cosigner, demanding to know more about Hunter Biden's prostitutes. When the DOJ didn't respond quickly enough, they sent off another letter, saying the House Oversight Committee was investigating whether DOJ "is upholding the rights of victims who were sexually exploited by Robert Hunter Biden (Hunter Biden)."

The episode was the essence of the House Republicans' assault on Biden. It had nothing to do with oversight of the president's official conduct. It was simply to legitimize whatever filth Greene and other right-wingers pulled from the dark web.

In an interview with the *New York Times* in March 2023, Comer admitted that he had little control over Greene, because she was such a darling of the right: "It's hard for a coach to tell LeBron James what he's doing wrong."

COMER, THE FACE OF THE PROBES OF BIDEN, QUICKLY ESTABLISHED HIMSELF as a bear of very little brain. He fired off a letter in February to Transportation Secretary Pete Buttigieg demanding answers from the National Transportation Safety Board. Buttigieg informed the clueless chairman that the independent NTSB is not part of the Transportation Department.

A week later, Comer decided it would be a good idea to attack Biden's *other* son, Beau, who died of brain cancer in 2015. Comer said on a Lou Dobbs podcast that "it was Beau Biden, the president's other son, that was involved in some campaign donations from a person that got indicted" and "Joe Biden was involved in some of these campaign donations." Comer suggested the president's late son should have been prosecuted—but "nothing ever happened," he complained.

No conspiracy idea was too wacky for Comer to embrace. After Russia released Brittney Griner in December, Comer suggested the WNBA star's release, after months in custody on drug charges, was tied to . . . Hunter Biden. "We fear that this administration's compromised because of the millions of dollars that Hunter Biden and Joe Biden have received from Russia and China," he told Fox News. "This bizarre prisoner swap that clearly was in the benefit of Russia is another example of why we need to investigate to see if, in fact, this administration is compromised."

When a Chinese spy balloon floated across U.S. airspace in February 2023, Comer speculated (on Fox News, of course) that it was biological warfare. "Is that bioweapons, weapons in that balloon? Did that balloon take off from Wuhan?" He said the dirigible should have been shot down "before it even reached the continental United States." He didn't say how he thought Canada might have reacted to the United States exploding a bioweapon over its territory.

The chairman later admitted he had no evidence for suggesting the balloon was a bioweapon. "I asked a question," he explained.

When the Secret Service found a small pouch of cocaine in the White House in an area of the complex used by tourists and visitors, Comer called it "a shameful moment in the White House's history." Other Republicans suggested the cocaine belonged to Hunter. After the Secret Service concluded that it couldn't ascertain which of the 500 people who had passed through that area left the drugs, McCarthy called it a cover-up, saying, "You can't tell me . . . that they don't know who delivered it there." He suggested it was covered up because "anything involving Biden Inc. gets treated differently."

This was an extraordinary act of projection. Comer and his colleagues worked furiously to identify the speck in Biden's eye while steadfastly ignoring the log in Trump's eye.

Comer and his colleagues, for example, had a conspicuous lack of interest in Trump's mishandling of classified documents, which eventually led to dozens of charges against the former president. Trump had retained thousands of documents on U.S. and foreign nuclear programs and other sensitive matters, showing them off to people without security clearances and trying to conceal them from investigators and his own lawyers.

Asked about whether his committee would be looking into this, Comer replied, "That will not be a priority." But when Biden's lawyers told authorities that a search of his home in Wilmington, Delaware, had found classified documents, Comer didn't hesitate. "We're probing it," he said. He dashed off a letter to the Secret Service demanding years' worth of visitor logs for Biden's private residence, even though such logs do not exist, then decried a "lack of transparency" when the nonexistent logs were not provided. Intelligence Committee chairman Mike Turner, likewise, who dismissed Trump's hoarding of classified documents as a "bookkeeping issue," demanded "a full and thorough review" of Biden's conduct.

Republicans, echoing Trump's false claim that he had declassified all the documents in his possession, claimed that Biden's actions were worse because, as Comer put it, "the vice president does not have the authority to declassify documents, so there's a big difference here."

That rationale blew up a few days later when it emerged that Trump's former vice president, Mike Pence, also had mishandled classified documents. So Comer approached reporters in the Capitol basement on Jan. 31 in an attempt to establish a new justification for probing Biden but not Trump. However, Comer succeeded only in confusing himself. "We're very concerned about who had access to Pence's documents," he said—then stopped. "I said Pence. I'm sorry. Let me start all over. We're very concerned about who had access to Biden's documents." Moments later, he added: "I want to be very clear, I was talking about Biden."

Comer, perhaps recognizing the absurdity of his distinction, attempted a new justification soon after this, returning to CNN for an interview with Kaitlan Collins. This time, he said the reason he wasn't looking into Trump's documents was because "there's a special counsel looking into everything at Mar-a-Lago."

Collins pointed out that "there's a special counsel looking into Biden as well."

"Pardon me for not having as much confidence in this special counsel appointed by [Attorney General] Merrick Garland on Joe Biden."

Collins checked him again: "But he appointed the special counsel into Trump as well."

"I'm against both special counsels!" blurted out Comer, contradicting what he had said just seconds earlier.

The Trump and Biden cases were similar only in the superficial sense: Both men had retained classified documents after leaving office. In Biden's case, there were dozens of sensitive documents, including entries in his personal notebooks; his lawyers alerted the government after finding them, and Biden cooperated with investigators. In Trump's case, detailed in a 32-count federal indictment, there were hundreds of sensitive documents, some stashed in a ballroom and a bathroom; he refused to turn over the documents, then worked with aides to destroy evidence, conceal security footage, and lie about it to investigators.

In Biden's case, special counsel Robert Hur portrayed the president as "an elderly man with a poor memory." But he concluded in February 2024 that no charges were warranted.

Never mind that Hur was a conservative who had been appointed U.S. attorney by Trump. House Republicans hauled Hur before the Judiciary

Committee to echo Trump's claims that Hur was part of a conspiracy protecting Biden with a "double standard" and a "two-tiered system of justice."

"WHERE'S HUNTER?" WENT THE POPULAR TAUNT AT TRUMP RALLIES DURING the 2020 campaign. House Republicans found the answer: He was everywhere!

Comer alleged that the president's son had control over, among other things: cobalt in Congo, fentanyl on the Mexican border, coronavirus in Wuhan, military and monetary policy tensions with China, international climate accords, war in Ukraine, the Biden administration's push for electric vehicles, human trafficking, and the sanctioning of Russian oligarchs.

At one news conference, ostensibly about Joe Biden's supposed wrongdoing, Comer and other senior House Republicans mentioned Hunter's name two dozen times. Reporters tried to ask questions about other topics. Comer cut them off. "If we could keep it about Hunter Biden, that would be great," he said.

First, Comer decided to probe Hunter Biden's artwork. In his first weeks as chairman, Comer dashed off a letter demanding information from the Georges Bergès Gallery about paintings done by the president's son—what the *Wall Street Journal* called a "mixture of ink and acrylic on metal, depicting abstract flowers and trees." In the letter, Comer (his training is in agriculture) played art appraiser, declaring prices for the younger Biden's work "exorbitant." He wanted prompt answers from Hunter Biden's dealer (art, not drugs).

While awaiting answers about Hunter's artwork, he also set up a hearing on another matter of national urgency: Hunter Biden's laptop. He led his committee the following day into a doomed attempt to prove that the FBI and the Biden campaign colluded with Twitter "to suppress and delegitimize information contained in Hunter Biden's laptop about the Bidens family business schemes." That's how Comer put it as he sat in front of a blown-up *New York Post* front page screaming "BIDEN SECRET EMAILS."

The hearing, on Feb. 8, 2023, dragged on for six hours—including an hourlong break in the middle when the power went out in the hearing room. In the darkness, somebody who sounded like Comer asked: "Now did Twitter do that?"

The conspiracies never end!

The committee members succeeded in mentioning Hunter Biden's name at least 82 times, a transcript showed. The hearing's stated purpose had been to prove that collusion between the FBI, the Biden campaign, and Twitter had suppressed the *New York Post*'s original reporting on Hunter's laptop. But the former Twitter officials who had been summoned as witnesses testified that neither entity spoke to them about Hunter Biden's laptop when Twitter, fearing that the *New York Post* story was based on hacked material or Russian propaganda, blocked it for all of 24 hours before reversing the ban and apologizing.

It turns out Comer had no evidence for his claim that there was a "coordinated cover-up" of Hunter Biden's laptop. "My, my, my," gloated Democrat Gerry Connolly of Virginia. "What happens when you hold a hearing and you can't prove your point?"

The Hunter hunters kept hunting, in hopes that they would stumble across that elusive link to the man they called "the Big Guy," the president.

IN THE SPRING, COMER SPENT WEEKS PROMISING THAT HE FINALLY HAD THE goods on the elder Biden. "Joe Biden's going to have a lot of explaining to do," he teased on Fox News on Apr. 11, promising a blockbuster news conference within two weeks.

He continued weekly to hype his upcoming announcement until, after a month of buildup, Comer and other Oversight Committee Republicans walked into the House television studio and revealed . . . a whole lot of nothing.

He had not found any evidence of wrongdoing by the president—or any evidence that he had any involvement in his son's businesses. Comer's months of digging through bank records had found $10 million in payments from companies run by foreign nationals that went to Biden family members and business associates and their "shell" companies. But Comer produced no evidence that these payments were illegal or that any official government actions were taken in exchange.

Said Comer: "We're going to continue to look."

After unwrapping his nothingburger, Comer gave the first question to a friendly reporter from the Rupert Murdoch–owned *New York Post*. But even the reporter sounded skeptical, asking whether Comer would eventually prove "that President Biden was directly involved." Comer gave the second question to the *Epoch Times*, a far-right publication that traffics in conspiracy theories.

The reviews, even from the right, were savage. "I'm not impressed with James Comer's Biden bombshell," tweeted former Trump adviser Sebastian Gorka.

Commentator Geraldo Rivera said on social media that Comer and colleagues were "struggling to find direct evidence of criminal conduct or corruption." He said the investigators need to "put up . . . or shut up."

On *Fox and Friends* on May 11, Comer got a dressing-down from host Steve Doocy. The charge of influence peddling is "just your suggestion," he told Comer. "You don't actually have any facts to that point. You've got some circumstantial evidence. And the other thing is, of all those names, the one person who didn't profit is—there's no evidence that Joe Biden did anything illegally."

They had no evidence. But in a sense, that didn't matter. If the purpose was to smear the president, insinuation and accusation could be just as useful.

Comer went on Fox News again on May 22, and this time he accidentally spoke the truth, baldly admitting that his committee's probe of the Biden family was motivated by politics. "You look at the polling, and right now Donald Trump is seven points ahead of Joe Biden," he said, and that was because "the American people are keeping up with our investigation."

This was obviously true—Trump was using Comer's probe for fundraising—but tactically unhelpful. McCarthy's first bid for the speakership, after all, had collapsed in 2015 when he admitted to Fox that the select committee investigating the Benghazi, Libya, terrorist attack was created to hurt Hillary Clinton in the polls.

Comer, suddenly on cleanup duty, returned to Fox News the next day to deny that he had said what he had said. "Look, when I was referencing poll numbers, it had nothing to do with Donald Trump," he lied.

Comer kept looking for the absent evidence of Joe Biden's wrongdoing, firing off subpoenas to Hunter's business associates, financial institutions, and the FBI.

He claimed to have found a "very credible" whistleblower who had information showing that Biden and his family may have received a bribe from a Chinese energy company. But then he came forward with an embarrassing admission: He couldn't find his whistleblower. "Well, unfortunately, we can't track down the informant," he confessed to Fox's Maria Bartiromo in mid-May. Months later, we learned why.

The whistleblower, Gal Luft, was on the lam after being indicted for acting as an illegal arms broker and an unregistered agent for China. This raised some obvious doubts about his credibility, so Republicans immediately alleged a new conspiracy theory: that the Biden administration was "trying to silence our witnesses" (as Nancy Mace of South Carolina alleged) and that the timing was not "coincidental," in Comer's telling.

But there was a small problem with the new conspiracy theory: Though the indictment had just been unsealed, Luft was actually charged all the way back on Nov. 1, 2022—before Republicans even took over the House.

In Comer's imagination, everybody was in on the plot. After Hunter Biden reached a deal with federal prosecutors in which he was to plead guilty to two minor tax crimes and admit to a gun charge—the deal later fell through and prosecutors filed charges—Comer declared it a "sweetheart deal" and said it "reveals a two-tiered system of justice." Comer felt this way even though the prosecutor, David Weiss, was a Trump appointee, and even though Weiss repeatedly stated that he had full authority to charge Hunter Biden however and wherever he saw fit.

With great fanfare, Comer brought two other "whistleblowers" before the Oversight Committee who would prove that Hunter had gotten favorable treatment because of his father. The two, both IRS agents (one dramatically advertised as "Whistleblower X"), did indeed testify that they believed prosecutors had gone easy on Hunter for political reasons. But once again, Comer's witnesses didn't have the goods. Their complaints about how prosecutors were handling the Hunter Biden case began in 2019—during the Trump administration.

So Trump's DOJ tried to throw the 2020 election to Biden by giving his son kid-glove treatment? Makes total sense.

Once again, Comer's committee was left with nothing but its own wild allegations. "The only thing missing is direct evidence that Joe Biden knew and participated in these bribery schemes," Arizona representative Paul Gosar admitted during the July 19 hearing.

The fabrications kept coming. The committee brought in Devon Archer, a Hunter Biden business partner, for a closed-door interview—and Republicans said the testimony was explosive. Colorado's Lauren Boebert claimed that Archer "confirmed today that the 'Big Guy' participated in more than 20 of Hunter's shady business deals."

And Comer asserted that Archer had confirmed that "Biden lied to the American people when he said he had no knowledge about his son's business dealings and was not involved."

But when the transcript came out, it showed that Archer had told the committee that none of the conversations involving Joe Biden had to do with Hunter Biden's business but were rather "casual" conversations about "niceties." Archer said Hunter had been peddling "an illusion of access to his father," not actual access.

But Comer was already off on a new invention. On the right-wing cable channel Newsmax at the end of August, he said Joe Biden "was using a pseudonym and he copied his son about a shady, shady transaction." But the "pseudonym" was actually an official White House email account of the sort that senior officials routinely use to avoid spam. It was yet another swing and miss.

THEATRICALLY OUTRAGED HOUSE REPUBLICANS HURLED SO MANY CONSPIRACY allegations at Biden that it had become a daily occurrence. Virtually every action the president took, or didn't take, was evidence of something suspect. He was accused of trying to take away Americans' hamburgers, at one point, followed by their beer. No accusation was too petty or picayune.

At the White House, the task of responding to the allegations fell to two men: Ian Sams for all things Hunter and Andrew Bates for everything else. One day I found Bates struggling with the latest accusation. "I'm just coming to grips with the fact that I work for a dog-petting monster," he told me. What happened? A couple of weeks earlier, Biden had visited Hawaii after the devastating fire that struck Maui. While touring the destruction, he met a Labrador retriever named Dexter, a search-and-rescue dog who was wearing booties to protect his paws from the scorching ground. Biden petted the animal—and scandal ensued.

The Republican National Committee swung into action. "Biden gets distracted by a dog: 'That's some hot ground, man!'" the GOP tweeted from its @RNCResearch account. The tweet included video of the "incident."

The Republican National Committee (RNC) was weirdly obsessed with Biden and his alleged crimes related to dogs. "Biden gets distracted by his dog on the balcony as he returns from Japan," the RNC tweeted in May. The month before, @RNCResearch mocked Biden for answering "a child's question about his dog." It also ridiculed Biden when the Irish premier's Bernese mountain dog barked at the president: "This dog wants nothing to do with Joe Biden."

Offensive though it was that Biden likes dogs, the RNC had exposed him for worse: enjoying ice cream. @RNCResearch had gone after him no fewer than 12 times for this deplorable behavior, tweeting out indefensible things Biden had said about ice cream, such as "I know some really great ice cream places around here" and "I got a whole full freezer full of Jeni's chocolate chip ice cream."

The goal, of course, was to portray Biden as doddering and feeble-minded, and any "evidence" would do. "Was Biden dozing off in Maui?" @RNCResearch tweeted, along with a video that showed Biden clearly not asleep. It also tweeted clips of Biden struggling with words—the result not of old age but of a lifelong stutter.

The account advertised itself as "exposing the lies, hypocrisy, and failed far-left policies of Joe Biden." Instead, the RNC faulted him for saluting an audience; for using the "short stairs" to board Air Force One; for smiling as he exited Marine One; for shaking hands after coughing into his (other) hand. "Joe Biden says the length of Barack Obama's signature is shorter than his. Obama's is 3 letters longer," the RNC mocked at one point. In fact, "Joseph R. Biden Jr." is longer than "Barack Obama." But even if it weren't, this was the best the RNC could come up with?

IN THE SINGULAR QUEST TO GET BIDEN, ANY CRITIC WAS TREATED AS CREDIBLE and designated a "whistleblower."

In early 2023, Florida's Matt Gaetz and Georgia's Marjorie Taylor Greene announced that they would be bringing in Tara Reade for a transcribed interview as part of a joint inquiry by the Oversight and Judiciary committees. Reade accused Biden in 2020 of sexually assaulting her in the 1990s, but now she had broadened her accusations against Biden and become an all-purpose critic of Biden's policies.

The logistics for the congressional inquiry, however, got a bit trickier two months later—when Reade defected to Russia.

"I'd like to apply for citizenship in Russia from the president of the Russian federation, Vladimir Putin," she said from Moscow on May 30 in an event hosted by the state-owned news agency Sputnik. "Hopefully Maria Butina can help me with that from the state Duma," she added; Butina, with whom Reade shared the stage, had been convicted in the United States of being an unregistered Russian agent and is now in the Russian parliament.

Reade said she stayed in Russia after Gaetz told her, "I'm worried about your physical safety in the United States." She spent the session in Moscow denouncing the United States for its "crashing" economy, inflation, homelessness, child poverty, decaying roads, hunger, poor medical care, and "evil" determination to "warmonger" in Ukraine.

Best of all, she expressed indignation that "I was accused when I first came forward of being a Russian asset." She seemed unaware of the irony that she was, at that very moment, the star of an actual Russian propaganda operation.

Replied the Sputnik moderator to the defector: "The attempts by the USA government to accuse you of ties with Russia is just outrageous."

The curious case of Comrade Reade was just one instance in which the Venn diagram of Republican political interests and Russian propaganda interests had shown an uncomfortable amount of overlap. GOP lawmakers had repeatedly been cautioned by national security officials that they were advancing, or were targets of, Russian disinformation.

This doesn't necessarily mean that the Republicans were wittingly spouting Russian propaganda. But, as the Reade performance illustrated, there was an undeniable similarity between the Russian attacks on President Biden and his policies and the Republican attacks. At the very least, House Republicans were willing to trumpet any accusation against Biden, no matter how dubious the source.

Reade called herself a "whistleblower" who will be "testifying...about how the DOJ and the FBI has [been] weaponized by the Biden administration against its own citizens." House Republicans created a "weaponization" committee chaired by Jim Jordan devoted to precisely that.

Reade alleged that the Biden administration was "infiltrating social media to suppress the truth" and particularly to "suppress" the *New York Post*'s reporting on Hunter Biden's laptop. Republicans had held numerous hearings in a fruitless quest to demonstrate that.

Reade alleged that in the "corruption" case against Biden, House investigators have "bank receipts and proof that unfortunately when Joe Biden was vice president, he was influence peddling and created shell companies." Comer had likewise alleged that in his "Biden family corruption investigation" he found that Biden arranged an "influence-peddling" scheme through "shell companies."

Reade suggested that the Hunter Biden laptop and the weaponization matters, despite a "complete media blackout," had caused a drop in Biden's "poll numbers." Comer had claimed that Biden's "poll numbers are low partly because the American people think he's corrupt, and they sense a cover-up."

And, of course, Reade said Americans are opposed to spending "so much money giving weapons to Ukraine." Many House Republicans, for their part, were vowing to block funds for Ukraine.

Reade later said she had been granted political asylum. "In our story, Russia is the hero," she said.

Reade had a strong motivation for her behavior. She wanted to be "a good citizen" of Russia. What was the House Republicans' excuse?

FIFTEEN YEARS AGO, I WAS IN THE HOUSE CHAMBER WHEN JOE WILSON, A South Carolina Republican, shocked the world by shouting two words at President Barack Obama: "You lie!" In the outcry that followed, House Republican leaders demanded Wilson apologize, which he did, calling the

White House and issuing a public statement offering "sincere apologies to the president for this lack of civility."

In retrospect, the episode looks almost quaint. Wilson's outburst began a fundamental change in how a president is received in the House chamber. Justice Samuel Alito shook his head and said "not true" during an Obama speech. Democrats groaned and booed during a Trump speech, and then-House Speaker Nancy Pelosi once ripped up her text after Trump finished. Trump called Democrats "treasonous" for failing to applaud him as much as he wanted.

By the time Biden gave his State of the Union address in 2023, the boorishness the House Republicans displayed made Joe Wilson look, by comparison, as though he had been operating under Emily Post's rules of etiquette.

McCarthy reportedly asked Biden in advance not to use the phrase "extreme MAGA Republicans," and Biden honored the request. The president's goodwill didn't end there. He opened by congratulating McCarthy and Senate Republican leader Mitch McConnell. He used the word "together" 20 times in the speech, hailing bipartisan achievements, offering to "sit down together" to resolve the debt ceiling standoff, and closing with a rallying cry: "We're the United States of America, and there's nothing—nothing—beyond our capacity if we do it together."

Republicans answered him with hooliganism and obscenity. Greene shouted "Liar!" at the president—not once, as Wilson had done, but over and over. As Biden talked about solving the debt standoff together, Greene shouted "Bullshit!" at Biden. Some closer to the front—GOP senators Mitt Romney and Lisa Murkowski among them—whipped their heads around in surprise. (Greene had already demonstrated her gravitas earlier in the day by posing for photographs while carrying a white helium balloon that looked like a miniature version of the Chinese spy balloon.)

House Republicans by the dozens groaned, booed, laughed, jeered, waved their hands dismissively at the president, and pointed their thumbs down—ignoring an attempt by McCarthy, seated behind Biden, to shush them. Several shouted, "Secure the border!" Ronny Jackson of Texas noisily chewed gum; Byron Daniels of Florida interrupted Biden with a series of taunts ("don't say it!"); Lauren Boebert of Colorado shook her head in

FOOLS ON THE HILL

disgust; others shared laughs about messages on their phone screens. In the middle of the mayhem, GOP leaders Steve Scalise, Tom Emmer, and Elise Stefanik sat stone-faced. When Biden spoke about deaths from fentanyl, Andy Ogles of Tennessee shouted: "It's your fault!"

And the shouting didn't end on the House floor. In Statuary Hall after the speech (where lawmakers go to talk with reporters) I caught up with Pat Fallon of Texas, who had been sitting next to Greene during the speech. Fallon's take: "He lied about the economy! He lied about the deficit! He lied about us cutting Medicare and Social Security ... He lied about the labor shortage! ... He lied about burger joints! ... He lied about policing ... He lied about Mr. Pelosi."

"So overall, you liked it?" I asked Fallon.

"I loved the ending, because it was over," Fallon replied, soon resuming his catalogue. "He said a couple of things like we're going to work together. He's lying there, too!"

Fallon shared with me and Joseph Morton of the *Dallas Morning News* three pages of scribbled notes he took during the address. Among his observations: Biden is a "SNAKE OIL SALESMAN" (and of course a "LIAR") who "MUMBLES" (Fallon thought this evidence of a "health issue"), engages in "climate alarmism" and "CLASS WARFARE," and talks like "A COMMUNIST—ACCUSE HIM OF CENTRAL CONTROL."

Even some of the more pugilistic Republicans recognized this was no way to behave. Ryan Zinke of Montana told us Biden's speech had been "cordial," but "the House at times was a little raucous, I thought, a little vocal. But that's the House in this period."

Yes, that is the House in this period. There are no longer grown-ups leading the House Republican majority to demand and enforce decency, as they did in Joe Wilson's moment of glory. In fact, the leaders are often the ones leading the indecency. McCarthy went on Fox News the day after the State of the Union and blamed the Republicans' outbursts on Biden. "Well, the president was trying to goad the members, and the members are passionate about it," McCarthy said. He offered no criticism of the "liar" and "bullshit" outbursts.

When it came to the House majority's treatment of Biden, no epithet was too vulgar, and no accusation too outlandish.

Chapter 12

"This Is What's Known as Luna-cy"

T HOUGH THE WILD ALLEGATIONS DIRECTED AT BIDEN WERE ENDLESS, and constantly reimagined to fit the news of the day, it would not be accurate to say that the new House majority was *solely* obsessed with Joe Biden. They used the majority's powers to slander others, too. For a group purporting to be concerned about the "weaponization of government," House Republicans sure seemed intent on turning their own patch of the federal government into a tactical nuke. The new majority was out for vengeance.

In one of their first acts, House Republicans changed the rules for the new Congress to revive something called the Holman Rule. The rule, which had been around since 1876 but was seldom used, allowed Congress to zero out the salary of federal employees who annoyed them. In 2023, the new House majority proceeded to make various attempts to cut the salaries of the Defense secretary, Homeland Security secretary, Transportation secretary, Education secretary, Health and Human Services secretary, and several others to $1 apiece. But this was only a symbolic threat, because the Democratic controlled Senate wasn't about to go along with the scheme.

The House Republicans had more clout when it came to exacting revenge on Democratic members of the House who had antagonized them. When Democrats had been in the majority, they had removed Marjorie Taylor Greene and Paul Gosar of Arizona from their committees—Greene for her online support for assassinating Nancy Pelosi and others, and

Gosar for posting an anime video in which he killed Congresswoman Alexandria Ocasio-Cortez of New York.

Republicans at the time threatened revenge, and immediately after taking control of the chamber they acted. Kevin McCarthy used his power as speaker to remove Democrat Adam Schiff of California from the Intelligence Committee, where he had served as chairman, in explicit revenge for his stewardship of Trump's first impeachment. He also removed Eric Swalwell of California, a highly visible critic of his Republican colleagues, suggesting that Swalwell had been compromised by a Chinese spy who had targeted him eight years earlier. Swalwell hadn't been accused of wrongdoing, and the House Ethics Committee, after investigating, took no action against him.

Swalwell, booted from Intelligence, kept his seat on the Homeland Security Committee, where he was now joined by the newly appointed Greene, whose committee memberships were restored by McCarthy. She promptly used her new perch to resume the smear of Swalwell, this time at an April 19 hearing featuring testimony from Homeland Security secretary Alejandro Mayorkas about the Biden administration's proposed 2024 budget.

Midway through the hearing, after Swalwell questioned Mayorkas about the effects of calls from GOP officials such as Trump and Greene to "defund the FBI," Greene began her five minutes of questioning with a sweet smile and a breathtaking libel.

"That was quite entertaining from someone that had a sexual relationship with a Chinese spy, and everyone knows it," she said.

Democrats demanded that her words be "taken down." There was no evidence that Swalwell had had a sexual relationship with the spy who targeted him in 2014. It was the very definition of slander.

Yet Republicans jumped to her defense. Chairman Mark Green, of Tennessee, ruled that Greene's slander was "not going to be stricken from the record." He went so far as to suggest the unsubstantiated innuendo was a "statement of fact." And when Democrats challenged the ruling, Republicans on the panel voted unanimously, in an 11–9 party-line tally, to defend Greene's defamation.

For Greene (the one who shouted "Bullshit!" at the president during the State of the Union), it was a typical display. But it made for an awkward

FOOLS ON THE HILL

moment a month later when Greene was taking her turn presiding over the House as speaker pro tempore. Somebody on the Democratic side had heckled House majority leader Steve Scalise when he was speaking about the debt ceiling standoff. Greene banged the gavel, called for order, and, instructed by the House clerk, read out the standard admonition for such occasions. "The members are reminded to abide by decorum of the House," she said.

Democrats erupted in laughter at this legislative equivalent of being called ugly by a pig.

Meanwhile, the new majority still wasn't finished harassing Schiff. In June, freshman Anna Paulina Luna of Florida, previously best known for her creatively curated resume, introduced a "privileged resolution" (which means it had to be taken up by the House) to censure and fine Schiff $16 million for his role in leading Trump's first impeachment. Scalise promptly pledged to "help it pass"—and put it on the floor.

Luna, full of confidence that her attack on her senior colleague would prevail, told *Politico*'s Olivia Beavers before the vote that she was acting against Schiff "at the suggestion of a member of leadership."

Scalise, GOP whip Tom Emmer, and GOP conference chair Elise Stefanik all voted with Luna. Alas for her, 20 Republicans retained more integrity than their leaders and joined with Democrats to kill Luna's censure gambit.

It was a temporary reprieve for good sense.

A week later, Republicans held another vote on Luna's resolution to censure Schiff, and this time not a single House Republican voted against censuring Schiff. What changed?

Well, there was a tweak to the language, removing a financial penalty. But there was a more important factor as well: House Republicans had received orders from on high. In between the first and second votes, Trump issued a threat saying that any Republican voting against censuring the "lowlife" Schiff "should immediately be primaried."

"The supreme puppet master," House minority leader Hakeem Jeffries of New York said during the censure debate, "threatened the other side of the aisle with primaries if they didn't bend the knee."

And bend they did.

The resolution itself was a clumsily worded exoneration of Trump in all matters: Schiff "spread false accusations that the Trump campaign colluded with Russia." Schiff "behaved dishonestly and dishonorably" in launching "the first impeachment of President Trump." Schiff gave a "false retelling of a phone call between President Trump and Ukrainian President Volodymyr Zelensky."

Since the nineteenth century, censures (there were only seven since 1890) had been about financial or sexual improprieties or other personal misconduct—not policy disputes. "We don't censure members over a difference of opinion," said Jamie Raskin of Maryland, leading the Democrats' defense of Schiff. Until now, that is, and this "embarrassing revenge tour," as Raskin put it. "We are seeing the complete ethical collapse of a once-great political party," he continued, into "an authoritarian cult of personality taking orders from an inciter of insurrection."

The first-term Luna, 34 years old, knew so little of the functioning of the House that she had to be reminded repeatedly while leading her side in the debate about the difference between "reserving" her time and "yielding" it. Her speeches sounded like social media rants: Schiff's "own political good was served by permanently destroying family relationships."

So now he's a home-wrecker?

Luna's obsession with Schiff was perverse—of the eight pieces of legislation she had introduced in her brief career to date, five involved Schiff—and Republicans of any stature had enough sense not to lend their voices to the sordid affair. While Democrats lined up to defend Schiff, Luna couldn't find enough speakers to fill her 30 minutes of the debate—or, as she called it, "these little fun games and comments back and forth." She pulled together an assortment of the usual extremists, most of whom weren't even in Congress when Schiff allegedly did the terrible things they accused him of doing.

Among them was Lauren Boebert, who called Schiff a "disgrace to our nation" and a "crook" before lapsing into gibberish: "I told the American people that he had to prove—he, that he had proof, that Trump, the Trump campaign, asking, uh, the Russians for help in a conspiracy."

Democrats took whatever time Raskin could spare—even 30 seconds—to fire off their best lines.

"This is what's known as Luna-cy," Massachusetts Democrat Jim McGovern offered.

"This is a partners' meeting of Insurrection LLC," Swalwell proposed.

Schiff, whose Senate campaign has reaped a financial bonanza from the censure shenanigans, did the honest thing: He thanked his persecutors. "You honor me with your enmity," he said.

"No matter how many false justifications or slanders you level against me, you but indict yourselves," Schiff added. "As Liz Cheney said, 'There will come a day when Donald Trump is gone, but your dishonor will remain.' Will it be said of you that you lacked the courage to stand up to the most immoral, unlawful and unethical president in history but consoled yourselves by attacking those who did?"

Arkansas Republican Rick Crawford, the speaker pro tempore, called for a voice vote on the resolution.

"Aye," called the few Republicans in the chamber.

"No," bellowed the Democrats who crowded their side of the aisle.

"In the opinion of the chair, the ayes have it," Crawford lied.

McGovern called out to Crawford: "I think you need a hearing aid."

That might help. But what these guys really needed was a conscience.

McCarthy took over the speaker's chair and called Schiff to the well to receive the Trump-ordered rebuke. Democrats crowded around Schiff, applauding and chanting, "Adam!" At McCarthy, they chanted "Shame!" and "Disgrace!" then heckled him as he tried to read the admonishment.

"I have all night," said McCarthy, though he quickly abandoned his attempt to gavel down the enraged Democrats and instead tried to talk over them.

Among the many shouts of protest coming from the hornet's nest of Democrats: "Do what the people elected you to do!"

What a novel concept.

LUNA MAY HAVE STOLEN THE SPOTLIGHT, BUT GREENE WAS DETERMINED TO seize it back. In a three-day spree, she filed articles of impeachment against four Biden administration officials, including FBI director Christopher Wray and Attorney General Merrick Garland. (In addition to the Mayorkas impeachment, other Republicans introduced impeachment articles against Vice President Kamala Harris and Defense Secretary Lloyd Austin.)

At the end of what she called "impeachment week," Greene gave a news conference where she announced "with the highest amount of solemnnenity [sic]" that she was also filing impeachment articles against Biden himself.

But Greene's leadership of the impeach-Biden movement was in serious jeopardy. Since she first filed articles of impeachment against the president more than two years earlier, no fewer than nine House Republicans had introduced or cosponsored Biden impeachment articles.

And then, out of nowhere, came Boebert. She discovered that she could vault ahead of all her rivals by using the same sort of "privileged resolution" Luna had used to censure Schiff. Using a privileged resolution, she would force the House to have an immediate vote to impeach Biden—dispensing with all those cumbersome and tedious preliminary steps such as, say, investigating the matter or presenting evidence.

Boebert rose in the House one evening after the last vote. "For what purpose does the gentlewoman from Colorado seek recognition?" asked the presiding officer, Russell Fry of South Carolina.

The gentlewoman sought recognition to unveil her parliamentary maneuver forcing a vote within 48 hours on House Resolution 503, "Impeaching Joseph R. Biden Jr., president of the United States, for high crimes and misdemeanors."

No impeachment proceedings. No investigation. No evidence. No crimes. Not so much as a parking ticket. Just a willy-nilly snap vote to impeach the president, because Boebert took issue with Biden's immigration policies. In her mind, "President Biden has intentionally facilitated a complete and total invasion at the southern border," she charged on the House floor.

At this, Greene flew into a fit of jealousy because Boebert had thought to use the maneuver to force an impeachment vote before Greene got a vote on her articles of impeachment against Biden. Boebert stole her impeachment articles, Greene whined to reporters. "A copycat," was Greene's kindergarten-level complaint.

The two women could be seen in a noisy altercation on the House floor. According to a *Daily Beast* account that Greene later confirmed, Congresswoman Jewish Space Lasers confronted Boebert and called her a "little bitch."

"I've donated to you, I've defended you. But you've been nothing but a little bitch to me," Greene said, "and you copied my articles of impeachment after I asked you to cosponsor them."

But Boebert was unmoved—because she was on a mission from God. She filed her impeachment resolution because "I am directed and led by Him . . . by the spirit of God," she told the evangelical cable outlet Victory Channel.

God could not be reached for comment.

McCarthy, in a closed-door meeting with Republicans, pleaded with them to oppose Boebert's flash-mob impeachment. "What majority do we want to be?" he admonished them, warning that impeachment mania could cause Republicans to lose their majority. He persuaded Boebert to accept a revised resolution sending Biden's impeachment through the Judiciary and Homeland Security committees first.

On the floor, Boebert exulted. "For the first time in 24 years, a House Republican-led majority is moving forward with impeachment proceedings against a current president," she said. "This bill allows impeachment proceedings to proceed."

Her GOP colleagues made clear on the floor that the vote was teeing up impeachment for this "corrupt" head of the "Biden crime family syndicate" who was responsible for the "murders of countless Americans." Vowed Chip Roy of Texas, the Republican floor leader for the impeachment debate: "We are just beginning."

As usual, McCarthy had only himself to blame for the chaos. The whole thing started with Luna's attack on Schiff. A responsible leader would have quashed such petty vindictiveness, but McCarthy's leadership team threw its support behind the censure resolution and helped rewrite it so that it would pass (although a couple of bright lights in the House GOP boasted that they had voted to "censor" Schiff).

He had unleashed a cycle of retribution that would, as mentioned earlier, curse the House for months. In the entire history of the Republic, the House had censured just 24 of its members. But in this Congress, lawmakers had filed formal censure resolutions 18 times in just 11 months.

A couple of weeks before the midterm elections in 2022, McCarthy had assured voters that House Republicans, if given the majority, wouldn't be so rash as to go on an impeachment binge. "I think the country doesn't like impeachment used for political purposes at all," he told *Punchbowl News* at the time. "I think the country wants to heal," he added, and avowed that he didn't think anybody in the Biden administration merited impeachment proceedings.

McCarthy had tried to stall his caucus's drive for Biden's impeachment by setting House committee chairs loose to launch a series of overlapping probes into whatever caught their fancy. As a consequence, at least three committees were investigating Hunter Biden. At least three committees were auditioning impeachment articles against Mayorkas. At least three committees were probing "censorship" of social media by the administration. Multiple committees were pursuing fanciful conspiracy theories involving public health officials and the supposed "weaponization" of the FBI, the Justice Department, and the rest of the government by the Deep State. And, of course, the committees were investigating anybody who investigated Trump—Justice Department special counsel Jack Smith, Manhattan district attorney Alvin Bragg, Fulton County district attorney Fani Willis.

As late as August 2023, two days before lawmakers left Washington for their summer recess, McCarthy told his House Republican caucus that they could not justify launching a formal "impeachment inquiry" into Biden over the unproven (and unfounded) allegations. Instead, any "impeachment inquiry" would be preceded by an impeachment "investigation." Leaving the meeting, McCarthy ally Don Bacon, of Nebraska, explained this half-measure to a group of us. "We're not ready for an inquiry," he said. "We're doing an investigation."

But, as the world would soon learn, McCarthy was not in charge of the House. That authority rested with Matt Gaetz, Marjorie Taylor Greene, and Donald Trump.

On Aug. 31, Greene, at a constituent gathering in Georgia, announced that she would not "vote to fund the government unless we have passed an impeachment inquiry." Later, Gaetz announced that he would speak on the House floor on Sept. 12, the first day the chamber reconvened after recess, to detail plans to seek McCarthy's ouster as speaker if he impeded the impeachment of Biden. Trump joined in the impeach-Biden lobbying.

McCarthy, whose main strength as a leader had always been his steadfast devotion to self-preservation, recognized that he was about to get trampled by the impeachment parade. So he stepped out in front of it and pretended to be the drum major, announcing a formal impeachment inquiry just an hour before Gaetz was scheduled to deliver his fateful speech on the floor denouncing McCarthy.

This set off a perverse competition to claim the credit for forcing McCarthy to bow and scrape. Was it Greene, who as a QAnon devotee and new congresswoman in January 2021 filed the day-one impeachment articles against Biden? Or was it Gaetz, subject of a newly revived House Ethics Committee investigation into allegations of sexual misconduct, illegal drug use, and corruption?

"When @SpeakerMcCarthy makes his announcement in moments, remember that... I pushed him for weeks," Gaetz posted on social media.

"Correction my friend," retorted MTG in her own post. "I introduced articles of impeachment against Joe Biden . . . on his very first day in office. You wouldn't cosponsor those and I had to drag you kicking and screaming."

While House Republicans embraced the evidence-free impeachment inquiry, a lone exception was Ken Buck of Colorado, a former prosecutor and a member otherwise in good standing of the Freedom Caucus.

"Without doubt, Hunter Biden's shady business deals undermined America's image and our anti-corruption goals, and his conduct was thoroughly reprehensible," he wrote in the *Washington Post*. "What's missing, despite years of investigation, is the smoking gun that connects Joe Biden to his ne'er-do-well son's corruption."

Accusing his colleagues of deploying a "gotcha narrative" with a "fictitious version" of events, he wrote: "Republicans in the House who are itching for an impeachment are relying on an imagined history . . .

It's a neat story, and one that performs well in certain media circles. But impeachment is a serious matter and should have a foundation of rock-solid facts."

Buck gave a similar message on MSNBC: "The time for impeachment is the time when there's evidence linking President Biden—if there's evidence linking President Biden—to a high crime or misdemeanor. That doesn't exist right now."

"Imagined history." "Fictitious version." For such truth-telling by Buck, Greene, who called for "a very tedious impeachment inquiry" (one wonders whether Ms. Gazpacho Police knew what "tedious" means), proposed that he should be stripped of his committee assignment. "I really don't see how we can have a member on Judiciary that is flat-out refusing to impeach," she told CNN. Greene, who sent out a solicitation inviting campaign contributors to join her "Impeachment Team," added: "It seems like, can he even be trusted to do his job at this point?"

Apparently not. Seven weeks later, Buck announced that he wouldn't run for reelection. Four months after that, he resigned before completing his term.

In Greene's House, there was no room for the truth.

HOUSE REPUBLICANS, STILL LACKING ANY EVIDENCE AGAINST BIDEN, continued their guilt-by-association efforts to tie him to his son's misdeeds.

The Judiciary Committee met on Sept. 20 to hear from Attorney General Garland on the subject of "Oversight of the U.S. Department of Justice." It would have been more accurately titled "Oversight of the President's Son."

A transcript of the proceedings revealed that the name "Hunter" was invoked 78 times. "So, Hunter Biden is selling art to pay for his $15,000 a month rent in Malibu," Gaetz informed the attorney general. "How can you guarantee that the people buying that aren't doing so to gain favor with the president?"

Things were off-kilter from the start. California Republican Darrell Issa led the Pledge of Allegiance by telling people in the room full of flags to "please face whichever flag is most appropriate for your direction."

Those in attendance faced north, south, east, and west, face-to-face and back-to-back.

It only got more confusing from there. "The fix is in!" Jim Jordan yelled at the beginning of his opening statement, and he didn't stop shouting for the rest of the hearing.

On Sept. 27, three days before the federal government's funding was to expire, Jason Smith called a news conference in the House TV studio. Had the chairman of the tax-writing House Ways and Means Committee come up with a last-minute plan to avert a government shutdown?

Um, no. Instead, Smith was announcing "new and alarming" accusations against Hunter Biden, and dumping another 700 documents about the presidential son's finances. A reporter asked about the wisdom of focusing on such "other priorities" as the federal government careened toward disaster.

"House Republicans can walk and chew gum," Smith replied. "We're pretty good at that."

How true! They can shut down the government and impeach Biden on bogus charges—all at the same time.

The next day, with the federal government 48 hours away from having its funding lapse, Republicans went right ahead with the first formal hearing of their impeachment inquiry.

The House Oversight Committee's Sept. 28 hearing, titled "The Basis for an Impeachment Inquiry of Joseph R. Biden Jr.," would have been the time, in a proper impeachment proceeding, for the investigators to bring in witnesses with firsthand knowledge of offenses committed by the accused. But in this fact-free impeachment, there were no such witnesses. So instead of facts, House Republicans brought hacks: three partisans who had no direct knowledge of the situation but who had already auditioned their anti-Biden arguments on Fox News.

There was tax lawyer Eileen O'Connor, a former member of Trump's presidential transition team who has held leadership roles in conservative and Republican groups. O'Connor has shared cartoons on social media expressing support for anti-vaxxers, alleging Deep State collusion with Vladimir Putin, decrying an immigrant "invasion," and celebrating the acquittal of Kyle Rittenhouse in the killing of two people in Kenosha, Wisconsin, during protests and riots over police misconduct in 2020.

Also at the witness table was accountant Bruce Dubinsky, who shared on social media a doctored photo of Joe Biden with the pouch of a jock strap covering his eyes, nose, and mouth. He also "liked" two Trump campaign ads, complaints about Trump's first impeachment, Trump's claims that there would be fewer covid cases if there were less testing, and criticism of the Jan. 6 committee.

And there was Jonathan Turley—of course. The go-to Republican witness regularly seemed to contradict his earlier positions to suit whichever argument his congressional Republican hosts were making at the moment. Ostensibly a constitutional lawyer, he was best known as a Fox News regular who falsely claimed that Dominion voting machines switched Trump votes to Biden in 2020. Among the headlines on his recent columns for Fox, the *New York Post*, and others was the headline "Joe and Jill Biden Finally Acknowledge 7th Grandchild for Most Obnoxious Reason." That's some quality constitutional lawyering.

Yet even this partisan panel couldn't deliver. Not one of them testified that House Republicans had met the threshold for impeaching a president. In fact, Turley said exactly the opposite: "I do not believe that the current evidence would support articles of impeachment."

Under questioning, Turley said the lawmakers needed to find a "linkage to the president"—a crazy idea! "Whether he participated, whether he encouraged it, we simply don't know, and we don't even know if this was an illusion or not," he said, telling the lawmakers that they had not established "that type of nexus."

Dubinsky, similarly, said "more information is still needed" in order to determine "whether or not the Biden family and its associates' businesses were involved in any improper or illicit activities, and whether those activities, if any, were connected to President Joe Biden."

After all these months, this was all they had?

"If the Republicans had a smoking gun or even a dripping water pistol," said Raskin, the ranking Democrat, "they would be presenting it today. But they've got nothing on Joe Biden."

Florida Republican Byron Donalds displayed what appeared to be a screen shot of a text message, which he claimed showed that Joe Biden was involved in Hunter Biden's business dealings. But Donalds omitted the actual context of the exchange: not Hunter Biden's business dealings but his alimony payments.

South Carolina's Nancy Mace, for her part, claimed that "we already know the president took bribes from Burisma." But they knew no such thing, and had no evidence.

Jason Smith, the Ways and Means chairman, cited a document related to a Hunter Biden search warrant, which Smith said was evidence of "the Biden Justice Department protecting the Biden brand." He neglected to note that the date of the document was Aug. 7, 2020—when it was the Trump Justice Department.

Smith, deeply troubled that Hunter Biden had "cashed in," evidently had seen nothing wrong in sending out a fundraising appeal the week before soliciting donations based on his role "leading the impeachment inquiry into Joe Biden." Comer sent a similar one after the hearing. Smith told GOP donors that "with your generous support, we will be able to expose Joe Biden and reveal the truth about this alleged corruption."

But the "corruption" remained entirely "alleged."

Publicly, right-wing commentators panned the hearing. Privately, Republican leadership aides agreed. "Picking witnesses that refute House Republicans' arguments for impeachment is mind blowing," a senior Republican staffer told CNN's Melanie Zanona. "This is an unmitigated disaster."

Their witnesses had undermined their case. Mace resorted to a barnyard obscenity—twice. Greene displayed a poster of a scantily clad woman and shouted random interruptions when others had the floor.

"As a former director of emergency management," Florida Democrat Jared Moskowitz told the committee, "I know a disaster when I see one."

The Biden impeachment disaster was temporarily overshadowed by another political disaster: the ouster of McCarthy. With the House shuttered for three weeks while they attempted to pick a new speaker, Republicans needed to create a diversion. And Comer had one! After Jordan's failed bid and before Emmer's failed bid, the Oversight Committee posted a bulletin on social media. "BREAKING," it said, with two siren emojis. "We have found a $200,000 DIRECT payment to Joe Biden."

But on further investigation, what they had was a check from the president's brother James Biden and his wife to Joe Biden. In the memo section, it said, clearly, "loan repayment."

On Nov. 1, Comer tried again. "BREAKING," the committee posted. "We've followed the money and identified how Joe Biden received $40,000 in laundered China money."

But this payment had already been reported, and it was another repayment of a loan that Biden made to his brother.

Comer admitted that it was "certainly plausible" that the loan repayments were, in fact, loan repayments.

Comer's wild allegations kept crumbling upon scrutiny, which may explain why he told reporters, regarding his impeachment inquiry, "I don't know that I want to hold any more hearings, to be honest with you." It was a striking admission of the failures of his previous hearings. Comer said he preferred closed-door depositions—from which he could selectively leak to create false impressions of guilt.

The new speaker, Mike Johnson, was just fine with all of this. In his first interview after becoming speaker, he told Fox News' Sean Hannity that "it looks and smells like" Biden received bribes.

At a subsequent news conference, he maintained that the impeachment inquiry was totally legit. "What you're seeing right now is a deliberate constitutional process that was envisioned by the founders, the framers of the Constitution," Johnson said. He said Comer and House investigators were working "very methodically and I would say outside the scope of politics."

This claim to be "outside the scope of politics" was followed by yet another appeal from Comer for campaign cash: "I'm once again asking for your help to defend my good name as I delve deeper into the belly of the corrupt beast that is ravaging our country: THE BIDEN CRIME FAMILY."

In early November, House Republicans finally got their long-awaited chance to grill the prosecutor overseeing the Hunter Biden case, David Weiss. But instead of holding a public hearing, as the Justice Department offered, they opted for a private deposition. Apparently, they feared another embarrassing spectacle in which they failed to produce any evidence of wrongdoing by Biden. And the fear turned out to be justified: Weiss repeated to the lawmakers that he had full decision-making authority in the case and didn't experience any interference.

Matt Gaetz acknowledged that the Republican inquisitors got "almost nothing" from the highly anticipated session.

And Comer was getting increasingly defensive.

On Nov. 9, the *Daily Beast*'s Roger Sollenberger published an article titled "James Comer, Like Joe Biden, Also Paid His Brother $200K." The article asserted that Comer and his brother operated a "shell company," that "Comer channeled extra money to his brother, seemingly from nothing," and that Comer had family agriculture interests at the same time he "held important positions in agriculture oversight."

There was no evidence that James Comer had done anything illegal— much like there was no evidence that Joe Biden did anything illegal. But the *Daily Beast* piece attached the same innuendo to Comer's dealings that Comer attached to Biden's dealings.

Shortly after the piece was published, at an otherwise sleepy Oversight Committee hearing on the General Services Administration, Florida Democrat Jared Moskowitz needled Comer over the propriety of his family business dealings and appearances of conflicts of interest.

"It has come out in the public that you also do business with your brother with potential loans," Moskowitz said, telling Comer "you owe it to the American people to explain."

Comer went wild. "That is bullshit!" he yelled from the dais. "All this bullshit that [the White House's] Ian Sams is trying to tell people that only dumb, financially illiterate people pick up on!" When Comer started a gratuitous attack on another Democrat on the panel, Dan Goldman, calling him "Mr. Trust Fund," Moskowitz tried to reclaim his time.

"No, I'm not going to give you your time back!" Comer shouted. "You look like a Smurf." (Moskowitz was wearing a light blue jacket and tie.)

Comer was out of control. "My father, who was a dentist, had some farmland . . . I'm one of the largest landowners . . . You've already been proven a liar."

"Mr. Chairman," Moskowitz observed, "this seems to have gotten under your skin."

Comer fancied the *Daily Beast* piece to be the result of "bullshit" peddled by Ian Sams, whose job in the White House counsel's office involved defending Biden against Comer's endless allegations. Comer went after the little-known Biden staffer so often that Sams's White House colleagues displayed in their office some of the childish insults Comer had directed at him: "That Ian Sams, the president's little weenie guy . . . a little guy like Ian Sams . . . He's not the most flattering person I've ever seen . . . Ian Sams is a clown."

To be guilty of bribery, as Republicans liked to suggest Biden was, there needs to be an official act done in exchange for the bribe—a quid pro quo. But not only had Comer failed to establish that Biden had received funds; he also failed to demonstrate that Biden had done anything in exchange for the funds he had not received.

On Fox Business on Nov. 28, right-wing host Maria Bartiromo was getting an update on the Oversight Committee's probe from Lisa McClain, a Michigan Republican and a member of the panel. "There could be some serious crime here," Bartiromo ventured. "Have you been able to identify any actual policy changes that Joe Biden made as a result of getting money from China?"

McClain shut her eyes for a moment, then replied: "The short answer is no. That's what we're trying to get to."

In reality, the House investigators hadn't demonstrated that Biden received "money from China," as Bartiromo claimed. Regardless, McClain's admission meant there was neither quid nor quo.

COMER, JORDAN, AND SMITH ESTABLISHED THEMSELVES AS THE THREE STOOGES of the House's Biden investigations, bumbling as they tried to make a case for their predetermined outcome of impeaching the president.

Judiciary's Jordan was clearly Moe, thundering but blundering in his repeated failures to prove Biden's "weaponization" of the government. Smith, in over his head at Ways and Means, was Larry, brainlessly reciting whatever script was in front of him. (He was famous for asking several years earlier at a committee hearing why Democrats have "not proposed a tax on the sun" to reduce skin cancer.) And Comer was Curly, perpetually getting a pie in the face when the "evidence" he produced was immediately debunked.

"BREAKING," Comer announced on social media on Dec. 4. This attempt at a bombshell, like the previous ones, came with siren emojis. "Hunter Biden's business entity, Owasco PC, made direct monthly payments to Joe Biden." But it turned out the payments, for all of $1,380, were actually repayments for a 2018 Ford Raptor truck Biden helped his son Hunter buy at a time when the younger Biden was broke because of his drug addiction.

Nyuk, nyuk, nyuk.

After that flop, the Three Stooges assembled in the echoey lobby of the Longworth House Office Building on Dec. 5 for a "media availability" on the impeachment inquiry. But all they did was recite their allegations before hustling away.

"No questions?" the *Washington Examiner*'s Reese Gorman called after them. "I thought this was a press conference."

Smith then gaveled in the Ways and Means Committee to hear once more from his IRS "whistleblowers." His first order of business: to close the meeting to the public and the press.

The ranking Democrat, Richard Neal of Massachusetts, made a motion for the hearing to remain open to the public. "You're not recognized," Smith replied.

Texas Democrat Lloyd Doggett asked to debate the Republicans' motion to kick out the public. "It's not debatable," Smith shot back.

Republicans repelled the Democrats' attempts at transparency in party-line votes; Smith ordered the room cleared of journalists and spectators. Republicans said they would release a transcript "upon completion of our meeting," but it didn't come out that day, or the next.

Their efforts to hide their proceedings from the public made it clear, if it weren't already, that the investigators had lost the plot in their attempt to implicate Biden. But would they press ahead anyway? Certainly! Woop, woop, woop, woop, woop, woop.

Failure was no deterrent. On Nov. 29, during a private caucus meeting at Republican National Committee headquarters, the majority whip, Tom

Emmer, told his colleagues that they would vote to ratify the impeachment inquiry that McCarthy had authorized.

Just a few weeks earlier, Johnson, shortly after assuming the speakership, had told Republican moderates in a closed-door meeting that there was insufficient evidence to begin formal impeachment proceedings, the *Washington Post*'s Jacqueline Alemany reported. This was unacceptable to the impeachment-happy members of his caucus, and Johnson quickly reversed himself. "A formal impeachment inquiry vote," he declared in December, "is something we have to do at this juncture."

At the Dec. 12 debate on the impeachment resolution before the Rules Committee, Democrats exhausted their thesauruses in denouncing the move: "sham," "stunt," "ludicrous," "lie," "pathetic joke," "colossal waste of time." "We are here because Donald Trump ordered you to be here," said the ranking Democrat, Jim McGovern.

Republicans didn't really try to conceal that they were motivated by revenge for Trump's impeachments. "You can't say that what was good enough for President Trump is no longer good enough for President Biden," said Guy Reschenthaler of Pennsylvania. "The Democrats shifted the standard. Frankly, now, impeachment, you could view it as almost a political exercise."

He elaborated: "Now we have a situation where impeachment, the standard of impeachment has been lowered to such a degree that, again, it's merely at this point, a political exercise. Not that this is a political exercise."

Of course not!

Pressed by Democrat Joe Neguse of Colorado to say which specific crime the Biden inquiry was investigating, Reschenthaler had no answer.

Members of the majority on the panel made their case by repeating their well-worn insinuations. To this, they added extraneous insults. Ralph Norman of South Carolina alleged that Biden was "cognitively gone," adding, "The man is not there . . . He doesn't know where he is." And yet at the same time Republicans alleged that he was the mastermind of the greatest political scandal in American history.

The debate on the House floor was no more illuminating. Comer, keeping his place in his speech with his finger, prattled on about "schemes" and "shell companies."

Norman offered a novel twist on the whole innocent-until-proven-guilty concept. "You cannot, just not, uh, say you are innocent and not have to prove it," he told the House.

And, as usual, the Republicans cited the sins of the son as justification for impeaching the father. "The son of the president of the United States is a tax cheat!" Byron Donalds thundered.

"You'll notice," McGovern responded, "my Republican friends never talk about Joe Biden. It's all Hunter Biden."

Donalds, ignoring House rules, heckled McGovern, shouting, "Didn't I just say Joe Biden?"

Democrat Swalwell congratulated Republicans for their dogged pursuit of the president's son. "I want to give James Comer some credit," he told the House, "because after 50,000 pages of depositions and secret hearings and closed hearings, I think, if we give him enough time, he is going to prove that Hunter Biden is Joe Biden's son."

The day before skipping town for their Christmas recess, House Republicans voted in an entirely party-line vote of 221–212 to formalize their impeachment inquiry.

For months, House Republicans had been demanding to hear from Hunter Biden. On Oct. 31, Comer had said on a podcast that he would soon be bringing in the remaining witnesses, including the president's son, "for depositions or committee hearings, whichever they choose."

Then Hunter Biden called his bluff. Biden's lawyer, Abbe Lowell, said his client would be happy to testify publicly before Congress. Comer immediately rejected the offer—"That won't stand with House Republicans"—and insisted the president's son instead submit to a closed-door inquisition.

Jamie Raskin needled the chairman for his sudden diffidence. "After wailing and moaning for ten months about Hunter Biden and alluding to some vast unproven family conspiracy . . . Chairman Comer and the Oversight Republicans now reject his offer to appear before the full committee and the eyes of the world?" he asked,

On Dec. 13, the day Hunter Biden had been summoned for his closed-door appearance before Comer's panel, Biden instead pulled into the Capitol driveway and stood on a patio called the Senate Swamp. "Here

I am, Mr. Chairman, taking up your offer, when you said we can bring these people in for depositions or committee hearings, whichever they choose," the president's son said in front of the cameras. "Well, I've chosen. I am here to testify at a public hearing."

But now Comer stood on the other side of the Capitol, in the Rayburn building, complaining to reporters that Biden had blown off the closed-door deposition. "The president's son does not get to set the rules," Comer told reporters after Hunter's remarks. Soon thereafter, Comer and Jordan announced "contempt of Congress proceedings" against Biden for insisting that his testimony be in public.

What were they trying to prevent Americans from seeing? That "my father was not financially involved in my business," as Hunter Biden declared outside the Capitol? That "MAGA Republicans" have taken "the light of my dad's love for me and presented it as darkness"?

As for his insistence that Hunter Biden testify in secret, Comer said: "This has been the most transparent, political—er, congressional investigation."

Nothing says "transparent" quite like "closed-door deposition"—an awkwardness even Fox News couldn't hide. "On this show, we've been calling for Hunter to go and sit in a chair on Capitol Hill in front of the TV cameras for the last year," host Steve Doocy said on *Fox and Friends*. "Now, Hunter's lawyer, Abbe Lowell, says he will do that, but Comer and Jim Jordan say, no, it's not negotiable, he's got to be in private."

That's not all the normally MAGA-friendly host had to say. "It looks like they've got the goods on Hunter Biden, but the Republicans have not made the case yet where Joe Biden profited from it," he told Fox viewers. "They haven't explained how it implicates Joe," he added, and "they have not shown Joe Biden did anything illegal."

Several Senate Republicans shared those doubts about the House's blind race to impeach. "I don't see the grounds," Shelley Moore Capito of West Virginia told *Politico*'s Anthony Adragna.

"There's been no evidence provided to the public yet or certainly to me to suggest an impeachment inquiry or impeachment itself is justified," said Romney.

"You're not going to have this president impeached based on the evidence that we've seen," offered Murkowski.

Chuck Grassley of Iowa told CNN's Manu Raju that "the facts haven't taken me to that point where I can say the president is guilty of anything."

On Jan. 10, their first day back in session after the Christmas break, members of the House Oversight Committee spent their time marking up legislation to hold Hunter Biden in contempt of Congress for refusing to appear before the committee—and there, appearing before the committee in the very front row of the audience, was Hunter Biden. The panel voted, along party lines, to hold him in contempt anyway, but not before voting, also along party lines, to support the right of Marjorie Taylor Greene to display pornographic photos of Hunter Biden with a prostitute.

"Who bribed Hunter Biden to be here today?" asked Republican Nancy Mace of South Carolina, one of the first to speak. "You are the epitome of white privilege," added Mace, who is white and the daughter of a U.S. army general, "coming in to the Oversight Committee, spitting in our face, ignoring a congressional subpoena to be deposed. What are you afraid of? You have no balls to come up here and—"

Thus began eight hours of chaos.

"If the gentlelady wants to hear from Hunter Biden, we can hear from him right now," Democrat Jared Moskowitz of Florida said, interrupting.

Lawmakers yelled over each other. Cries of "Order!" broke out.

"I think that Hunter Biden should be arrested right here, right now and go straight to jail," Mace opined.

Andy Biggs, an Arizona Republican, suggested that his colleagues shouldn't "act like a bunch of nimrods."

Moskowitz called for a vote "to hear from Hunter right now." Republicans declined.

After several minutes of this, Hunter Biden and his lawyer left the room—just as Greene was getting ready to speak. "I was about to speak to him!" she called after him. "What a coward!"

Mace's claim that Hunter Biden had "no balls" was undermined rather vividly by Greene, who again displayed for the committee posters showing him engaging in sex acts with a prostitute. They were the same images she had displayed at a 2023 hearing, with genitals minimally obscured and leaving nothing to the imagination. Raskin objected. "This is not the Jerry Springer Show," he protested.

Comer called the sex photos "appropriately censored evidence"—and 21 Republicans on the committee, in a party-line vote, upheld Greene's display of the sex shots, which she insisted were not "revenge porn."

Moskowitz retaliated, displaying a blow-up poster of Donald Trump posing with Jeffrey Epstein. He blasted the hypocrisy of the Republicans' prurient fascination with Hunter Biden while "the guy you all kneel to associates himself with a pedophile."

Louisiana Republican Clay Higgins demanded that Moskowitz's words be struck from the record—not the ones about Trump and the pedophile but the ones about Republicans kneeling to Trump. "I kneel to Christ!" Higgins screamed, not long after voting to uphold pornography in the hearing room.

At the core of the bogus impeachment case against Biden was an allegation that, as vice president, he had been bribed by an executive at the Ukrainian energy company Burisma, where Hunter Biden was on the board. In exchange for a $5 million payment, the allegation went, Biden pressured Ukraine to remove a prosecutor, Viktor Shokin, who was investigating corruption at Burisma. The claim had been endlessly debunked: Shokin was the corrupt one, Europeans and the United States had all been pushing for his ouster, and Biden's involvement had nothing to do with Burisma, which Shokin wasn't even investigating. Then there was the small matter of there being no evidence of any bribe being paid.

Comer had rolled out the explosive charge in May 2023, claiming a "whistleblower" had raised concerns "that then–Vice President Biden allegedly engaged in a bribery scheme with a foreign national." He continued: "The American people need to know if President Biden sold out the United States of America to make money for himself." Fox News dutifully repeated the outrageous allegation 1,400 times over the following four months.

Comer demanded documents from the FBI that would supposedly

corroborate the bribe, and he threatened to hold the FBI's Wray in contempt of Congress if he didn't turn them over.

The FBI tried to discourage Comer from reading too much into the claim, raising doubts about its reliability and noting that it had investigated the claim during the Trump administration and decided that it wasn't worthy of further action.

But House Republicans continued to raise the Burisma bribery allegation, and Jordan called the confidential informant's accusation "the most corroborating evidence we have."

That "evidence" collapsed in spectacular fashion in February 2024, when the confidential FBI informant, Alexander Smirnov, was indicted by federal prosecutors for fabricating the entire thing. He was apparently doing the bidding of Russian intelligence, with which, a court filing showed, he had numerous ties.

When Hunter Biden appeared for his deposition two weeks later, on Feb. 28 (he had by now consented to the closed-door session rather than a public hearing), it was apparent to all that there was nothing left of the House Republicans' impeachment case.

Moskowitz usually wore loud ensembles and sneakers to work. But for the Hunter Biden deposition, the Democrat came in all black: suit, tie, and shoes. "My colleagues and I are witnessing the death of the fake, faux, frivolous Joe Biden impeachment inquiry," he said by way of explaining his somber garb. "In fact, as a Jewish American, when this is over I will say the mourner's kaddish for this impeachment inquiry."

To the extent there ever was life in the case against the president, it had finally died after a long illness.

But more fitting than the mourner's kaddish would have been to offer a Panikhida, the Russian Orthodox prayer service for the dead. For the House Republicans' yearlong attempt to impeach Biden, it was now clear, was based at least in part on a Russian disinformation campaign—and House Republicans went along with it, either as useful idiots or as knowing accomplices.

Smirnov had been indicted. He joined the Republican sleuths' other key witness, Gal Luft, who, as noted earlier, was a fugitive from justice, charged with arms trafficking and illegal lobbying work for China.

Republicans had also relied on the accounts of two of Hunter Biden's former business partners, one of whom had been sentenced to prison for defrauding a Native American tribe; House investigators went to visit at a prison in Alabama.

Of course, Republicans didn't actually need any evidence to impeach the president if they had the votes. But even the impeachment ringleader, Comer, had tiptoed away from this goal. He told a group of us staking out the Hunter Biden deposition that "the purpose of this investigation [is] to create legislation"—legislation to stop "the Bidens from continuing to enrich themselves."

Wagging two index fingers, Comer admonished: "The American people do not want families to peddle access to the tune of $200,000." Asked whether his legislation would also target the Trump family, which peddled access to the tune of billions of dollars, Comer ignored the question as he walked away.

The fabricated "bribery" allegation was just the latest case of MAGA Republicans trumpeting Kremlin propaganda. They let Russia off the hook for its hacking of the Democratic National Committee and its extensive efforts to influence American social media to Trump's benefit in 2016, dismissing it as the "Russia hoax."

During Trump's 2019 impeachment for trying to strong-arm Ukraine into providing dirt on Biden for the 2020 campaign, House Republicans defended Trump by echoing Russian propaganda claiming that Ukraine, not Russia, was the country that had tried to meddle in the U.S. election.

Trump adviser Rudy Giuliani tried to inject disinformation from an active Russian agent into the 2020 campaign, and two of his associates who worked on the effort have been convicted.

More recently, in February 2024, Tucker Carlson and other Trump allies promoted Russian propaganda about its invasion of Ukraine. Senator Tommy Tuberville of Alabama claimed that "Russia is open to a peace agreement, while it is DC warmongers who want to prolong the war." Carlson, visiting Moscow, called the city "so much nicer than any city in my country."

And, of course, Speaker Johnson and his House Republicans, some of them citing Russia's talking points, were at that very moment blocking funds for Ukraine's war effort that the Senate had overwhelmingly supported.

They didn't seem to care that they were serving as Putin's pawns. A dozen or so witnesses had already testified to House impeachment investigators that the president was not involved in his son's businesses. The investigators produced no evidence showing that the elder Biden benefited in any way from his son's businesses nor took any official action to help his son.

Yet Comer wanted so much to believe otherwise that he was willing to take the word of the indicted Smirnov over that of the FBI and of the prosecutor Weiss. Weiss's court filing said that Smirnov acknowledged ties to Russian intelligence agencies, and that he had met in December 2023 with a Russian official "who controls groups that are engaged in overseas assassination efforts." Smirnov was "actively peddling new lies that could impact U.S. elections after meeting with Russian intelligence officials in November."

Comer whipped up a new conspiracy with Fox Business's Maria Bartiromo, suggesting Smirnov had been indicted not because he fabricated the bribery allegation but because he told the truth. "Alexander Smirnov was another whistleblower," Bartiromo, a Trump ally, said, arguing that Smirnov had told the FBI that Biden "accepted bribe money—and now he's being indicted."

Comer said he thought the matter "suspicious" and the indictment "very concerning," because he had "zero" trust in the FBI. "The FBI paid him to be a spy in Russia," the chairman argued. "They indicted him because he was communicating with Russia, but that's what they paid him for." Comer went on to defend the truth of claims Smirnov had made. "The part that has never been confirmed is about Joe Biden . . . and look, we're still looking."

And looking. And looking.

Comer, speaking to reporters in the lobby before the Hunter Biden deposition, was pressed repeatedly by NBC's Ryan Nobles to give evidence of a single official action Biden supposedly took to benefit his son.

Comer, after a couple of failed attempts, abandoned his argument entirely and instead attacked the journalist. "You can defend Joe Biden all day long! You can be on his legal defense team!"

"You're not answering my question," Nobles replied. "I'm asking you what specific action did he take as an elected public official?"

"Calm down, calm down," Comer countered. "All the angry liberals."

In the closed-door deposition, Republicans grilled the president's son about crucial matters such as his divorce, his drug addiction, and his use of speakerphones. Hunter Biden, rather than evading questions and taking the Fifth, went on the offensive, asking why they had not investigated Trump son-in-law Jared Kushner's influence peddling.

Biden, labeling the Republicans "dupes in carrying out a Russian disinformation campaign waged against my father," scolded them: "You have trafficked in innuendo, distortion, and sensationalism—all the while ignoring the clear and convincing evidence staring you in the face. You do not have evidence to support the baseless and MAGA-motivated conspiracies about my father because there isn't any."

Finally, at day's end, Hunter Biden departed with lawyer Abbe Lowell, who told reporters: "It seems to me that the Republican members wanted to spend more time talking about my client's addiction than . . . any question that had anything to do with what they call their impeachment inquiry."

As they walked out the door, a reporter from the Tucker Carlson–founded *Daily Caller* shouted after them: "Mr. Biden! Was the cocaine at the White House yours?"

Had they a scintilla of shame, House Republicans would have shut down their embarrassing caper. But there was no longer such a thing as shame. Comer declared that "we've been very effective in getting the truth to the American people."

It sounded better in the original Russian.

COMER COULDN'T QUITE COME TO TERMS WITH HOW SPECTACULARLY HIS previous impeachment probe had flamed out. He called yet another hearing, this one relying on the testimony of a onetime business associate of Hunter Biden who separately engaged in multiple securities fraud schemes. Comer had to get special permission from House leadership for Jason Galanis to testify remotely because, as Comer explained, "He is unable to attend the hearing in-person as he is currently in federal custody." But once again, neither Galanis nor the other witness, another Biden business associate, named Tony Bobulinski, had anything incriminating. Hunter Biden, invited by Comer to testify, sent his regrets; he had no incentive to throw Comer a lifeline.

Raskin, at the hearing, openly mocked Comer and "his ace MAGA detectives" for coming up empty. Comer, in desperation, said he would invite the elder Biden to testify before his panel. "We need to hear from the president himself," the hapless chairman said.

Replied Ian Sams at the White House: "LOL . . . This is a sad stunt at the end of a dead impeachment. Call it a day, pal."

Comer and the other impeachment leaders knew they had nowhere near the votes to impeach Biden. Even a Newsmax anchor asked Jordan why he hadn't given up: "It kind of seems like you're chasing your tail at this point on the impeachment inquiry because this is not going to go anywhere."

"Fair question," Jordan allowed.

Comer, in one more face-saving attempt, said he would send "criminal referrals" to the Justice Department instead of impeaching Biden. A brilliant plan—except that he had uncovered no crimes, and Biden's Justice Department was unlikely to prosecute Biden for crimes he didn't commit.

In the end, Comer ended where he had begun: with a conspiracy theory. On Fox News Radio, he offered an explanation for why impeachment failed. Attorney General "Garland's working with the Deep State, who's working with the liberal mainstream media to try to indoctrinate into people's minds that there's no evidence."

There couldn't possibly be another explanation.

HOUSE REPUBLICANS HAD BY NOW HAD A YEAR TO REFLECT ON THEIR VULGAR antics during Biden's 2023 State of the Union address. The day before Biden delivered his 2024 address, Johnson, in a closed-door meeting with his Republican caucus, urged his colleagues to show "a high standard of decorum," *Axios*'s Andrew Solender reported, and not to act like hooligans during the speech.

He might as well have asked them not to breathe.

Greene, who disrupted Biden in 2023 with her cry of "bullshit," promised more of the same. "How can we be concerned about decorum when Congress has put the American people $34 trillion in debt?" she asked, raising the possibility that she didn't know what the word "decorum" means. "I think decorum is already broken."

On the night of March 7, just minutes into the speech, as Biden was talking about the Trump administration's failures during the covid pandemic, Wisconsin Republican Derrick Van Orden bellowed from the back of the chamber: "Lies!"

When Biden spoke about forcing the wealthiest Americans to "pay your fair share in taxes," Greene, wearing a red Make America Great Again baseball cap autographed on the bill by Donald Trump, shouted out: "Tell Hunter to pay his taxes!"

And when Biden spoke about the bipartisan border security legislation that Republicans killed at Trump's behest, the Republican side erupted in boos, jeers, and screaming at the commander in chief.

The lawmakers' invited guests in the gallery joined in the general abuse of the president. Biden mentioned crime—and a man started screaming about the withdrawal from Afghanistan. Biden spoke about the 30,000 Palestinians killed in Gaza—and another heckler shouted: "Says who?"

Adding to the Republicans' tawdry treatment of this once solemn ritual of democracy, the expelled George Santos could be seen cavorting on the floor, wearing a glittery shirt and shoes, receiving well-wishes from his former GOP colleagues. And Texas Republican Troy Nehls served as a human billboard throughout the speech, standing in the chamber wearing a T-shirt that showed Trump's mug shot with the message "Never Surrender."

Many others in the House majority took Johnson's call for "decorum" to the other extreme. They were so determined not to react to Biden that they refused to applaud even the most anodyne, patriotic sentiments.

"Let's remember who we are. We are the United States of America!" Biden cried.

On the Republican side: crickets.

He called for federal funds to go only for "American products ... built by American workers, creating good-paying American jobs."

Again, Republicans sat on their hands.

"We all come from somewhere, but we're all Americans," Biden offered. Even this produced almost no applause from Republican lawmakers.

Johnson, in his seat behind Biden, didn't heed his own admonition to be "respectful of the institution." He rolled his eyes at Biden, shaking his head, contorting his face into pained expressions, and shrinking into his chair.

That was the thing about this House Republican majority. Whether it was their failure to keep the House functioning, their failure to make a case against Biden, or their failure to uphold even a minimal standard of decency, there simply was no learning curve. It was all combat, all the time—and all in the service of one man.

Chapter 13

"We Need a
National Divorce"

Donald Trump could not have asked for a nicer arraignment-day gift.

On June 13, 2023, during the very same hour in which the former president surrendered to federal authorities in Miami to face charges of mishandling national security secrets—his second of four arraignments—his Republican allies in the House were officially embracing as heroes and martyrs the people who had sacked the Capitol on Jan. 6, 2021, in hopes of overturning Trump's election defeat.

In the Capitol complex, Matt Gaetz, with sidekick Marjorie Taylor Greene and four other far-right lawmakers, held a "hearing" that lauded participants in the riot, family members of other Jan. 6 participants, and organizers of the attempted overthrow of the 2020 vote.

Technically, Gaetz had no authority to call such a hearing, because he wasn't a committee chairman. But Kevin McCarthy, desperate to win over the extremists in his caucus, let it happen anyway.

Gaetz did his all to make the proceedings look official. There were congressional seals on his nameplate and on the big screen behind him. A meeting room in the Capitol Visitor Center was arranged to appear like a committee room, with lawmakers facing the witnesses. Gaetz advertised the "field hearing" as part of how "the 118th Congress is investigating the weaponization of the federal government."

He impersonated a chairman. "I'm going to call this field hearing on January 6 to order," he began, and he sprinkled in official-sounding phrases such as "You are recognized," "Thank you for your written testimony," "I'm going to recognize myself for questions," and "Your time has expired." The others played along ("Thank you for the opportunity to testify," "I yield back"). Gaetz said testimony would be available "for the official record of the House" or for "work in the Judiciary Committee, upon which I serve, or the Oversight Committee." C-SPAN carried the proceedings live.

The invited witnesses?

The wife of Ronald McAbee, who is awaiting trial for allegedly attacking a police officer and dragging him into the mob while wearing a black vest that said "SHERIFF."

Underwear model John Strand, sentenced to two years and eight months for being part of the mob that breached the Capitol on Jan. 6 and pushed past police officers.

Activist Brandon Straka, sentenced to home detention and probation and fined for his Jan. 6 actions.

The aunt of Matthew Perna, who committed suicide while awaiting sentencing for his role in breaching the Capitol.

Ed Martin, an organizer of the "Stop the Steal" effort leading up to Jan. 6.

Jeff Clark, the Trump Justice Department official who tried to get states to toss the election results.

The lawmakers hailed them all.

"To all of you, my condolences," said Paul Gosar, who added tenderly that "you know how I feel about Ashli" Babbitt, the woman shot by police as she breached the last line of defense protecting lawmakers in the House chamber.

"This is heartbreaking," added South Carolina Republican Ralph Norman, "the way you all have been treated."

Greene added "my deepest sympathy for each of you and all the pain and suffering that you've all had to go through because of this government." She told them that they were the victims of "sick, evil people" and that she and other lawmakers had a "constitutional duty to object to Joe Biden's fraudulent electoral college votes because we all believed that the election had been stolen."

Gaetz opened the hearing with a video suggesting FBI culpability in the Jan. 6 attack. He claimed he "became aware of evidence" that the Justice Department had evidence of "fraud in the election" but Attorney General Bill Barr—Trump's attorney general—"was suppressing evidence."

Gosar blamed the attack on "people undercover, whether it be antifa, FBI, whatever." Norman suggested that the FBI was framing people who weren't involved in the attack.

Another lawmaker, Troy Nehls of Texas, offered his view that people in charge in the Capitol (Democrats, presumably) "hid the intelligence" showing that an attack was coming: "It's like they wanted this to happen." Nehls added that "I believe Ashli Babbitt was murdered that day," and he said he hoped Trump would return to power and send the officer who shot her before a grand jury. Another participant, Colorado's Lauren Boebert, had also asserted that Babbitt was "murdered" by Capitol Police.

From the witness table came howls of "wrongful conviction" and "fascism." From the dais came a cry of "tyranny." From both came attacks on judges, juries, and prosecutors. People in the audience wore T-shirts saying rioters had been "murdered by Capitol police." In the hallway, keeping the peace, were two Capitol Police officers, guarding the people accusing them of murder.

Straka, who on Jan. 6 yelled "Go, go, go" to the mob as they tried to breach the Capitol and "Take it, take it" when rioters grabbed a shield from a police officer, "testified" to Gaetz's panel that "we, the defendants of Jan. 6, need to be able to have some sort of voice."

And now they had that voice: the 221 members of the House Republican Conference who let this abomination occur.

This is how House Republicans used their majority: to rewrite the history of the Jan. 6 insurrection, to lionize those who attacked American democracy, to demonize those who tried to uphold the rule of law—and even to encourage outright violence.

Days before Trump's arraignment in Miami, Louisiana Republican Clay Higgins issued military-style orders on Twitter: "President Trump said he has 'been summoned to appear at the Federal Courthouse in Miami on Tuesday, at 3 PM.' This is a perimeter probe from the oppressors. Hold. rPOTUS has this. Buckle up. 1/50K know your bridges. Rock steady calm. That is all."

Dartmouth College professor Jeff Sharlet, who follows the language of the far right, interpreted Higgins's code in *The Atlantic:* "rPOTUS" referred to the "real" president. "1/50K" is the 1:50,000 scale used on military maps. "Know your bridges" meant "knowing the approaches to your location—especially bridges, which can be seized."

Two days later, Higgins backed away—slightly—from the violence he was teeing up when he told Trump supporters to make their preparations and "buckle up." He tweeted: "Patriots, we've manipulated the MSM [mainstream media] to establish deep commo"—that's psyops—"now copy this . . . do NOT trip the wire they've laid for you. Maintain your family. Live your life. Know your bridges. Hold."

The Louisianan, with his checkered background in law enforcement, identified himself as a member of the Three Percenters, a far-right group involved in the Jan. 6 attack on the Capitol, and he also spoke at a rally of the Oath Keepers, another group later involved in the insurrection. And now he was a member of Congress issuing militia-coded calls to arms on social media.

Higgins wasn't alone. Also on Twitter, Andy Biggs, an Arizona Republican, responded to the Trump indictment with violent language: "We have now reached a war phase. Eye for an eye."

THE MOST DISTINGUISHING CHARACTERISTIC OF THE HOUSE REPUBLICAN majority of 2023 was its thorough Trumpification. At a time when Trump was down and out, House Republicans as a group did more than any other to restore him as the unquestioned leader of the party. They rallied impulsively to his side after each of his four indictments, without even a moment to consider the substance of the charges. They also, to a far greater extent than Republicans in the Senate or in governorships, mimicked, amplified, and tried to validate his paranoid claims about a Deep State conspiracy within the federal government, his ludicrous claims that the election had been stolen, his rewriting of Jan. 6, and his claim that the government had been "weaponized" against him and his supporters by Democrats.

To the extent the federal government had been "weaponized" by anyone, Trump was the one wielding the weapon. During his time in the White House, Trump wanted the IRS to investigate four senior officials at the FBI who had been part of the probe into Russia's interference in the 2016 election. Two of them—James Comey and Andrew McCabe—were actually audited. He called for criminal investigations or actual charges against Barack Obama, Joe Biden, Hillary Clinton, John Kerry, and other prominent Democrats. He withheld military aid from Ukraine to pressure the country to announce a probe of Biden, and when he lost the election, he used his position to try to overthrow the election results.

He threatened to do even worse if he was returned to power. Trump and his allies drafted plans to invoke the Insurrection Act to use the military to put down domestic protests. They threatened to use criminal and regulatory sanctions against unfriendly journalists and media outlets, and former staffers he considers disloyal. Lifting the language of Nazi Germany, he called his political opponents "vermin" and said immigration was "poisoning the blood" of the United States. Asked by Fox News' Sean Hannity to provide reassurance that he wouldn't abuse his power by seeking retribution against opponents, Trump said he wouldn't be a dictator—"except for Day One."

A few Republicans dared to speak out about the dangers of worshipping the "Orange Jesus," as Tennessee Republican Mark Green dubbed Trump, in Liz Cheney's account. "Too many Republican leaders are lying to America," Colorado Republican Ken Buck said, "claiming that the 2020 election was stolen, describing January 6 as an unguided tour of the Capitol and asserting that the ensuing prosecutions are a weaponization of our justice system." Of these "self-serving lies," he continued: "These insidious narratives breed widespread cynicism and erode Americans' confidence in the rule of law. It is impossible for the Republican Party to confront our problems and offer a course correction for the future while being obsessively fixated on retribution and vengeance for contrived injustices of the past."

Buck could say such things because he was quitting. He made the remarks in a Nov. 1 video announcing his retirement.

COME ON, BE HONEST: WHO AMONG US HAS NOT HAD AN EXTRAMARITAL affair with a porn star? It is the rare person indeed who can truthfully say he or she has not. And that is why I admonish you: Let he who has not lied about using campaign funds to pay hush money cast the first stone!

When Manhattan district attorney Alvin Bragg in March 2023 brought the first indictment against Trump, in the Stormy Daniels case, MAGA World raced to circle the wagons. But special recognition had to go to those who not only attacked Bragg's prosecution but also defended Trump's behavior with the adult-film actress as totally and completely normal.

"Settlements like this, whatever you think of them, are common both among famous people, celebrities and in corporate America," Fox News' Tucker Carlson (mis)informed his viewers on March 20. "Paying people not to talk about things, hush money, is ordinary in modern America."

Carlson's surrender to Trump was epic. A couple of weeks earlier, old text messages had come out in which Carlson called Trump "a demonic force, a destroyer," and said, "I hate him passionately." But suddenly Carlson was back to defending some of Trump's seediest behavior as utterly routine.

It wasn't just Carlson, of course. It was also the elected Republican officials who collectively decided after Bragg brought the indictment that it was in their interest to bring Trump back from the political dead. Once again, Trump used a fabrication to revive his flagging standing. And once again, congressional Republicans fell for it.

Just a week previously, leading Republicans were daring to hope that Trump's sway was ebbing. Polls showed Florida governor Ron DeSantis within striking range of Trump in the GOP presidential primary, and challengers DeSantis and Mike Pence took Trump on directly. Then Trump changed all that with just one post on his social media site on Saturday morning, March 18, announcing his expectation that he "WILL BE ARRESTED ON TUESDAY." He wrote: "PROTEST, TAKE OUR NATION BACK!"

In reality, he wasn't arrested on Tuesday. Or Wednesday. Or Thursday. But House Republicans didn't wait to see whether Trump was speaking the truth. They did as he commanded, leaping to his defense—and, in the process, returning him to his previous place of dominance atop the Republican Party. Suddenly, it was all about Donald Trump—again.

Within just a few hours of Trump's claim that he would be arrested three days later, Kevin McCarthy announced that House Republicans were launching investigations into the "outrageous abuse of power" by Bragg and his attempt "to subvert our democracy by interfering in elections with politically motivated prosecutions."

On March 20, three House committee chairmen fired off a letter to Bragg summoning him to testify before Congress and demanding that he produce six years' worth of documents—all because he was "reportedly about to engage" in "the indictment of a former president." Never mind that Bragg hadn't yet done so. House Republicans were using their power to interfere in a criminal investigation of state law on the basis of Trump's erroneous claim.

Things only deteriorated from there.

By the dozen, House lawmakers and their Fox allies denounced Bragg by calling him "a hired hit man by George Soros" (Eric Burlison, Republican of Missouri) or by saying Bragg, who is Black, is "listening to his master, George Soros" (Fox host Rachel Campos-Duffy).

Matt Gaetz called on DeSantis to "stop any sort of extradition of President Trump from the state of Florida." Mark Green, chairman of the House Homeland Security committee (and the one who brought us the phrase "Orange Jesus"), apparently mistook Bragg for a federal prosecutor. "Daniel Ortega arrested his opposition in Nicaragua and we called that a horrible thing," he said. "Mr. Biden, Mr. President, think about that."

House GOP conference chief Elise Stefanik likewise called the investigation by a county D.A. "the epitome of the weaponizing of the federal government."

Inevitably, Republicans quickly found themselves not only denouncing the prosecutor but defending Trump's behavior. McCarthy vouched for Trump by saying that the hush money paid to Daniels "was personal money" and that Trump "wasn't trying to hide" it—claims that were challenged by the available facts. Fox host Jesse Watters did him one better in Trump's defense, telling viewers: "There's no proof Trump slept with Stormy. There's no baby."

Senate Republicans voiced public concern that their House counterparts had gone too far in their prosecutorial meddling. "I would hope they would stick to the agenda they ran on," said Senator John Cornyn of Texas.

Senator Shelley Moore Capito, a West Virginia Republican, put it best when she told *Punchbowl News:* "The House is gonna do what the House is gonna do."

And what it did was put Trump back in unquestioned command of the Republican Party.

When the indictment came down a week later, House Republicans didn't just defend Trump. They aped Trump.

"Political Persecution," Trump alleged in his statement.
"Political persecution," parroted Diana Harshbarger of Tennessee, Josh Brecheen of Oklahoma, Claudia Tenney of New York, and Paul Gosar of Arizona.

"Blatant Election Interference," Trump announced.
"This is unprecedented election interference," echoed Stefanik.
"An attempt to interfere in our Presidential election," echoed McCarthy.

"Witch hunt," complained Trump.
"Witch hunt," repeated George Santos, Lauren Boebert, Ralph Norman, Matt Gaetz, and more.

"Weaponizing our justice system," Trump inveighed.
"Weaponizing," chorused majority leader Steve Scalise, David Rouzer of North Carolina, Austin Scott and Rich McCormick of Georgia, and more.

Trump blamed George Soros, the progressive Jewish billionaire. Harshbarger, Gosar, and Wesley Hunt of Texas (along with Senators Rick Scott and Ron Johnson) blamed Soros.

They mimicked Trump in other ways, too.

In their vulgarity: "Enough of this witch hunt bullshit," tweeted Greene. "This is complete and utter bullshit," asserted Brian Mast of Florida.

In ALL CAPS: "WITCH HUNT!" screamed Ronny Jackson of Texas. "Alvin Bragg is a NATIONAL EMBARRASSMENT."

In demanding vengeance: "Hunter Biden: Call your lawyers," suggested Darrell Issa of California. "The House of Representatives will hold Alvin Bragg and his unprecedented abuse of power to account," declared McCarthy. "When Trump wins, THESE PEOPLE WILL PAY!!" tweeted Jackson.

In voicing Deep State conspiracy theories: "The Regime occupying our country and systematically killing America is most afraid of President Donald J. Trump," warned Gosar.

And in stoking paranoia among the unstable: "If they can come for him, they can come for anyone," tweeted Andy Biggs of Arizona.

The message from House Republicans was clear: We are all Trumpians now.

On Apr. 17, Chairman Jim Jordan took his House Judiciary Committee on a field trip to Manhattan in his capacity as unofficial cheerleader for Donald Trump's legal defense. The plan was to hold a hearing showing that Bragg, the man who indicted Trump, had, in just one year on the job, single-handedly turned New York City into an apocalyptic hellhole of violent crime. The hearing's official purpose: to "examine how Manhattan District Attorney Alvin Bragg's pro-crime, anti-victim policies have led to an increase in violent crime and a dangerous community for New York City residents."

But, as with seemingly all things Jordan touched, the proceedings quickly devolved into chaos.

Audience members heckled Democrats on the Judiciary Committee's panel: "You're a scumbag! . . . You guys are scumbags, all of you!" As one demonstrator was being led out by police, he shouted at the ranking Democrat, Jerry Nadler: "You're a disgrace, Ralph Nader!"

Republican witnesses joined in the disruption, interrupting Democrats (one of whom, Georgia's Hank Johnson, referred to them as "props in a MAGA Broadway production" put on by Republicans acting "like jack-booted thugs"). "Don't insult my intelligence!" one witness screamed at Democrats. "That's why I walked away from the plantation of the Democratic Party."

Members of the majority were barely more temperate. Texas Republican Troy Nehls recommended that people "use deadly force" if they fear for their lives. "I would encourage residents . . . to defend yourself. You are given that God-given right, and that means pulling out a weapon and put two at center mass," he said, pointing at his chest. "You'll reduce recidivism, won't you? And you won't have a repeat offender." His recommendation came just days after a Kansas City man opened fire on a Black teenager who rang his doorbell because he had accidentally come to the wrong address to pick up his siblings.

And there were the incessant insinuations that Bragg was "handpicked and funded by George Soros," as Trump put it. Dozens of Republicans—including at least 10 on the Judiciary Committee, by my count—echoed the spurious charge. (Soros contributed to a political action committee, Color of Change, that helped several candidates, including Bragg.)

If the antisemitic implications weren't clear enough in the constant charge that the Jewish billionaire manipulates the D.A. with his money, those attending the field hearing were greeted on their way into the building by a man holding a large poster with two dollar signs, a Jewish star, and the word "Soros." Yet even after that greeting, Mike Johnson, the future speaker, referred four times to Soros and spoke of Bragg as "bought and paid for by George Soros," and Gaetz denounced the "Soros-ization of the U.S. justice system."

New York Democrat Dan Goldman, who is Jewish, reminded the assembled that many consider such "smears" to be antisemitic.

Soon after, Wesley Hunt let it be known what he thought of that admonition. "Why do these Soros-funded district attorneys put criminals first and victims last?" he asked. "It's who they are."

And after the hearing, three Republicans on the panel—North Carolina's Dan Bishop, Wisconsin's Tom Tiffany, and Hunt—fired off tweets again repeating the Soros smear. "Today in New York," Hunt tweeted, "we heard the heartbreaking stories of Americans who mourn a loved one lost to the rising violent crime brought to you by Democrats and paid for by George Soros."

So Soros money was killing people? There really was no bottom.

WITH EACH NEW LEGAL BLOW, REPUBLICANS TIGHTENED THEIR EMBRACE OF Trump. On May 9, a Manhattan jury awarded $5 million to E. Jean Carroll, who accused Trump of sexually abusing and defaming her. Senator Marco Rubio, a Florida Republican, called the jury "a joke." (A second jury later awarded her $83 million more.)

Then, in June, came Trump's second indictment, in the federal criminal probe by special counsel Jack Smith into his mishandling of classified documents. The detailed, 37-count indictment was damning, alleging that Trump kept documents, including nuclear secrets and White House intelligence briefings, and showed them off on multiple occasions to people who did not have security clearances. He then tried to destroy camera footage and other evidence, and to conceal documents, even from his own lawyers, the prosecutor said. In the Senate, Republican leaders voiced little support for Trump, with GOP whip John Thune calling the charges "very serious" and Cornyn calling them "not good."

But in the House, McCarthy had no such integrity, instead hewing closely to the Fox News assessment of the situation, as expressed in an on-screen "news alert": "Wannabe dictator speaks at the White House after having his political rival arrested."

McCarthy began by calling the indictment a "brazen weaponization of power" and a "grave injustice." He threatened to block funding for a new FBI headquarters in retaliation. He accused Biden of stealing classified documents from a secure facility, and he said that Trump's handling of documents (piled in a bathroom) was superior to Biden's storage method (in a garage) because "a bathroom door locks."

The privacy-lock defense! But did McCarthy not comprehend that garage doors also have locks?

Jack Smith, as a special prosecutor, was protected from political influence. But within weeks various House Republicans were making plans to harass him. In mid-July, Gaetz said he would introduce legislation "to DEFUND Jack Smith's witch hunt against President Trump." In a tactic that would become popular among Trump-aligned Republicans, he accused Smith of doing precisely what Trump had actually done—"attacking our democracy and engaging in election interference."

On Aug. 1, Smith delivered another indictment against Trump, the former president's third, this time on charges related to the Jan. 6 insurrection. Greene, joining calls to defund the special prosecutor, called the indictment a "communist attack" and said she would "vote for Trump even if he's in jail." McCarthy and Oversight Committee chairman James Comer both endorsed a conspiracy theory in which Smith was trying to "divert attention" from the Hunter Biden investigation.

A couple of weeks later, Fulton County district attorney Fani Willis delivered Trump his fourth indictment, this time in a racketeering case involving 18 co-defendants over their attempt to subvert the 2020 election in Georgia. This was another serious case, as demonstrated by the guilty pleas made by four of the defendants. But House Republicans brought out the standard complaints. "WITCH HUNT," said Jordan. McCarthy called it a "desperate sham" by a "radical DA." Stefanik declared this case, too, to be "election interference" against Trump.

During the third week of August, the House Judiciary Committee formally opened an investigation into Willis for the alleged misuse of federal funds—nearly identical to an investigation of Bragg already underway. Two weeks later, the Judiciary Committee announced that it was investigating "prosecutorial abuse" by Smith. House Republicans were now formally investigating all the prosecutors who had brought charges against Trump. And the verbal harassment continued. In November, the militia-friendly Clay Higgins of Louisiana warned Smith that "his days are numbered, and American patriots are not going to stand idly by, good sir, and allow our republic to dissolve." (Higgins protected himself by saying that those patriots seeking to number Smith's days should do so "peacefully.") For good measure, Stefanik also filed a judicial ethics complaint against the judge presiding over Trump's civil fraud trial, who ruled that Trump had indeed committed fraud. The House GOP Conference chairwoman said the judge had "clear judicial bias" and had "weaponized lawfare" against Trump.

Talk about "weaponized": In their scorched-earth defense of Trump, congressional Republicans had used their positions to attack judge and jury—not to mention every one of the prosecutors.

KEY TO THEIR ADVOCACY FOR TRUMP WAS A WHITEWASHING OF THE JAN. 6 riot. Even before they took over the gavel, House Republicans released a "report" on the insurrection with a counterfactual narrative in which Trump merely encouraged his supporters to march "peacefully" on the Capitol. Greene, speaking at a New York Republican dinner in December 2022, informed the group that if she and Steve Bannon had organized the Jan. 6 insurrection, "we would have won. Not to mention, it would've been armed." (In fact, the insurrectionists were armed—with bear spray, clubs, and various other objects they used in the deadly rampage—and several of those on the Ellipse that day carried guns.)

McCarthy gave the green light to a new probe designed to challenge the conclusions of the Jan. 6 committee. The man in charge of the new panel, Georgia Republican Barry Loudermilk, chairman of the House Administration Committee, declared in March 2023 that Americans "didn't see the other side" of the insurrection. "I think the truth is going to be somewhere between the violent videos and the supposedly peaceful actions there," he said. As part of his investigation, Loudermilk called in former acting Capitol Police chief Yogananda Pittman to testify about the insurrection—and Democrats weren't allowed to attend.

Greene and others took field trips to a D.C. jail where some of the accused rioters were awaiting trial. They demanded "Justice for J6" and asserted that the prisoners had been maltreated. McCarthy, who originally had said that the police officer who fatally shot Ashli Babbitt during the riot "did his job" that day, sat down with Babbitt's mother, Micki Witthoeft, who led the effort to rebrand her death as murder. Witthoeft and a few others, wearing T-shirts announcing "Ashli Babbitt, Murdered by Capitol Police," regularly positioned themselves in the TV camera shot at House hearings.

Central to the whitewashing: reinventing Jan. 6 as a false-flag operation, an inside job perpetrated by the FBI. At a hearing on July 12 with FBI director Christopher Wray, Troy Nehls of Texas invoked the conspiracy theory, popular on the far right, that a man named Ray Epps was an undercover FBI agent who instigated the violence on Jan. 6 in order to discredit Trump. (After the riot, Epps was arrested, and pleaded guilty, for his role in the attack.)

"Shame on you!" Nehls said to Wray. Nehls called the Jan. 6 investigation "a political witch hunt against the greatest president in my lifetime." Coming to the defense of people convicted for their actions during the insurrection, he claimed the FBI "is more concerned about searching for and arresting Grandma and Grandpa for entering the Capitol building that day than pursuing the sick individuals in our society who prey on our children."

Before the hearing, the Associated Press's Farnoush Amiri reported that Republicans planned to screen a video showing the "FBI planting the pipe bombs outside the DNC on Jan. 6." Tom Massie of Kentucky did screen the video, but he stopped short of fingering the FBI, suggesting only that there was some unspecified conspiracy involving law enforcement. (Massie, no legal scholar, at one point told Wray his behavior "may be lawful, but it's not constitutional.")

Darrell Issa of California told Wray that he was "going to make the assumption" that there were "more than 10" FBI informants in the crowd on Jan. 6. Wray had said no such thing.

Patiently, Wray tried to disabuse the Republicans of their fantasies. No, the FBI doesn't investigate parents for attending school board meetings. No, there weren't undercover FBI agents in the crowd on Jan. 6. Actually, the FBI has opened more investigations into violence by abortion rights supporters than by abortion opponents.

"This notion that somehow the violence at the Capitol on January 6 was part of some operation by FBI sources and agents is ludicrous," Wray responded, "and is a disservice to our brave, hardworking, dedicated men and women."

It was no use. The conspiracy theorizing got stranger and stranger. At another hearing with Wray, on Nov. 15, Greene demanded that the FBI, which she erroneously asserted was part of the Department of Homeland Security, "stop targeting innocent grandmothers and veterans who walked through the Capitol on January 6" as part of an "event." And Higgins of Louisiana alleged (with an accompanying poster) that he had identified two "ghost buses," painted white, that were "nefarious in nature and were filled with FBI informants dressed as Trump supporters deployed onto our Capitol on January 6."

Your party is drowning in disinformation and conspiracy theories. Who you gonna call? Ghost buses.

Early in 2023, McCarthy, making good on one of the many promises he made to the right wing in order to win the speakership, handed over 41,000 hours of Capitol security camera footage from Jan. 6, 2001, to Fox News host Tucker Carlson. He didn't bother to consult with the Capitol Police, who worried that their security measures would be compromised by the release, or with the House sergeant at arms.

Carlson (predictably) manipulated the Jan. 6 security footage McCarthy gave the propagandist, creating the false appearance that the bloody insurrection was "mostly peaceful."

"I didn't see what was aired," McCarthy asserted.

Senate Republican leader Mitch McConnell, in an implicit rebuke of McCarthy, blasted the Carlson propaganda while holding up a statement from the Capitol Police chief denouncing Fox's "outrageous," "false," and "offensive" portrayal of the insurrection.

McCarthy said he "didn't see" that, either.

After Carlson aired his phony portrayal of the insurrection, several Senate Republicans spoke up about Fox's lies: "inexcusable" and "bullshit" (Thom Tillis of North Carolina), "whitewashing" (Lindsey Graham of South Carolina), and "dangerous and disgusting" (Mitt Romney of Utah). McConnell called it "a mistake" for Fox to portray the insurrection "in a way that's completely at variance with what our chief law enforcement official here in the Capitol thinks."

But then there was McCarthy, found by reporters just outside the speaker's office, which the supposedly "peaceful" insurrectionists had ransacked that terrible day. "Do you regret giving him this footage so he could whitewash the events of that day?" asked CNN's Manu Raju.

"No," McCarthy replied, adding some gibberish about "transparency" (which was the very opposite of Carlson's fabrication).

"Do you agree with his portrayal of what happened that day?" Raju pressed.

"Look," McCarthy said. "Each person can come up with their own conclusion."

Given a choice between fact and fiction, between law and anarchy, between democracy and thuggery, the speaker of the House proclaimed his agnosticism. In doing so, he threw the power of the speakership behind the insurrectionists and against the constitutional order he had sworn to uphold. McCarthy's leadership team even endorsed Carlson's fakery, promoting a link to the segment from the House GOP conference's official Twitter account with four alarm emojis and a "MUST WATCH" recommendation. GOP caucus chairwoman Stefanik claimed Carlson's propaganda "demolished" the "Democrats' dishonest narrative" about Jan. 6, while Massie went on Carlson's show to congratulate him on his deception.

Even Fox chairman Rupert Murdoch expressed some regret over the network's role in perpetuating Trump's Big Lie, saying Fox should have been "stronger in denouncing it." In April 2023, shortly after Fox paid $787 million to settle the Dominion defamation lawsuit (Fox hosts had falsely claimed the company's voting machines switched votes to Biden), the network ousted Carlson—to a hail of protests by House conservatives. Yet McCarthy expressed no regret about putting himself before his country.

The Senate majority leader, Chuck Schumer, charged on the Senate floor that McCarthy had "done more than any party leader in Congress to enable the spread of Donald Trump's Big Lie." But Schumer hadn't yet had the chance to see how Mike Johnson would handle the job. After Johnson succeeded the ousted McCarthy as speaker in November, he immediately set out to release the Jan. 6 security footage more broadly.

In early December, after a Republican caucus meeting in the Capitol basement, Johnson gave the press an update on the footage. The release had been slowed, he explained, because "we have to blur some of the faces of persons who participated in—in the events of that day, because we don't want them to be retaliated against and—and to be charged by the DOJ and to have other, you know, concerns and problems."

It was as clear a statement as there could be on where the new speaker's allegiance lay: protecting those who sacked the Capitol from being brought to justice for their crimes. Johnson was openly siding with the insurrectionists against the United States government he had sworn an oath to defend.

The Justice Department already had the non-doctored footage, as Johnson's spokesman later acknowledged, so presumably the speaker meant for his face-blurring operation to prevent members of the public from identifying anybody in the violent mob ("persons who participated in the events of that day") whom law enforcement may have overlooked. Sure, they attacked the seat of government in their bloody attempt to overthrow a free and fair election, but let us respect their privacy! After all the yammering from the right about transparency, Johnson, too, was manipulating the footage—not to protect the Capitol's security defenses but to protect the attackers.

Originally, Johnson had been no fan of Trump. "The thing about Donald Trump is that he lacks the character and the moral center we desperately need again in the White House," he wrote on Facebook in 2015 as a state legislator. "I am afraid he would break more things than he fixes," Johnson wrote in posts uncovered by Annie Karni and Steve Eder of the *New York Times*. "He is a hot head by nature, and that is a dangerous trait to have in a Commander in Chief."

But as soon as Johnson won the speaker's gavel, he raced to endorse Trump's return to power—even though the speaker presides over the Republicans' nominating convention and therefore has historically remained neutral. "I'm all in for President Trump," he said on CNBC on Nov. 14.

The new speaker had little choice but to do so, unless he was prepared to become the former speaker. He had to keep up with the likes of Stefanik, the GOP conference chairwoman and a leading Trump sycophant in the caucus. At one caucus meeting in the fall of 2023, she told colleagues that she would help those who had endorsed Trump to receive a "Trump badge" that they could place on their online fundraising pitches, *Punchbowl News'* Jake Sherman reported. The "badge" had boosted her own receipts by 25 percent, she told them.

Johnson had also learned from McCarthy's failure to be an adequate suck-up to Trump. Certainly McCarthy had tried. McCarthy famously flew to Mar-a-Lago soon after the Jan. 6 insurrection, helping to revive Trump's political fortunes. As Liz Cheney recounted in her book, *Oath and Honor*, McCarthy explained to her that the former president was "depressed" and needed a pick-me-up: "Trump's not eating, so they asked me to come see him."

But McCarthy suffered a lapse in June 2023 when he admitted, in an interview on CNBC (the same network on which Johnson would later profess his undying devotion to Trump), that Trump may not be "the strongest" candidate for Republicans. Trump's allies reacted furiously, and McCarthy quickly backtracked, repeatedly calling Trump strong, stronger, and strongest.

Trump didn't forget, and when hardliners were ousting McCarthy in the fall, Trump didn't lift a finger to help him.

HOUSE REPUBLICANS SPENT A GOOD CHUNK OF THEIR FIRST YEAR IN POWER trying to validate Trump's paranoid allegations that a Deep State within the federal bureaucracy was conspiring against him and his followers.

On Jan. 10, 2023, in one of their first acts, they approved, in a party-line vote on the House floor, a Select Subcommittee on the Weaponization of the Federal Government. On the floor, the committee's proponents didn't hide their conspiracy beliefs. "Mr. Speaker, today we are putting the Deep State on notice. We are coming for you," Dan Bishop proclaimed, in meandering remarks that included his thoughts on the FBI's spying on Frank Sinatra, John Lennon, Martin Luther King Jr., and Muhammad Ali. It was during this debate that Montana's Ryan Zinke, the former Trump cabinet secretary, gave his unhinged soliloquy on the existence of the Deep State.

With the panel's creation, QAnon conspiracy beliefs went from a message board for the paranoid to the official policy of the new House Republican majority. Under the chairmanship of the voluble Jim Jordan, a former wrestler who usually eschewed a jacket to show just how scrappy he was, the new Judiciary subcommittee had an extraordinary mandate that allowed it to interfere in active criminal investigations—including, potentially, investigations into themselves. Six House Republicans, after all, had requested pardons from then-president Trump for their role in trying to overturn the 2020 election.

"I think we need to call this the Tinfoil Hat Committee," Democrat Jim McGovern remarked during the Jan. 10 debate.

Even as they debated the creation of the Deep State committee, Republicans spun new fantasies. Texas Republican August Pfluger rose to object to "the assertion I just heard, that MAGA Republicans are domestic terrorists, the assertion that this is happening throughout the country."

Nobody in the debate had said any such thing. "Will the gentleman yield?" McGovern asked, to challenge the claim.

"I will not," Pfluger replied.

On Feb. 9, the new subcommittee held its first hearing, and one thing was abundantly clear: The weaponization panel's weapon of choice would be the blunderbuss.

Republicans managed to turn Room 2141 of the Rayburn House Office Building, the Judiciary Committee hearing room, into the main ballroom of a QAnon convention. The witnesses—including world-class conspiracy purveyors Senator Ron Johnson (R-Ivermectin) and former congresswoman Tulsi Gabbard (I-Ukraine Bioweapons Labs)—might as well have been auditioning to guest-host Tucker Carlson's show.

It is possible that, by random chance, one of the witnesses may have said something that is factually true, but any pellet of accuracy was lost amid all the errant slugs that ricocheted crazily out of their muzzles. They revisited the "Russian collusion hoax" perpetrated by the "fake dossier," Fusion GPS, Peter Strzok, and Lisa Page. They conjured an "engineered" Trump impeachment and a "coordinated effort" to "sabotage any public revelation of Hunter Biden's laptop." They alleged maltreatment of Jan. 6 insurrectionists and suggested that embedded federal agents provoked the crowd to attack the Capitol. They went back a decade to revive the debunked charge that the Obama administration's IRS harassed the Tea Party for political reasons.

They imagined that the U.S. government funded the creation of the covid-19 virus, that the World Health Organization has been "captured by the Chinese government," and that doctors have been wrongly "vilified" for treating the virus with hydroxychloroquine and other bogus treatments. They fantasized about a government cover-up of harms caused by covid vaccines. They imagined that ordinary people are being labeled "domestic terrorists" for asking questions at school board meetings or for flying the 13-star early American flag. Jordan, the chairman, asserted that "the FBI views the Betsy Ross flag as a terrorist symbol." In reality, it is one of the flags flown at FBI headquarters.

Above all, the witnesses testified to their own victimhood. Eighty-nine-year-old senator Chuck Grassley, an Iowa Republican, recited a long list of Democratic colleagues who were out to get him as part of a "triad" that also involves partisan journalists and the FBI. Gabbard, who left the Democratic Party for Fox News after a failed presidential campaign, expressed her outrage that Hillary Clinton said mean things about her and "Mitt Romney accused me of treason." (Apparently, the senator from Utah and 2012 Republican presidential nominee is part of the vast left-wing conspiracy.)

Ron Johnson showed why he had gained the nickname "RonAnon" when he testified about a conspiracy so huge it included "most members of the mainstream media, big tech, social media giants, global institutions and foundations, Democrat Party operatives and elected officials," all working "in concert" with "corrupt individuals within federal agencies" to "defeat their political opponents and promote left wing ideology and government control over our lives."

With so much accomplished in its first hearing, the weaponization committee needed only one more thing to complete its work: a scintilla of evidence.

Things did not improve after the first hearing. Conservatives complained about Jordan's slow start and lack of results. Jordan responded by firing off yet more subpoenas and even more outrageous allegations. This was not surprising, for Jordan, if nothing else, knew how to fight. He had faced a serious threat to his political career when several of the wrestlers he had coached at Ohio State University alleged that he had knowingly turned a blind eye to sexual abuse by the team's doctor. Jordan saved himself with a no-holds-barred campaign to discredit his accusers. He ran his committees in a similar fashion—with questionable moves, slashing attacks, and constant yelling.

When his weaponization panel assembled for its second hearing, on March 9, the pressure on Jordan was showing. Still lacking evidence that conservatives had been victimized by the government, he instead spent much of the hearing shouting at Democrats. While the ranking

Democrat, Delegate Stacey Plaskett of the Virgin Islands, delivered her opening statement criticizing the proceedings, Republicans interrupted with laughs and heckling (the word "crazy" could be heard). Mike Johnson interrupted Plaskett midsentence, calling her "out of line" and demanding that her description of the day's witnesses be "struck down."

"I'm not striking down that, and I get to have an opinion," she replied.

"You don't get to determine what's struck down!" said Johnson.

Jordan leaped in. "You do get an opening statement and it's about over."

Then Jordan, though he had already given his statement, launched into a fist-shaking tirade: "I'm talking now . . . You guys don't care! You don't care! . . . You don't want the American people to see! You don't want the American people to see! What happened! The full video! Transparency! You don't want that!"

Jordan's disjointed harangue continued at length.

"Is this your question time?" Plaskett inquired.

"No! I'm responding to your ridiculous statements!" Jordan shouted back.

"Okay," Plaskett said, "well, let's get on with it."

"Oh, so now you want to get on with it!" Jordan roared. He shouted his way through the introductions, botching his lines.

It continued similarly from there. Johnson interrupted again. The Republican witnesses interrupted to argue with Democrats on the panel. Jordan repeatedly granted himself impromptu rebuttals of Democratic lawmakers. "You've got the wrong understanding!" he shouted at Virginia Democrat Gerry Connolly, going on a tangent about a "left-wing journalist" and Black Lives Matter.

It was all sound and fury signifying nothing but the obvious fact that, once again, Jordan hadn't delivered the goods. He had decided that, after Republicans spent the last seven years attacking the credibility of the "fake news" media as the "enemy of the people," his best move would be to hold a hearing at which his only two witnesses were . . . journalists? Not just any journalists, but two of the ones Elon Musk had handpicked to go through the private files of former Twitter executives in hopes of proving that the company had conspired with the supposed Deep State to suppress the voices of conservatives.

Alas for Jordan, the so-called Twitter Files proved to be less than the bombshell Musk promised, and Republican questioning of the two—Matt Taibbi and Michael Shellenberger—broke no new ground.

Jordan, at the hearing, styled himself a champion of the First Amendment, protecting the two journalists from inquiries by "the Biden administration FTC [Federal Trade Commission]" into whether Musk had given them access to Twitter consumers' private data. But there was a problem here, too: Because of Twitter's past abuses, the FTC has exercised its legal authority to police privacy violations at the company since 2011—a decade before it was "the Biden administration FTC."

Another "weaponization" hearing, and still no gun and no smoke—just a lot of steam coming out of Jordan's ears.

The reviews of Jordan's second hearing, even from the right, were murderous. "Jordan is overextended and short-staffed, biting off much more than he can chew," Mike Davis, a former chief counsel to Chuck Grassley when he was chairman of the Senate Judiciary Committee, wrote on Twitter. "This is doomed to fail."

Davis, head of a conservative judicial advocacy group, told the *Washington Post* that Jordan merely "took an adapted screenplay from journalists' tweet thread," and he suggested that "Jordan should hand off the committee to a lawmaker who has the time to do it."

Fox's Jesse Watters pleaded on the air: "Make me feel better, guys. Tell me this is going somewhere. Can I throw someone in prison? Can someone go to jail? Can someone get fined?"

A host at right-wing Epoch TV remarked about Jordan's panel being "once again all talk."

The failure was all the more pronounced because Comer's Oversight Committee had already held a hearing about supposed "censorship" at Twitter, and that session had also been an embarrassment, failing to prove collusion between the FBI, the Biden campaign, and Twitter. The worst case of government interference that came up at the hearing had been done by the Trump White House, which in September 2019 wanted Twitter to remove a tweet by model Chrissy Teigen that called Trump a "pussy ass bitch."

Instead of identifying government abuse, the hearing became a recitation of right-wing grievances. Lauren Boebert shouted about how her Twitter account was suppressed by the "sinister overlords" of "fascist Twitter" because she made "a freaking joke about Hillary Clinton."

Nancy Mace used the hearing to inform the former Twitter executives that the covid vaccine caused her tremors, asthma, and "occasional heart pain that no doctor can explain."

"I'm a member of Congress and you're not," Marjorie Taylor Greene taunted the witnesses.

Clay Higgins accused the former Twitter executives of "knowingly and willingly" interfering with the 2020 election—and said they would soon be arrested.

Jordan's panel tried a third time, on March 30. This time, he brought in Louisiana attorney general Jeff Landry and Republican senator Eric Schmitt, a former Missouri attorney general, to rehash details of a 2022 lawsuit they had filed alleging the Biden administration pressured social media companies to restrict content.

Apparently, Jordan worried that, once again, his witnesses' wild allegations ("the Biden administration has led the largest speech censorship operation in recent American history") wouldn't stand up to scrutiny. So this time he settled on an elegant solution: He hustled the pair out of the room after they read their opening statements, without allowing for any questions. Democrats howled that this violated committee rules. The hearing quickly devolved, like the others, into parliamentary skirmishes, shouting, and personal vitriol.

"They have scurried away with your complicity," Massachusetts Democrat Stephen Lynch scolded Jordan. "You couldn't find two people to defend their statements? That's pretty disgraceful."

Early in his tenure as the weaponization committee chairman, Jordan promised that a symphony of "whistleblowers" would expose dramatic instances of wrongdoing by the feds. But then came a *New York Times* report in March 2023 that the first three of these self-described whistleblowers Jordan was bringing forth were financially supported by a pro-Trump organization and were "a group of aggrieved former FBI officials who have trafficked in right-wing conspiracy theories" about Jan. 6 and more. A 316-page report by committee Democrats said the first three "whistleblowers" to participate in transcribed interviews before the panel had no firsthand evidence of misconduct—but these former FBI officials did subscribe to cockamamie ideas. "Each endorses an alarming series of conspiracy theories related to the Jan. 6 Capitol attack, the Covid vaccine, and the validity of the 2020 election," the report said. "One has called repeatedly for the dismantling of the F.B.I. Another suggested that it would be better for Americans to die than to have any kind of domestic intelligence program."

In May, the day before Jordan's panel was to hold a hearing featuring testimony by the whistleblowers, the FBI warned Jordan that two of the supposed whistleblowers scheduled to appear before his panel had had their security clearances revoked after they "espoused alternative theories" about the 2021 Capitol insurrection. It had concerns about the "allegiance to the United States" of one of them and said another had mishandled sensitive information and given an unauthorized interview to a "Russian government news agency." A third scheduled witness had engaged in "criminal trespass" on the Capitol grounds on Jan. 6, the FBI said.

But that didn't deter Jordan. He went ahead with the hearing anyway, on May 18. There, with cameras rolling, the chairman thanked the Jan. 6 conspiracy theorists for their "commitment to . . . the rule of law."

Clearly, the weaponization panel needed a different weapon. Jordan turned to Robert F. Kennedy Jr., the anti-vaccine gadfly who was at the time mounting a long-shot Democratic presidential primary challenge to Biden. Kennedy, like previous witnesses before the subcommittee, was an avid conspiracy theorist, arguing, among other things, that childhood vaccines cause autism, that Wi-Fi causes "leaky brain," that chemicals in the water supply might turn children transgender, that AIDS may not be caused by HIV, that Republicans stole the 2004 election, and that 5G networks are used for mass surveillance.

Days before his July 20 appearance before the weaponization panel, Kennedy alleged that covid-19 was a "bioweapon" that was "ethnically targeted" to spare "Ashkenazi Jews and Chinese," and he tied it to "ethnic bioweapons." This followed Kennedy's previous suggestion that public health restrictions during covid had been worse than life for Jews in Nazi Germany, because under the Nazis "you could hide in an attic, like Anne Frank did."

Despite the obvious antisemitism, and despite the embarrassments at the select subcommittee's first four hearings, Jordan went ahead with the RFK Jr. hearing anyway. Kennedy, at the hearing, labeled the charges of bigotry "defamations and malignancies that are used to censor me."

Tom Massie tried to defend Kennedy's vile comments, entering into the record a medical study that Kennedy said supported his claims. But the study said nothing about ethnic targeting or bioweapons.

Republicans on the panel accepted at face value Kennedy's claims that he was a victim of government censorship—claims he incongruously repeated in his many media appearances, in tweets to his 2 million followers, and, of course, in this televised congressional hearing, carried live on Fox News. Unhelpfully to the Republicans, Kennedy also testified that he had been censored by the Trump administration.

Jordan opened the hearing with an example of the "censorship" of RFK Jr.: a 2021 tweet in which Kennedy said baseball great Hank Aaron's death was "part of a wave of suspicious deaths among elderly closely following administration of covid vaccines."

Jordan said Kennedy was "just pointing out facts" in the tweet, yet the Biden administration was "trying to censor the guy who's actually their Democratic primary opponent."

In reality, Aaron's death, from natural causes, wasn't suspicious. And Kennedy wasn't Biden's primary opponent in 2021. More to the point, as committee Democrats noted, Twitter never took down the tweet, which remains online to this day. Apparently, both Jordan and Kennedy had lost their minds. Must be something in the water.

Jordan was out of ideas. He waited four months before holding another hearing. And when he eventually held his sixth and final hearing of 2023, in November, it was a rerun.

The weaponization panel invited back two journalists who had testified at an earlier hearing to testify again about actions at Twitter in 2021 that were supposedly part of a "government censorship effort," as Jordan called it.

"Republicans are holding the same hearing all over again," said Plaskett, the ranking Democrat. It was actually the panel's second rerun: It had already called an assistant attorney general from Louisiana to testify, twice.

Plaskett told the audience that "this committee has heard closed-door testimony from 29 witnesses," both government and social media officials, asserting that "the alleged collusion and supposed censorship claimed by the Republicans has not taken place. But Republicans won't release that testimony."

Instead, they simply staged a reprise to repeat the same accusations. But this time, they had lost their audience. I was one of only three reporters at the press table. There was only one photographer in the well. And the seats in the audience were mostly empty, save for a few right-wing activists.

In one of many turn-back-time moments during the hearing, Stefanik asked one of the returning journalists, Michael Shellenberger: "What was the most alarming thing that you came across during your review of internal Twitter documents?"

Shellenberger's answer? It was the nonprofit "Aspen Institute trying to persuade people not to cover the Hunter Biden laptop story in August and September of 2020."

That's the most alarming thing? After a year of pratfalls, those trying to prove the existence of a weaponized Deep State were right back where they started.

Other committees fared no better in their efforts to validate Trump's paranoid claims.

Special counsel John Durham, appointed by the Trump administration, spent four years doing his darnedest to uncover wrongdoing by those who handled the Justice Department's probe of Trump's involvement with Russia. But he took only two cases to trial—and lost both. He secured just one conviction, a guilty plea by a low-level FBI lawyer on a tangential charge that didn't result in prison time. And even that misbehavior had already been uncovered by DOJ's inspector general. When Durham finally released his findings in May 2023, he said he had found "troubling violations of law and policy," but no evidence that they were politically motivated. Rather, he cited "confirmation bias," which he called "mostly unintentional."

So House Republicans called bull on Durham. When he came before the House Judiciary Committee on June 21, they trashed the man they had spent the last four years building up.

Andy Biggs told Durham "so many of us are underwhelmed" with his findings. "We're baffled, just utterly baffled, that more people have not been held accountable for their crimes. These are crimes!"

Next, Matt Gaetz called Durham's findings "silly" and "laughable." "It seems like you weren't really trying to expose the true core of corruption," the congressman said, accusing Durham of being "part of the cover-up."

Durham called that "offensive"—but Gaetz wasn't done. "You didn't charge [former FBI deputy director] Andrew McCabe. You didn't convict the lyin' Democrats or the lyin' Russians," he went on. "For the people like the chairman who put their trust in you, I think you let them down, you let the country down, and you are one of the barriers to the true accountability that we need."

Chairman Jordan (who led the overall Judiciary Committee at the same time he led the weaponization subcommittee) pretended that Durham had uncovered a great conspiracy. Jordan endeavored to tie together everything from Peter Strzok to parents being treated as "terrorists" at school board meetings. "They will even take your kids' clothes!" Jordan warned, without elaboration.

But just then it was the chairman who had no clothes.

The Judiciary Committee generated even more paranoia when it hosted Biden's attorney general, Merrick Garland, on Sept. 20.

Victoria Spartz treated Garland to a rambling speech about the Jan. 6, 2021, attack on the Capitol, which she said involved police "throwing the smoke bombs into the crowd with strollers with kids."

Biggs condemned Garland "because you didn't file those charges" against people "who were involved in the 2020 summer riots."

It didn't seem to matter to either lawmaker that both of those events happened during the Trump administration.

New Jersey Republican Jeff Van Drew suggested that Garland viewed "Catholics that go to church" as "violent extremists."

Garland, who had lost family members in the Holocaust, responded, "The idea that someone with my family background would discriminate against any religion is so outrageous, so absurd."

But not as absurd as Wisconsin Republican Tom Tiffany, who demanded answers from the attorney general on ... naked bicycling. "There was a World Naked Bike Ride in Madison, Wis., just a couple of months ago," Tiffany said, "and I sent you a letter two months ago asking if you had a problem with that because it exposed a 10-year-old girl, by the race organizer, the bike organizers, to pedaling around Madison, Wisconsin, naked. Do you think that's a problem?"

Garland brazenly disavowed any involvement by the Deep State in naked bike rides. "It sounds like you're asking about a question about state and local law enforcement," he pointed out.

BOTH THE OVERSIGHT AND JUDICIARY COMMITTEES HAD THREATENED IN THE summer of 2023 to hold FBI director Christopher Wray in contempt of Congress for failing to hand over documents they demanded. But there was some truth to the charge. Wray did seem to have contempt for at least some members of Congress—and it was well earned.

"Insane." "Absurd." "Ludicrous." Those are the actual words Wray used to describe House Republicans' crackpot conspiracy theories when he appeared before the Judiciary Committee on July 12.

"The American people fully understand," Wyoming Republican Harriet Hageman informed Wray, "that you have personally worked to weaponize the FBI against conservatives."

Right. Hageman, the election denier who ousted Liz Cheney in a primary, would have us believe that Wray—a senior political appointee in the George W. Bush Justice Department, clerk to a noted conservative judge, contributor to the Federalist Society, Donald Trump–appointed head of the FBI—was part of a conspiracy to persecute conservatives. "The idea that I'm biased against conservatives seems somewhat insane to me, given my own personal background," he replied.

Mike Johnson told Wray that his FBI "suppressed conservative leaning free speech" on topics such as the (unconfirmed) theory that covid-19 leaked from a Chinese lab.

"The idea that the FBI would somehow be involved in suppressing references to the lab-leak theory is somewhat absurd," Wray answered, pointing a finger, "when you consider the fact that the FBI was the only—the only—agency in the entire intelligence community to reach the assessment that it was more likely than not that that was the explanation for the pandemic."

It was a righteous effort. But here's what was especially insane, absurd, and ludicrous: No matter how many refutations Wray and others provided, the Republicans were convincing people to believe their lies—and they were proud of the deception.

Johnson, the lead-off questioner at the hearing, told Wray about a recent NBC News poll in which "only 37 percent of registered voters now view the FBI positively," down from 52 percent in 2018. "That's a serious decline in the people's faith, and it's on your watch," he told Wray.

Several other Republicans joined him in gloating about the FBI's poor standing in public opinion. "We're seeing the polling numbers," said Alabama's Barry Moore. "The FBI is tanking."

Gaetz taunted: "People trusted the FBI more when J. Edgar Hoover was running the place."

Wesley Hunt and Nathaniel Moran of Texas also needled Wray about the FBI's popularity. "You're not aware of those numbers?" Moran needled.

The Republicans were well aware of "those numbers"—because they were the ones who assassinated the reputation of the nation's premier law enforcement agency. While support for the FBI wasn't low among all Americans, it was at rock bottom among Republicans—only 17 percent of whom had a positive view of the FBI in the NBC poll, compared to 58 percent of Democrats.

Now why would that have happened? Well, maybe it was because they had been fed an endless diet of lies and conspiracy theories about the FBI by elected Republicans and their Murdoch mouthpieces. These lies— and similar ones told about the Justice Department, public health agencies, the IRS, and even the military—served Republicans' short-term interest of discrediting the Biden administration. But the lies also destroyed the right's support for the most basic functions of government that conservatives had long supported, such as law and order and national defense. Maybe that was the goal.

When Wray walked into the House Judiciary hearing room that day in the summer of 2023, he entered a parallel universe. A few seats down, next to the woman with the "Biden's Laptop Matters" phone cover, Ivan Raiklin, a self-styled "Deep State Marauder," rose to heckle Wray: "Sir, can you stop violating our First, Fourth and Fifth Amendments?" Jordan ordered a recitation of the Pledge of Allegiance, which ended in a few women wearing T-shirts claiming Ashli Babbitt had been murdered shouting "Justice for all!" (They did this often at hearings.)

Jordan opened with an ode to paranoia: "American speech is censored. Parents are called terrorists. Catholics are called radicals. And I haven't even talked about the spying that took place of a presidential campaign or the raiding of a former president's home."

Gaetz accused Wray of "protecting the Bidens," of being "blissfully ignorant as to the Biden shakedown regime," of "whitewashing the conduct of corrupt" people, and of operating a "creepy personal snoop machine" at the FBI.

"Amen!" called out one of the Ashli Babbitt women when Gaetz finished.

Spartz accused Wray of a passel of crimes: "unlawful surveillance of American citizens, intimidation of American citizens, potential cover-ups of convenient political figures and potential set ups of inconvenient political figures."

Republicans invoked the "Russian collusion hoax" and the Steele dossier. Most sinister were the attempts to pin Jan. 6 on the FBI. Each time Wray batted down a wacky accusation, Republicans popped up with another.

Chip Roy spoke of a "tyrannical FBI storming the home of an American family."

Dan Bishop accused the FBI of being the "agent of a foreign power."

Tiffany alleged that the FBI "interfered with the elections in both 2016 and 2020" and that Wray was in "denial" to say otherwise.

And Hageman saw Wray's FBI doing the "dirty work" of "mass censorship" to "suppress the First Amendment" as part of a supposed "two-tiered justice system that has been weaponized to persecute people."

It was, to coin a phrase, an "absurd" spectacle to watch this law-and-order conservative being attacked by MAGA lawmakers set on undermining the rule of law. Various House Republicans had already issued demands to "defund the FBI" (Marjorie Taylor Greene even sold T-shirts with the slogan), and on the day before the Wray hearing, Jordan, the Judiciary chairman, had sent a letter to House Appropriations Committee chairwoman Kay Granger requesting that she "eliminate any funding for the FBI that is not absolutely essential." (For good measure, he also asked her to block some funds for the Bureau of Alcohol, Tobacco, Firearms, and Explosives.)

Were Republicans to succeed in their demands to defund the FBI, Wray told the Judiciary Committee, they would leave Americans more vulnerable to fentanyl cartels, violent criminals, gangs, sex predators, foreign and domestic terrorists, cyberattacks, and Chinese spies. But House Republicans were answering to a higher authority.

The order had come out from Mar-a-Lago in early April. "DEFUND THE DOJ AND FBI," Trump demanded on Truth Social after his indictment.

Like good little boys and girls, House Republicans joined the defund-the-FBI movement.

"We must defund and dismantle the FBI," proclaimed Biggs.

"We have to defang and defund them," said Gaetz.

"It's far past time to cut their budget," added Bishop.

"The only way to rein them in is to cut their budget," agreed Comer.

House Republicans even rewrote a ceremonial resolution praising law enforcement to avoid anything that might be seen as support for the FBI. As *Punchbowl News* noted, the National Police Week resolution originally offered "sincere gratitude and appreciation to the Nation's law enforcement officers." The House GOP changed that to say "local law enforcement officers deserve our respect and profound gratitude."

Democrats on the Judiciary Committee repeatedly tried to add language saying that federal law enforcement deserved that same respect and gratitude—but Republicans on the panel blocked them, saying it wasn't "germane." In the House Republicans' quest, only one consideration was germane: trashing the federal government and all who worked in it.

WAY BACK IN JANUARY 2023, AFTER THE 15-BALLOT CONTEST TO SELECT A speaker, a CNN poll found that about three-quarters of Americans, including nearly half of Republicans, thought House Republican leaders weren't paying enough attention to the country's most pressing problems. So those Republicans made haste to rectify the situation. They brought to the floor a resolution condemning the Russian Revolution. Of 1917.

Before you call Bolshevik on Republican leaders for being 106 years out of date, I should note, in fairness, that their resolution also took issue with more recent events: Joseph Stalin's Ukraine famine, Mao Zedong's Great Leap Forward, and Pol Pot's killing fields. For those who haven't kept up with current affairs, those happened, respectively, in 1932–1933, 1958–1960, and 1975–1979. Still awaiting legislative action by the new House majority: a condemnation of Genghis Khan's Siege of Merv in 1221 and the Romans' sack of Carthage during the Third Punic War, in the second century BCE.

The Republicans' late hit on 20th-century atrocities served a 21st-century partisan aim—specifically, the absurd accusation that Democrats were trying to import the "horrors of socialism" to the United States. "Congress denounces socialism in all its forms and opposes the implementation of socialist policies in the United States," the resolution concluded.

It was some good old-fashioned Red-baiting, in the year 2023.

"Socialism is the greatest threat to our economy and freedom and must be defeated," Texas Republican Roger Williams warned the House, calling the fictional menace "alarming and scary."

Another Texan, Jodey Arrington, joined the GOP caterwauling, saying the Biden administration had seized "control of the means of production" from private industries. "God have mercy on our country!"

And New York's Mike Lawler felt qualified after one month in office to declare that the Democratic Party "has been taken over by a radical socialist ideology."

Most Democrats went along with the resolution—it's not a good look to be on the same side of a vote as Pol Pot—but not before they had some fun with the Red-scare revivalism.

California Democrat Maxine Waters pointed out that the pandemic-era Paycheck Protection Program would qualify as a socialist program, then asked consent to insert into the record the names of all Republican lawmakers who requested PPP loans and forgiveness.

North Carolina Republican Patrick McHenry, leading the antisocialist forces on the floor, leaped to his feet. "I object!" he said.

FOOLS ON THE HILL

But even McHenry, who as chairman of the House Financial Services Committee was tasked with leading Republicans in the antisocialist debate, felt sheepish about the whole thing. "This is not my resolution," he assured the Rules Committee. "This came straight to the House floor rather than through the committee markup . . . What I would have preferred in this resolution was a defense of capitalism."

The antisocialism resolution was the most absurd thing to come before the House since . . . well, a couple of days earlier, when Republicans on the House Judiciary Committee used the panel's organizational committee to adopt a new provision calling for the Pledge of Allegiance to be recited before each hearing.

Jerry Nadler, the ranking Democrat, pointed out that "we pledge allegiance every day on the floor, and I don't know why we should pledge allegiance twice on the same day. To show how patriotic we are?"

Mike Johnson rebutted Nadler: "I've not seen Mr. Nadler on the floor when the pledge is done."

"I pledged allegiance dozens of times," Nadler responded.

Rhode Island Democrat David Cicilline proposed an amendment: that the person leading the pledge cannot be "an individual who supported an insurrection against the government of the United States."

The debate—a screaming match at times—lasted 43 minutes. "In the House Judiciary Committee, we have opposition to pledging allegiance to the flag of the United States!" Chip Roy bellowed.

Future speaker Johnson said the episode proved that Democrats had a "completely different world view."

The pledge provision passed, on a party-line vote. Moments later, the committee opened its first hearing of the year.

"Mr. Chairman, point of order," Cicilline interjected. "Are we not going to begin the hearing with the Pledge of Allegiance?"

"We already had it," Chairman Jordan responded.

Cicilline pointed out that the previous pledge had been offered at the organizational meeting, but this was a hearing.

"If the gentleman is insisting on doing that, I would welcome Mr. Cicilline to lead the Judiciary Committee in the pledge," Jordan said.

And so he did.

The attempts to portray the U.S. government as full of socialists and disloyal people unwilling to pledge allegiance were downright silly—but they served a deadly serious purpose. They were part of a broader effort by Republicans to encourage Americans to see enemies everywhere within their government.

In its first days in power, the new majority used its authority in committee rooms and on the House floor to undermine trust in government on various fronts:

Falsely claiming lazy bureaucrats were refusing to go to work, denying Americans their tax refunds, passports, and benefits.

Falsely insinuating that the government was forcing Americans to take covid-19 vaccines that were both deadly and useless.

Falsely asserting that the Biden administration was in effect killing Americans by encouraging fentanyl smugglers to enter the country across "open borders."

Falsely declaring the only Muslim on the House Foreign Affairs Committee a threat to national security and booting her from the panel in a party-line vote.

And, for extra credit, summoning the ghosts of Stalin and Mao to suggest that the administration was promulgating an ideology of mass murder.

The bureaucrats are cheating you. The vaccine is killing you. Immigrants are drugging your children. Muslims are endangering you. And the bloodthirsty socialists are destroying your way of life. The new majority was using the levers of power to stoke paranoia.

In March, four Georgia Republicans—Greene, McCormick, Loudermilk, and Buddy Carter—got wind that the Bureau of Alcohol, Tobacco, Firearms and Explosives was conducting a (routine) inspection of a gun dealer in Georgia. So the four of them showed up to confront the bureau's agents, and they floated a conspiracy theory that the agents had come from Democratic states and had organized the inspection because Ron

DeSantis was planning a visit there. "The government has been weaponized!" Greene declared. "That's where we step in and make sure the government is not out of control."

The new House majority was determined to inspire contempt for federal workers. In its first significant legislative action, the new House majority voted to rescind $80 billion in funding for the IRS, much of it intended to improve customer service at the agency. A couple of weeks later, many of those same Republican lawmakers went to the House floor with a new grievance: They were angry about—wait for it—poor customer service at the IRS.

"The American people have suffered" while waiting "for months for their tax refunds," Comer declared on the House floor.

Too bad the IRS couldn't run an irony audit on these guys.

Republicans, some of whom were still scaring Americans with the bogus claim that 87,000 armed IRS agents would be breaking down their doors, now had a new conspiracy theory: The IRS's backlogs were caused by teleworking. (Naturally, the backlogs had absolutely nothing to do with the fact that the IRS had had its budget slashed by 15 percent since 2010 while the number of returns jumped by nearly 10 million annually.)

Therefore, the new majority passed a bill ordering IRS employees and all federal workers to return to teleworking levels that existed in 2019—before the pandemic forever changed the way people work. The title of the bill was as jumbled as its goal: the Stop Home Office Work Unproductive Problem Act—a word soup created to generate the acronym "SHOW UP." "This title does some real violence to the English language," Maryland Democrat Jamie Raskin observed during the debate.

It wasn't really about teleworking. It was about encouraging Americans to loathe federal workers. "This legislation asks every member to ask a simple question," Comer told the House. "Do you put the needs of your constituents first, or do you put the preferences of federal bureaucrats first?"

Virginia Foxx, chairwoman of the Education and Workforce Committee, blamed "bureaucrats in Washington" for making it so that "delay and disarray might as well have become hallmarks of federal agencies and departments."

The sentiment was much the same at a hearing Comer held that same week on waste and fraud in pandemic relief programs. There, he bemoaned taxpayer dollars "wasted by bureaucrats whose only priority is getting money out the door."

Lauren Boebert picked up the theme: "How the heck were these bureaucrats so dang incompetent?"

And over at the Rules Committee, Norman said bureaucrats "are not getting the work done"—something he knew because he "just hired a girl who'd been with Social Security for 25 years."

A girl.

Raskin protested the "implied contempt" for federal workers in Republicans' statements. But really, the contempt was explicit. "They're surely collecting their paychecks," said a sneering Steve Scalise, the majority leader. "It's long past time that they show up for work."

The complaint that federal workers wouldn't work was contradicted by another complaint—that federal workers were working hard to kill Americans with lethal vaccines. The new majority passed a bill aimed at striking down the "tyrannical" requirement that healthcare workers get vaccinated. This time they were targeting the Centers for Disease Control and the National Institutes of Health, and they came armed with vials of disinformation about how the vaccines "do nothing" except kill people.

"No American should stand for this type of authoritarianism," South Carolina Republican Jeff Duncan told the House.

"We're living under medical malpractice martial law," alleged Massie.

From there, the covid conspiracy theorists went on to accuse federal officials of an elaborate scheme to conceal the origin of the virus.

Nobody knew for sure how the novel coronavirus came to be. Among the U.S. intelligence community, five agencies believed it crossed over into humans from animals, while two (Wray's FBI, later joined by the Energy Department) thought it leaked from a lab in Wuhan, China. Scientists tended to favor the animal-origin theory, but there, too, opinion was split.

Then, in a reality all their own, were the Republicans on the House Select Subcommittee on the Coronavirus Pandemic. They embraced the lab-leak theory as gospel. Some of them even claimed it was a Chinese bioweapon, an idea resoundingly rejected by scientists. And they accused U.S. public health officials of an elaborate conspiracy, involving cover-ups and bribery, to suppress these "facts."

It was yet another reminder that there was no cure for long covidiocy.

On July 11 the select subcommittee held a hearing, "Investigating the Proximal Origin of a Cover Up," to prove their conspiracy theory. They hauled in two scientists on whose work the National Institutes of Health relied, to accuse them of being involved in a cover-up because they argued that the animal-origin theory was the most probable. "We as a committee have formed what we feel is most important in understanding all the information that's brought forward to us, and that information points directly to a lab leak," Pennsylvania Republican John Joyce, a dermatologist, informed the virologists.

Greene, whose own technical expertise was in Jewish space lasers, suggested that the virus was a Chinese bioweapon, and she falsely declared that "the I.C. [intelligence community] believes that the origin of covid-19 is from the lab. Most of the intelligence community believes that." She accused the virologists of using "pro-China talking points" and told them "it's important to recognize that it probably came from the lab."

Next came Texas Republican Ronny Jackson, the "candyman." He advised the virologists that their animal-origin theory was "ridiculous" and that it "sounds like engineering" was responsible for creating the virus—engineering funded by the National Institutes of Health. "What a lot of people think is going on here is that Dr. Anthony Fauci and Francis Collins realized that they'd been implicated in the production or in the creation of this virus and they were doing everything they could, including getting both of you to come on board as tools or vehicles, to undermine that theory."

McCormick, too, blamed human engineering, saying, "We can stop gain-of-function research when we admit that that's where the disease came from." And the panel's chairman, Ohio Republican (and podiatrist) Brad Wenstrup, proposed that "scientific integrity was disregarded in favor of political expediency, maybe to conceal or diminish the government's relationship with the Wuhan Institute of Virology."

The two scientists, Kristian Andersen of Scripps Research and Robert Garry of Tulane Medical School, tried to rebut the wild allegations: "The scientific evidence for this pointing to a single market in the middle of Wuhan is overwhelming." The grant with which they were allegedly bribed had been awarded before the pandemic, they pointed out. The virus on which gain-of-function research was conducted "could not have led to" covid-19. Their own initial suspicion that the virus came from a lab was "unsupported" by the scientific process. Fauci and Collins had no role in their conclusions.

After eighteen months of sleuthing, the select subcommittee struck out, failing to find evidence that the United States funded research that created the virus, or that Fauci tried to suppress the lab-leak theory.

Yet some House Republicans had already decided that the conspiracy went even deeper. In May 2023, Ralph Norman held a news conference outside the Capitol "to express strong opposition to efforts now underway by the Biden Administration, Chinese Communist Party, and the World Economic Forum that would surrender U.S. sovereignty to the unaccountable bureaucrats at the World Health Organization."

At the same press conference, Maryland Republican Andy Harris warned the assembled reporters of the need to get "out of the World Health Organization before it finishes off America."

Ronny Jackson said that the Biden administration was trying "to make us part of some world governance."

Florida's Anna Paulina Luna mentioned a 13-year-old WHO paper that she said promoted "early childhood masturbation," adding: "If you support this, I think that you're a pervert and you need to stay completely away from children."

While they spun their conspiracies, a heckler began questioning Paul Gosar about his far-right politics and Boebert about her divorce. Clay Higgins and Arizona Republican Eli Crane chased the man, and Higgins pulled him away from the proceedings as the heckler shouted, "This is assault!" Higgins followed this manhandling with another of his coded tweets. "Activist was a 103M. Threatening," he wrote, using police code for a disturbance by a mentally ill person.

Speaking of 103M, House Republicans imagined Deep State conspiracies wherever they looked. The House Energy and Commerce Committee spent more than a year investigating the National Institutes of Health, and the committee's chairwoman, Cathy McMorris Rodgers, announced that she had uncovered "unprecedented" wrongdoing, with Anthony Fauci and others serving in an "unlawful" manner, under "a complete breakdown of accountability." The actual offense? McMorris Rodgers had a quibble with how the paperwork was handled for the reappointments of certain officials.

Greene, never one to be outdone in the conspiracy department, used social media to revive the case of Seth Rich, the Democratic National Committee staffer who was slain in 2016 in what police said was an attempted robbery. Fox News reached a settlement, reportedly worth millions of dollars, with Rich's family to settle a lawsuit in 2020 over its false reporting that Rich leaked Democratic Party emails and that Democrats may have been involved in his killing. Seven years after the slaying and three years after Fox paid for its lies, Greene was still promoting the conspiracy theory.

All that was left was for House Republicans to accuse the Deep State of hiding the existence of little green men from space—and that's precisely what they did.

The House Oversight Committee's national security subcommittee called a hearing on July 20, 2023, to study "unidentified anomalous phenomena," the curiosity formerly known as UFOs. The panel brought in as its star witness one David Grusch, a former Defense Department intelligence official who claimed:

That there are "quite a number" of "nonhuman" space vehicles in the possession of the U.S. government.

That one "partially intact vehicle" was retrieved from Italian dictator Benito Mussolini in 1933 by the United States, acting on a tip from Pope Pius XII.

That the aliens have engaged in "malevolent activity" and "malevolent events" on Earth that have harmed or killed humans.

That the U.S. government is also in possession of "dead pilots" from the spaceships.

That a private defense contractor is storing one of the alien ships, which have been as large as a football field.

That the vehicles might be coming "from a higher dimensional physical space that might be co-located right here."

That the alien landing in Roswell, New Mexico, was real, and the Air Force's debunking of it was a "total hack job."

And that the United States has engaged in a nearly century-long "sophisticated disinformation campaign" (apparently including murders to silence people) to hide the truth.

Alas, Grusch had no documents, photos, or other evidence to corroborate any of his fantastic claims. It's classified!

Several Republicans on the panel greeted his out-of-this-world claims with total credulity, using them as just more evidence that the Deep State was lying to the American people, covering up the truth and could never be trusted. Their anti-government vendetta had gone intergalactic.

"There has been activity by alien or nonhuman technology and/or beings that has caused harm to humans?" asked Missouri's Eric Burlison.

Grusch said what he "personally witnessed" was "very disturbing."

"You've said that the U.S. has intact spacecraft," Burlison continued. "You've said that the government has alien bodies or alien species. Have you seen the spacecraft?"

Grusch said the nonclassified setting prevented him from divulging "what I've seen firsthand."

"Do we have the bodies of the pilots?" Mace wanted to know.

"Biologics came with some of these recoveries, yeah," Grusch told her, and the remains were "nonhuman."

Mace asked whether, "based on your experience," Grusch believed "our government has made contact with intelligent extraterrestrials."

"Classified," Grusch replied.

Just over a year earlier, a House Intelligence subcommittee had held a similar hearing on "unidentified aerial phenomena" (UAP), but with dramatically different results. The panel's bipartisan leadership said the matter should be taken seriously to protect pilots and to make sure enemies didn't develop breakthrough weapons. But they assured the public there was no evidence of "anything nonterrestrial in origin," and they cautioned against conspiracy theories. In addition, Sean Kirkpatrick, the head of the Pentagon's All-Domain Anomaly Resolution Office, where Grusch worked, testified to senators in April 2023 that his UAP-hunting office "has found no credible evidence thus far of extraterrestrial activity, off-world technology or objects that defy the known laws of physics." NASA has said likewise.

At the start of the House Oversight hearing in July 2023, Robert Garcia, the subcommittee's ranking Democrat, reminded colleagues of Kirkpatrick's testimony. One of the other witnesses, David Fravor, a retired Navy commander, told the subcommittee that the government is "not focused on little green men." But this Republican majority had yet to meet a conspiracy theory it wouldn't amplify, so it was only a matter of time before it landed on Roswell and Area 51.

Some of the House's leading conspiracy theorists—Republicans Matt Gaetz, Paul Gosar, Virginia Foxx, James Comer—took seats on the dais, whether or not they were on the subcommittee. Many in the audience, who lined up for a seat in the room, applauded the beaming witnesses when they entered.

Even some on the Democratic side complained about the overclassification of UAPs. The lack of public information allowed Republicans on the subcommittee to indulge, for more than two hours, in otherworldly accusations of a government cover-up.

Luna proposed that the government is trying "to gaslight Americans into thinking that this is not happening." Biggs accused the government of "misdirection," and Mace suggested the United States acted "unlawfully."

"The cover-up goes a lot deeper" than politics, Tim Burchett argued, vowing "to uncover the cover-up" perpetrated by the Pentagon and the intelligence community. "You can't trust a government that does not trust its people." Burchett said he would like to visit Area 51 or other locations purportedly housing alien spaceships, but "as soon as we announce it, I'm sure the moving vans pull up."

Asked by Burchett whether he knew people who had been "harmed or injured in efforts to cover up or conceal this extraterrestrial technology," Grusch said, "Yes, personally."

"Anyone been murdered?" Burchett asked.

Grusch said he had to be "careful" about answering.

Burchett even complained that members of the subcommittee "were denied access to the SCIF," the sensitive compartmented information facility in the Capitol where classified material can be discussed.

So Kevin McCarthy was also part of the cover-up?

"I don't trust anything in this town," complained Burlison.

But Burlison trusted Grusch completely, even relying on the witness to explain the "interdimensional potential" of nonhuman spacecraft— which Grusch obligingly illustrated with his index finger.

"You can be projected, quasi-projected from higher dimensional space to lower dimensional," he explained. "It's a scientific trope that you can actually cross, literally, as far as I understand, but there's probably guys with PhDs who would probably argue about that."

Yeah, they probably would.

The conspiracy theorists kept after the space invaders. In November, five right-wing House Republicans, joined by a token Democrat, held a press conference to promote legislation requiring more public disclosures about UFOs. "Whether it's little green men, American technology or worse, technology from the CCP [Chinese Communist Party], we need to know," announced Tennessee's Andy Ogles. "The truth is out there." But, he said, it was being concealed by the Deep State and a Pentagon "more concerned about pronouns and woke agendas."

THE CONSTANT PARANOIA AND NEVER-ENDING CONSPIRACY THEORIES SOUNDED, well, crazy. But the problem is that they had an effect. Polls showed a sizable chunk of Americans accepted that Biden was corrupt, that the charges against Trump were political, that the 2020 election was stolen. The *Washington Post* reported that universities and government agencies scaled back programs to counter the spread of online misinformation in response to claims by Jim Jordan and others that right-wing views were being censored. State and local election officials, facing threats and harassment, quit their jobs by the hundreds.

And still Republicans kept hacking away at Americans' confidence in government institutions, government workers, even democracy itself. Election Night 2022 revived failed Republican candidates' biennial allegations of "fraud," "criminal" behavior, "corruption," "cheaters," and "crooks."

House Republicans used their newly acquired gavels to add legitimacy to the fraud claims. On March 28, 2023, the House Administration Committee staged a hearing titled "Government Voter Suppression in Luzerne County, Pennsylvania," under the authority of chairman Barry Loudermilk of Georgia, who also was in charge of GOP efforts to rewrite the history of the Jan. 6 insurrection.

Loudermilk used the forum to repeat Donald Trump's lies about the 2020 election. Citing "rumors, whether founded or unfounded, that there were problems with the general election in 2020" in his home state of Georgia, he said this resulted in "losing the faith and confidence of the American people in their electoral system." One of the witnesses voiced skepticism that Biden had really won the election.

The purpose of this hearing, though, was to spread doubts about the 2022 election, suggesting that Luzerne County, which ran out of ballot paper at several precincts, was engaged in "voter suppression." The losing candidate in the race for Pennsylvania's Eighth Congressional District, Republican Jim Bognet, raised the possibility that "county election administrators purposely did not provide enough paper" and then tried to "cover up" what they had done.

Virginia Republican Morgan Griffith speculated that "a normal person" would "immediately assume" that election officials committed "some kind of criminal offense."

But the conspiracy theories, once again, dissolved under scrutiny. Ten of the 11 council members in Luzerne, a Republican county, were Republican. The local D.A. investigating the paper shortage was a Republican. The number of ballots in question, even by the Republican National Committee's estimate, wasn't nearly large enough to alter the outcome of the election. And there was an obvious explanation for the ballot-paper screw-up. Before the 2020 election, the median experience of officials in the election office was more than 17 years, the Allentown *Morning Call* reported. For the 2022 election—after an unprecedented volume of abuse and threats heaped on election workers by Trump's supporters caused massive turnover nationwide—the median was just 1.5 years. The county had been through half a dozen election directors and five deputy directors over five years.

It was a classic case of Republicans sabotaging the functioning of government—and then triumphantly gloating that government had failed. In this case, they did it in service of the lie that elections are rigged against Republican voters.

Where does all the Deep State paranoia end? As always, Marjorie Taylor Greene had thoughts on this. "We need a national divorce," she tweeted in February 2023, as the new House got down to business. "We need to separate by red states and blue states and shrink the federal government. Everyone I talk to says this. From the sick and disgusting woke culture issues shoved down our throats to the Democrat's [sic] traitorous America Last policies, we are done."

As the old saying goes, nothing succeeds like secession.

There were a couple of problems with Greene's civil war cry—not least that she hails from what is currently a blue state, which went for Biden and has two Democratic senators. There was also the small matter of her secession talk being, as Utah's Republican governor, Spencer Cox, put it, "destructive and wrong and—honestly—evil."

Greene ended the year in much the same spirit of sedition. A few days after the House adjourned for Christmas, she posted online a photo of herself with the "QAnon shaman," Jacob Chansley, who had been sentenced to 41 months in prison for his role in the Jan. 6 attack on the Capitol. The "Biden regime's DOJ wrongfully prosecuted him for innocently and nonviolently walking through the Capital [sic]," she wrote, calling his conviction a case of how "the politicized and weaponized DOJ hunts and persecutes it's [sic] perceived political enemies" and "continues it's [sic] perversion of justice."

"This is really about punishing Americans who dared to use their 1st amendment—their free speech to protest against the government," she wrote.

Chansley was part of the mob that attacked the Capitol in a violent attempt to nullify a free and fair election. If sacking the seat of the United States government is "free speech," as Greene and her colleagues would have it, then the civil war she craves has already begun.

THE NEW YEAR BROUGHT THE PRESIDENTIAL PRIMARY SEASON—AND A CORresponding effort among House Republicans to bolster their man.

On Feb. 6, 2024, Gaetz introduced a one-sentence resolution: "Expressing the sense of the House of Representatives that former President Donald J. Trump did not engage in insurrection or rebellion against the United States." No fewer than 70 of his Republican colleagues signed on as co-sponsors.

Their resolution was brief, but their event rolling it out went on for more than an hour and included a mention of just about every conspiracy theory of the Trump era, and before.

"Fake dossier!"

"Russia collusion hoax."

"Deep State."

"Witch hunt!"

"Woke mob."

"Antifa!"

"Hunter Biden's laptop."

Their purpose, to the extent they had one at their news conference, was to attack the assembled journalists. "What we have seen is mass hysteria caused by you, the reckless leftist media," Andy Biggs of Arizona informed us. Eli Crane of Arizona told us: "You don't have the balls to write the truth!"

The House Republicans' ongoing obsession with testicles (both Greene and Mace having previously suggested that their male colleagues might lack these organs) was best left to the Freudians. Of more concern was their ongoing determination to rewrite the history of Jan. 6.

"President Trump and his supporters were vilified for doing nothing more than exercising their First Amendment rights," Diana Harshbarger of Tennessee said of the rioting, which injured 140 police officers and resulted in several deaths.

"There was not an insurrection that took place on Jan. 6th," Matt Rosendale of Montana said of the mob that sacked the Capitol to stop the certification of Biden's win.

Eric Burlison of Missouri said events like Jan. 6 occurred all the time when he was in the Missouri legislature: "We would call what happened on that day 'a Wednesday' in the Missouri capitol."

Greene made clear that she didn't know what the word "insurrection" meant, because she complained to the "liars" in the media: "When Joe Biden was inaugurated and this entire Capitol complex was surrounded with 30,000 National Guard troops, none of you stood there and called that an insurrection. Oh, no. You all stayed silent."

And Anna Paulina Luna declared that once House Republicans passed their resolution, it would no longer be permissible for "sociopath" journalists like us to call the insurrection an insurrection. "Once we have this on the floor, if you continue to push this, you guys are all going to be guilty of breaching House privileges, okay?" she said. "Because we're saying that it didn't happen."

And if House Republicans say so . . .

Gaetz's resolution set off a predictable round of one-upmanship, as other Republicans tried to prove their fealty to the leader. Ten days after Gaetz's resolution, Andy Ogles of Tennessee introduced a resolution of more than 2,000 words stating that "the United States would benefit enormously from having Donald J. Trump inaugurated once again as the president." It read like a barstool rant, with references to the Deep State, "opportunistic left-wing activists," and "leftist media outlets (plus their Republican-in-name-only allies), along with a refresher on the "Steele dossier" and Hunter Biden's laptop.

Not to be outdone, Guy Reschenthaler of Pennsylvania, a member of GOP leadership, sponsored H.R. 7845, "to designate the Washington Dulles International Airport in Virginia as the 'Donald J. Trump International Airport.'" It had only six cosponsors—none of them from Virginia—but there was a certain logic to it. With Trump planning to surrender Ukraine to Russia, it seemed inappropriate to have a major airport named after a fierce Cold Warrior such as John Foster Dulles, secretary of state in the Eisenhower administration. But couldn't Reschenthaler cut out the middleman and just name the airport Putin International?

So necessary was it to demonstrate fealty to Trump, and Trumpism, that House Republicans subordinated everything to the task—even the rule of law and national security. After the Supreme Court in January 2024 issued a temporary ruling siding with the Biden administration in a border enforcement dispute with Texas (the high court later ruled for Texas), Chip Roy asserted that the high court's order was "unconscionable and Texas should ignore it." Never mind that two conservative justices joined in the order.

Roy suggested that an appropriate response would be to "tell the court to go to hell."

Reacting to the same ruling, Clay Higgins sounded a new call to arms, posting on social media that "the feds are staging a civil war, and Texas should stand their ground."

Greene, reprising her secessionist theme, announced: "Now the Biden admin[istration] is at WAR with Texas."

House Republicans staged a press conference and a hearing to encourage Texas to fight the administration—and the Supreme Court. Brian Babin of Texas, implying treason by the Biden administration, praised his state because it "stood its ground against an invasion and an administration that clearly wants the opposing forces to win." And an earthy Randy Weber, also of Texas, said of the Supreme Court: "Maybe we ought to tell them to go butt a stump." Even as they impeached Alejandro Mayorkas for "failure to enforce the law" at the border, they were loudly encouraging Texas to ignore the law at the border and the highest court in the land.

These dime-store Confederates went beyond simply rejecting the authority of the Supreme Court. They were at the same moment actively sabotaging the government they were elected to serve. This was the same moment in which House Republicans, at Trump's order, killed the Senate's bipartisan border security bill—thereby blocking the United States from mounting an effective response to a historic surge of migrants at the southern border—so Trump could have an election issue. This wasn't "America First." It was Trump first.

Next came the subordinating of national security to Trump's whims. In April, the House was finally working toward agreement to extend section 702 of FISA, the surveillance program. The authority was set to expire in a week, and FBI chief Wray said that the loss of the power would be "devastating" to national security.

Yet at 1:43 a.m. on April 10, hours before the House was to begin debate on extending the program, Trump torpedoed the effort with an all-caps post on Truth Social: "KILL FISA, IT WAS ILLEGALLY USED AGAINST ME, AND MANY OTHERS. THEY SPIED ON MY CAMPAIGN!!!"

That was entirely false. The expiring section of FISA that lawmakers were racing to renew was entirely separate from the section of the law used to monitor a Trump campaign adviser in 2016—which is what had drawn Trump's pique.

But the truth didn't matter. After Trump's false, middle-of-the-night attack on the vital program, 19 House Republicans once again used a procedural vote to block the renewal from coming to the floor. If you've lost track, this was the seventh time Republicans had thrown the chamber into chaos by using the previously unheard-of practice of defeating the "rule" on the floor.

After this latest humiliation, majority whip Tom Emmer, the man in charge of counting votes, was asked whether he was surprised by the failure.

"We don't whip rules," Emmer replied.

Asked *Politico*'s Anthony Adragna: "Should you start?"

Leaving a House Republican Conference meeting after the FISA debacle, Ohio Republican Max Miller, a former Trump aide, told reporters the closed-door session was "pure chaos."

Trump's former attorney general Bill Barr told *The Hill* that Republicans were "crazy and reckless" for endangering "our principal tool protecting us from terrorist attacks." Finally, after House leaders placated Trump by proposing a shorter-term extension, he relented, and they passed the extension on a second try.

"Pure chaos." "Crazy and reckless." These have been the hallmarks of governance under MAGA Republicans' control of the House of

Representatives. There will be more of that, and worse, if voters return Trump and his legislative servants to power on Election Day 2024.

Eventually, even the primary source of the chaos and craziness had had enough of the House Republicans' shenanigans. On May 8, just before the House was to vote on Marjorie Taylor Greene's motion to vacate Johnson's speakership, Trump posted a cease-and-desist notice on his Truth Social site. He explained that while a motion to oust Johnson might be appropriate "at some point," this was not the time. "We are leading in the Presidential Polls by a lot," he wrote, with his whimsical capitalization. "But if we show DISUNITY, which will be portrayed as CHAOS, it will negatively affect everything!"

It was a candid request from the boss: Suspend the craziness long enough to fool the voters. This deterred all but a few of Johnson's Republican critics, making it easy for Democrats to table the motion and save Johnson's speakership.

Just six days later, Johnson showed Trump his gratitude. He traveled to New York to accompany Trump to his hush-money trial, then stood in front of the cameras outside the courthouse to denounce the trial, and the criminal justice system generally. This set off a rush by fellow House Republicans, and a few MAGA senators and state office holders, to do the same. Several of them even dressed as Trump mini-mes, in blue-gray suits, white shirts and red ties; one, Troy Nehls, wore a tie with Trump's face plastered on it. Each dutifully echoed their leader's ejaculations.

> "This is a sham trial!" said Trump, inside the courthouse.
> *"Sham of a trial," parroted Johnson, outside the courthouse.*
> *"Sham trial," repeated Andy Biggs.*
> *"A crooked sham trial," said Bob Good.*
> *"This is a sham," echoed Cory Mills.*

> "There's no crime!" said Trump, inside the courthouse.
> *"There's no crime here," repeated Johnson, outside the courthouse.*
> *"There is no crime," said Byron Donalds.*
> *"What is the crime?" asked Lauren Boebert.*

"It's election interference!" proclaimed Trump.
"It is election interference," chorused Johnson.
"Election interference," said Gaetz and Good.
"Election interference at its finest!" said Mills.

Biden is "weaponizing the Department of Justice," announced Trump.
"Weaponized against President Trump," Johnson echoed.
"Weaponized DOJ," chorused Boebert.
"Weaponization against our president," repeated Mills.

As a large group of House Republicans spoke outside the courthouse, somebody held a hand-lettered sign behind them with a pithy summary of the moment. "BOOTLICKERS," it said.

The worst, by far, was Johnson, second in line to the presidency and the highest-ranking officer of the legislative branch, using his position to spread lies. Without a shred of evidence, he alleged that "the judge's own daughter is making millions of dollars" off the trial. He claimed a prosecutor in the case had "recently received over $10,000 in payments from the Democratic National Committee." He alleged that, in Trump's classified documents case, prosecutors "manipulated documents" and "might have tampered with the evidence"—conduct "so egregious" that it caused that trial to be "indefinitely postponed." Each of these was false or, at best, deeply distorted. For good measure, Johnson even offered an inflated count of the crowd size at a recent Trump rally—just to please the boss.

"The people are losing faith right now in this country, in our institutions," Johnson said. "They're losing faith in our system of justice. And the reason for that is because they see it being abused as it is being done here in New York."

No, Mr. Speaker. The people are losing faith in our institutions because you and others sworn to uphold those institutions are instead attacking them in order to appease your patron. The damage you are doing will outlive us all.

ACKNOWLEDGMENTS

Long before Kevin McCarthy suffered his ritual humiliations on the House floor, before the world had heard of George Santos, and before people associated the name "Mike Johnson" with somebody other than a contestant on the Bachelorette, the *Washington Post*'s Editorial Page editor, David Shipley, threw his wholehearted support behind my idea to write my column from Capitol Hill for a year and to develop what I saw there into a book. This project could not have happened without him. A team of top-notch *Post* editors, particularly Chris Suellentrop, David Von Drehle, and Mike Larabee, improved my work every week.

Also before we knew that the House Republican majority would execute one pratfall after another, Pronoy Sarkar, my editor at Little, Brown, saw the potential for humor and horror in the project. Pronoy is a gifted editor and an elegant thinker, and he was indispensable in helping me to organize my thoughts and to structure the narrative. This ideal match was made by my agent, Rafe Sagalyn, who has somehow had the patience to represent me for the last quarter century, for which I am most grateful. Little, Brown executive editor Alexander Littlefield generously stepped in at a critical time and, as I write this, is expertly shepherding the book to market. Pronoy, Alex, and I were aided by a strong supporting cast at Little, Brown, particularly Sofia Sanchez, Katharine Myers, Michael Noon, Mario Pulice, and Bryan Christian. I'm tickled that the inimitable Barry Blitt agreed to draw the cover, and that the Associated Press's Scotty Applewhite, dean of Capitol Hill photographers, shot the jacket photo. My researcher, Maggie Duffy, a real pro, helped extensively with sourcing and rolled with all of the difficult tasks and deadlines thrown at her.

The *Post* has an exceptionally strong team covering Congress, and I was blessed to have them as colleagues, especially my old pal Paul Kane, the bureau chief, and Marianna Sotomayor, Leigh Ann Caldwell, and Jacqueline Alemany. They shared their considerable knowledge with me (though, to be clear, they are not to be blamed for any of the opinions in the book). My friends Chris Orr, Eric Weinberger, and Kristin Wilson did me the huge favor of reading the manuscript, giving me their sage advice and counsel.

The people now running the House are uniquely unimpressive, but the current congressional press corps is perhaps the best there ever has been. *Punchbowl*'s Jake Sherman and *Politico*'s Olivia Beavers have the place wired, tweeting out verbatim quotes from closed-door party meetings as if they were sitting in the room. Many others contribute to the functioning of this awesome machine, including Lisa Desjardins, John Bresnahan, Manu Raju, Arthur Delaney, Ben Jacobs, Carl Hulse, Chad Pergram, Max Cohen, Billy House, Sahil Kapur, Reese Gorman, Kadia Goba, Juliegrace Brufke, Andrew Solender, Melanie Zanona, and several more. I've cited their work often in the text and in the notes, and I follow them closely on social media—and you should, too, if you want to know what's really going on in Congress.

All those who cover the House owe a debt of gratitude to the staff of the House Daily Press Gallery. Ed Kachinske and Kristine Michalson were my companions at many a stakeout and reliable sources of institutional wisdom (though never of opinions—they are nonpartisan). Reporters couldn't do our jobs without them and the rest of the gallery staff, including Danny Kim, Justin Supon, and Jill Ornitz.

The mayhem on the Hill was more easily endured because of my grounding at home. My wonderful daughter, Paola Milbank, a junior at Yale with a keen sense of justice and interest in policy, inspires me and gives me hope for the future. My step-kids, the wise and goofy Sadie and Jasper Delicath, provide the happy soundtrack of my domestic life. And my wife, the pollster Anna Greenberg, to whom I dedicate this book, makes everything possible. She is my toughest editor, my fiercest champion, and my best friend, and she teaches me something new about politics—and life—every day.

NOTES

PROLOGUE

2 *They screamed "Bullshit!"*: Katie Rogers, "After Shouts of 'Liar' and Worse, Biden Takes On His Detractors in Real Time," *New York Times*, February 8, 2024, https://www.nytimes.com/2023/02/08/us/politics/biden-state-of-the-union.html.

2 *"Our Republican House majority"*: Matt Cannon, "Marjorie Taylor Greene Blasts Her Own 'Failed' Party," *Newsweek*, April 9, 2024, https://www.newsweek.com/marjorie-taylor-greene-blasts-failed-party-mike-johnson-speech.

3 *"One thing"*: Emily Brooks, "Chip Roy Gets Heated over Spending Strategy: 'We're Pissing It All Away,'" *The Hill*, November 15, 2023, https://thehill.com/homenews/house/4311429-chip-roy-gets-heated-over-spending-strategy-were-pissing-it-all-away/.

3 *"We're a party"*: Burgess Everett and Sarah Ferris, "Congress Officially Avoided a Shutdown—but GOP Hardliners Still Caused One," *Politico*, October 23, 2023, https://www.politico.com/live-updates/2023/10/23/congress/congress-avoided-a-shutdown-this-month-eight-republicans-shut-it-down-anyways-00123082.

3 *"The amount of damage"*: Erin B. Logan and Faith E. Pinho, "Jordan Out of Speaker Race; as New Candidates Line Up, GOP 'in a Very Bad Position,' McCarthy Warns," *Los Angeles Times*, October 20, 2023, https://www.latimes.com/politics/story/2023-10-20/jim-jordan-house-speaker-friday.

3 *"We're a ship"*: Makini Brice and David Morgan, "Republican Steve Scalise's Quest to Be US House Speaker Ends Before Liftoff," Reuters, October 13, 2023, https://www.reuters.com/world/us/republican-steve-scalise-path-us-house-speaker-turbulent-time-2023-10-11/.

3 *"We are a broken conference"*: Zachary Basu, "House GOP's 'Broken' Conference Sees No Way Out of Speaker Crisis," *Axios*, October 12, 2023, https://www.axios.com/2023/10/12/steve-scalise-speaker-house-republicans-gop.

3 *"You keep running lunatics"*: Dave Goldiner, "NY Republican Fellow GOP Members as 'Clown Show' as Congress Hurtles Toward Government Shutdown," *Daily News*, September 19, 2023, https://www.nydailynews.com/2023/09/19/ny-republican-fellow-gop-members-as-clown-show-as-congress-hurtles-toward-government-shutdown/.

3 *"We need to . . . get"*: Mark Harper, "Volusia Congressmen Back Jim Jordan's Bid for Speaker of the House in First Round of Voting," *Daytona Beach News-Journal*, October 17, 2023, https://www.news-journalonline.com/story/news

/nation-world/2023/10/17/jim-jordan-vote-congressmen-michael-waltz-cory
-mills-lend-support/71217176007/.

3 *"This is embarrassing"*: "Kevin McCarthy Calls House Speaker Chaos
   'Embarrassing' for GOP," *Axios*, October 22, 2023, https://www.axios.com
   /2023/10/22/kevin-mccarthy-house-speaker-gop-chaos.

3 *"We put sharp knives in the hands of children"*: Russell Berman, "'We Put Sharp
   Knives in the Hands of Children,'" *The Atlantic*, October 7, 2023, https://www
   .theatlantic.com/politics/archive/2023/10/kevin-mccarthy-congress-tom
   -cole-interview/675566.

3 *"serious issues"*: Manu Raju, "GOP Rep. Tony Gonzales to me after 5 Rs joined
   Ds to block defense bill," X, September 19, 2023, https://twitter.com/mkraju
   /status/1704233150417625257.

3 *"look like a bunch of idiots"*: Eden Villalovas, "Republican Says GOP Bickering
   over Next Speaker Makes 'Us Look Like a Bunch of Idiots,'" *Washington
   Examiner*, October 13, 2023, https://www.washingtonexaminer.com/news
   /2451649/republican-says-gop-bickering-over-next-speaker-makes-us-look
   -like-a-bunch-of-idiots/.

3 *"This is a continuation"*: Emily Brooks and Mychael Schnell, "Republicans
   Rudderless as Speaker Mess Consumes House," *The Hill*, October 13, 2023,
   https://thehill.com/homenews/house/4253701-republicans-rudderless
   -speaker-mess-house/.

3 *"This is the worst"*: Arthur Delaney, "Mike Kelly R-Pa likened the situation
   to a football team calling a play in the huddle," X, October 12, 2023,
   https://twitter.com/ArthurDelaneyHP/status/1712545588787687710?s=20.

5 *"Chaos follows Trump"*: Byron York, "Nikki Haley, Donald Trump, and 'Chaos
   Follows Him,'" *Washington Examiner*, December 19, 2023, https://www
   .washingtonexaminer.com/daily-memo/2621663/nikki-haley-donald-trump
   -and-chaos-follows-him/.

5 *"kidney punch"*: Jennifer Bowers Bahney, "'No!' Kevin McCarthy Vehemently
   Denies He Dished Out 'Kidney Punch' to Fellow Republican," *Mediaite*,
   November 14, 2023, https://www.mediaite.com/politics/no-kevin-mccarthy
   -vehemently-denies-he-dished-out-kidney-punch-to-fellow-republican/.

5 *"scumbags"*: Matthew Choi, "Tony Gonzales Openly Blasts Fellow
   Republicans as 'Scumbags' and Klansmen," *Texas Tribune*, April 22, 2024,
   https://www.texastribune.org/2024/04/22/tony-gonzales-republicans-matt
   -gaetz-scumbags/.

6 *"like Nagasaki and Hiroshima"*: Neil Vigdor, "Republican Congressman Says of
   Gaza: 'It Should Be Like Nagasaki and Hiroshima,'" *New York Times*, March
   31, 2024, https://www.nytimes.com/2024/03/31/us/politics/tim-walberg-gaza
   -nagasaki-hiroshima.html.

6 *"exact opposite"*: Kelly Garrity, "GOP Congressman Tempers 'Nagasaki and
   Hiroshima' Comments on Gaza: 'I Used a Metaphor,'" *Politico*, March 31, 2024,
   https://www.politico.com/news/2024/03/31/gop-congressman-nagasaki
   -hiroshima-comments-gaza-00149862.

6 *"just happened to be walking through the building"*: Ellie Quinlan Houghtaling,
   "Mike Johnson Has Most Unhinged Defense Yet of January 6," *New Republic*,
   April 2, 2024, https://newrepublic.com/post/180336/mike-johnson-unhinged
   -defense-january-6.

6 *"the truth why"*: Clarissa-Jan Lim, "Kevin McCarthy Says Fellow Lawmaker Ousted Him as Speaker to 'Stop an Ethics Complaint,'" MSNBC, April 10, 2024, https://www.msnbc.com/top-stories/latest/kevin-mccarthy-matt-gaetz -ethics-investigation-rcna147214.

6 *"Go fuck yourself"*: Ben C. Jacobs, "It sounds like Mike McCaul told Darrell Issa to go fuck himself," X, March 19, 2024, https://x.com/Bencjacobs/status /1770194112924230003.

6 *"God is sending America"*: Theresa Maher, "Greene: Earthquakes and Eclipses a Sign from God to 'Repent,'" *The Hill*, April 5, 2024, https://thehill.com /homenews/house/4576923-greene-earthquakes-eclipses-sign-god/.

7 *"notably less effective"*: Patrick W. Buhr, Craig Volden, and Alan E. Wiseman, "Polarization and Lawmaking Effectiveness in the United States Congress," Center for Effective Lawmaking, January 2024, https://thelawmakers.org/wp -content/uploads/2024/01/CEL-Polarization-and-Lawmaking-Effectiveness -in-the-United-States-Congress-paper.pdf.

CHAPTER 1: "AN ABSOLUTE DISASTER FOR THE REPUBLICAN PARTY"

11 *"I'm very optimistic"*: Democracy 2022: Election Coverage, Fox News, November 8, 2022, https://archive.org/details/FBC_20221109_020000_Fox _News_Democracy_2022_Election_Coverage/start/2040/end/2100.

13 *Aides, desperate to keep some semblance:* Olivia Beavers and Hailey Fuchs, "McCarthy's Victory Party Fizzles," *Politico*, November 9, 2022, https://www .politico.com/news/2022/11/09/mccarthy-house-gop-00065882.

13 *"That is a searing indictment"*: The Recount (@therecount), "Fox News' Marc Thiessen: The midterm results are 'a searing indictment of the Republican Party,'" Twitter, November 9, 2022, https://twitter.com/therecount/status /1590233789137289218.

15 *"I've spent my whole life chasing"*: "Emotional Boehner Promises New Way Forward for GOP," ABC News, November 3, 2010, https://abcnews.go.com /Politics/john-boehner-emotional-house-republican-leader-promises-gop /story?id=12040640.

15 *"The RED WAVE did not happen"*: Christopher Brito, "'The RED WAVE Did Not Happen': Texas Republican Mayra Flores Projected to Lose House Seat," CBS News, November 9, 2022, https://www.cbsnews.com/news/elections-2022 -texas-house-republican-mayra-flores-projected-to-lose-seat-no-red-wave/.

16 *Majewski presented himself:* Brian Slodysko and James Laporta, "Ohio GOP House Candidate Has Misrepresented Military Service," Associated Press, September 22, 2022, https://apnews.com/article/2022-midterm-elections -afghanistan-ohio-campaigns-e75d2566635f11f49332bd1c46711999.

16 *During the campaign, Majewski had visited:* Riley Rogerson, "How This Nutty Ohio Primary Is Dividing the GOP," *Daily Beast*, January 30, 2024, https://www.thedailybeast.com/nutty-ohio-primary-between-craig-riedel-jr -majewski-derek-merrin-is-dividing-the-gop.

16 *"four combat deployments"*: Deena Winter, "Congressional Candidate Tyler Kistner Has Repeatedly Suggested He Saw Combat, but He Didn't," *Minnesota Reformer*, October 5, 2022, https://minnesotareformer.com/2022/10/05

/congressional-candidate-tyler-kistner-has-repeatedly-suggested-he-saw
-combat-but-he-didnt/.

17 *"eroding the white population":* Andrew Kaczynski, "GOP Congressional
Candidate Said US Suffered from Women's Suffrage and Praised
Organization Trying to Repeal 19th Amendment," CNN, September 21, 2022,
https://www.cnn.com/2022/09/21/politics/john-gibbs-womens-suffrage-19th
-amendment-kfile/index.html.

17 *"I think that's an insult to Banana Republics":* Olafimihan Oshin, "GOP House
Hopeful: Calling US a Banana Republic 'an Insult to Banana Republics
Across the Country,'" *The Hill*, August 15, 2022, https://thehill.com
/homenews/campaign/3602989-gop-house-hopeful-calling-us-a-banana
-republic-an-insult-to-banana-republics-across-the-country/.

17 *"it wouldn't surprise me":* Ned Oliver, "Scoop: Spanberger Rival Yesli Vega
Doubts Pregnancy After Rape," *Axios*, June 27, 2022, https://www.axios.com
/2022/06/27/yesli-vega-pregnancy-rape-audio-recording.

18 *"on the brink of being taken over":* Ernest Luning, "Recently Minted Republican
Challenges Michael Bennet for Colorado Senate Seat," *Colorado Politics*,
June 8, 2021, https://www.coloradopolitics.com/elections/2022/recently
-minted-republican-challenges-michael-bennet-for-colorado-senate-seat
/article_1b24bea8-c885-11eb-b5d5-b319a6e5288a.html.

18 *"is a manufactured crisis":* Adam Sexton, "Chris Pappas, Karoline Leavitt Say
Whether Passing Climate Legislation Is a Priority," WMUR, October 20,
2022, https://www.wmur.com/article/leavitt-pappas-cd1-new-hampshire
-climate-change/41726178.

18 *"we would need a panel":* Amanda Terkel and Kevin Robillard, "GOP Candidate
Robert Burns Proposed Abortion Panels in 2018," *HuffPost*, September 16,
2022, https://www.huffpost.com/entry/robert-burns-abortion-panels-life
-mother-risk_n_63236cdfe4b000d988596f0a.

18 *"intelligence operation":* Evan Watson, "A Closer Look at the Trump-Endorsed
Republican Candidate for US House Seat in Southwest Washington," KGW,
October 6, 2022, https://www.kgw.com/article/news/politics/elections/joe
-kent-washington-3rd-district-house-candidate/283-47cb370d-18c3-4347-9af6
-11a69c02683e.

19 *firearms cause:* "Number of Murder Victims in the United States in 2022, by
Weapon Used," Statista, https://www.statista.com/statistics/195325/murder
-victims-in-the-us-by-weapon-used/.

19 *"I stand by them":* Dana Milbank, "Think You Already Know Crazy? Meet the
House GOP Class of '22," *Washington Post*, November 22, 2022, https://www
.washingtonpost.com/opinions/2022/10/07/republican-house-candidates
-2022-crazy/.

CHAPTER 2: "VOTING FOR THE CRAZIEST
SON OF A BITCH IN THE RACE"

21 *Ogles had merely participated in nondegree:* Phil Williams, "REVEALED:
Tennessee Congressman Andy Ogles Didn't Want You to See His College
Transcript! We Got It Anyway," NewsChannel 5, February 27, 2023,
https://www.newschannel5.com/news/newschannel-5-investigates

/tennessee-congressman-andy-ogles-didnt-want-you-to-see-his-college
-transcript-we-got-it-anyway.

22 *"could not be corroborated"*: Glenn Kessler, "Tennessee Congressman
    Andrew Ogles's Résumé Is Too Good to Be True," *Washington Post*, March
    10, 2023, https://www.washingtonpost.com/politics/2023/03/10/tennessee
    -congressman-andrew-ogless-rsum-is-too-good-be-true/.

22 *Ogles took in $25,000 in a GoFundMe campaign:* Phil Williams, "REVEALED:
    What Did Andy Ogles Do with Nearly $25,000 Meant for a Child Burial
    Garden? He Won't Say," NewsChannel 5, March 15, 2023, https://www
    .newschannel5.com/news/newschannel-5-investigates/what-did
    -congressman-andy-ogles-do-with-nearly-25-000-meant-for-child-burial
    -garden-he-wont-say.

22 *"raised as a Messianic Jew"*: Jacqueline Alemany and Alice Crites, "The Making
    of Anna Paulina Luna," *Washington Post*, February 10, 2023, https://www
    .washingtonpost.com/politics/2023/02/10/anna-paulina-luna-republican
    -biography/.

23 *$4,000 of campaign cash:* Roger Sollenberger, "GOP Candidate Bankrolled Jan.
    6 Riot Trip with Campaign Cash," *Daily Beast*, June 27, 2021, https://www
    .thedailybeast.com/gop-candidate-bankrolled-jan-6-riot-trip-with-campaign
    -cash.

23 *"aggressively shoving the books around"*: Olivia Herken, "Library Staff Felt
    'Threatened' After GOP Candidate Complained About Pride Month Display,"
    La Crosse Tribune, August 22, 2021, https://lacrossetribune.com/news/local
    /library-staff-felt-threatened-after-gop-candidate-complained-about-pride
    -month-display/article_1de09ffd-892a-535f-b1ce-ad43a2732df6.html.

23 *"totally unfazed"*: Stephanie Grisham, "Stephanie Grisham: I Told the
    Trumps My Relationship with a White House Staffer Had Turned Abusive.
    They Didn't Seem to Care," *Washington Post*, October 5, 2021, https://www
    .washingtonpost.com/opinions/2021/10/05/stephanie-grisham-abusive
    -relationship-trump-white-house/.

23 *Interior Department's inspector general:* Linda Qiu, "Ryan Zinke Broke Ethics
    Rules as Interior Secretary, Inquiry Finds," *New York Times*, February 16,
    2022, https://www.nytimes.com/2022/02/16/us/politics/ryan-zinke-ethics
    .html.

24 *"it is my pleasure to give you a 40mm grenade"*: Morgan Phillips
    (@_phillipsmorgan), "Rep @CoryMillsFL is passing out grenades to
    fellow House members," Twitter, January 26, 2023, https://twitter.com
    /_phillipsmorgan/status/1618648723764170753.

24 *"sold tear gas"*: Amber Phillips, "Four Takeaways from the New York
    and Florida Primaries," *Washington Post*, August 24, 2022, https://www
    .washingtonpost.com/politics/2022/08/24/four-takeaways-new-york-florida
    -primaries/.

24 *allegedly kicking a dog and cutting its belly:* Daniel Lippman, "GOP Operative
    Who Allegedly Kicked a Dog Hired as Top Aide to New Congressman,"
    Politico, December 13, 2022, https://www.politico.com/news/2022/12/13/gop
    -operative-brandon-phillips-00073724.

25 *"Norfolk Southern's DEI . . . policies directing"*: Acyn (@Acyn), "Rep. Mike
    Collins (R-GA) wonders if diversity, equity, and inclusion contributed

Norfolk Southern train derailment," Twitter, March 8, 2023, video, 0:20, https://twitter.com/Acyn/status/1633487321810051072?s=20.

25 *"cruel and aggressive conduct"*: Michael Scherer, "Top GOP Congressional Candidate in Texas Accused of Abusing Teenage Daughter of Estranged Husband," *Washington Post*, November 9, 2021, https://www.washingtonpost .com/politics/texas-gop-congressional-candidate-abuse-allegations/2021/11 /09/0cbdcdb6-4191-11ec-9ea7-3eb2406a2e24_story.html.

26 *"causing a disturbance"*: John Aguilar, "Lauren Boebert Escorted Out of 'Beetlejuice' Musical in Denver After 'Causing a Disturbance,'" *Denver Post*, September 12, 2023, https://www.denverpost.com/2023/09/12/lauren -boebert-removed-beetlejuice-musical-denver/.

26 *Former Democratic senator Heidi Heitkamp:* Victor Nava, "Rep. Matt Rosendale Threatens Legal Action over Ex-Senator's 'Rumor' He Impregnated 20-Year-Old Staffer," *New York Post*, February 26, 2024, https://nypost.com/2024/02/26 /us-news/rep-matt-rosendale-threatens-legal-action-over-ex-senators-rumor -he-impregnated-staffer/.

27 *"tried to pull me by my waist"*: Judy Kurtz, "Nancy Mace Tells Prayer Breakfast She Told Fiancé 'We Don't Got Time for That This Morning,'" *The Hill*, July 27, 2023, https://thehill.com/blogs/in-the-know/4123527-nancy-mace-tells -prayer-breakfast-she-told-fiance-she-dont-got-time-for-that-this-morning/.

27 *was known as "Candyman"*: Catie Edmondson and Michael D. Shear, "Congressman Harassed Staff and Got Drunk as White House Doctor, Watchdog Says," *New York Times*, March 3, 2021, https://www.nytimes.com /2021/03/03/us/politics/ronny-jackson-white-house-doctor.html.

27 *At a rodeo outside Amarillo:* Patrick Svitek, "Bodycam Video Shows Confrontation Between U.S. Rep. Ronny Jackson and Law Enforcement," *Texas Tribune*, August 14, 2023, https://www.texastribune.org/2023/08/14 /ronny-jackson-dps-bodycam-video/.

28 *alleged misconduct:* Bryn Stole, "Under Congress Police Reform Package, Clay Higgins' Own Policing Career Might've Drawn Closer Scrutiny," nola.com, June 27, 2020.

28 *"animals"*: T. Reese Shapiro, "Tough-Talking Captain in Louisiana Sheriff's Office Resigns After Calling Black Suspects 'Animals' in Viral Video," *Washington Post*, February 29, 2016.

28 *"I'll drop any 10 of you"*: Bryn Stole and Jerry Dicolo, "Clay Higgins Says on Facebook That Armed Demonstrators 'Won't Walk Away' from Louisiana Protests," *Acadiana Advocate*, September 1, 2020, https://www.theadvocate .com/acadiana/news/article_77138836-ecc4-11ea-a8d0-772b482469cb.html.

28 *"covenant marriage"*: Isaac Stanley-Becker, "House Speaker Mike Johnson Used Faith in Campaign Against Gay Rights," *Washington Post*, October 26, 2023, https://www.washingtonpost.com/politics/2023/10/26/mike-johnson -house-speaker-lgbtq-religion/.

28 *Paul Gosar, a former dentist with extensive ties:* Andrew Kaczynski and Em Steck, "Rep. Paul Gosar's Lengthy Ties to White Nationalists, Pro-Nazi Blogger and Far-Right Fringe Received Little Pushback for Years," CNN, March 6, 2022, https://www.cnn.com/2022/03/06/politics/republican-paul -gosar-white-nationalists-kfile/index.html.

28 *prescribed the deworming drug ivermectin:* Ovetta Wiggins and Meagan Flynn, "Rep. Andy Harris, a Doctor, Says He's Prescribed Ivermectin as a Covid-19

Treatment," *Washington Post*, October 19, 2021, https://www.washingtonpost
.com/local/md-politics/harris-prescribes-ivermectin-covid/2021/10/19
/7f2c4a9a-304c-11ec-a1e5-07223c50280a_story.html.

29 *"losing the gavel"*: Kipp Jones, "Congressman Andy Biggs Mocks Pelosi Getting
Bashed with a Hammer at GOP Watch Party," *Mediaite*, November 8, 2022,
https://www.mediaite.com/politics/congressman-andy-biggs-mocks-pelosi
-getting-bashed-with-a-hammer-at-gop-watch-party/.

29 *"pure insanity"*: Jacqueline Alemany, Emma Brown, and Amy Gardner, "Rep.
Scott Perry Played Key Role in Promoting False Claims of Fraud," *Washington
Post*, June 23, 2022, https://www.washingtonpost.com/national-security
/2022/06/23/scott-perry/.

30 *"You're a fucking piece of shit traitor"*: Josh Feldman, "'F*cking Piece of Sh*t
Traitor, I Hope You Die': GOP Congressman Shares Disturbing Voicemail
He Got After Voting for Infrastructure Bill," *Mediaite*, November 8, 2021,
https://www.mediaite.com/tv/fcking-piece-of-sht-traitor-i-hope-you-die
-gop-congressman-shares-disturbing-voicemail-he-got-after-voting-for
-infrastructure-bill/.

30 *"didn't want to run for Congress"*: Olivia Beavers and Daniella Diaz, "GOP's
Houck Problem Hits a Leadership Group Chat," *Politico*, August 24, 2023,
https://www.politico.com/newsletters/huddle/2023/08/24/gops-houck
-problem-hits-a-leadership-group-chat-00112718.

30 *Gaetz joined Illinois Republican Mary Miller:* Melanie Zanona (@MZanona),
"GOP primary drama: Mary Miller & Gaetz endorsed a challenger to
Mike Bost," X, December 12, 2023, https://twitter.com/MZanona/status
/1734687552597336538.

31 *8 percent of voters had effectively elected 83 percent:* Karen Tumulty, "Who Elects
These Clowns, Exactly? As It Turns Out, Almost None of Us," *Washington Post*,
September 29, 2023, https://www.washingtonpost.com/opinions/2023/09/29
/house-shutdown-primaries-voters/.

32 *The nonpartisan Pew Research Center found:* Drew DeSilver, "The Polarization
in Today's Congress Has Roots That Go Back Decades," Pew Research Center,
March 10, 2022, https://www.pewresearch.org/short-reads/2022/03/10/the
-polarization-in-todays-congress-has-roots-that-go-back-decades/.

33 *"They're voting for the craziest son of a bitch"*: Jessie Walker, "Thomas Massie's
Unified Theory of Ron Paul, Rand Paul, and Donald Trump," *Reason
Magazine*, March 15, 2017, https://reason.com/2017/03/15/thomas-massies
-unified-theory-of-ron-pau/; Thomas Massie (@RepThomasMassie), "I've
been quoted & misquoted," Twitter, May 8, 2018, https://twitter.com
/repthomasmassie/status/993885780782272513?lang=da.

CHAPTER 3: "LOOK, THERE'S A LOT OF FRAUDS IN CONGRESS"

35 *2,500 dogs and cats:* Grace Ashford and Michael Gold, "Who Is Rep.-Elect
George Santos? His Résumé May Be Largely Fiction," *New York Times*,
December 19, 2022, https://www.nytimes.com/2022/12/19/nyregion/george
-santos-ny-republicans.html.

37 *"a lot of frauds in Congress"*: Tony Gonzales, interview by Margaret Brennan,
Face the Nation, CBS News, January 8, 2023, transcript, https://www.cbsnews
.com/news/tony-gonzales-face-the-nation-transcript-01-08-2023/.

37 *Santos claimed to be the victim of a "witch-hunt":* Long interview with broadcaster Piers Morgan in February 2023, "'I've Been a Terrible Liar' - Piers Morgan GRILLS George Santos," YouTube, https://www.youtube.com/watch?v=I7p -6HHUgl4.

40 *"such a moron":* Rebecca Shabad and Frank Thorp V, "Pelosi, McCarthy Trade Barbs over Return of House Mask Mandate," NBC News, July 28, 2021, https://www.nbcnews.com/politics/congress/pelosi-mccarthy-trade-barbs -over-return-house-mask-mandate-n1275301.

41 *accused CBS of doctoring it:* Scott Pelley, "The Impeachment Inquiry: 'We Could Not Ignore What the President Did,'" CBS News, September 30, 2019, https://www.cbsnews.com/news/nancy-pelosi-on-trump-impeachment -inquiry-ukraine-president-phone-call-and-the-whistleblower-in-60-minutes -interview/.

41 *"who fought to the death in Ramadi":* Dana Milbank, "Kevin McCarthy: Say What?," *Washington Post*, June 17, 2014, https://www.washingtonpost.com /opinions/dana-milbank-house-gop-leader-kevin-mccarthy-has-an-odd-way -with-words/2014/06/17/2009ac42-f65c-11e3-a606-946fd632f9f1_story.html.

42 *"Only Kevin":* Melanie Zanona and Lauren Fox, "Inside McCarthy's Struggle to Lock Down the House Speakership," CNN, January 2, 2023, https://www .cnn.com/2023/01/02/politics/kevin-mccarthy-house-speaker-struggle/index .html.

43 *"constant stream of text messages":* Jonathan Swan and Catie Edmondson, "How Kevin McCarthy Forged an Ironclad Bond with Marjorie Taylor Greene," *New York Times*, January 23, 2023, https://www.nytimes.com/2023/01/23/us /politics/kevin-mccarthy-marjorie-taylor-greene.html.

44 *The winner: Greene, with a bid of $100,000:* Olivia Beavers (@Olivia_Beavers), "NEW: During GOP conference today, House Rs did about a 15-min fundraising auction for chapstick used by Speaker McCarthy," Twitter, May 23, 2023, https://twitter.com/Olivia_Beavers/status/1661013857824014339.

44 *"my mother's Jewish background beliefs":* Matthew Kassel, "Meet the Next Jewish Republican Congressman from Long Island," *Jewish Insider*, November 10, 2022, https://jewishinsider.com/2022/11/george-santos-long-island -queens-congress-midterms/.

44 *He took his act to WNYC's* Brian Lehrer Show: George Santos, interviewed by Brian Lehrer, "Meet Your New Member of Congress," *Brian Lehrer Show*, November 21, 2022, https://www.wnyc.org/story/meet-your-new-member -congress/.

45 *"In the middle of Fifth Avenue":* Gustaf Kilander, "Video Emerges of George Santos Saying He's the Victim of an Assassination Plot," *Independent*, January 24, 2023, https://www.the-independent.com/news/world/americas/us -politics/george-santos-video-attempted-murder-b2268120.html.

45 *Two days later,* The Forward, *a Jewish publication:* Andrew Silverstein, "Congressman-Elect George Santos Lied About Grandparents Fleeing Anti-Jewish Persecution During WWII," *The Forward*, December 21, 2022, https://forward.com/news/529130/george-santos-jewish-lie-genealogy -records/.

46 *"I said I was 'Jew-ish'":* Victor Nava and Carl Campanile, "Liar Rep.-Elect George Santos Admits Fabricating Key Details of His Bio," *New York Post*,

December 26, 2022, https://nypost.com/2022/12/26/rep-elect-george-santos
-admits-fabricating-key-details-of-his-bio/.

47 *zero to $11 million:* Maureen Daly, "Santos Filings Now Claim Net Worth
of $11 Million," *North Shore Leader,* September 2023, https://www
.theleaderonline.com/single-post/santos-filings-now-claim-net-worth-of-11
-million.

47 *Santos's faked résumé:* Dana Milbank, "Think You Already Know Crazy?
Meet the House GOP Class of '22," *Washington Post,* November 22, 2022,
https://www.washingtonpost.com/opinions/2022/10/07/republican-house
-candidates-2022-crazy/.

47 *"Senior House Republicans were apparently aware":* Nava and Campanile, "Liar
Rep.-Elect George Santos Admits Fabricating Key Details of His Bio."

49 *"Mitt Romney . . . tells me, a Latino gay man":* Darragh Roche, "George Santos
Compares Himself to Rosa Parks," *Newsweek,* July 10, 2023, https://www
.newsweek.com/george-santos-compares-himself-rosa-parks-1811848.

49 *"Now that everybody's canceling me":* George Bowden, "George Santos Tells
Piers Morgan: 'I've Been a Terrible Liar,'" BBC News, February 20, 2023,
https://www.bbc.com/news/world-us-canada-64712914.

50 *An Economist/YouGov poll in Santos's district:* Kaitlin Lewis, "The Bipartisan
Public Has Spoken, and George Santos Should Quit: Poll," *Newsweek,*
January 11, 2023, https://www.newsweek.com/bipartisan-public-has-spoken
-george-santos-should-quit-poll-1773148.

50 *"This was not the will of the voters":* Alexandra Hutzler and Lauren Peller, "NY
Congressman Joins Residents of Santos' District to Call for Probe of His
Finances," ABC News, January 17, 2023, https://abcnews.go.com/Politics/ny
-congressman-joins-residents-santos-district-call-probe/story?id=96482320.

51 *Santos wrote thank-you notes to his GOP colleagues:* Olivia Beavers (@
Olivia_Beavers), "Rep. SANTOS giving thank you letters to members for
voting to refer Dem's expulsion res to Ethics panel," Twitter, May 22, 2023,
https://twitter.com/Olivia_Beavers/status/1660736101990924289.

CHAPTER 4: "A SPEAKER HAS NOT BEEN ELECTED"

62 *"I'm not afraid of the civil war in the GOP":* Stephen K. Bannon, "Episode
2300: Fighting Back with the 'MTG Wing' of the Party," *War Room Podcast,*
November 14, 2022, https://www.audible.com/es_US/pd/Episode-2300
-Fighting-Back-With-The-MTG-Wing-Of-The-Party-Podcast/B0BMBDR541.

62 *"after he knew that he was facing somebody":* Dana Milbank, "Is Kevin
McCarthy Okay?," *Washington Post,* December 16, 2022, https://www
.washingtonpost.com/opinions/2022/12/16/kevin-mccarthy-republican
-party-leadership-speaker/.

64 *I wrote after the 2016 elections:* Dana Milbank, "For Democrats to Recover,
Nancy Pelosi and Her Team Should Go," *Washington Post,* November 25, 2016,
https://www.washingtonpost.com/opinions/for-democrats-to-recover-nancy
-pelosi-must-go/2016/11/25/ec1c8944-b31f-11e6-be1c-8cec35b1ad25_story
.html.

65 *"Nobody trusts McCarthy to pass anything":* Ryan Lizza, Rachael Bade, and
Eugene Daniels, "The Hill's Big Choice: Omnibus or Struggle Bus?," *Politico,*

November 30, 2022, https://www.politico.com/newsletters/playbook/2022
/11/30/the-hills-big-choice-omnibus-or-struggle-bus-00071313.

65   *"it's too much to ask"*: Burgess Everett and Sarah Ferris, "December Spending
Gloom Falls on GOP: 'I'm So Disgusted,'" *Politico*, December 14, 2022,
https://www.politico.com/news/2022/12/14/gop-spending-gloom-mccarthy
-mcconnell-00073778.

65   *"for Kevin's sake . . . some Republicans just feel"*: Joseph Zeballos-Roig and Kadia
Goba, "Senators Aren't Ready to Let Kevin McCarthy Negotiate a Big Boy Bill
Just Yet," *Semafor*, December 15, 2022, https://www.semafor.com/article/12
/15/2022/congress-isnt-ready-to-let-kevin-mccarthy-and-and-the-house-gop
-negotiate-a-big-boy-bill-just-yet.

74   *Next, in a moment captured by the C-SPAN cameras:* Theresa Driley, "User Clip:
That Time Rodgers Lunged at Gaetz in the House," C-SPAN, January 6, 2023,
video, 1:26, https://www.c-span.org/video/?c5050136/user-clip-time-rodgers
-lunged-gaetz-house.

75   *"burn the whole place down"*: Lisa Mascaro and Stephen Groves, "Hard-Right
Republicans Push Closer to a Disruptive Federal Shutdown," Associated
Press, September 21, 2023, https://apnews.com/article/government
-shutdown-mccarthy-house-republicans-spending-cuts
-deff84c0e2ff7d3bd076b8c38e14cca4.

CHAPTER 5: "WHAT A TURD SANDWICH THIS 'DEAL' IS"

79   *"We haven't passed one of the must-pass bills this year"*: Natalie Andrews, "Kevin
McCarthy Boasts of GOP Unity, but Tests Loom on Spending Cuts, Trump,"
Wall Street Journal, March 21, 2023, https://www.wsj.com/articles/kevin
-mccarthy-boasts-of-gop-unity-but-tests-loom-on-spending-cuts-trump
-89e660c2.

82   *Representative Ken Calvert, a California Republican:* Andrew Solender, "House
Republicans in the Dark on McCarthy's Shadow Document," *Axios*,
January 10, 2023, https://www.axios.com/2023/01/10/republicans-mccarthy
-house-rules-addendum.

82   *"we don't have any idea what promises were made"*: Nancy Mace, interviewed
by Margaret Brennan, "Transcript: Rep. Nancy Mace on 'Face the Nation,'"
CBS News, January 8, 2023, https://www.cbsnews.com/news/nancy-mace
-transcript-face-the-nation-01-08-2023/.

83   *"secret three-page addendum"*: Jake Sherman and John Bresnahan, "McCarthy's
First Test," *Punchbowl News*, January 9, 2023, https://punchbowl.news/archive
/1923-punchbowl-news-am/.

83   *"weaponization of the federal government"*: Aaron Blake, "GOP Gives the
Freedom Caucus the Keys to the Car," *Washington Post*, January 25, 2023,
https://www.washingtonpost.com/politics/2023/01/25/house-freedom
-caucus-committees/.

83   *"Bring the Tiger"*: Olivia Beavers (@Olivia_Beavers), "Told NRCC's theme
this year is to bring the tiger. If it sounds familiar . . . it's from the bad lip
reading video during speakership battle re: the line 'I brought the tiger,'"
Twitter, January 25, 2023, https://twitter.com/Olivia_Beavers/status
/1618278688344387598.

84 *"out of bounds"*: "Leaders of House China Panel Denounce Attack on Rep Judy Chu," Associated Press, February 26, 2023, https://apnews.com/article /politics-united-states-government-judy-chu-raja-krishnamoorthi-mike -gallagher-578818d8dc270d50627146304b0de8e4.

89 *"committee of the whole"*: Paul Kane, "So Much for That Promise: Debt Bill Talks Again Done in the Backroom," *Washington Post,* April 22, 2023, https://www .washingtonpost.com/politics/2023/04/22/debt-ceiling-mccarthy/.

90 *"doesn't do anything to balance the budget"*: Leigh Ann Caldwell and Theodoric Meyer, "House GOP Leaders' Debt Ceiling Pitch," *Washington Post,* April 25, 2023, https://www.washingtonpost.com/politics/2023/04/25/house-gop -leaders-debt-ceiling-pitch/.

91 *"Because now I'm not president"*: "Transcript of CNN's Town Hall with Former President Donald Trump," CNN, May 11, 2023, https://www.cnn.com/2023 /05/11/politics/transcript-cnn-town-hall-trump/index.html.

91 *"Let me be very clear"*: "Speaker McCarthy News Conference on the Debt Limit," C-SPAN, May 22, 2023, video, 20:08, https://www.c-span.org/video /?528265-1/speaker-mccarthy-news-conference-debt-limit.

92 *"I think my conservative colleagues"*: Joseph Zeballos-Roig, "Matt Gaetz Embraces Role as Hostage Taker as House Leaders Brace for Debt Limit Fallout," *Semafor,* May 24, 2023, https://www.semafor.com/article/05/24/2023/matt-gaetz -embraces-role-as-hostage-taker-as-house-leaders-brace-for-debt-limit-fallout.

93 *"I see the path"*: Manu Raju (@mkraju), "News—For the first time, Speaker McCarthy sounding positive about direction of debt talks," Twitter, May 18, 2023, https://twitter.com/mkraju/status/1659206660169273347.

95 *"Everyone loves dessert, and that's impeachment"*: Juliegrace Brufke (@ juliegraceb), "Rep. Marjorie Taylor Greene likens raising the debt ceiling to a 'shit sandwich' but is a lean yes," Twitter, May 30, 2023, https://twitter.com /juliegraceb/status/1663670150078386178.

98 *"Now we are allowed to say it: We rolled them"*: Erik Wasson (@elwasson), "'Now we are allowed to say it: we rolled them' said Democrat Brad Sherman," Twitter, May 31, 2023, https://twitter.com/elwasson/status /1664088476814376962?s=43&t=BdcI9Vl1vn-oooeVGjV_2Q.

99 *"This is fabulous"*: "House Republican News Conference on Debt Limit Vote," C-SPAN, May 31, 2023, video, 40:40, https://www.c-span.org/video/?528450-1 /house-republican-news-conference-debt-limit-vote.

101 *"House Republicans couldn't pass gas"*: Jordain Carney, Katherine Tully-McManus, and Daniella Diaz, "Mayorkas, Wray to Testify at Judiciary," *Politico,* June 7, 2023, https://www.politico.com/newsletters/huddle/2023/06 /07/mayorkas-wray-to-testify-at-judiciary-00100705.

102 *"resolve those issues"*: Jake Sherman and John Bresnahan, "Scalise Says Republicans Are Angry at McCarthy," *Punchbowl News,* June 8, 2023, https://punchbowl.news/archive/6823-punchbowl-news-am/.

CHAPTER 6: "THIS PLACE IS CRAZIER THAN USUAL"

103 *"Did you or did you not decriminalize public urination"*: Dana Milbank, "Finally, Republicans Tackle the No. 1 Issue in Washington," *Norman Transcript,* April 5, 2023, https://www.normantranscript.com/opinion/national-column

-finally-republicans-tackle-the-no-1-issue-in-washington/article_79b245de
-d257-11ed-825f-5fbe1970abed.html.

105 *In Election Day exit polls in 2022:* "Exit Polls 2022," NBC News, November 8,
2022, https://www.nbcnews.com/politics/2022-elections/exit-polls?icid
=election_nav.

107 *"the single mom who's working two shifts":* "Republicans Ready to Change
Washington and Help Hardworking Families," press release, Congressman
Steve Scalise, January 10, 2023, https://scalise.house.gov/press-releases
/Scalise%3A-Republicans-Ready-to-Change-Washington-and-Help
-Hardworking-Families.

108 *"most dishonest, demagogic rhetoric":* Kevin Freking, "House GOP Kicks Off
Majority with Vote to Slash IRS Funding," Associated Press, January 9, 2023,
https://apnews.com/article/politics-united-states-government-internal
-revenue-service-us-republican-party-house-of-representatives
-64692090ef20e35a59ba1ea7d21a9eea.

109 *"Phoenix, Holly and Angel":* Kendall Tietz, "U.S. Congresswoman Demands
Late-Term Abortionist Have His Medical License Revoked: 'Ignored for
a Year,'" Fox News, March 30, 2023, https://www.foxnews.com/media/us
-congresswoman-demands-late-term-abortionist-medical-license-revoked
-ignored-year.

110 *"We're just sick of every appropriations bill":* Andrew Solender, "Abortion
Threatens Another House GOP Spending Bill," *Axios,* November 8, 2023,
https://www.axios.com/2023/11/08/abortion-fsgg-spending-bill-house
-republicans.

112 *less than a fifth want more lenient laws:* Jeffrey M. Jones, "Majority in U.S.
Continues to Favor Stricter Gun Laws," Gallup, October 31, 2023, https://news
.gallup.com/poll/513623/majority-continues-favor-stricter-gun-laws.aspx.

112 *"stabilizing braces":* "The Nashville Shooter Used a Gun with an Arm Brace.
House Republicans Want to Make It Easier to Get One," *Everytown for Gun
Safety,* March 29, 2023, https://www.everytown.org/press/the-nashville
-shooter-used-a-gun-with-an-arm-brace-house-republicans-want-to-make-it
-easier-to-get-one/.

112 *"Democrats were going to turn this tragic event":* Emily Brooks, "House Judiciary
Postpones Pistol Brace Rule Markup After Nashville Shooting," *The Hill,*
March 27, 2023, https://thehill.com/homenews/house/3920835-house
-judiciary-postpones-pistol-brace-rule-markup-after-nashville-shooting/.

114 *In one study, nearly a quarter of teachers said:* Hannah Natanson, "'Slavery
Was Wrong' and 5 Other Things Some Educators Won't Teach Anymore,"
Washington Post, March 6, 2023, https://www.washingtonpost.com/education
/2023/03/06/slavery-was-wrong-5-other-things-educators-wont-teach
-anymore/.

117 *"Democrats are a party of pedophiles":* Lesley Stahl, "Representative Marjorie
Taylor Greene: From the Far-Right Fringe to the Republican Party's Front
Row," CBS News, April 2, 2023, https://www.cbsnews.com/news/marjorie
-taylor-greene-far-right-republican-transcript-60-minutes-2023-04-02/.

118 *"a clear but ugly signal":* Jennifer Shutt, "LGBTQ Project Funding in Two States
Stripped by U.S. House Republicans from Spending Bill," *Louisiana Illuminator,*
July 18, 2023, https://lailluminator.com/2023/07/18/lgbtq-project-funding-in
-two-states-stripped-by-u-s-house-republicans-from-spending-bill/.

118 *the words "Dead Faggot":* Dana Milbank, "In the House, It's Open Season on LGBTQ Americans," *Washington Post,* July 21, 2023, https://www.washingtonpost.com/opinions/2023/07/21/house-gop-lgbtq-bigotry-discrimination/.

119 *"covid was intentionally released":* Dana Milbank, "There Ain't No Cure for Long Covidiocy," *Washington Post,* March 3, 2023, https://www.washingtonpost.com/opinions/2023/03/03/select-subcommittee-coronavirus-pandemic-covidiocy/.

119 *"You crack me up":* Philip Bump, "A Child in Marjorie Taylor Greene's District Died of Covid. She's Still Attacking Masks and the Vaccine," *Washington Post,* July 22, 2021, https://www.washingtonpost.com/politics/2021/07/22/child-marjorie-taylor-greenes-district-died-covid-shes-still-attacking-masks-vaccine/.

120 *"covid will be mostly gone by April":* Marty Makary, "We'll Have Herd Immunity by April," *Wall Street Journal,* February 18, 2021, https://www.wsj.com/articles/well-have-herd-immunity-by-april-11613669731.

120 *"actively harmful":* Eran Bendavid and Jay Bhattacharya, "Is the Coronavirus as Deadly as They Say?," *Wall Street Journal,* March 24, 2020, https://www.wsj.com/articles/is-the-coronavirus-as-deadly-as-they-say-11585088464.

124 *shouted "Slava Ukraini!":* John Bowden, "Zelensky Invokes US Fighting in Battle of the Bulge as He Insists Ukraine Is 'Alive and Kicking' in Address to Congress," *Independent,* December 21, 2022, https://ca.sports.yahoo.com/news/zelensky-invokes-us-fighting-battle-035100750.html.

126 *"I have a real concern of the aggression of Russia":* "House Republican Retreat Opening News Conference," C-SPAN, March 19, 2023, video, 58:54, https://www.c-span.org/video/?526814-1/house-republican-retreat-opening-news-conference.

128 *This went on for the better part:* Burgess Everett, "Tuberville Staffer Asks Anti-Abortion Groups to Float Primaries Against Republicans Who Oppose Military Holds," *Politico,* November 2, 2023, https://www.politico.com/live-updates/2023/11/02/congress/tuberville-staffers-anti-abortion-group-ask-00124994.

128 *"sodomy-promoting General Milley":* Corbin Bolies, "Rep. Gosar's Homophobic Sunday Rant Is Deranged—Even for Him," *Daily Beast,* September 24, 2023, https://www.thedailybeast.com/rep-paul-gosars-homophobic-rant-on-mark-milley-is-derangedeven-for-him.

CHAPTER 7: "THE DYSFUNCTION CAUCUS AT WORK"

135 *"If it continues":* Leigh Ann Caldwell and Theodoric Meyer, "Swing-District Republicans Strike Back," *Washington Post,* July 3, 2023, https://www.washingtonpost.com/politics/2023/07/03/swing-district-republicans-strike-back/.

136 *"I'm opposed to a shutdown":* Jake Sherman and Andrew Desiderio, "McCarthy Eying Disaster Relief on CR, Exacting Price for Ukraine Aid," *Punchbowl News,* September 7, 2023, https://punchbowl.news/archive/9723-punchbowl-news-am/.

138 *"You think I'm scared":* Marianna Sotomayor, Leigh Ann Caldwell, Amy B. Wang, and Jacqueline Alemany, "After Chaotic Week, House Heads Home

with Government Shutdown on Horizon," *Washington Post*, September 14, 2023, https://www.washingtonpost.com/politics/2023/09/14/house -republicans-speaker-shutdown-chaos/.

138 *"Him starting an impeachment inquiry"*: "Daniella Diaz and Jordain Carney, "Impeachment Won't Solve McCarthy's Spending Problem," *Politico*, September 12, 2023, https://www.politico.com/newsletters/huddle/2023/09 /12/impeachment-wont-solve-mccarthys-spending-problem-00115417.

139 *"Matt is upset"*: Melanie Zanona, Annie Grayer, and Manu Raju, "Kevin McCarthy Stares Down Another Right-Wing Revolt," CNN, September 14, 2023, https://www.cnn.com/2023/09/14/politics/kevin-mccarthy-right-wing -revolt/index.html.

140 *baby changing table:* Matt Laslo (@MattLaslo), "Found on a baby changing table in restroom underneath House floor," X, September 19, 2023, https://twitter.com/MattLaslo/status/1704194792760951011.

142 *"Unfortunately, real leadership takes courage"*: Victoria Spartz (@RepSpartz), "Today, Rep. Spartz issued the following statement on her opposition to the proposed CR deal and lack of real leadership by @SpeakerMcCarthy," X, September 18, 2023, https://twitter.com/RepSpartz/status /1703755976300536106?s=20.

142 *"Oh my God, I'm going"*: Heather Caygle (@heatherscope), "Speaker McCarthy asked about Matt Gaetz constant Twitter threats to try to oust him," X, September 18, 2023, https://twitter.com/heatherscope/status /1703900606467830136.

142 *"You want me to follow that clown show?"*: Alex Griffing, "'It's a Clown Show': Moderate Republican Rips GOP Colleagues, This Is What Happens When 'You Keep Running Lunatics,'" *Mediaite*, September 19, 2023, https://www .mediaite.com/politics/its-a-clown-show-moderate-republican-rips-gop -colleagues-this-is-what-happens-when-you-keep-running-lunatics/.

143 *"It feels like Festivus"*: Sahil Kapur, Scott Wong, Ali Vitali, and Rebecca Kaplan, "Republican Infighting Paralyzes the House as Some Call a Shutdown Inevitable," NBC News, September 19, 2023, https://www.nbcnews.com /politics/congress/republican-infighting-paralyzes-house-call-shutdown -inevitable-rcna105882.

143 *"There's yelling, there's screaming"*: Marianna Sotomayor, Leigh Ann Caldwell, Paul Kane, and Amy B. Wang, "House Flounders as GOP Fails to Appease Hard-Right Members on Funding," *Washington Post*, September 19, 2023, https://www.washingtonpost.com/politics/2023/09/19/house-republicans -spending-vote/.

143 *"we've got five clowns"*: Connor O'Brien, "Hardliners Block Defense Spending Bill as GOP Civil War Worsens," *Politico*, September 19, 2023, https://www .politico.com/news/2023/09/19/gop-block-defense-spending-bill-00116810.

143 *"showed just how broken we are"*: Manu Raju (@mkraju), "Gonzales added: 'I think today's vote showed just how broken we are. There's no doubt in my mind we're headed for a shutdown,'" X, September 19, 2023, https://twitter .com/mkraju/status/1704233688504914227.

144 *"I don't quit"*: Chad Pergram, "The Speaker's Lobby: The Hitchhiker's Guide to a Possible Government Shutdown," Fox News, September 20, 2023, https://www.foxnews.com/politics/speakers-lobby-hitchhikers-guide -possible-government-shutdown.

145 *ravages of a shutdown:* Annie Grayer and Melanie Zanona, "House Republicans Vow to Continue Impeachment Inquiry Even If Government Shuts Down," CNN, September 26, 2023, https://www.cnn.com /2023/09/26/politics/impeachment-inquiry-shutdown?cid=external -feeds_iluminar_google.

148 *"We're just screaming at each other":* Andrew Solender and Juliegrace Brufke, "GOP Tensions Flare as McCarthy Grasps for Shutdown Solution," *Axios,* September 29, 2023, https://www.axios.com/2023/09/29/republicans -government-shutdown-continuing-resolution.

150 *Honest!:* George Santos (@MrSantosNY), "Here's someone actually putting her neck out there to defend the actions of an insurrectionist," X, October 1, 2023, https://twitter.com/MrSantosNY/status/1708497346219086062.

CHAPTER 8: "LET'S GET OUR POOP IN A GROUP, PEOPLE"

156 *"eight selfish assholes":* Andrew Solender (@AndrewSolender), "McCarthy supporters have nothing nice to say about the eight Republicans who voted to remove him," X, October 3, 2023, https://twitter.com/AndrewSolender /status/1709380487385428394.

157 *"brag about how he would crush ED":* Melanie Zanona and Manu Raju, "House Devolves into Angry Round of Retribution Following McCarthy's Ouster," CNN, October 4, 2023, https://www.cnn.com/2023/10/04/politics/house -republican-anger-speaker-fight/index.html.

157 *"the next speaker is going to be subjected":* Igor Bobic (@igorbobic), "Sen. Cornyn calls effort to oust McCarthy 'disgraceful,'" X, October 3, 2023, https://twitter .com/igorbobic/status/1709304274327380000.

157 *"This is potentially a setback of weeks":* "GOP Lawmaker Says McCarthy Ouster Was Fundraising Move," CBS, October 4, 2023, https://www .cbsnews.com/video/gop-lawmaker-says-mccarthy-ouster-was-fundraising -move/.

160 *Democrats "tried to do everything":* "Full Transcript of 'Face the Nation,'" CBS News, October 1, 2023, https://www.cbsnews.com/news/face-the-nation-full -transcript-10-01-2023/.

162 *"I did not have access to my phone":* Dana Milbank, "Opinion: House Republicans Collapse into Anarchy," *Washington Post,* October 14, 2023, https://www.washingtonpost.com/opinions/2023/10/13/scalise-jordan-house -gop-speaker-chaos/.

163 *"I personally cannot, in good conscience":* Joan E. Greve and Lauren Gambino, "House Remains Without Speaker as Republican Holdouts Block Scalise," *The Guardian,* October 12, 2023, https://www.theguardian.com/us-news/2023 /oct/12/us-house-speakership-steve-scalise.

165 *"great opportunity" for Republicans:* Mike Roe, "RNC Chair Ronna McDaniel Tells Fox News That Israel Attacks Are a 'Great Opportunity for Our Candidates,'" *The Wrap,* October 7, 2023, https://www.thewrap.com/ronna -mcdaniel-fox-news-israel-attack-hamas-iran.

166 *"It's time to take the sharp knives away":* Andrew Solender (@AndrewSolender), "Rules Committee Chair Tom Cole makes the case to raise the threshold for the motion to vacate: 'I think it's time to take the sharp knives away

from the children,'" X, October 9, 2023, https://twitter.com/AndrewSolender /status/1711542674015068394.

168 *"If you see smoke, it's not a speaker"*: Ali Vitali (@alivitali), "'If you see smoke it's not a speaker, someone just set the place on fire,' GOP Rep. Ronny Jackson with a literally 🔥 vibe check," X, October 12, 2023, https://twitter.com /alivitali/status/1712534316914245838.

168 *"This is the worst team"*: Arthur Delaney and Jonathan Nicholson, "'We Are a Broken Conference': Republicans at Standstill After Speaker Nominee Drops Out," *HuffPost*, October 12, 2023, https://www.huffpost.com/entry/steve -scalise-republican-house-speaker_n_65285a13e4b0a304ff6f8311.

170 *"snowflakes"*: Juliegrace Brufke (@juliegraceb), "Moderates are growing increasingly irritated with the tactics Jordan allies are using to pressure them into voting for him," X, October 15, 2023, https://twitter.com /juliegraceb/status/1713694255841992765?s=20.

170 *Missouri's Ann Wagner:* Olivia Beavers (@Olivia_Beavers), "'Absolutely not,' said Rep. Ann Wagner, a Scalise ally, when I asked if she will support Jordan for speaker," X, October 12, 2023, https://twitter.com/Olivia_Beavers/status /1712642712384491800.

171 *vulgar voice messages:* Olivia Beavers (@Olivia_Beavers), "Taking it to a different level, Bacon tells me his wife even received multiple anonymous emails and texts from people over the past few days w/ implied message: vote Jordan or be booted," X, October 17, 2023, https://twitter.com/Olivia_Beavers /status/1714426340084986074.

171 *"I hope your kids fucking burn alive"*: Audrey Fahlberg, "GOP Congressman Shares Voicemails from Jordan Backers Threatening His Family: 'I Hope Your Kids F∗∗∗ing Burn,'" *National Review*, October 25, 2023, https://www .nationalreview.com/news/gop-congressman-shares-voicemails-from-jordan -backers-threatening-his-family-i-hope-your-kids-fing-burn/.

177 *"worst job in America"*: "Jordan Does Not Appear to Have Votes for Speakership; Rep. Jim Jordan Loses First Speaker Vote; Rep. Carlos Gimenez (R-FL) Discusses House Speakership Vote," CNN, October 17, 2023, https://transcripts.cnn.com/show/se/date/2023-10-17/segment/04.

177 *Gaetz and Mike Bost of Illinois:* Olivia Beavers, Jordain Carney, and Sarah Ferris, "House GOP Drowning as Crisis Reaches Breaking Point," *Politico*, October 19, 2023, https://www.politico.com/news/2023/10/19/house-gop -speaker-mccarthy-gaetz-00122617.

177 *McHenry reportedly threatened to resign:* Scott Wong and Rebecca Kaplan, "In the Latest Sign of House Chaos, the Temporary Speaker Is Threatening to Quit," NBC News, October 19, 2023, https://www.nbcnews.com/politics /congress/patrick-mchenry-house-speaker-pro-tempore-threaten-quit -rcna121314.

177 *"too many men here with no balls"*: Nancy Mace (@RepNancyMace), "This is exactly what's wrong with this place—too many men here with no balls," X, October 19, 2023, https://twitter.com/RepNancyMace/status /1715170523691254095.

180 *"I want to know which one of you have the balls"*: Jordain Carney, Olivia Beavers, and Daniella Diaz, "House GOP Speaker Field Drops to 8 Hopefuls—but Still Has Little Hope of an Easy Endgame," *Politico*, October 23, 2023, https://www

.politico.com/live-updates/2023/10/23/congress/the-candidate-forum
-00123117.

181 *"get right with Jesus"*: Jake Sherman (@JakeSherman), "NEW from me and @
bresreports—Rep. RICK ALLEN, Georgia Republican, told TOM EMMER
in close House GOP conference meeting that . . . ," X, October 24, 2023,
https://twitter.com/JakeSherman/status/1716936383657656762?s=20.

181 *"You mean the backup to the backup"*: Max Cohen (@maxpcohen), "Vibe
check, courtesy of Dusty Johnson: 'I hope we knock ourselves out of this
doom loop,'" X, October 24, 2023, https://twitter.com/maxpcohen/status
/1716910079172346249.

183 *"It was absurd last week"*: Ben Jacobs, "The Nice Guy Who Finished First:
Mike Johnson Made It to Speaker Mostly by Not Making Enemies," *New York
Magazine*, October 25, 2023, https://nymag.com/intelligencer/2023/10/house
-speaker-mike-johnson-the-nice-guy-who-finished-first.html.

184 *Chip Roy, a Freedom Caucus ringleader:* Erik Wasson, "Conservative
Lawmaker Chip Roy Working on Plan to Avoid US Shutdown," Bloomberg
News, September 14, 2023, https://www.bloomberg.com/news/articles
/2023-09-14/conservative-lawmaker-roy-working-on-plan-to-avoid-us
-shutdown.

185 *"Shut up! Shut up!"*: Rachel Scott, "Republicans Boo ABC Reporter over
Question," ABC News, October 25, 2023, https://abcnews.go.com/Politics
/video/republicans-boo-abc-reporter-question-104279018.

185 *"We're not talking about any issues"*: Jacqueline Alemany (@JaxAlemany),
"Just asked newly minted Speaker Johnson whether he believes the 2020
was stolen. He declined to answer before walking away," X, October 25, 2023,
https://twitter.com/JaxAlemany/status/1717258646621458940.

CHAPTER 9: "IT'S THE SAME CLOWN CAR WITH A DIFFERENT DRIVER"

187 *"hits for a 'Bachelorette' contestant"*: Paul Kane, "A Historic Gamble: Mike
Johnson's Unpaved Path to House Speaker," *Washington Post*, October 25,
2023, https://www.washingtonpost.com/politics/2023/10/25/mike-johnson
-speaker-who-history/.

187 *"same-sex deviate sexual intercourse"*: Andrew Kaczynski and Allison Gordon,
"New Speaker of the House Mike Johnson Once Wrote in Support of the
Criminalization of Gay Sex," CNN, October 27, 2023, https://www.cnn.com
/2023/10/25/politics/mike-johnson-gay-sex-criminalization-kfile/index.html.

187 *"People are curious: What does Mike Johnson"*: "Speaker Mike Johnson Defends
Stance on Social Issues: 'Go Pick Up a Bible, That's My Worldview,'" Fox
News, October 27, 2023, https://www.foxnews.com/media/speaker-mike
-johnson-defends-stance-social-issues-pick-bible-worldview.

188 *"I reject that being a Christian Nationalist"*: Tim Dickinson, "The Christian
Nationalist Machine Turning Hate into Law," *Rolling Stone*, February 23,
2023, https://www.rollingstone.com/politics/politics-features/christian
-nationalists-national-association-christian-lawmakers-1234684542/.

188 *"the American colonies imposed the death penalty for sodomy"*: Kyle Mantyla,
"AFA's Jameson Taylor Chastises Sen. Cruz for Criticizing Uganda's

Draconian Anti-LGBTQ Law," *Right Wing Watch*, June 15, 2023, https://www
.rightwingwatch.org/post/afas-jameson-taylor-chastises-sen-cruz-for
-criticizing-ugandas-draconian-anti-lgbtq-law/.

188 *"a label across their forehead":* Right Wing Watch (@RightWingWatch), "Right-
wing pastor Andrew Wommack claims that being gay is 'three times worse
than smoking,'" Twitter, May 21, 2021, https://twitter.com/RightWingWatch
/status/1395769165282222090?s=20#google_vignette.

188 *blamed gay people for Noah's flood:* Nina Liss-Schultz, "The Mastermind
Behind Ohio's New "Heartbeat" Abortion Bill Is Too Extreme for Christian
Talk Radio," *Mother Jones*, December 9, 2016, https://www.motherjones.com
/politics/2016/12/ohio-heartbeat-abortion-janet-porter/.

188 *governed under biblical law by Christians:* Payton Armstrong, "Mike Johnson
to Speak at Christian Nationalist Conference," *Media Matters*, December 4,
2023, https://www.mediamatters.org/congress/mike-johnson-speak
-christian-nationalist-conference-alongside-extreme-right-wing-media.

188 *"we're coming to a Red Sea moment":* Molly Olmsted, "Mike Johnson Claims
That God Prepared Him to Be a 'New Moses,'" *Slate*, December 7, 2023,
https://slate.com/news-and-politics/2023/12/mike-johnson-christian
-nationalist-lawmakers-moses.html.

189 *"Tell her to go chase so-called Jewish space lasers":* Mychael Schnell, "CHIP
ROY responds to this dig from MTG," X, November 2, 2023, https://x.com
/mychaelschnell/status/1720067788834804156.

189 *"whore":* Zachary Petrizzo, "MTG Is Trashing Lauren Boebert as a 'Whore' to
GOP Colleagues," *Daily Beast*, November 10, 2023, https://www.thedailybeast
.com/marjorie-taylor-greene-is-trashing-lauren-boebert-as-a-whore-to-gop
-colleagues.

191 *"ungovernable":* Sahil Kapur, Scott Wong, and Julie Tsirkin, "'We're
Ungovernable': House Republicans Nix Votes on Two Funding Bills as
Shutdown Deadline Nears," *NBC News*, November 9, 2023, https://www
.nbcnews.com/politics/congress/-ungovernable-house-republicans-nix-votes
-two-funding-bills-shutdown-d-rcna124441.

192 *"I'm going to get out my unicorn":* Mike Collins (@RepMikeCollins), "This is
my team," X, November 6, 2023, https://twitter.com/RepMikeCollins/status
/1721578075270299993.

192 *"clear as mud":* Olivia Beavers and Jordain Carney, "Confusion Reigns as
House GOP Inches Toward Shutdown Deadline," *Politico*, November 7, 2023,
https://www.politico.com/live-updates/2023/11/07/congress/spending
-confusion-reigns-in-house-gop-00125768.

193 *"I'm getting anxious":* Dana Milbank, "The House Is Most Definitely Not in
Order," *Washington Post*, November 11, 2023, https://www.washingtonpost
.com/opinions/2023/11/10/new-speaker-mike-johnson-censure-resolutions
-tlaib-shutdown/.

194 *"Impeach that person, censure that person":* Jake Sherman and John
Bresnahan, "Santos Is Probably Done," *Punchbowl News*, November 17, 2023,
https://punchbowl.news/archive/111723-punchbowl-news-am/.

195 *"lunged towards me":* Claudia Grisales (@cgrisales), "Have NEVER seen
this on Capitol Hill: While talking to @RepTimBurchett after the GOP
conference meeting . . . ," X, November 14, 2023, https://twitter.com/cgrisales
/status/1724452392811286565.

195 *"You got no guts"*: Manu Raju et al., "Burchett Accuses McCarthy of Elbowing Him in the Kidneys as Former House Speaker Denies It," CNN, November 14, 2023, https://www.cnn.com/politics/live-news/federal-government -shutdown-funding-11-14-23/h_8b6fe0f1a6b7b45bcdff4a5bdb9416d6.

196 *"In a fight, I'm gonna bite"*: Anthony Adragna, "Markwayne Mullin Is Unbowed After Nearly Coming to Blows in a Hearing Tuesday," *Politico*, November 15, 2023, https://www.politico.com/live-updates/2023/11/15 /congress/mullins-biting-commentary-00127321.

197 *"It's the same clown car with a different driver"*: Sarah Ferris, Olivia Beavers, and Jordain Carney, "'Same Clown Car with a Different Driver': House GOP Goes off the Rails," *Politico*, November 15, 2023, https://www.politico.com/news /2023/11/15/the-house-gop-is-stuck-on-a-failure-loop-00127418.

198 *"Not much of a honeymoon in this job"*: Mychael Schnell, "House Votes to Avert Government Shutdown," *The Hill*, November 14, 2023, https://thehill.com /homenews/house/4309779-house-votes-avert-shutdown/.

200 *both men had opposed:* Jake Sherman, "Johnson in Florida for Cash and Official Event with Buchanan," *Punchbowl News*, November 27, 2023, https://punchbowl.news/article/johnson-in-florida-with-vern-buchanan -fundraising/.

200 *Max Miller called him a "joke":* Olivia Beavers, "Speaker Johnson Singed by a Blast of Conservative Fury," *Politico*, November 29, 2023, https://www.politico .com/news/2023/11/29/speaker-johnson-singed-by-a-blast-of-conservative -fury-00129180.

200 *"belongs in jail":* Mia McCarthy, "Divisions Leave Florida's House Republicans Powerless," *Politico*, November 29, 2023, https://www.politico .com/news/2023/11/29/divisions-leave-floridas-house-republicans -powerless-00129200.

200 *"Fuck you," McCarthy reportedly told Trump:* Jacqueline Alemany and Leigh Ann Caldwell, "McCarthy Privately Recounts Terse Phone Call with Trump After Ouster," *Washington Post*, November 30, 2023, https://www .washingtonpost.com/politics/2023/11/30/donald-trump-kevin-mccarthy -phone-call/.

201 *"It often seems that the more Washington does":* Kevin McCarthy, "I'm Leaving the House but Not the Fight. My Work Is Only Getting Started in My Next Chapter," *Wall Street Journal*, December 6, 2023, https://www.wsj.com /articles/kevin-mccarthy-my-next-chapter-house-gop-retirement-california -e4e593d7.

201 *"not rational":* Andrew Desiderio (@AndrewDesiderio), "After Speaker Johnson told Hill leaders he can't pair Ukraine aid with anything less than H.R. 2, Senate Republicans are now taking shots at Johnson," X, December 5, 2023, https://twitter.com/AndrewDesiderio/status/1732046014276931590 ?s=20.

201 *"this is not a traditional negotiation":* Sahil Kapur, Kate Santaliz, and Frank Thorp V, "Immigration Talks Collapse, Threatening to Sink Aid to Israel and Ukraine," NBC News, December 4, 2023, https://www.nbcnews.com/politics /congress/immigration-talks-collapse-threatening-sink-aid-israel-ukraine -rcna127942.

203 *Congress got even less done in 1931:* Jonathan Nicholson, "The Least Productive Congress Since the Great Depression," *HuffPost*, November 15, 2023,

https://www.huffpost.com/entry/least-productive-congress-since-great
-depression_n_65553d38e4b0e4767012b6df.

204 *"proven to be unwilling or unable"*: Andrew Desiderio, Jake Sherman, and John Bresnahan, "Do We Have Immigration Movement?," *Punchbowl News*, December 13, 2023, https://punchbowl.news/article/white-house-senate -negotiations-border-ukraine/.

204 *"fucking lying"*: Jake Sherman (@JakeSherman), "NEW—Some fireworks over FISA in House Republican Conference meeting," X, December 11, 2023, https://twitter.com/JakeSherman/status/1734353184070447442.

204 *"prayerfully consider electing someone else"*: Juliegrace Brufke, "Scoop: House Freedom Caucus Drama Erupts over Its Next Leader," *Axios*, December 11, 2023, https://www.axios.com/2023/12/12/house-freedom-caucus-leader -drama-bob-good.

213 *"I believe our joint history shows the folly"*: David Cameron, "David Cameron: Pass Ukraine Funding for the Sake of Global Security," *The Hill*, February 14, 2024, https://thehill.com/opinion/international/4465907-david-cameron -pass-ukraine-funding-for-the-sake-of-global-security/.

215 *It was precisely what House Republicans:* Jake Sherman and John Bresnahan, "Johnson and House Republicans Face Reality," *Punchbowl News*, March 6, 2024, https://punchbowl.news/archive/3624-punchbowl-news-am/.

CHAPTER 10: "MY OPINION OF A WHITE NATIONALIST"

223 *"people of color"*: Bryan Metzger, "GOP Congressman Declares Amendment Has 'Nothing to Do' with 'Colored People' on the House Floor," *Business Insider*, July 13, 2023, https://www.businessinsider.com/eli-crane-colored -people-joyce-beatty-house-floor-ndaa-2023-7.

223 *"white supremacy snipe hunt"*: Jon Jackson, "Matt Gaetz Wants Congress to Decide if U.S. Should Go to War with Russia," *Newsweek*, May 11, 2022, https://www.newsweek.com/matt-gaetz-congress-decide-war-russia -1705734.

223 *"I question either her loyalty or her competence"*: Anthony Adragna, "Hakeem Jeffries Is Pushing Back After Lance Gooden Questioned the 'Loyalty or Competence' of Judy Chu for Defending a Chinese-American Biden Appointee," *Politico*, February 23, 2023, https://www.politico.com/minutes /congress/02-23-2023/jeffries-gooden-judy-chu/.

224 *"has betrayed the trust of our visit"*: Katherine Tully-McManus, "Kim's Burden of Education," *Politico*, April 12, 2023, https://www.politico.com/newsletters /huddle/2023/04/12/kims-burden-of-education-00091595.

224 *The Republican Conference chairwoman, Elise Stefanik:* "Stefanik Raises $150K at Fundraiser with Paladino," *Punchbowl News*, April 5, 2023, https://punchbowl .news/archive/4523-punchbowl-news-am/.

224 *Hitler was "the kind of leader we need today"*: Eric Hananoki, "Hitler Is the Kind of Leader We Need Today. We Need Somebody Inspirational," *Media Matters*, June 9, 2022, https://www.mediamatters.org/diversity -discrimination/carl-paladino-hitler-kind-leader-we-need-today-we-need -somebody.

226 *"We cannot have these kangaroo courts"*: Andrea Mitchell, "Rep. Victoria Spartz: House 'Becoming Like a Theater Full of Actors in the Circus,'" MSNBC,

January 25, 2023, https://www.msnbc.com/andrea-mitchell-reports/watch
/rep-victoria-spartz-house-becoming-like-a-theater-full-of-actors-in-the
-circus-161766469767.

226 *"Speaker McCarthy needs to stop 'bread and circuses'"*: Congresswoman Victoria
Spartz, "McCarthy Needs to Stop 'Bread and Circuses' in Congress and Start
Governing," press release, January 24, 2023, https://spartz.house.gov/media
/press-releases/spartz-issues-statement-proposed-committee-removals
-mccarthy-needs-stop-bread.

227 *"she should resign in disgrace"*: J. Patrick Coolican and Max Nesterak,
"Republicans Smeared Ilhan Omar over a Faulty Translation.
Here's What She Really Said," *Minnesota Reformer*, February 1, 2024.
https://minnesotareformer.com/2024/02/01/republicans-smeared-ilhan
-omar-over-a-faulty-translation-heres-what-she-really-said/.

229 *"I don't even want to call it the Palestinian flag"*: Laura Ingraham, "Max Miller:
'I Will Not Tolerate Hate or Antisemitism in the Halls of Congress,'" *The
Ingraham Angle*, Fox News, October 10, 2022, video clip, 3:32, https://www
.foxnews.com/video/6338813818112.

230 *"I call them Americans"*: Richard Banks, "Tuberville Defends Hold on Defense
Nominations, Says Pentagon Wrong to Screen Out White Nationalists,"
WHBM, May 8, 2023, https://wbhm.org/2023/tuberville-defends-hold
-on-defense-nominations-says-pentagon-wrong-to-screen-out-white
-nationalists/.

230 *"I look at a white nationalist as a Trump Republican"*: Sean Keeley, "Tommy
Tuberville Doubles Down on Dumb Comments," *The Comeback*, May 11,
2023, https://thecomeback.com/politics/tommy-tuberville-trump
-republicans-white-nationalists.html?utm_source=mj-newsletters&utm
_medium=email&utm_campaign=daily-newsletter-07-01-2023.

232 *"stay in power"*: Gabe Ortiz, "Border Patrol Union President Goes on Fox News
to Spew White Supremacist 'Replacement Theory,'" *Daily Kos*, April 6, 2022,
https://www.dailykos.com/stories/2022/4/6/2090450/-After-appearing-in
-violent-ad-Border-Patrol-union-head-pushes-white-supremacist-conspiracy
-theory.

233 *"to turn all the illegals into voters"*: Speaker Mike Johnson (@Speaker
Johnson), "HERE'S THE ANSWER for all who have asked why in the world
the Democrats would intentionally open our borders," Twitter, May 12, 2022,
https://twitter.com/SpeakerJohnson/status/1524726171421794304.

233 *Cochise County sheriff Mark Dannels*: Isaac Stone Simonelli, "How AZCIR
Identified Arizona's 'Constitutional Sheriffs,'" Arizona Center for
Investigative Reporting, October 20, 2022, https://azcir.org/news/2022/10/20
/azcir-identified-criteria-constitutional-sheriffs/.

235 *"Trying to ban legitimate asylum claims"*: Marianna Sotomayor and Theodoric
Meyer, "Early Rift over Immigration Exposes House GOP's Tough Path to
Consensus," *Washington Post*, January 23, 2023, https://www.washingtonpost
.com/politics/2023/01/23/house-republicans-immigration-legislation/.

235 *In truth, illegal immigration from Canada*: "Border Patrol's Swanton Sector
Apprehensions & Encounters Reach Historic Highs," U.S. Customs and
Border Protection, press release, February 13, 2023, https://www.cbp
.gov/newsroom/local-media-release/border-patrol-s-swanton-sector
-apprehensions-encounters-reach-historic.

237 *"Next week, get the popcorn"*: Karoun Demirjian, "Key Republican Tells Donors He Will Pursue Impeachment of Mayorkas," *New York Times*, April 18, 2023, https://www.nytimes.com/2023/04/18/us/politics/republicans-mark-green -mayorkas-impeachment.html.

240 *a crisis in East Palestine, Ohio:* Committee on Oversight and Accountability, letter to the Secretary of the Department of Transportation, February 24, 2023, https://oversight.house.gov/wp-content/uploads/2023/02/2023-02-24 -Letter-DOT-Norfolk-Southern-Derailment.pdf.

241 *"cognizable basis here for impeachment"*: "Jonathan Turley: Republicans Don't Have a Basis to Impeach Mayorkas," Fox News, January 29, 2024, https://www.foxnews.com/video/6345814125112.

245 *"We cannot allow this man to remain in office"*: "Chairman Green Delivers Opening Statement in Impeachment Markup," Homeland Security Republicans, January 20, 2024, https://homeland.house.gov/2024/01/30 /chairman-green-delivers-opening-statement-in-impeachment-markup-the -actions-and-decisions-of-secretary-mayorkas-have-left-us-with-no-other -option/.

245 *"charade"*: Speaker Mike Johnson (@SpeakerJohnson), "Nancy Pelosi Isn't Worried about a Rigged Trial," Twitter, December 17, 2019, https://twitter .com/SpeakerJohnson/status/1210426145042247681?s=20.

245 *"Democrats sat on the articles for four weeks"*: "Rep. Green Statement on Transmission of Impeachment Articles to Senate," Dr. Mark Green, Press Releases, January 15, 2020, https://markgreen.house.gov/2020/1/rep-green -statement-on-transmission-of-impeachment-articles-to-senate.

CHAPTER 11: "WELL, UNFORTUNATELY, WE CAN'T TRACK DOWN THE INFORMANT"

247 *"In so doing, Joseph R. Biden threatened"*: H.R. 57, "Impeaching Joseph R. Biden, President of the United States, for Abuse of Power by Enabling Bribery and Other High Crimes and Misdemeanors," 117th Cong., 1st sess., https://www .congress.gov/bill/117th-congress/house-resolution/57/text.

250 *"He spoke of his frustration"*: Eric Cortellessa, "Inside House Republicans' Plan to Investigate Hunter Biden as a 'National Security Threat,'" *Time*, October 3, 2022, https://time.com/6218879/hunter-biden-investigations-james-comer -house-republicans/.

250 *"I would like to let the committee"*: Committee on Oversight and Accountability, "Hearing with IRS Whistleblowers About the Biden Criminal Investigation," 118th Cong., 1st sess., July 19, 2023, https://oversight.house.gov/hearing /hearing-with-irs-whistleblowers-about-the-biden-criminal-investigation/.

251 *Buttigieg informed the clueless chairman:* Secretary Pete Buttigieg (@ SecretaryPete), "I am alarmed to learn that the Chair of the House Oversight Committee thinks that the NTSB is part of our Department," X, February 24, 2023, https://twitter.com/SecretaryPete/status /1629250264745103368.

251 *"it was Beau Biden"*: Tommy Christopher, "GOP Oversight Chair Comer Attacks US Attorney for Not Prosecuting Biden's Son—Now-Deceased Beau Biden," *Mediaite*, March 1, 2023, https://www.mediaite.com/news/gop

-probes-chair-comer-attacks-us-attorney-for-not-prosecuting-bidens-son-now
-deceased-beau-biden/.

251 *"We fear that this administration's compromised"*: Steve Benen, "Key GOP
Lawmaker Tries to Connect Britney Griner, Hunter Biden," MSNBC,
February 12, 2022, https://www.msnbc.com/rachel-maddow-show
/maddowblog/key-gop-lawmaker-tries-connect-britney-griner-hunter-biden
-rcna61268.

251 *When a Chinese spy balloon floated:* Justin Baragona, "GOP Rep Warns That
Chinese Balloon May Have 'Bioweapons' from 'Wuhan,'" *Daily Beast,*
February 3, 2023, https://www.thedailybeast.com/gop-rep-james-comer
-warns-that-chinese-balloon-may-have-bioweapons-from-wuhan.

251 *"I asked a question":* Justin Baragona, "CNN Forces GOP Rep to Admit There's
'No Evidence' Spy Balloon Had 'Bioweapons,'" *Daily Beast,* February 7, 2023,
https://www.thedailybeast.com/cnn-forces-rep-james-comer-to-admit-theres
-no-evidence-spy-balloon-had-bioweapons.

252 *"You can't tell me . . . that they don't know":* Charles Creitz, "White House
Cocaine Mystery Shows 'Biden, Inc.' Always Gets Special Treatment:
McCarthy," Fox News, July 13, 2023, https://www.foxnews.com/media/white
-house-cocaine-mystery-shows-biden-gets-special-treatment-mccarthy.

252 *Trump's former vice president, Mike Pence:* "Representative Comer on Classified
Documents Investigation," C-SPAN, January 31, 2023, https://www.c-span.org
/video/?525690-101/representative-comer-classified-documents-investigation.

253 *"there's a special counsel looking into everything at Mar-a-Lago":* Kaitlan Collins
(@kaitlancollins), "Our interview this morning with House Oversight Chair
James Comer," X, February 7, 2023, https://twitter.com/kaitlancollins/status
/1622947818209001474.

253 *In Trump's case, detailed in a 32-count federal indictment:* Washington Post staff,
"Read the Superseding Indictment Bringing New Charges Against Trump,"
Washington Post, July 27, 2023, https://www.washingtonpost.com/national
-security/2023/07/27/trump-superseding-indictment-document/.

254 *"BIDEN SECRET EMAILS":* Emma-Jo Morris and Gabrielle Fonrouge,
"Smoking-Gun Email Reveals How Hunter Biden Introduced Ukrainian
Businessman to VP Dad," *New York Post,* October 14, 2020, https://nypost.com
/2020/10/14/email-reveals-how-hunter-biden-introduced-ukrainian-biz-man
-to-dad/.

255 *"Joe Biden's going to have a lot of explaining to do":* Fox and Friends, April 11, 2023,
https://video.snapstream.net/Play/1Y4ZY06Ahj6J2HXTguGzzN?accessToken
=dti3yw0mn7img.

258 *"Biden lied to the American people":* "Biden Crime Family," Conservative
Political Action Conference, August 4, 2022, https://www.c-span.org/video
/?522151-109/conservative-political-action-conference-rep-jim-jordan.

258 *"was using a pseudonym":* "Rep. Comer to Newsmax: Biden Was Most
'Corrupt' VP in History," Newsmax, August 29, 2023, https://www.newsmax
.com/newsmax-tv/james-comer-joe-biden-corrupt/2023/08/29/id/1132486/.

259 *"dog-petting monster":* Dana Milbank, "Biden Eats Ice Cream and Pets Dogs?
Totally Unfit to Serve," *Washington Post,* September 8, 2023, https://www
.washingtonpost.com/opinions/2023/09/08/rnc-x-twitter-attacks-biden-dogs
-ice-cream/.

CHAPTER 12: "THIS IS WHAT'S KNOWN AS LUNA-CY"

268 *Schiff "behaved dishonestly and dishonorably":* "Censuring Adam Schiff, Representative of the 30th Congressional District of Congress," H.R. 521, June 16, 2023, https://www.govinfo.gov/content/pkg/BILLS-118hres521ih /html/BILLS-118hres521ih.htm.

271 *Victory Channel:* Right Wing Watch (@RightWingWatch), "Rep. Lauren Boebert claims that she is forcing a House vote on impeaching President Biden," X, June 21, 2023, https://twitter.com/RightWingWatch/status /1671520330408501255.

273 *"Correction my friend":* Dana Milbank, "Speaker Matt Gaetz Has Big Plans for the House," *Washington Post,* September 15, 2023, https://www .washingtonpost.com/opinions/2023/09/15/biden-impeachment-inquiry -house-gop-mccarthy-gaetz-greene/.

273 *"gotcha narrative":* Ken Buck, "My Fellow Republicans: One Disgraceful Impeachment Doesn't Deserve Another," *Washington Post,* September 15, 2023, https://www.washingtonpost.com/opinions/2023/09/15/congressman -ken-buck-biden-impeachment/.

274 *"That doesn't exist right now": Inside with Jen Psaki,* MSNBC, September 10, 2023, https://www.msnbc.com/inside-with-jen-psaki/watch/gop-rep-blasts-absurd -mtg-comments-on-impeachment-192642118000.

276 *Dominion voting machines switched:* Steve Inskeep (@NPRinskeep), "Can't stop thinking about this," Twitter, November 13, 2020, https://twitter.com /NPRinskeep/status/1327356909943480321.

276 *"Joe and Jill Biden Finally Acknowledge 7th Grandchild":* Jonathan Turley, "Joe and Jill Biden Finally Acknowledge 7th Grandchild for Most Obnoxious Reason," Fox News, July 29, 2023, https://www.foxnews.com/opinion/joe-jill -biden-acknowledge-7th-grandchild-obnoxious-reason.

277 *"with your generous support":* "Stand with the GOP," *Punchbowl News,* September 21, 2023, https://punchbowl.news/smith-email/.

278 *"BREAKING," it said, with two siren emojis:* GOP Oversight (@gopoversight), Instagram, October 20, 2023, https://www.instagram.com/gopoversight/reel /CyoqDmhuUPT/.

278 *"it looks and smells like" Biden received bribes:* Philip Bump, "Mike Johnson Points to a Biden Impeachment, Even If the Facts Do Not," *Washington Post,* October 27, 2023, https://www.washingtonpost.com/politics/2023/10/27 /mike-johnson-points-biden-impeachment-even-if-facts-dont/.

279 *the* Daily Beast*'s Roger Sollenberger:* Roger Sollenberger, "James Comer, Like Joe Biden, Also Paid His Brother $200K," *Daily Beast,* November 9, 2023, https://www.thedailybeast.com/james-comer-like-joe-biden-also-paid-his -brother-dollar200k.

283 *"for depositions or committee hearings, whichever they choose":* Justin Baragona, "James Comer Seems to Forget He Said Hunter Biden Could 'Choose' Public Hearing," *Daily Beast,* November 29, 2023, https://www.thedailybeast.com /james-comer-seems-to-forget-he-said-hunter-biden-could-choose-public -hearing.

284 *"They haven't explained how it implicates Joe":* Colby Hall, "Republicans Have 'Not Shown' Joe Biden 'Did Anything Illegally,'" *Mediaite,* November 28, 2023, https://www.mediaite.com/tv/gop-rep-admits-to-maria-bartiromo

-theres-no-evidence-of-biden-policy-changes-as-a-result-of-getting-money
-from-china/.

284 *"I don't see the grounds"*: Anthony Adragna, "Senate Republicans Wary
as House Moves Toward Formal Biden Impeachment Inquiry," *Politico*,
December 12, 2023, https://www.politico.com/live-updates/2023/12/12
/congress/senate-gop-wary-biden-probe-00131262.

286 *"The American people need to know"*: "Grassley, Comer Demand FBI Record
Alleging Criminal Scheme Involving Then-VP Biden," press release,
Committee on Oversight and Accountability, May 3, 2023, https://oversight
.house.gov/release/grassley-comer-demand-fbi-record-alleging-criminal
-scheme-involving-then-vp-biden/.

288 *defrauding a Native American tribe:* "Jason Galanis Sentenced to More Than
14 Years in Prison for Defrauding Tribal Entity and Pension Funds of Tens
of Millions of Dollars," United States Attorney's Office, Southern District
of New York, August 11, 2017, https://www.justice.gov/usao-sdny/pr/jason
-galanis-sentenced-more-14-years-prison-defrauding-tribal-entity-and
-pension-funds.

CHAPTER 13: "WE NEED A NATIONAL DIVORCE"

298 *"President Trump said he has 'been summoned'"*: Clay Higgins (@
RepClayHiggins), "President Trump says he has 'been summoned to appear
at the Federal Courthouse in Miami on Tuesday, at 3 PM,'" X, June 8, 2023,
https://twitter.com/RepClayHiggins/status/1666978397027803142.

298 *Dartmouth College professor Jeff Sharlet:* Jeff Sharlet, "The Congressman Telling
Trump Supporters to 'Buckle Up,'" *The Atlantic*, June 11, 2023, https://www
.theatlantic.com/ideas/archive/2023/06/the-congressman-telling-trump
-supporters-to-buckle-up/674367/.

298 *"Patriots, we've manipulated the MSM"*: Clay Higgins (@RepClayHiggins),
"Patriots, we've manipulated the MSM to establish deep commo,"
X, June 10, 2023, https://twitter.com/RepClayHiggins/status
/1667557694163632128?lang=en.

298 *a member of the Three Percenters:* Sharlet, "The Congressman Telling Trump
Supporters to 'Buckle Up.'"

298 *Oath Keepers:* Lamar White Jr., "Captain of the Militia," *Bayou Brief*, August 13,
2018, https://www.bayoubrief.com/2018/08/13/captain-of-the-militia/.

298 *"We have now reached a war phase"*: Andy Biggs (@RepAndyBiggsAZ),
"We have now reached a war phase. Eye for an eye . . . ," X, June 9, 2023,
https://twitter.com/RepAndyBiggsAZ/status/1667241900938502146?lang
=en.

299 *"except for Day One"*: Michael Gold, "Trump Says He Wouldn't Be a Dictator,
'Except for Day 1,'" *New York Times*, December 5, 2023, https://www.nytimes
.com/2023/12/05/us/politics/trump-fox-news-abuse-power.html.

300 *"Settlements like this"*: "Tucker Carlson: 'Paying People to Not Talk About
Things, Hush Money, Is Ordinary in Modern America,'" *Media Matters*,
March 20, 2023, https://www.mediamatters.org/fox-news/tucker-carlson
-paying-people-not-talk-about-things-hush-money-ordinary-modern
-america.

300 *"WILL BE ARRESTED ON TUESDAY"*: Michelle L. Price, Jill Colvin, and Eric

Tucker, "Trump Says He Expects to Be Arrested, Calls for Protest," Associated Press, March 18, 2023, https://apnews.com/article/trump-arrested-indicted-hush-money-manhattan-prosecutor-a48428984cf99d23f46b4157b34160ae.

301 *"outrageous abuse of power" by Bragg:* Kevin McCarthy (@SpeakerMcCarthy), "Here we go again—an outrageous abuse of power by a radical DA who lets violent criminals walk," X, March 18, 2023, https://twitter.com/speakermccarthy/status/1637108358208421888?s=46&t=JjZ0HYOqxLjGtjkLnr-3YA.

301 *"listening to his master, George Soros":* Decoding Fox News (@DecodingFoxNews), "Former MTV reality star, Rachel Campos-Duffy, says that New York DA, Alvin Bragg, a Black man, must be listening . . . ," X, March 20, 2023, https://twitter.com/DecodingFoxNews/status/1637925978474160130.

302 *"There's no proof Trump slept with Stormy":* Nikki McCann Ramirez, "Fox News Struggles to Defend Trump's Stormy Daniels Hush Money," *Rolling Stone*, March 20, 2023, https://www.rollingstone.com/politics/politics-news/fox-news-struggles-defend-trump-stormy-daniels-hush-money-1234700569/.

302 *"The House is gonna do":* "Senate Shrugs at House GOP's Trump Defense," *Punchbowl News*, March 22, 2023, https://punchbowl.news/archive/32223-punchbowl-news-am/.

302 *"Political Persecution":* Max Greenwood, "Trump Lashes Out at Indictment, Says He's 'Completely Innocent,'" *The Hill*, March 30, 2023, https://thehill.com/homenews/campaign/3926877-trump-lashes-out-at-indictment-says-hes-completely-innocent/.

305 *"Wannabe dictator speaks at the White House":* David Bauder, "Fox News Says It 'Addressed' Onscreen Message That Called Biden a 'Wannabe Dictator,'" Associated Press, June 14, 2023, https://apnews.com/article/fox-wannabe-dictator-biden-trump-speech-1a9750c5dfcfb0a6482f3c51674ae08f.

307 *"we would have won":* Aaron Blake, "Marjorie Taylor Greene's Jan. 6 'Joke' Has Been Building for a Long Time," *Washington Post*, December 12, 2022, https://www.washingtonpost.com/politics/2022/12/12/greene-january-6-punchline/.

307 *Micki Witthoeft:* Ryan J. Reilly, Ryan Nobles, and Liz Brown-Kaiser, "Kevin McCarthy Met Ashli Babbitt's Mom Ahead of GOP Visit with Jan. 6 Prisoners," NBCNews.com, March 23, 2023, https://www.nbcnews.com/politics/congress/kevin-mccarthy-met-ashli-babbitts-mom-ahead-gop-visit-jan-6-prisoners-rcna76419.

308 *"FBI planting the pipe bombs":* Dana Milbank, "Republicans Celebrate Their Successful Deception of Voters," *Washington Post*, July 14, 2023, https://www.washingtonpost.com/opinions/2023/07/14/fbi-conspiracy-theories-house-gop-wray-hearing/.

309 *"mostly peaceful":* Emily Brooks, Dominick Mastrangelo, and Rebecca Beitsch, "Tucker Carlson Shows the First of His Jan. 6 Footage, Calls It 'Mostly Peaceful Chaos,'" *The Hill*, March 6, 2023, https://thehill.com/homenews/media/3887103-tucker-carlson-shows-the-first-of-his-jan-6-footage-calls-it-mostly-peaceful-chaos/.

309 *"in a way that's completely at variance":* Luke Broadwater and Stephanie Lai, "Republican Lawmakers Split over Carlson's False Jan. 6 Claims," *New York*

Times, March 7, 2023, https://www.nytimes.com/2023/03/07/us/republicans
-tucker-carlson-jan-6.html.

309 *"Do you regret giving him this footage"*: Manu Raju (@mkraju), "McCarthy
last night defended his decision to give Jan. 6 footage to Tucker Carlson," X,
March 8, 2023, https://twitter.com/mkraju/status/1633441946810085378.

310 *"stronger in denouncing it"*: Jeremy Barr, Sarah Ellison, and Rachel Weiner,
"Murdoch Admits Some Fox Hosts 'Were Endorsing' Election Falsehoods,"
Washington Post, February 27, 2023, https://www.washingtonpost.com/media
/2023/02/27/rupert-murdoch-testimony-fox-dominion/.

311 *"The thing about Donald Trump is that he lacks"*: Annie Karni and Steve Eder,
"Johnson Said in 2015 Trump Was Unfit and Could Be 'Dangerous' as
President," *New York Times*, November 14, 2023, https://www.nytimes.com
/2023/11/14/us/politics/mike-johnson-donald-trump.html.

311 *"He is a hot head by nature"*: Karni and Eder, "Johnson Said in 2015 Trump Was
Unfit and Could Be 'Dangerous' as President."

311 *"I'm all in for President Trump"*: "House Speaker Mike Johnson on 2024
Election," CNBC, November 14, 2023, https://www.cnbc.com/video/2023/11
/14/house-speaker-mike-johnson-on-2024-election-im-all-in-for-president
-trump.html.

311 *"Trump badge"*: Jake Sherman (@JakeSherman), "INSIDE HOUSE GOP
MEETING | ELISE STEFANIK, House GOP conference chair, said she
has received a 25% bump in digital fundraising," X, November 29, 2023,
https://twitter.com/JakeSherman/status/1729866575451460032.

312 *Trump may not be "the strongest"*: Kevin Breuninger, "Trump May Not Be the
Strongest GOP Presidential Candidate, Kevin McCarthy Says," CNBC, June
27, 2023, https://www.cnbc.com/2023/06/27/trump-may-not-be-strongest-gop
-candidate-kevin-mccarthy.html.

316 *"took an adapted screenplay from journalists' tweet thread"*: Jacqueline Alemany,
"Jordan's Weaponization-Panel Game Plan Draws Critique from Some on the
Right," *Washington Post*, March 10, 2023, https://www.washingtonpost.com
/politics/2023/03/10/jim-jordan-house-weaponization-panel/.

316 *"once again all talk"*: Jeff Carlson (@themarketswork), "Worthwhile Thread.
Is it once again all talk & no action from the GOP—this time from the
Weaponization Committee?" X, February 28, 2023, https://twitter.com
/themarketswork/status/1630664553037197312?s=46&t=ghs6jNpp28YDRkrjk
-7G9g.

317 *Jordan promised that a symphony of "whistleblowers"*: Luke Broadwater and
Adam Goldman, "G.O.P. Witnesses, Paid by Trump Ally, Embraced Jan. 6
Conspiracy Theories," *New York Times*, March 2, 2023, https://www.nytimes
.com/2023/03/02/us/politics/house-weaponization-committee-jan-6.html.

318 *"Russian government news agency"*: Alan Feuer, "F.B.I. Revokes Security Clearances of 3 Agents over Jan. 6 Issues," *New York Times*, May 17, 2023, https://www
.nytimes.com/2023/05/17/us/politics/fbi-security-clearance-jan-6.html.

318 *"criminal trespass"*: Letter from Christopher Dunham, FBI, to Jim Jordan,
House of Representatives, May 17, 2023, *Politico*, https://www.politico.com/f
/?id=00000188-2c91-d5ba-a7fe-fedfd3160000.

318 *a "bioweapon" that was "ethnically targeted"*: Ruby Cramer, "Robert F. Kennedy
Jr. Suggests Covid Was Designed to Spare Jews, Chinese People," *Washington*

Post, July 15, 2023, https://www.washingtonpost.com/nation/2023/07/15
/robert-kennedy-jr-covid-conspiracy/.

319 *"you could hide in an attic":* Andrew Jeong, "Robert F. Kennedy Apologizes
for Saying the Unvaccinated Have Less Freedom Than Anne Frank Did,"
Washington Post, January 25, 2022, https://www.washingtonpost.com/nation
/2022/01/25/rfk-kennedy-jr-anne-frank-anti-vax/.

325 *a CNN poll found that about three-quarters:* Ariel Edwards-Levy, "Nearly Three-
Quarters of Americans Think House GOP Leaders Haven't Paid Enough
Attention to Most Important Problems," CNN, January 26, 2023, https://www
.cnn.com/2023/01/26/politics/cnn-poll-house-gop-leadership/index.html.

333 *with Rich's family to settle a lawsuit in 2020:* Ben Smith, "Fox Settled a Lawsuit
over Its Lies. But It Insisted on One Unusual Condition," *New York Times,*
January 17, 2021, https://www.nytimes.com/2021/01/17/business/media/fox
-news-seth-rich-settlement.html.

336 *universities and government agencies scaled back programs:* Naomi Nix, Cat
Zakrzewski, and Joseph Menn, "Misinformation Research Is Buckling Under
GOP Legal Attacks," *Washington Post,* September 25, 2023, https://www
.washingtonpost.com/technology/2023/09/23/online-misinformation-jim
-jordan/.

338 *The county had been through half a dozen election directors:* Carter Walker, "A
Deficit of Experienced Voting Officials Could Mean Trouble for Pa.'s 2024
Election," Allentown *Morning Call,* February 21, 2024, https://www.mcall
.com/2024/02/21/a-deficit-of-experienced-voting-officials-could-mean
-trouble-for-pa-s-2024-election/.

338 *"We need a national divorce":* Marjorie Taylor Greene (@mtgreenee), "We need
a national divorce. We need to separate by red states and blue states and
shrink the federal government," X, February 20, 2023, https://twitter.com
/mtgreenee/status/1627665203398688768?lang=en.

INDEX